PORTRAIT
OF AN ERA

An Illustrated History of Britain 1900 - 1945

PORTRAIT
OF AN ERA

An Illustrated History of Britain 1900 - 1945

WITH A FOREWORD BY
JULIET GARDINER

Reader's Digest | gettyimages

CONTENTS

FOREWORD

This is the story of the making of modern Britain, a half century punctuated by wars, but in part redeemed by unprecedentedly rapid social and scientific progress. It is a dizzyingly rich panorama that unfolds, from the Boer War and the death of Queen Victoria to 'coming home' from the Second World War. These events bookend and exemplify the period: the terminus of one world and the anticipation – indeed, the realisation – of changes that would transform in myriad ways the political, economic and social structure of Britain, its place in the world and the life of its people.

It is the contrast of these years that make them so endlessly intriguing. And that contrast threads across the decades. The long, lingering, golden Edwardian summer enjoyed by the upper and middle-classes, the confident plutocrats, their money made in commerce and spent on glamour and excess, compared to conditions for the swelling urban masses – 13 million lived in Britain's towns and cities by 1900, the poorest housed in malodorous, overcrowded slums, their children ill-fed, bare-footed and put to work long hours at 12 years old. Rural poverty could be equally invidious, eking out a living on the land as cheap food imports increasingly undercut livelihoods – and always the looming spectre of the workhouse.

The Edwardian world was blown apart by the First World War. General Ferdinand Foch, who ended the war as supreme commander of the Allied armies, said of the peace agreement signed in 1919 'This is not peace, it is an armistice for 20 years'. And so it proved. The grieving of a nation when the guns fell silent soon turned to disappointment and anger that such supreme sacrifice was not rewarded with better housing and employment. Some were single-minded in their wish to forget through the pursuit of fun. Others hoped to forge a new world: suffragettes who had turned into patriotic munitionettes in wartime were determined not to allow the wider horizons that women had glimpsed shrink back into their limited pre-war world. They wanted opportunities – of education, of work and some choice in how many babies they bore.

A striking contrast of the Thirties was between the long-term unemployed in traditional industrial heartlands, many of them dependent on the hated Means Test, and those in the 'new' industries who enjoyed rising wages fuelling a housing and consumer boom. It was a nation united by the wireless and the BBC, by the 'dream palace' cinemas, but divided by politics: between those who sought a solution to Britain's ills in fascism or communism and those for whom these movements threatened the peace and stability of Europe. Yet when war came in 1939, the British proved staunchly united in the face of German attrition.

Portrait of an Era: 1900 to 1945 vividly sketches this procession of events and people with a splendid collection of photographs and a powerful narrative full of fascinating detail. Here are the burning issues of the first half of the 20th century – questions of Empire and trade, independence for Ireland, education, employment, a raft of social change that made Britain a fairer place and, of course, war. A dense and varied crowd of politicians, reformers, renegades, stars and 'ordinary' people take their turns at centre stage to bring to life the most epic half century this country has ever lived through.

Juliet Gardiner

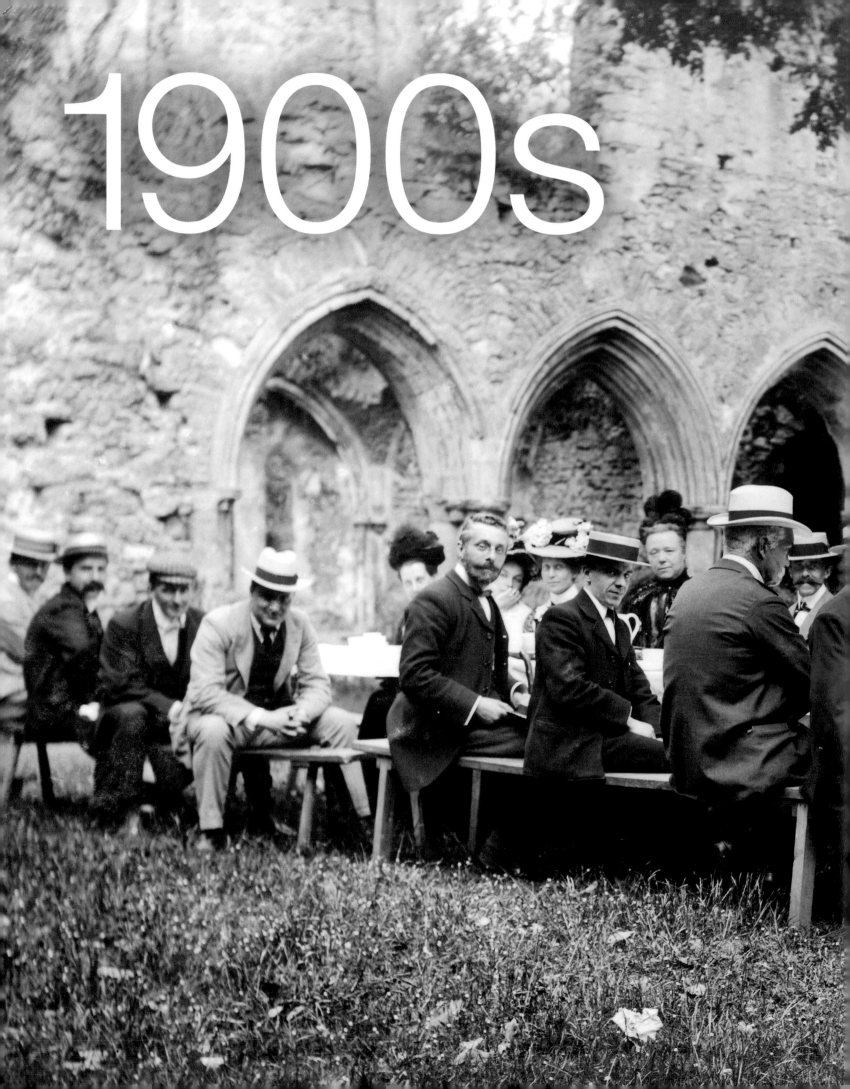

1900s

1900s

A NEW AGE DAWNS

Revellers celebrating New Year's Eve on 31 December, 1899, did so with more than the usual degree of enthusiasm and trepidation. They were entering the new century with a sense that an era was passing. The Victorian Age, which had seen Britain rise to a pinnacle of imperial grandeur, was in its 63rd year. The Queen herself was 80 years old – older than any previous British monarch save for her grandfather George III, who had died aged 81. Few people could recollect a time when Victoria had not been on the throne, and as mortality crept upon her, they regarded the future with a vague sense of foreboding.

REGAL SPLENDOUR Queen Alexandra, Edward VII's Danish-born consort, in a formal portrait with her pageboys taken on the day of her husband's coronation – 9 August, 1902.

SNAPSHOT OF THE NATION

On the surface, the British had little enough to fear. The past 100 years had been Britain's century, and no-one yet realised that the new one would belong to the USA. Victoria ruled over an empire on which the sun famously never set, and its bounds had continued to grow over the past 20 years as the nation took its share of the spoils from the European 'scramble for Africa'. In 1899 competing white claims to lands in the southern part of the continent had embroiled the country for a second time in war with the Boers, settlers of Dutch extraction. The British public, having expected a quick victory, were surprised when the hardy farmers took the military initiative, inflicting early reverses on British troops. But few people expected success to be long delayed.

Domestically, at first sight the situation seemed serene. In the long years of Victorian prosperity, Britain had experienced a sustained demographic boom. At the turn of the new century there were almost 37 million people in the United Kingdom, excluding Ireland, a figure that had nearly doubled since the first modern UK census of 1841, early in Victoria's reign. It was a young population, with more than 40 per cent of the total below the age of 20; the downside of this statistic lay in a much lower life expectancy of around 50 years and in particular the high toll of infant mortality, with one baby in eight dying before reaching its first birthday. Divorce remained a rarity, with fewer than a thousand decrees

TAKING THEIR EASE
Looked at retrospectively, the Edwardian era seemed to pass in a golden glow, a permanent summer, leaving later generations with the impression that people spent the whole decade lazing about and having fun, like the group below enjoying a picnic near Hereford in 1901. Much of this later nostalgia came from the stark contrast with the horrors of what was soon to come: the First World War and the trenches of the Western Front would blow the Edwardian way of life to smithereens. Yet for now, the quarter of the population who did not have to live by manual labour enjoyed standards that were genuinely comfortable. For this minority, income tax rates of 5 per cent and the ready availability of low-paid servants were a recipe for the good life.

IN THE BACKSTREETS

For the urban poor, life was a far cry from the ease of the leisured classes. Skilled workers with secure jobs enjoyed home comforts and a respectable lifestyle, but millions of other city-dwellers struggled to make any kind of living at all. Not everyone succeeded; at a time when the only welfare was provided by the Poor Law and the workhouse, pioneering sociological studies showed that between a quarter and a third of the entire population of Britain regularly went hungry. Overcrowding was another problem. In London's East End, where this photograph was taken, a third of the population lived in accommodation housing more than two people to a room. Yet even here there were positive aspects to city life in Edwardian times: in particular, the low crime rate and strong sense of community meant that children mostly played in the street without fear.

granted each year, although this reflected the complexity, expense and general unacceptability of divorce rather than the national state of marital contentment. Crime levels were extraordinarily low, with only 300 offences recorded for every 100,000 people; by the end of the 20th century – when admittedly police record-keeping was vastly more comprehensive – the figure was approaching 9,000.

The urban drift

Victoria's reign had seen an ongoing drift from the countryside. In 1871 almost two-thirds of Britain's population had lived in communities of less than 50,000 – small country towns or villages, for the most part. Thirty years later the situation had been reversed, with roughly two-thirds now living in cities. Some 13 million people were crammed into the five largest conurbations, of which the biggest was Greater London, the largest city in the world, with almost 7 million inhabitants.

The people in the great urban agglomerations were rigidly divided on class lines. Almost three-quarters of the population earned their living as manual workers – a figure that would be halved by the end of the century. More than 2 million women were employed in domestic service, along with half a million men. Life at the bottom of the pile was grim indeed. Social researchers estimated that almost one third of the population lived in poverty, earning too little to feed themselves to adequate nutritional standards, let alone to enjoy the wider amenities of life. The result was widespread sickliness and infirmity, which became all too evident to the authorities during the Boer War: out of the 20,000 men who volunteered to fight, some 6,000 were rejected as unfit for military service.

For a minority of the population, life could be very good indeed. The rich lived magnificently, exuding a showy opulence that marked them out as the chosen elite of the world's greatest power. The aristocracy enjoyed almost regal splendour, while even middle-class families had servants to look after them. One typical office administrator, the secretary to the board of directors of an iron and shipping works in Jarrow, kept a cook, a housemaid, two other maids and a governess for his children. The lower middle classes clung to the skirts of privilege by nurturing a cult of respectability that distinguished them from the working masses. One Islington resident recalled for an oral historian how his father, a Post Office clerk with a young family, always took particular care to be well groomed. 'He wore a bowler hat and never wore shabby clothes. He never worked in his shirt sleeves and there were no Christian names used at work.'

Deceptive appearances

To the casual observer, then, the late Victorian world was settled and secure, but the more thoughtful of Britain's citizens regarded the future with a certain apprehension, even anxiety. There was a feeling that many of the pillars on which the social framework rested were being gradually undermined. True, Britain remained the world's greatest economic power, but it was being challenged; Germany and the USA had both grown faster than Britain in industrial might since 1870. The countryside was in a state of decline, with cheap imported American grain undercutting British wheat and refrigerated meat and dairy products coming in from Argentina, Australia, New Zealand and northern Europe. Even the family, that great bulwark of Victorian values, was no longer what it had been. The birth-rate had been falling, and the typical number of children had declined from the five or six of earlier times to a mere three or four, causing concerns that Britain was slipping behind the prolific Germans in demographic terms too.

LONG SHE REIGNED OVER US
Seen here in 1900, at the age of 80, Queen Victoria had already become the longest-reigning British monarch. By the time of her death in January 1901 she had been on the throne for 63 years, 7 months and 2 days – more than 4 years longer than the previous record-holder, George III. She had outlived two sons and one daughter; her eldest daughter, also Victoria, would die later the same year. In her last years, Queen Victoria spent much of her time either at Osborne House on the Isle of Wight or at Balmoral in the Scottish Highlands. The contrast with her successor, the extrovert Edward VII, could hardly have been greater.

A NATION MOURNS

Against all such worries the abiding presence of the Queen seemed a reassuring counterweight. The heartfelt celebrations that greeted her Diamond Jubilee in 1897 had demonstrated the depth of the public's affection. So stories of her declining strength were met with alarm. A pall of gloom fell over the nation on 22 January, 1901, when news spread that the Queen was dead.

As was her custom, Victoria had gone to Osborne House on the Isle of Wight for the Christmas holidays. It was there, at 6.30 in the evening, that she finally succumbed to a cerebral haemorrhage. She was attended at her bedside not just by her eldest son Edward but also by her eldest grandson, Kaiser Wilhelm II of Germany, who was holding her hand when she passed away.

'I felt her death far more than I should have expected. She was a sustaining symbol and the wild waters are upon us now.'

Henry James, writer

In accordance with her wishes, Victoria was laid to rest dressed in white and wearing her wedding veil. She had left instructions, too, on the contents of her coffin, including her beloved husband Albert's dressing gown and a photograph of her longtime favourite, the Scots ghillie John Brown, which was placed in her left hand. Her funeral – a military affair, with the coffin drawn through London by eight white and bay horses – was attended by most of Europe's ruling elite, the kings of Greece and Portugal, five crown princes and 14 princes among them.

Working people showed their grief in the traditional way. 'Even poor little houses that faced onto the street put a board up and painted it black,' one observer recalled of the East End of London. 'All the shops had black shutters up, and everyone felt as if they'd lost somebody.' Up and down the country people sensed that an era had ended and speculated on what the new reign might bring.

FINAL JOURNEY
Queen Victoria died at Osborne House on 22 January, 1901. After lying in state there for ten days, her body was carried across the Solent to Portsmouth in the royal yacht *Alberta*, sailing between two lines of warships which fired their guns at one-minute intervals. From Portsmouth the coffin was carried by train to Victoria Station, then in horse-drawn procession through the streets to Paddington to allow the public to say a final farewell; almost a million people travelled to London for the occasion. In Paddington a second train was waiting to take Victoria to Windsor, where a team of sailors pulled the hearse up to the castle for the private funeral – the horses originally envisaged for the job proved too skittish. The white wreath on the front of the royal locomotive below was in accordance with Victoria's own wishes; she had come to dislike mourning black.

INTO THE EDWARDIAN ERA

One reason for concern on the Queen's death was the character of the new king. Edward was 59 years old, and his past life had been touched by more than a whiff of scandal. Some of the nation's best minds regarded his accession with disquiet. Rudyard Kipling called him a 'corpulent voluptuary'. The novelist Henry James wrote to a friend that the nation had 'dropped to Edward … fat Edward … Edward the Caresser', adding 'I mourn the safe, motherly old middle-class queen who held the nation warm under the folds of her big, hideous, Scotch-plaid shawl.'

Worries about Edward's temperament had started early in his life. The second child and eldest son born to Victoria and Albert, he grew up in the shadow of the

Queen's adored husband. Christened Albert Edward after his father, he was always known within the royal family as 'Bertie'. To train him for his future role Victoria entrusted his upbringing to a succession of disciplinarian tutors. He quickly proved a disappointment. Victoria privately dismissed him as having 'a small, empty brain', while Albert confided in a letter to a friend that 'I never in my life met with such a thorough and cunning lazybones'. Having failed to distinguish himself as a student first at Oxford and then Cambridge universities, Edward spent a brief spell on manoeuvres with the army in Ireland, where fellow officers hid an actress in his tent – a jape that backfired badly when his mother got to hear of it.

In the vain hope of forestalling further sexual escapades, he was encouraged at the age of 21 to marry Alexandra, daughter of King Christian IX of Denmark, whose relatively austere upbringing recommended her to Victoria as a suitable consort for her son. Beautiful, kindly and high-spirited, the young princess proved indeed to be a dignified and supportive partner to whom Edward remained deeply attached for the rest of his life. Yet the genuine affection he felt for Alexandra did nothing to inhibit his pursuit of extra-marital adventures. There was a scandal in 1869 when Sir Charles Mordaunt, a wealthy country squire and Member of Parliament, threatened to cite Edward as a co-respondent in a divorce case. His wife Harriet was just one of a string of society beauties whose names were linked with the high-living prince, among them the actress Lillie Langtry, the singer Hortense Schneider, and the eccentric Daisy, Countess of Warwick, who ended her days as a convert to socialism. Most famously of all, Edward was long involved with Alice Keppel, wife of a complaisant aristocrat and remembered today as a

PLAYBOY PRINCE
Edward VII's accession saw a sea change in the image of the British monarchy. Where his mother was the incarnation of respectability, the pleasure-loving prince surrounded himself with a social set that enthusiastically embraced horse-racing, gambling and a constant round of house parties. He is pictured above decorously shaking a leg with other guests at Mar Lodge near Braemar in the Highlands. Such gatherings allowed Edward plenty of opportunities to rendezvous with a long succession of mistresses, of whom Alice Keppel (left) was the best-known. Edward's other passions included motor-cars; he is seen here (right) seated alongside the future Lord Montagu of Beaulieu, a leading pioneer of the automobile age, in Montagu's 12-horsepower Daimler.

grandmother of Camilla, Duchess of Cornwall. Edward's relationship with this beautiful socialite was sufficiently well-known to prompt Winston Churchill, a rising young politician at the time of Edward's accession, to ask ironically in a letter to a friend, 'Will the Keppel be appointed First Lady of the Bedchamber?'

By the time of Edward's marriage to Alexandra, his father Albert was already dead and the Prince was heir to the throne, much to the alarm of his widowed mother, who considered him too frivolous to handle affairs of state. 'What will become of the country if I die?' Victoria privately worried. 'If Bertie succeeds, he would spend his life in one whirl of amusements.' As heir apparent for six decades, Edward did much to justify his mother's fears. The Marlborough House set, named after his London residence, gained a reputation for high living. Their behaviour came into the public spotlight in the Royal Baccarat Scandal of 1891, which led to Edward being called to give evidence in court as a witness in a libel trial. Even though he himself was not accused of wrongdoing, his behaviour attracted widespread criticism.

Edward's day finally comes

There were legitimate reasons, then, for Victoria's concern, and on his accession events did not seem to augur well for the new reign. His coronation, set for 5 July, 1902, had to be delayed when he suffered a life-threatening bout of appendicitis, and he was not formally crowned until August. The ceremony itself was saved from disaster in the most unlikely circumstances when the Master of Horse, who was responsible for getting the royal party safely to Westminster Abbey, had a

CORONATION CITY

For Edward's subjects, the first coronation in 65 years was something to celebrate. It was planned for July 1902, which allowed a suitable time for mourning as well as for making the necessary arrangements, and by then he was already firmly established in the nation's affections. The decorations enlivening London for the ceremony, like those on Queen Victoria Street (below), reflected a genuine mood of rejoicing. It helped that, as J B Priestley noted, Edward 'enjoyed being a king'. He took genuine pleasure in public appearances and he was soon being familiarly toasted in pubs and clubs as 'Good Old Teddie!'. Shortly before the intended date the King became acutely ill and the ceremony was postponed. The royal guests who had flocked to London from across Europe went home and the banquet was cancelled, providing an unexpected bounty for London's poor. As the royal chef later wrote, 'It was the poor of Whitechapel and not the foreign kings, princes and diplomats who had the *consommé de faisan aux quenelles*, the *côtelette de bécassines à la Souvaroff* and many other dishes ...'.

6582.

A POPULAR KING

Despite Victoria's fears, Edward proved immediately popular when he came to the throne, appealing to a public weary of the high moral tone of the old Queen's reign. But although Edward cultivated a less formal, more approachable manner than his mother as ruler of Britain, he remained a stickler for etiquette. Those who failed to share his dress sense sometimes suffered when they got it wrong; he once refused to allow an aide to accompany him to an art exhibition because he was wearing a tailcoat, commenting 'I thought everyone must know that a short jacket is always worn with a silk hat at a private view in the morning'. He would have felt very much at ease, then, in his coronation robes. In this formal portrait Edward is shown wearing the Crown of St Edward, said to be based on that worn by Edward the Confessor in the 11th century. The lighter Imperial State Crown was used in the actual ceremony, which eventually took place in Westminster Abbey on 9 August, 1902. Although primarily a domestic affair, it was celebrated with all the pomp and circumstance befitting a ruler who bore the titles Emperor of India and King of the United Kingdom and Dominions. The event left an enduring legacy in the anthem 'Land of Hope and Glory', which first saw the light of day as Edward's 'Coronation Ode'.

premonition in a dream. He saw the carriage becoming stuck in the arch separating Horse Guards Parade from Whitehall and subsequent investigation revealed that resurfacing of the roadway during Victoria's long reign had indeed reduced the clearance to below the required level. Urgent road repairs were undertaken to allow the carriage to pass freely

Presages notwithstanding, something unexpected happened once Edward eventually reached the throne. Invested with the aura of royalty, the scapegrace prince started to exude a benignly avuncular presence. Abandoning his first name Albert, with all its loaded associations, he chose to reign as Edward – a change that signalled a more general willingness to turn his back on his mother's legacy.

Victoria's beloved Osborne House was given to the Navy as a training college, and Edward abandoned her custom of teatime receptions in favour of evening courts.

In some ways Edward's style of kingship confirmed his mother's worst fears. His annual round was a constant cycle of pleasures, interspersed only when necessary with the expected regal duties. Christmas and the New Year were spent at Sandringham House in Norfolk, followed by a week's shooting in the country before the King returned to London for the State Opening of Parliament, then held in February. In early March Edward set out for Paris and Biarritz, followed perhaps by a cruise on the royal yacht. He was back in England by May, in time to preside over the London season, including such highlights as the Ascot and Goodwood race meetings and the June presentation of the year's crop of debutantes. At the start of August he was on the yacht again for the Cowes Regatta, after which it was time for his annual cure at Marienbad, a spa in Bohemia. Then there was a short stay in London, followed by Doncaster race week, with shooting and deer stalking at Balmoral in the month of October. The closing months of the year were divided between Buckingham Palace, Sandringham and Windsor.

> Edward became 'the most popular king England had known since the early 1660s, the first years of Charles II's Restoration'.
>
> J B Priestley, writer

Edward's subjects, then, were never under any illusions but that he liked to enjoy himself. Yet his hedonism suited the spirit of the times. Far from disapproving, as Victoria had feared, people came to see Edward as a reassuringly human figure whose taste for the comforts of life mirrored their own, albeit on a grander, more luxurious scale. Genial and good-hearted, this new Merry Monarch became identified with his time; the 1900s would be remembered as the Edwardian Era, a compliment that none of his immediate successors would share.

UNFINISHED BUSINESS – THE SECOND BOER WAR

The political system that the King found himself presiding over was something less than a democracy, at least by present-day standards. Barely a third of the adult population had the vote – more precisely, some two-thirds of the men and none of the women. The unelected House of Lords, mostly hereditary peers, had almost as much legislative power as the elected House of Commons, having the ability to reject bills approved by the lower house (although convention demanded that it should not exercise that right in respect of the Chancellor's annual budget). As one Liberal wit put it: 'The House of Lords represent nobody but themselves, and they enjoy the full confidence of their constituents.'

Edward also inherited Victoria's last prime minister, the bearded, myopic Lord Salisbury, who was already 70 years old and six years into his third term of office. An aristocratic Conservative of the old school, he regarded his chief field of expertise as foreign policy. He had been an architect of the 'splendid isolation' that had seen Britain avoid entanglements with Continental allies in favour of the unencumbered pursuit of its own imperial ambitions. It was fitting, then, that the great matter of Salisbury's final term was a colonial conflict.

Unlike most of the imperial ventures of Victoria's reign, the Boer War was fought against opponents of European origin. The Boers were white farmers, mostly from Dutch or German ethnic backgrounds, who had been contesting control of southern Africa with the British for many years past. The immediate cause of hostilities lay in Her Majesty's government's support for mainly British migrant workers who had flocked to the autonomous Boer republic of the Transvaal following the discovery of gold and diamonds there in the 1880s. The dispute over the civil rights of these *uitlanders* (foreign immigrants) offered convenient cover for British ambitions to incorporate the mineral-rich Boer state of Transvaal and its sister republic, the Orange Free State, within a British-dominated federation. When negotiations came to nothing, the two sides went to war.

The British under siege

In the first months of the fighting, the Boer forces surprised their powerful opponents by taking the offensive, and soon substantial British forces were cooped up under siege in the towns of Mafeking, Kimberley and Ladysmith, all within Britain's imperial territory. Initial attempts to relieve the garrisons resulted in

EARLY BOER SUCCESS
It was Britain's opponents who took the initiative when the fighting began in October 1899 and to begin with they had considerable success. Below, a crowd of onlookers turn out to watch a trainload of British prisoners of war arriving in the Boer capital, Pretoria. The Boers were unconventional fighters. They had no standing army, no uniforms and no formal military training. All men and boys over the age of 14 – for the most part farmers and smallholders – were required to fight, bringing their own arms and horses with them. They were skilled marksmen and they also had modern weapons shipped in from Europe, mainly Germany, in the years before the war. They used commando-style tactics, employing small groups of snipers to divert attention from their main forces, and proved masters of camouflage. It was in response to this that the British forces adopted khaki rather than the traditional scarlet uniforms, which had made them easy targets in the veldt.

TROOP SURGE
The response to early setbacks in the war was to send out more troops. By January 1900 some 180,000 men had been assembled from all corners of the Empire – the largest array of fighting men Britain had ever sent overseas. As they drove north toward the besieged town of Mafeking, they met heavy resistance. The soldiers above, under the command of Lord Methuen, are in action at Honey Nest Kloof. When Mafeking was relieved on 17 May, 1900, the news (left) triggered rejoicing across Britain.

significant British defeats, notably at Colenso and Spion Kop, and it was only after massive reinforcements arrived in early 1900 that the tide of battle began to turn.

Kimberley was the first siege to be lifted, on 15 February, 1900, followed by Ladysmith on 28 February; both had stood firm for four months. The news was greeted with rejoicing back in Britain, but when Mafeking was finally relieved – on 17 May, after holding out for 217 days – the British public reacted with almost hysterical joy. A new word, 'mafficking', was coined to describe the scenes of jubilation in all the major cities. The garrison's commander, Colonel Robert Baden-Powell, became a national hero. Further successes followed, and by late 1900 the Orange Free State had been annexed and imperial troops had marched into the Transvaal's capital, Pretoria.

THE ROAD TO PRETORIA

Early in 1900 a new commander arrived in South Africa to direct the British war effort. Field Marshal Lord Roberts (left) was a 67-year-old veteran of many campaigns. He had won the Victoria Cross 41 years earlier for gallantry in the Indian Mutiny and had also seen active service in Afghanistan. He was able to use the vastly increased troop numbers available to him to turn the tide of battle, forcing the surrender of the Boer general Piet Cronjé with 4,000 men at Paardeberg before moving on to capture Bloemfontein, capital of the Orange Free State. The road then lay open to Pretoria. Although the going was not quite as easy as suggested by the cigarette advertisement at bottom left, Boer resistance by then had been largely broken. After brushing aside a force of some 800 marksmen at the Zand River (right), the British entered the capital unopposed on 5 June, 1900. Roberts subsequently saw fit to declare the war over – prematurely, as it turned out, for a whole new phase was about to begin with the Boer forces adopting guerrilla tactics.

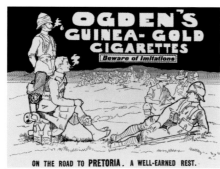

ON THE ROAD TO PRETORIA. A WELL-EARNED REST.

Premature peace

The British commander in South Africa, Field Marshal Lord Roberts, felt satisfied enough with the situation to declare the war over. One consequence of the change in fortune was an upsurge in patriotic support for the government of the day back in Britain. In the 'Khaki Election' that took place in the autumn of 1900, Salisbury's Conservatives – often referred to at the time as 'Unionists' because of their alliance over the previous 15 years with defecting Liberal Unionists opposed to Irish Home Rule – were convincingly returned to power for a fresh term in office, although with a marginally reduced majority over the opposition Liberal Party. Conditions seemed set for a swift end to hostilities and for the subsequent incorporation of the troublesome Boer farmers into an expanded British imperium.

The Boers thought otherwise. Although their armies had been defeated, their resistance was not and they pursued a bitter guerrilla campaign for another two years. In response, the British army brought in Lord Kitchener – who had recently avenged the death of General Gordon at Khatoum with victory at Omdurman in the Sudan – to take over from Roberts.

continued on page 28

BEHIND BRITISH LINES

Learning from the mistakes of the Crimean War, the British army was better equipped to cope with battlefield casualties in the Boer conflict than it had been in Florence Nightingale's day. The Royal Army Medical Corps, which had been set up the year before the Second Boer War started, provided officers and men to staff field hospitals where the wounded were treated (right). They were helped by stretcher-bearers – including the young Mohandas Gandhi, who had been working in Durban as a lawyer at the time – and by volunteer nurses (left). In all, some 22,000 soldiers were treated for wounds over the course of the war. Disease proved a far greater menace than the fighting, accounting for more than twice as many deaths. Spread by crowded and insanitary living conditions – the two soldiers mending cavalry equipment below were relatively well housed – dysentery and enteric fever took a terrible toll, not least in tented hospitals like this one (left), set up with Boer permission outside Ladysmith to treat the sick and wounded of the besieged town.

Britain's concentration camp shame

Kitchener introduced a savage scorched-earth policy to deprive the Boer fighters of local support, burning farmsteads and forcibly moving wives and children into tented internment centres – concentration camps. Overcrowded and underfunded, the camps became breeding grounds of epidemic disease. Malnutrition was endemic. By the end of the war, some 26,000 Boer women and children would die in these concentration centres, and several thousand more black Africans succumbed as prisoners in separate camps.

Although Kitchener's tactics proved militarily effective, they were hugely controversial. The war had always been regarded with hostility abroad, where it was seen as a land-grab engineered by British imperialists eager to get their hands on the Transvaal gold and diamonds. The Boers' political leader, President Paul Kruger, received a hero's welcome when he travelled to Europe in search of diplomatic support. For a time Britain was so unpopular on the Continent that an intended visit by the Prince of Wales, the future Edward VII, to the Paris Universal Exhibition of 1900 was abandoned for fear of a hostile reception.

Divided opinions

Public opinion in Britain became aroused when reports on the camps began to circulate, largely due to the investigations of the welfare campaigner Emily Hobhouse. Soon the nation was divided between supporters of the war and protesters eager to bring it to a speedy end. The opposition Liberal Party took up the anti-war cause under the inspiration of a fiery young MP from north Wales,

BITTER EXILE
The British military authorities had considerable difficulty knowing what to do with the thousands of prisoners they took in the course of the war. Fearing that prison camps in the occupied lands would be obvious targets for raiders seeking to set the captives free, they sought alternative solutions. At first ships were used as temporary internment centres. When that expedient proved insufficient, the next step was to send captured fighters abroad. Some 5,000 men and boys, including the Boer general Piet Cronjé, were despatched to St Helena, the tiny mid-Atlantic island where Napoleon's life had ended. A similar number were sent to Ceylon (now Sri Lanka), and smaller contingents to other parts of the Indian subcontinent; the group above – mainly old men and young boys – were photographed at Kakul in what is now Pakistan. In the later stages of the war, non-combatant civilians were herded into concentration camps – a term newly minted at the time – to prevent them from offering support to the guerrilla fighters; many thousands died of starvation and disease.

QUEST FOR AN ELUSIVE PEACE
Despite British expectations of a quick settlement after the fall of Pretoria, the war dragged on for another two years. The Boers could no longer muster sufficient forces to confront their opponents in pitched battle, but they were not prepared to concede. Instead, they drew on their superior knowledge of local terrain and adopted guerrilla tactics, raiding supply lines and attacking isolated outposts. British commanders found it hard to counter these mobile raiders. Eventually more than 50,000 troops were committed to manning a network of fortified blockhouses, each one designed to house from six to eight guards. At the same time the British made overtures to the Boer commanders, offering peace terms that were initially rejected. The Boer and British leaders met for the first time in March 1901 to discuss a settlement (below); Kitchener is seated second from right.

'When is a war not a war? When it is carried on by methods of barbarism in South Africa.'

Sir Henry Campbell-Bannerman, Liberal Party leader, June 1901

David Lloyd George. He did not mince his words, stating publicly 'We have now taken to killing babies'. And Sir Henry Campbell-Bannerman, the mild-mannered Liberal leader, left no doubt that Lloyd George had his full support.

The divisions in the nation came to a head that December when Lloyd George was invited to address an anti-war rally in Birmingham. The city was the political stronghold of Joseph Chamberlain, a passionate advocate of empire whose defection to the Conservatives 15 years earlier over Irish Home Rule had split the Liberal Party and lost them power. To Chamberlain and his supporters, Lloyd George was little more than a traitor and his presence in the city was taken as a slap in the face by the pro-war lobby. Chamberlain himself privately commented that 'If Lloyd George wants his life, he had better keep away from Birmingham …

VICTORY CELEBRATION
On 31 May, 1902, crowds stretch as far as the eye can see in the City of London to celebrate the end of the Boer War. By the terms of the Treaty of Vereeniging, signed that day, Britain annexed the two formerly independent Boer republics – the South African Republic and the Orange Free State – which thus became part of the British Empire. But victory came at a high price. More than 6,000 British troops had been killed in battle, and more than twice that number had died of disease; Boer civilians had suffered even more heavily. In cash terms, the war had cost over £200 million, a huge sum at the time.

If he doesn't go, I will see that it is known that he is afraid. If he does go, he will deserve all he gets.' On the night Birmingham's town hall was packed with Chamberlain loyalists. The Welsh orator got no further than the first few sentences of his speech, in which he protested at the Union Jack, 'the pride and property of our common country', being turned instead 'into Mr Chamberlain's pocket handkerchief'. That was enough, and the crowd stormed the stage. Lloyd George was smuggled out of a back door disguised in a policeman's uniform. In the ensuing fighting two people, one of them a police constable, were killed.

The end at last
The last Boer guerrillas surrendered in May 1902 and the Treaty of Vereeniging officially ended the war. The Boer republics ceased to exist as independent entities and the Union of South Africa was born. For Britain it had been an expensive victory – almost 20,000 soldiers had lost their lives – and it now agreed to provide some £3 million in reconstruction funds. Just seven years later, the Boer republics would win a new constitution and a return to limited self-government. The settlement at least healed the rift between pro and anti-war factions at home. The rest of the decade was to be a time of peace, in which the clash between conservatives and progressives would be fought over domestic social issues.

ANTICIPATING THE FUTURE

In 1901 a rising young author greeted the new century with a work of prophecy. Thirty-four years old at the time, H G Wells had already established a reputation as a science-fiction pioneer with such novels as *The Time Machine*, *The Invisible Man* and *The War of the Worlds*. Now, in a work entitled *Anticipations of the Reaction of Mechanical and Scientific Progress upon Human Life and Thought*, he set out his vision of the world as it might be in the year 2000. It was an extraordinarily prescient vision of technological change, showing how the future looked to a far-sighted individual as the Victorian era came to an end.

One of Wells's most inspired insights was to realise, at the dawn of the automobile era, how profoundly the new development would affect the future world. He foresaw that motor vehicles powered by 'explosive engines' employing gas or petrol would put an end to the 19th-century 'Age of Coal and Steam'. At a time when legislation still limited cars to 12 miles per hour, he predicted the

coming of motor trucks carrying goods in bulk, motor buses replacing the horse-drawn omnibuses and carriages of his time, and 'hired or privately owned motor carriages' capable of travelling 300 miles or more in a day. These wonders would travel on roads exclusively reserved for motor transport, surfaced with 'very good asphalt sloped to drain', that would cross one another by means of flyovers and underpasses to combat the risk of congestion at junctions.

Extending his vision, he foresaw the outward spread of cities and the start of long-distance commuting, forecasting that 'it is not too much to say that the London citizen of the year AD 2000 may have a choice of nearly all England and Wales south of Nottingham and east of Exeter as his suburb'. In time, Wells predicted, all Britain short of the Scottish Highlands would come to be linked in a single, loose urban region, criss-crossed with telephone poles and dotted with wooded areas and 'islands of agriculture'. The boundaries between city and country life would fade until 'to receive the daily paper a few hours late, to wait a day or so for goods one has ordered will be the extreme measure of rusticity'.

He proposed the growth of telesales and mail-order to stock 'the convenient home of the future, with its numerous electrical and mechanical appliances, and the various bicycles, motor-cars, photographic and phonographic apparatus that will be included in its equipment'. The house would probably be 'warmed in its walls from some power-generating station'. He sketched the trend to en-suite facilities, suggesting that 'every bedroom will have its own bath-dressing room' equipped with hot and cold water. Meanwhile in the kitchen the days of the cook 'working with a crimsoned face and bare, blackened arms' were numbered, for 'with a neat little range, heated by electricity and provided with thermometers, with absolutely controllable temperatures and proper heat screens, cooking might very easily be made a pleasant amusement'. Wells even predicted green roofs: chimneys would disappear, making 'the roof a clean and pleasant addition to the garden spaces of the home'.

From prediction to science fact

At the very time when Wells was making his predictions, scientists and engineers were at work helping to create the technological future of his imaginings. In 1901 the Italian-born Guglielmo Marconi sent the first wireless message across the

TECHNOLOGICAL ADVANCES
For far-sighted observers the world in 1900 was already growing smaller. Trains and ocean-going liners had reduced travel times, and they would soon be shrunk further by the coming of aviation. Telephone exchanges like this one in Manchester were humming with activity, and providing new work opportunities for women. Radio would soon supply a medium for almost-instant delivery of messages; Marconi's first transatlantic transmissions took place early

in the decade, bringing competition for the existing ocean-crossing telegraph cables. For the average householder, such developments were less significant at the time than devices that helped in the home. Gas lighting was widespread in cities by the turn of the century, and soon there was growing interest in electrical appliances like the ones above (top left) advertised in a Northampton newspaper in 1908. Yet the market remained small; by 1910 just 2 per cent of British homes had electricity.

Atlantic, from a transmission station in Ireland to a kite-supported antenna in St Johns, Newfoundland. In 1902 Oliver Heaviside proposed the existence of a layer of gas in what is now known as the ionosphere that would not allow electromagnetic waves to escape into space; it is this band, now known as the Heaviside Layer, that bounces radio signals back to Earth, making global broadcasting possible. Even more radically, the New Zealand-born physicist Ernest Rutherford was making fundamental discoveries about the nature of matter; revealed to the world in his 1904 book *Radioactivity*, these would pave the way for the splitting of the atom. The world was indeed changing, even if most people could only sense the coming transformations dimly.

EXPLORERS IN ANTARCTICA

The heroic age of Antarctic exploration got underway in 1897 with a Belgian expedition that unintentionally became the first to over-winter in the Antarctic Circle when its ship became icebound in the Bellingshausen Sea. The first British-financed expedition set out the following year; led by the Norwegian Carsten Borchgrevnik, it spent the winter on the Antarctic mainland at Cape Adare. In 1901 Captain Robert Falcon Scott (right) led a more ambitious venture; their equipment included a tethered observation balloon used for aerial surveys (left). Besides undertaking scientific work, Scott led a sledge team consisting of himself, Ernest Shackleton and Edward Wilson on a journey further south than anyone before them, coming within 500 miles of the South Pole. The three-man team is pictured above celebrating Christmas 1902, shortly before returning to base camp. The other great Antarctic enterprise in the decade was the 1907-9 *Nimrod* expedition led by Shackleton (top left). Basing himself, like Scott before him, in McMurdo Sound, Shackleton took a different route to within 100 miles of the Pole before bad weather and the prospect of starvation forced him and his team to return to base. As the decade ended the Pole had not yet been achieved, but the Antarctic was fixed in the public imagination as an arena that tested the limits of human endurance.

KEEPING A STEADY COURSE

By the summer of 1902 Lord Salisbury, now 72 years old and in ailing health, was ready to step down from the premiership. He did not look far for a successor. Arthur Balfour, the rising star of the Conservative Party, was the obvious choice – he was also Salisbury's nephew.

STEADY AS SHE GOES Onlookers watch the launch of the battlecruiser HMS *Indomitable* from Glasgow docks in March 1907. Britain was still a world leader in shipbuilding at the time.

ARTFUL ARTHUR – THE NEW PM

Balfour owed his promotion to his uncle, Lord Salisbury, who had chosen him as his parliamentary private secretary in 1878 and then, in 1887, made him Chief Secretary for Ireland – a shock appointment said to have given rise to the expression 'Bob's your uncle!' (coined for Robert, Lord Salisbury). Balfour took a carrot-and-stick approach to Ireland. On the one hand he sought to subdue the desire for Home Rule by alleviating poverty and helping Irish tenants to buy the land they farmed. On the other, he sought to end nationalist protest by bringing in legislation to ban boycotts and intimidation; when police enforcing the new law killed three demonstrators, nationalists dubbed him 'bloody Balfour'.

At Westminster, his tenure as Irish secretary was generally considered a success, establishing his credentials as a potential Conservative leader. He enhanced his claim by his eloquence and subtlety as a parliamentary speaker. Nobody ever doubted his intelligence, least of all Balfour himself, who once said of a colleague 'If he had a little more brains he'd be a half-wit'. He was also perhaps the only British premier to write books on metaphysics, notably a *Defence of Philosophic Doubt*, and a study of theology entitled *The Foundations of Belief*.

BACHELOR BALFOUR
Conservative Prime Minister Arthur Balfour had been born into the enchanted circle of well-connected families who dominated politics in late Victorian times. His mother was the daughter of the 2nd Marquess of Salisbury and his father was a millionaire Scottish landowner and MP. His father died when Arthur was just 8 years old, leaving him one of the wealthiest heirs in Britain. He studied at Eton and at Trinity College, Cambridge, and became an MP at the age of 26, with a seat in Cabinet before he was 40. One of the few major setbacks in his seemingly charmed life was the death from typhus of Mary Lyttelton, a cousin and the love of his life whom he had hoped to marry. Perhaps this sadness helps to explain why, for all his gifts, he remained an aloof figure who once declared: 'Nothing matters very much, and most things don't matter at all.' One of his few passions was golf; for a time he was captain of the Royal and Ancient Golf Club of St Andrews.

CHANGE IN THE CLASSROOM

By 1900 Britain had many more primary schools than three decades earlier, when the Education Act of 1870 had set out to promote state schooling. Yet politicians and employers alike felt that the nation was falling behind its Continental rivals, and in particular Germany. Balfour described the school system as 'chaotic, ineffectual, and utterly behind the age'. By the terms of the 1870 Act, the administration of schools in England and Wales was devolved to some 2,500 separate school boards. The vast majority of state-school pupils finished their education at age 12; barely 2 per cent went on to any kind of secondary study at all. As a result a new Education Bill was introduced which passed into law in 1902. This scrapped the school boards set up since 1870 and instead placed all state-funded schools under the control of newly established local education authorities, which were given powers to vet teaching standards and promote secondary learning. The system brought in under the 1902 Act is the basis of state education in England and Wales to this day.

NON-CONFORMIST ANGER

Uncontroversial though it may now seem, Balfour's 1902 Education Act roused deep passions at the time. Most of the opposition came from Methodists and other Non-conformist religious groups who saw the measure as a surreptitious way of providing tax-financed subsidies for Church of England schools. A Baptist minister named John Clifford led the anti-campaign, staging large-scale demonstrations like the march below on the Thames Embankment in London. The National Passive Resistance Committee led by Clifford encouraged supporters to refuse to pay the education rates, and over 170 people eventually went to prison for doing so. The bill itself went through 59 days of heated debate in Parliament before it was passed into law. Resentment of the Act melted away once its provisions came into effect.

In his term as Prime Minister, Balfour's main achievement was the Education Act of 1902, which laid the foundations of the modern state education system in England and Wales (Scotland had its own system). The measure built on its 1870 predecessor, by which school boards had been set up in order to construct schools and provide elementary education for children up to the age of 12. In practice, more children had continued to attend so-called 'voluntary' institutions, mostly run by the Church of England, than the new board schools. Balfour's bill sought to bring British practice into line with the best Continental models. It abolished the school boards and instead placed all schools, whether voluntary or state-supported, under local authority control. It also encouraged county councils to promote secondary education, with the result that the number of state-aided schools for teenagers doubled within five years of the 1902 Act coming into force.

Surprising as it may seem today, the Education Act proved controversial, mainly because it provided state funding for Church schools. Non-conformists railed against what they termed 'religion on the rates', seeing the grants as a surreptitious way of providing government financial support for the Anglican establishment. Yet the changes brought in by the Act quickly bedded down and were never subsequently challenged. In effect, Balfour's move provided a ladder

by which more able pupils from the lower-middle and working classes could pursue their studies beyond the age of 12. By 1910 there were over 150,000 students in state-supported secondary institutions.

Forging foreign alliances

The changes that took place in British foreign policy in the Balfour years had long-term significance. The main drift was away from Salisbury's position of 'splendid isolation' towards closer ties with selected overseas allies. Britain had been forced into cooperation with foreign powers in 1900, when the Boxer Rebellion erupted in China. Angered by the level of overseas involvement in China, and with the sanction of the dowager-empress Cixi, the Boxer rebels (the Chinese name translates as the 'Righteous and Harmonious Fists') attacked and killed Christian missionaries and Chinese Christians, and besieged the foreign legations in Beijing. The uprising was eventually put down by a multinational force that brought together troops from eight countries, with Britain, Japan and Russia the biggest contributors. Cooperation with Japan was subsequently extended into a full-scale alliance, signed in London's Lansdowne House in 1902.

The Continental opposition to Britain's involvement in the Boer War had shown just how exposed the nation's position had become within Europe. Through the diplomacy of Otto von Bismarck, the German Chancellor, two blocs of alliances had formed in the previous decades, one linking Germany with Austro-Hungary and Italy, the other comprising France and Russia. For a time, Salisbury and Balfour hesitated between the two: Germany was the rising power, but it also showed a competitive urge that made it a potential threat.

So Balfour was already inclining towards the notion of alliance with France when it was announced that Edward VII would visit Paris as part of a 1903 tour of European capitals. There was apprehension in advance of the visit and little warmth in the reception that the King received on first arrival. Then, on a visit to the theatre, Edward noticed a French actress in the foyer whom he had previously seen on the London stage. Abandoning protocol, he made his way over to kiss her hand, complimenting her on a performance that represented 'all the grace and spirit of France'. This exhibition of gallantry was widely reported in the press the following morning, triggering a burst of enthusiasm for the British King. He was subsequently applauded on a visit to the Longchamp race-course and cheered on his way to a state banquet at the Elysée Palace.

By the end of Edward's visit, relations between the two nations were appreciably warmer, paving the way for the 1904 agreements known as the Entente Cordiale. This historic rapprochement established an Anglo-French alliance that would last through two world wars. It marked a joint awareness of the growing might of

MAKING FRIENDS
A French cartoon of President Emile Loubet and Edward VII, on the occasion of the King's visit to Paris in 1903, reflects a new spirit of political friendship between the two nations. Previously, Anglo-French relations had been distinctly frosty. Conflicting colonial ambitions had brought them to the brink of war over the Fashoda crisis of 1899. There was also disagreement over the Boer War, for which Britain was widely condemned in France, as across most of Europe. But by 1903, stimulated in part by fear of the growing might of Germany, both had reason to seek a *rapprochement* and old rivalries were set aside. Britain's closer ties with France were due in no small part to the influence of the King, himself a keen Francophile who enjoyed a holiday every year at Biarritz on the Bay of Biscay. His 1903 visit to the French capital turned into an extraordinary personal triumph.

FACES OF EMPIRE

'My name is George Nathaniel Curzon, I am a most superior person …' So began a well-known rhyme describing Baron Curzon of Kedleston (left), Viceroy of India from 1899 to 1905. Highly educated and much travelled, the aristocratic statesman became obsessed with the danger that Russian territorial ambitions were thought to present to the northern frontier of the British Raj. Responding to rumours that Russian influence was on the rise in Lhasa, the Tibetan capital, he determined to counter it by force. He despatched a military expedition to Tibet in 1903 under the command of Francis Younghusband (above), a career military officer who shared Curzon's passion for adventurous journeys through little-known regions. Younghusband's incursion was met by fierce resistance, but the British imperial troops reached the Tibetan capital in August 1904. Yet the achievement brought no political gains and proved expensive both in cash and in lives, particularly Tibetan ones.

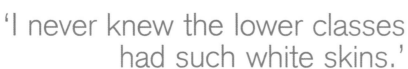

'I never knew the lower classes had such white skins.'

Lord Curzon, on seeing soldiers bathing

Germany, as well as a desire to avoid colonial clashes of the type that had soured relations between the two powers in the closing decades of the 19th century.

The new mood of conciliation eventually extended to include France's ally Russia, despite a tragic incident in the North Sea in October 1904. Having become embroiled with Japan in the Far East, the Tsar dispatched his Baltic fleet to sail halfway round the world to confront the enemy in the Pacific Ocean. The ships happened by night on a group of Hull trawlers fishing on the Dogger Bank. Mistaking them for Japanese torpedo boats, Russian warships opened fire, sinking one of the trawlers. Three British fishermen were killed and others were wounded. The Russians also fired on one another, causing further casualties.

At a time of heightened tension, this tragic farce could have been the spark for war. But although there was much anger in Britain, the incident was settled through diplomatic channels. The Russian government agreed to pay £66,000 in compensation – a huge sum at the time – and the responsible officers were disciplined. A statue was erected in Hull commemorating the dead fishermen. Anglo-Russian relations were not permanently damaged and within three years of the unfortunate clash diplomats from both sides were signing an entente of their own, calming the fears of Russian encroachment on India that had for so long caused friction between the two great powers.

DIVISIONS OVER EMPIRE

In the wider world beyond Europe, policy continued to be dominated by imperial matters. By 1900 the British Empire was, in geographical terms, nearing its greatest extent. The new decade saw further expansion. On 1 January, 1900, the government took over lands in West Africa that had been administered privately by the Royal Niger Company; these were combined with the small Niger Coast Protectorate to form the colony of Southern Nigeria. In the same year an amorphous protectorate was proclaimed over Northern Nigeria; military action was subsequently required to extend British control over the emirate of Kano.

Incursion into Tibet

Lord Curzon, the autocratic Viceroy of India, launched an altogether more ambitious venture when he dispatched a force several thousand strong under Major Francis Younghusband into the mountains of Tibet. Younghusband set out in the hope of negotiating a trade agreement and countering Russian influence, always feared as a potential threat on the northern borders of the Raj. When the Dalai Lama refused to respond, Curzon sent more troops, many of them Gurkhas and Pathan hill people from the other side of the border, with instructions to march on Lhasa, a forbidden city then virtually unknown in the West.

The Tibetans chose to resist, and an extraordinary campaign ensued as the imperial force pressed forward through some of the world's most difficult terrain. The defenders fought bravely, but had no answer to British Maxim guns; several thousand Tibetans died while inflicting a couple of hundred fatalities on the invaders. Younghusband eventually reached his destination in August 1904, eight months after setting out from base camp, only to find that the Dalai Lama,

Thubten Gyatso, had fled to Outer Mongolia. Younghusband imposed a punitive settlement on the Dalai Lama's deputy, which was never in fact fully implemented, then withdrew to India. The incursion, although a remarkable feat of arms, achieved little except to further humiliate China, which had proved incapable of defending the Tibetan territory that nominally came under its protective aegis.

Anti-imperialist views

The Tibetan expedition proved controversial back in London, where the appetite for colonial adventure was much reduced in the wake of the Boer War. A current of liberal opinion now viewed all such enterprises as greedy and unproductive. In 1902, J A Hobson had published *Imperialism*, a highly influential book in which he argued that the scramble for colonies in the late 19th century had not been driven by any real national interest but rather by international financiers interested in quick profits. Such views lay behind a fierce wave of agitation that opposed Balfour's decision, in the wake of the Boer War, to allow indentured Chinese labour into South Africa to work the Witwatersrand gold mines.

The natural home of such hostility to unbridled imperialism was the Liberal Party, and as long as the Conservatives remained in power, the imperial cause was firmly in the ascendant. Its greatest champion was Joseph Chamberlain, who would declare in a 1906 speech, 'England without an empire! Can you conceive it? England in that case would not be the England we love.'

Chamberlain's 'imperial preference'

Yet Chamberlain's very enthusiasm for the imperial cause would itself become deeply divisive in the Conservative Party. Ever since the repeal of the Corn Laws in 1846, Victorian Britain had remained wedded to the cause of free trade. For much of that time the nation had prospered, but by 1900 British merchants were feeling the pinch of serious competition from overseas, with the greatest challenge coming from the rising economies of Germany and the USA. Chamberlain thought he saw an opportunity to boost the Empire at the same time as bolstering Conservative support in the business community and generating government revenue for social welfare initiatives to boot. Promoting what he viewed as a win-win solution, he proposed a system of customs tariffs on goods imported from countries beyond the Empire's bounds.

As opponents both within and outside the Conservative Party were quick to point out, there were obvious disadvantages to Chamberlain's strategy of Imperial Preference, as it was known. On the one hand it would encourage the erection of similar trade barriers against British goods in the countries to which it applied; and on the other, it would increase the cost of imports from lands outside the Empire, and these included some of Britain's major trading partners. In particular, huge

continued on page 49

POPULAR PREFERENCE
Joseph Chamberlain being greeted by supporters in the run-up to the 1906 general election. His policy of Imperial Preference – creating preferential trade tariffs for empire-made goods – was seen by its opponents as an attack on free trade and it split the Conservative Party, contributing more than any other factor to the Liberal victory in the election. It was the second time that Chamberlain had caused such a rift: 20 years earlier he had left the Liberals over the issue of Irish Home Rule, taking a considerable section of the party with him.

A WORLDWIDE WEB OF TRADE

Seaborne trade, like the goods seen here piled up in Liverpool docks, was the lifeblood of Edwardian Britain – literally so, as the nation had come to rely on food imports to keep the population from going hungry. Even the production of favourite staples like Cadbury's cocoa (below) presupposed regular deliveries of raw beans from colonies in Africa. There were worries, though, that Britain's international position in terms of both trade and manufacturing was deteriorating; while manufacturing exports had increased by 30 per cent between 1885 and 1900, those for Germany had grown twice as fast over the same period and the value of US exports almost doubled. The discontent of manufacturers about such competition from foreign produce was one of the main forces that drove the protectionist campaign for Imperial Preference, begun by Joseph Chamberlain. Ultimately, the campaign was divisive and led to a humiliating defeat for the Conservatives at the general election of January 1906. The Liberal Party were returned to power on a policy pledging to continue free trade.

CADBURY'S COCOA

THE·OLDEST·AND·STILL·THE·BEST

YOUNG WINSTON
By the time this portrait of Winston Churchill was taken in 1904, he had already packed more adventure into his first three decades than most politicians see in a lifetime. He was born at Blenheim Palace on 30 November, 1874, the eldest son of the Conservative MP Lord Randolph Churchill and his beautiful American wife Jennie, daughter of the New York financier Leonard Jerome. At first Winston pursued a military career, seeing active service in Malakand (now in Pakistan) and in the Sudan, where he participated in a cavalry charge at the Battle of Omdurman. Covering the Boer War as a newspaper correspondent, he was captured and subsequently escaped from a prisoner-of-war camp, trekking almost 300 miles to safety through hostile territory. He was elected as a Conservative MP in the Khaki Election of 1900, but later crossed the House to the Liberals over the issue of Imperial Preference, which he opposed.

'He [Balfour] saw a great deal of life from afar.'

Ramsay MacDonald, leader of the Labour Party

amounts of wheat were brought into the country from the USA, as well as beef from Argentina and dairy products from Denmark and the Netherlands. The inevitable result would be a substantial hike in the cost of food.

In the years between 1903 and 1905 the Conservatives split down the middle over the issue of preferential tariffs. In its way, Imperial Preference was as divisive for the party as the question of relations with the European Community would be almost a century later in the 1990s. Free-traders, including Balfour's Chancellor of the Exchequer, C T Ritchie, passionately opposed the protectionist policy. Finding his plans stymied by such opposition, Chamberlain announced his intention to resign from the Cabinet.

Balfour had refused to commit himself to either side in the argument, seeking to straddle the growing divide. Now, he accepted Chamberlain's decision to resign, but sought to balance it by also forcing the resignation from the Cabinet of Ritchie and another prominent free-trader, Lord Balfour of Burleigh, the Secretary for Scotland. Other demissions followed and in 1904 a rising young Conservative MP, just 29 years old and recently back from adventures in the Boer War, crossed the floor to join the Liberal Party over the issue. His name was Winston Churchill.

Balfour's bane – a gift to the Liberals

The split that was tearing the Unionists apart failed to bring out the best in their leader. Prime Minister Balfour was often accused of viewing the world with lofty intellectual detachment and in this moment of crisis his instinct was to look for a middle way between free trade and protectionism. So he proposed a policy of retaliatory tariffs that would only apply to nations that themselves placed duties on British imports. The result was an unsatisfactory compromise that pleased neither side of the party.

Meanwhile, Chamberlain was using his new-found freedom from the restraints of Cabinet membership to carry the crusade for Imperial Preference across the country. Adopting the slogan 'Tariff Reform Means Work for All!', he attracted vast crowds with his oratory. Soon a newly formed Tariff Reform League was expensively touting the virtues of his plan, and something like open warfare had broken out between protectionists and free traders within the Unionist ranks. Balfour's authority was fatally weakened.

In this extremity the Prime Minister made a fateful decision. Believing that the Liberals, who had divisions of their own, might be unable to form a functioning government, he resigned from office in December 1905, hoping that a renewed mandate from the public would restore his authority in the party. But the prospect of power concentrated Liberal minds. Before the year was out their leader Henry Campbell-Bannerman was ensconced as Prime Minister in Balfour's place, at the head of a Cabinet committed to free trade.

In the general election that followed, in January 1906, the Conservatives and Unionists were routed, losing more than half their seats and putting an end to two decades of predominantly Tory rule. The Liberals were returned to power with 397 out of the 670 available seats, the greatest electoral victory in their history. In the general rout even Balfour lost his seat in Manchester East; he rapidly returned to the House via a safe seat in the City of London, but no-one doubted the depth of the humiliation he had suffered.

PRESS BARONS AND MUSIC HALL DUCHESSES

One reason why Imperial Preference had achieved such traction was the noisy backing it received from much of the British press. The development of mass-market journalism catering for the newly literate class emerging from the board schools had been one of the most significant innovations of the past two decades. The pioneer of the movement was the publisher George Newnes whose weekly *Tit-Bits*, presenting itself as a digest of the most interesting news snippets from all the world's periodicals, built up a circulation of over half a million readers.

One man to see the possibilities was Alfred Harmsworth. By the age of 23 he had launched a rival to *Tit-Bits* called *Answers to Correspondents*. The publication thrived on promotions, which Harmsworth did much to pioneer, including one promising 'a pound a week for life' – the answer given by a tramp on the Embankment when the budding publishing mogul asked him what he most dreamed of possessing. Other weeklies followed, and they were successful enough to encourage Harmsworth to move into daily newspapers. Starting with the *London Evening News*, which he bought in 1894, he went on to found the

PIONEERS OF MASS JOURNALISM
Between them, Alfred Harmsworth (above left) and Arthur Pearson (above) created mass-market journalism in Britain. They were almost exact contemporaries, being born and dying within a year of one another. In other respects, they had very different lives. Pearson was educated at Winchester and had the easier childhood of the two, but in later life lost his sight to glaucoma. Harmsworth, later ennobled as Lord Northcliffe, was the son of an alcoholic barrister. Northcliffe ruffled many feathers during his career – Lloyd George once said of him 'Even the Almighty formed a Trinity, Northcliffe is a Unitarian'. But even so, Lloyd George appointed him director of propaganda in his First World War Cabinet.

VOICE OF THE PEOPLE

Born in 1870, the eldest of 12 children, Matilda Alice Victoria Wood – known as Tilly – became famous as the singer Marie Lloyd, seen here in a portrait taken in about 1900. Her parents lived in the Hoxton district of inner-city London, earning their living making artificial flowers on piecework for an Italian dealer. Encouraged by an aunt who was a dancer, Marie began performing in public from the age of 5 and started her professional career aged just 15. Within a year, she was earning up to £100 a week – a huge sum at the time – in the big West End music halls.

Marie Lloyd remained a star until her death in 1922, popular with fellow performers as well as audiences. In the so-called 'Music-Hall War' of 1907, when music hall performers went on strike for better pay and conditions, Lloyd came out in support of the strikers, stating 'We [the stars] are fighting not for ourselves but for the poorer members of the profession, earning 30 shillings to £3 a week'. The strike ended in arbitration and the performers winning a minimum-wage agreement.

Daily Mail two years later. Right from the start the *Mail* threw itself behind the Unionist cause. Its hero was Joseph Chamberlain, its villains were anyone perceived to stand in the way of the Empire, a notable target being Emily Hobhouse who campaigned against the treatment of civilian prisoners in concentration camps in the Boer War.

Soon Harmsworth was successful enough in the newspaper business to attract competitors and in 1900 another entrepreneur, Arthur Pearson, established the *Daily Express* to compete with the *Mail*. A clergyman's son educated at Winchester School, Pearson introduced the innovation – radical at the time – of putting news on the paper's front page, rather than advertisements.

Harmsworth responded in 1903 with the *Daily Mirror*, originally targeted at a female audience and boasting 'an all woman staff for an all woman readership'. When that experiment failed, he relaunched the paper with a male editor, a reduced cover price and a new, tabloid format, stipulating that no story should run to more than 250 words. Other elements of Harmsworth's formula for the *Mirror* included the use of sub-headings to break up lengthy columns of text, the substitution of photographs for old-fashioned line drawings, and the introduction of gossip columns, household hints, competitions and special offers.

For his services to the media, Harmsworth was made 1st Viscount Northcliffe in Balfour's dissolution Honours List in 1905. He had earlier joked 'When I want a peerage I will pay for it like an honest man', and he did in fact receive it after investing large amounts of money in a local newspaper in Manchester, where Balfour had his seat, promising to make it 'the leading Conservative organ of the North'. In the years that followed he moved into quality journalism, buying up *The Observer* and then *The Times*. At first he struggled to raise the circulation of that ailing colossus, but eventually quadrupled its readership, primarily by the expedient of reducing the cover price to 1 penny.

Throughout the decade Harmsworth was a noisy, energetic presence who livened up the press of the day. He had few doubts of his own importance, yet the extent of the political influence of his publications is uncertain. Few of the causes that he campaigned for – whether to boost British aviation, or to persuade readers of the benefits of wholemeal bread – had much success, and the Liberal landslide of 1906 was won despite the hostility of all the Northcliffe newspapers.

Music to remember

The Edwardian age saw the last great flowering of music hall, with stars like George Robey, Harry Lauder, Vesta Tilley, Harry Champion, Little Tich and above all the great Marie Lloyd, all in their prime. In an age without radio, television, cinema or the internet, the demand for live entertainment was huge, and the music halls set out to fill it. In 1900 there were around 50 of them in the Greater London region alone and well over 200 in the rest of the country, with half a dozen each in Birmingham, Glasgow and Liverpool. Once raucous, music halls had become far more respectable since the 1880s, when legislation confined the sale of alcohol to licensed bars behind the stalls and circle. The subsequent reduction in drunkenness had turned the halls more into centres of family entertainment.

A typical variety bill included a dozen or so short acts, so stars moved from venue to venue, appearing in as many as four theatres in a single night. Alongside singers and stand-up comics there might be acrobats and dancers, notably the Tiller Girls, whose high-kicking, linked-arm precision routines were learned in a special school set up by the entrepreneur John Tiller. Even hard-up customers could afford a few pence for a seat in the gallery, where they sat crammed onto benches without back supports – as one audience member later recalled, 'you often got someone's feet in your back or orange peel down your neck'.

The plus side of the enforced intimacy in the audience was a wonderful sense of community that seasoned performers used to their advantage. Harry Lauder's winning combination of Lowland Scots wit and sentimental balladry would eventually make him the first British artist to sell more than a million records. Yet no-one worked the halls more effectively than Marie Lloyd, who attracted admirers from all backgrounds. The poet T S Eliot wrote of her 'genius' and her 'capacity for expressing the soul of the people'. To her core working-class audience, Marie was family. They loved her for the sentiment of her songs, for her Cockney humour and mildly risqué double-entendres – and for never forgetting where she came from. She retained her popularity to the end; when she died in 1922, more than 100,000 people paid their respects at her funeral procession.

Signs of change – moving pictures

Significantly for the future, moving pictures were just beginning to establish a foothold. The very first public film show in Britain had taken place at the Regent Street Polytechnic in London in 1896, and moving pictures were still a novelty in the early 1900s. Entrepreneurs with projectors toured small towns, putting on

'SCOTLAND'S GREATEST AMBASSADOR'
The singer-comedian Harry Lauder was born in Edinburgh in 1870, the same year as Marie Lloyd. He went to work part-time in a flax mill at the age of 13, following his father's death, but his natural talent as a comedian, singer and songwriter shone through. His show-business career began in local talent shows, graduating to music hall in Glasgow. He was an instant success when he first performed in London in 1900 and went on to international stardom, delighting audiences as far afield as the USA, where he performed many times, and Australia. His songs include 'Roamin' in the Gloamin' and 'Keep Right On to the End of the Road', which he wrote following the death of his son in the First World War, when he took to the road himself to pioneer entertainment for the troops. The epithet of 'Scotland's greatest ever ambassador' was bestowed by Winston Churchill.

FOREVER YOUNG
Peter Pan, J M Barrie's timeless creation, made his debut on the London stage on 27 December, 1904. This photograph (right) is of Stephanie Stephens in the role in 1906. The convention of Peter being played by a young woman, as in the tradition of pantomime principal boys, dates back to the very first performance. It got around the practical difficulty of finding young male actors suitable for the part, particularly as the children of the Darling family, whom Peter befriends, had to be even younger.

shows in improvised venues. The first purpose-built picture house was opened in Colne, Lancashire, in 1907 by a former magic-lantern showman. By the following year the new entertainment was generating enough excitement to cause tragedy, when 16 children were crushed to death as a crowd of 400 fought to enter a 'moving-picture show' held in a rented church hall in Barnsley.

J B Priestley would later describe a visit to one of the early cinemas – 'a certain Theatre-de-Luxe, where for sixpence you were given an hour or so of short films, a cup of tea and a biscuit'. He was unimpressed, comparing the experience unfavourably (as did T S Eliot) with the camaraderie of the music hall. Yet the future would belong to the flickering images on the silver screen.

THE GAP BETWEEN RICH AND POOR

The Conservative electoral debacle of January 1906 represented something of a watershed in the Edwardian era. In retrospect, the years of Tory rule under Lord Salisbury and Balfour can be seen politically as a continuation of the late Victorian consensus. The mood changed after the Liberal landslide, when a fresh awareness of the great divide that split British society came to the fore. In a time of general prosperity, observant citizens became more conscious than ever before of the yawning gap that separated the rich from the poor.

For the wealthiest section of society the decade was a time of conspicuous consumption, a term coined by the sociologist Thorstein Veblen in 1899 to describe the behaviour of America's new rich. Taxation was far less of a burden than it was to become in later years: income tax was levied at just 5 per cent and only on incomes above £160 a year. Fewer than a million out of the 33 million residents of England and Wales paid any income tax at all. Around 400,000 people declared annual incomes of more than £400 – sufficient to support a comfortably upper-middle-class lifestyle.

In Britain, the tone was set by royalty itself, for in contrast to Victoria's style of relatively modest respectability, Edward radiated an appetite for lavish enjoyment. At the top of the wealth pyramid came the elite who made up 'society', described by the Liberal critic C F G Masterman as 'an aggregation of clever, agreeable, often lovable people, whose material wants are satisfied by the labour of unknown workers in all the world, trying with a desperate seriousness to make something of a life spared the effort of wage-earning'.

EN ROUTE TO THE REGATTA
Ladies dressed in elegant summer finery and gentlemen in blazers and boaters make their way along the platform at Henley railway station, en route for the annual rowing regatta. Held over the first weekend in July, the event was a fixture of the summer season. Competitors as well as spectators belonged to 'polite' society – the rules specifically excluded 'mechanics, artisans or labourers' from participating, along with anyone 'who engaged in any menial activity'. The prohibition against the working classes was only dropped in 1937.

DRESSING FOR DINNER
For the well-to-do the formal dinner was a much-prized Edwardian institution. In society circles, according to Sir Charles Petrie, 'private dinner parties of 18 or 20 people were the rule rather than the exception, and the small dinner was unknown'. Hostesses were only able to contemplate such events thanks to the ready availability of servants to prepare and serve the food. For the most part, male guests still wore tailcoats; dinner jackets, known contemptuously as 'bum-freezers', were considered daringly modern. This group, photographed in 1909, were about to dine before attending a masonic ball.

The summer season

One focus for such efforts was the London season, which ran from the end of April to late July. Among the chief purposes of the 'season' was the finding of suitable husbands for eligible daughters, and a dizzying round of social occasions was provided for the purpose. One socialite recalled 'There were a minimum of four balls every night – six balls possibly', all listed in *The Times*. It was also *de rigueur* for debutantes to be presented at court at glamorous evening ceremonies.

For the older generation the season meant a round of parties rubbing shoulders with a familiar circle of friends and acquaintances, varied by visits to the opera, theatre and events such as the Royal Academy Summer Exhibition. There were sporting occasions like the Oxford–Cambridge boat race and the Eton–Harrow cricket match at Lord's, and excursions to Ascot or Goodwood for the racing. Husbands might seek sanctuary in the gentlemen's clubs of Pall Mall, while a growing number of wives attended all-female establishments. There was horseriding along Rotten Row in Hyde Park, where the riders could see their peers and be seen by them, and might also catch a glimpse of the celebrated team of zebras that drew the carriage of the financier Leopold de Rothschild.

There was time, too, for shopping. By the 1900s the big department stores were coming into their own. Harrods, Whiteleys, Barkers of Kensington, Peter Jones and John Lewis were joined in 1909 by Selfridges, established at the unfashionable end of Oxford Street by the American entrepreneur Gordon Selfridge. The fashion-conscious made trips to Paris to buy designs by Doucet, Paquin and Worth. Life *à la mode* demanded that a considerable amount of time be spent on dressing. Ladies of the *beau monde* might change their outfit three times or more in a day: a tailored costume was worn for morning calls and shopping, a looser tea gown could be worn for informal afternoon entertaining, then a spectacular silk or satin evening dress for the ball or theatre, worn with jewellery and perhaps a tiara.

Country living

When the season was over, society dispersed to country houses scattered across the land. For the men one of the main attractions was the shooting, and animal life was slaughtered on an industrial scale. Lord Ripon, a champion shot, accounted for over half a million head of game in his lifetime, all carefully annotated in his game books. Victor Cavendish, a Liberal Unionist MP and (as the Duke of Devonshire) a future Colonial Secretary, recorded a bag of 9,000 birds from a week's entertaining at Bolton Abbey.

Another major preoccupation was food – the Edwardian age was notable for the gargantuan appetites of the rich. Breakfast in the country might feature a choice of poached or scrambled eggs, bacon, ham, sausages, devilled kidneys and haddock, displayed on salvers and kept warm by spirit lamps. There would also

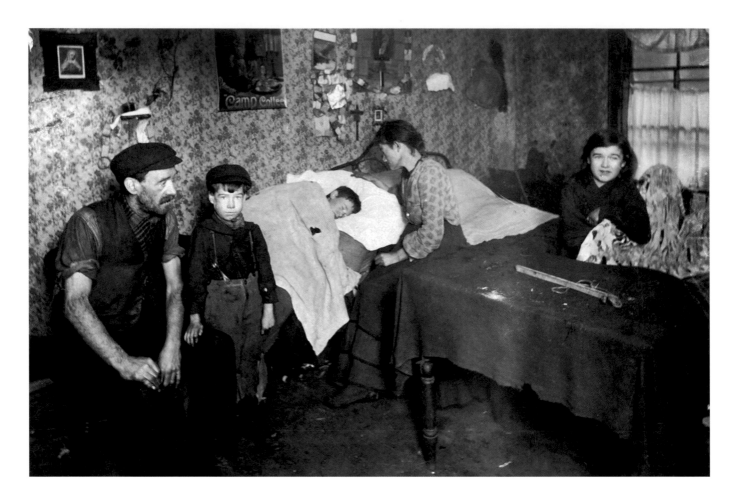

be cold meats ranging from pressed beef and tongue to roast pheasant and grouse, plus the usual range of porridge, scones, toast, marmalade and fruit. Evening dinners could run in exceptional circumstances to as many as 12 courses. One formal dinner in London, given by the Conservative 1900 Club for colonial premiers, catered for 1,600 diners with, among other delicacies, 200 whole salmon, 2,500 quails, 25,000 asparagus spears, 1,400 bottles of champagne and 300 bottles each of whisky, Chartreuse and brandy. Not surprisingly in view of such indulgence, the Edwardian era saw a fashion for taking the waters at health spas; Edward VII's favourite was Marienbad, just one of many Continental locations favoured by the gentry.

A world apart

Needless to say, the world inhabited by the poor was separated from the graciousness of country-house living by much more than the long drives and high walls that hid the great estates. Although this world, too, had its areas of privacy, it was in general more studied and observed than ever before, and the result was a growing awareness of poverty as a social problem that needed to be addressed.

Charles Booth had begun a pioneering study of the working classes in London in the late 1880s; it was published over the years in 17 volumes, the last of which appeared in 1903. Meanwhile Seebohm Rowntree, a scion of the Quaker chocolate dynasty, had been conducting a detailed survey of deprived families in York, which was published in 1901. Rowntree defined a living wage as being 7 shillings a week for a single man, or 21 shillings 8d for a family of five. According to his

MEAN STREETS
Life for poor working families, like this one (above) photographed in their home in about 1900, was difficult at best. Long hours and low wages combined with bad living conditions to make sickness almost endemic. Poor housing with inadequate services was a persistent problem – in Birmingham, for example, there were areas where 30 people shared a single tap. In the most deprived parts of the cities, renting rooms jointly and bed-sharing were not unknown; three people might rent the same bed in eight-hour shifts. Manual workers struggled to earn enough to support their families; the poor generally had more children than the rich – mining families, for example, averaged more than seven children compared to three or four in an upper-middle-class family. The result was chronic malnutrition among the poor, only marginally eased by charitable hand-outs. These women and children (right) were queuing with jugs outside a soup-kitchen in Bury, Lancashire.

observations, between a quarter and a third of the population of the city fell below this 'poverty line'. A similar conclusion was reached by the curiously titled Inter-Departmental Committee on Physical Deterioration, set up by Parliament in the wake of the Boer War; in 1904 it reported that a third of British schoolchildren regularly went hungry. Such studies revealed that poor families were in general larger than middle-class ones and many lived in unhealthily cramped conditions. Overcrowding was particularly bad in the city slums; the proportion of people living two or more to a room rose from a national average of 8.6 per cent to over 30 per cent in the East End and 59 per cent in parts of Glasgow.

In marked contrast to the feasts of the rich, the poor relied on bread as their staple. In an age before domestic gas or electricity was widely available, cooking was time-consuming and expensive, so a slice of bread spread with a scraping of butter, lard or beef dripping, or perhaps with jam or a wedge of cheese, served regularly as a meal. Even so, most households except the very poorest would manage to afford a joint, usually of beef, for Sunday dinner. Contrary to popular prejudice – it was a widely held belief among the comfortable classes, for example, that if the workers were given baths, they would only use them for storing coal – hard-up families were often thrifty. A researcher in Lambeth discovered that most households there saved between 2.5 and 10 per cent of their income in funds designed to cover funeral expenses for family members.

STREET URCHINS
Dirty, barefoot children, like these young mites outside their slum-terrace home, were a common sight in city streets. As a result of overcrowding and malnutrition, many were in poor health; rickets, consumption, diptheria and whooping cough all took a heavy toll on the young. Surveys showed that a third of state-school pupils regularly went hungry. The Liberal government sought to address the problem by passing the Provision of Meals Act in 1906, which permitted local authorities to provide subsidised food. Compulsory medical inspections in schools were introduced a year later, although treatment for the sick was not provided until 1912.

The cost of a burial might be manageable and planned for, but there was little that even the most prudent could do in the face of prolonged sickness or accident. At a time of minimal health and safety regulation, injury at work was common and disasters causing fatalities occurred all too frequently: an explosion in 1909 at the Burns Pit in West Stanley, County Durham, killed 168 people. Those who suffered lesser injuries often opted to look after themselves, for doctors' visits were expensive. If a doctor was called, he would sometimes do minor operations *in situ*, setting broken arms or legs on the kitchen table.

The 'people of the abyss'

For those who could not find work, the usual option was the workhouse. Conditions there were deliberately grim to discourage people from choosing to live on the public purse. Not surprisingly, some preferred to trust themselves to the streets; in London alone there were an estimated 35,000 vagrants in Edwardian times. There, too, the authorities made life as difficult as possible, closing the parks at night to ensure that the homeless had to keep moving or risk arrest. H G Wells called those trapped in the lower depths of society the 'People of the Abyss'. As awareness of the plight of the unemployed and the poor spread, reformers reached out to help, demanding basic social welfare measures such as pensions and national insurance. In the wake of the Liberal electoral victory of 1906, such calls became too loud to ignore.

LAST STOP: THE WORKHOUSE

For people with no jobs and no money, the only choice was begging or the workhouse, known familiarly at the time as 'the spike'. Conditions inside were grim, deliberately so to deter the poor from entering and living at the expense of rate-payers. Inmates had to take a cold bath on arrival, and families were split up – mothers often only saw their children once a week. Able-bodied inmates were given work to do – for the women that often meant the workhouse's washing (above). Hygiene was generally poor: a survey in 1909 found 56 girls sharing a single tub of water and half a dozen towels; another institution had two small basins for 120 inmates and the toilets were locked at night. Food was not tempting, but for many it was no worse than the fare outside. Portions were weighed out by a warder – typically 6oz (170g) of bread a day with ¾ pint (400ml) of a porridge called skilly.

1900s

TIME FOR CHANGE

Some general elections merely confirm a party's hold on the country, or switch power between rival groups with broadly similar views. Others – like Clement Attlee's Labour victory in 1945 or Margaret Thatcher's Conservative triumph of 1979 – mark a decisive shift in the nation's political orientation. The Liberal victory of January 1906 was just such an election, bringing an end to two decades of Conservative rule and putting Britain in the hands of reformers with a thirst for radical change.

UP AND AWAY Well-dressed onlookers at the Hurlingham Club in Fulham watch balloonists rise into the sky in 1908. Ballooning was more than a popular pastime: the Royal Engineers maintained a balloon factory for aerial observation, first at Aldershot then at Farnborough.

A NEW DIMENSION IN POLITICS

At first sight the Liberal Party leader, Sir Henry Campbell-Bannerman, seemed an unlikely revolutionary. Sixty-nine years old at the time of the 1906 election, he was a genial, avuncular figure, admired less as a parliamentary orator than as an efficient political operator who had held his party together in difficult times. Born Henry Campbell, the son of a successful Scottish merchant who rose to be Lord Provost of Glasgow, he had agreed to accept the second barrel to his name as a precondition of inheriting a rich uncle's legacy. He grew up within the Liberal fold, was an MP by the age of 32 and went on to serve as Gladstone's Chief Secretary for Ireland then subsequently as Secretary for War, before being chosen to head the party in 1899. A Europhile before the term was invented, he spent at least six weeks on the Continent each summer, regularly frequenting Edward VII's favourite spa, Marienbad. Otherwise he divided his time between London and Perthshire, where he had a small estate. There, he indulged a fondness for animals, keeping a long-lived African grey parrot and, in his later days, some 30 French bulldogs.

TAKING THE CASE TO THE PEOPLE
The Liberal landslide of January 1906 was something of a self-inflicted wound for the Conservatives, whose leader, Arthur Balfour, had chosen to step down from office in December 1905 with almost two years of his term still to run. Balfour gambled that the Liberals would be too busy arguing among themselves to form an interim government while an election was called, but far from splitting the opposition, the call to office drew the Liberal Party together. Would-be MPs, like the Liberal candidate campaigning below, took their message to the voters with enthusiasm and conviction. The Liberals won in a landslide, gaining a 241-seat majority over their chief rivals, the Conservative and Liberal Unionists, and a clear majority in the Commons overall. They viewed the result as a mandate for social change. As for Balfour, he lost his seat in Manchester East and had to wait for a safe Tory seat to come up in the City of London to be re-elected to Parliament.

CB, as he was known to his colleagues, has a claim to be Britain's first Prime Minister, as the term, used informally for many years, only received official recognition shortly after he took office. He was in charge for little more than two years, but in that time he proved a competent leader with an astute and generous political brain behind his 'hail-fellow-well-met' manner. Early in his stewardship he signalled his mastery of the Commons with a devastating attack on his predecessor, Arthur Balfour, freshly re-seated after suffering defeat in the main election. 'He comes back', CB told assembled MPs, 'with the same airy graces, the same subtle dialectics, the same light and frivolous way of dealing with great questions. He little knows the temper of the new House of Commons if he thinks these methods will prevail here ... I say, enough of this foolery!'

The attack struck home because the mood of Parliament had indeed changed. Balfour himself admitted as much when he wrote to an acquaintance: 'What is going on here is a faint echo of the same movement which has produced massacres in St Petersburg, riots in Vienna and Socialist processions in Berlin.' No such revolutionary dramas accompanied the Liberal takeover, but there was a feeling that the old order was crumbling. As J B Priestley would one day put it, 'this 1906 election took politics into a new dimension'.

Progressive Liberalism

The novelty in the progressive Liberalism that now came to the fore lay chiefly in its willingness to look to the state to set social policy. The expanding appetite for bigger government drew on many sources. A growing awareness of the plight of the poor played a part, sparked by the writings of Charles Booth and Seebohm Rowntree, and by the sorry condition of many Boer War recruits. Equally important was the belief, shared by some members on the Conservative side of the House, that Britain was falling behind its foreign competitors – in particular Germany. There, the impeccably unradical Chancellor Otto von Bismarck had already introduced old-age pensions and health and accident insurance for workers, not so much out of compassion for their plight as from fear that they might otherwise turn to Socialism. Winston Churchill, re-elected to Parliament in the 1906 election as a Liberal MP, had Bismarck's example very much in mind when he argued that 'the minister who applies to this country the successful experience of Germans in social organisation may or may not be supported at the polls, but he will at least have a memorial which time will not deface'.

The result was a growing conviction that the government would have to take a lead in protecting the weak and providing for those who could not look after themselves. Earlier administrations had been fearful of state intervention – even in times of emergency. When famine in India threatened millions with starvation in 1900, Balfour had turned down requests for additional aid on the grounds that it would encourage 'financial irregularity and extravagance ... the most fruitful parent of social troubles'. The parliamentary class of 1906 were less concerned with balancing budgets than with the need to address fundamental flaws in the nation's social fabric. Reform was the order of the day.

LIBERAL LEADER
Described by an admirer as 'a gay old dog with a twinkle in his eye', the Liberal Prime Minister Sir Henry Campbell-Bannerman was a committed reformer. His taste for the good life also enabled him to establish an easy rapport with Edward VII, helping to reconcile the King to the new government's radical programme. In the event CB's short premiership was dogged by ill health, which forced him to resign from office in April 1908. Too sick to move from 10 Downing Street, he died there three weeks later, the only former prime minister to do so.

This new-found zeal for changing the status quo did not at first extend to Ireland. Remembering too well the divisions of Gladstone's day, Campbell-Bannerman's administration continued with Balfour's approach of limited reform, introducing measures to encourage the use of the Irish language, to establish an Irish national university, and to improve primary education and housing. Government motivation for more radical change would not reappear until 1910, when the Liberals, re-elected as a minority government, became dependent once more on the support of Irish MPs – and Home Rule became a pressing issue.

Children's Charter

In marked contrast, the reformers passionately embraced the cause of disadvantaged children across Britain, producing a body of legislation sometimes referred to collectively as the Children's Charter. In 1906 an Act of Parliament encouraged local authorities to provide free meals for needy pupils. The following year compulsory medical examinations were introduced in schools. Then, in 1908, came the Children Act, a wide-ranging piece of legislation designed to prevent the

PICKING UP BAD HABITS
A young girl shares a drink in a pub (left), while young strawberry-pickers puff away on cigarettes during a work break (above). Juvenile drinking and smoking were major causes of concern. The Band of Hope, a temperance movement, had some 2 million supporters by 1900; its campaigning helped to persuade the Conservative government to ban the sale of alcohol, unless in a sealed container, to children under 14. Smoking was considered a prime cause of 'physical deterioration', a leading social issue of the day, and groups like the Boys' Brigade and International Anti-Cigarette League had members sign pledges to refrain from the habit. The Liberal government took up the cause in the Children Act of 1908, which included measures banning young people from entering pubs or buying tobacco.

NANNY STATE

Nannies were a fixture in affluent families in the Edwardian years, taking on not just the physical, but also often the emotional demands of motherhood. Nannies were officially known as 'nurses' and their domain was the nursery, where they sometimes had a subordinate nurserymaid to help them. In the grander aristocratic houses, nannies often remained in attendance for decades on end, raising successive generations until they finally became a permanent – and often much-loved – part of the household. In such circumstances it was not uncommon for children to grow up feeling closer to their nanny, who looked after them, than to their actual mother or father, who might well be distant figures whom they saw only occasionally. Winston Churchill had such an upbringing. When, during a stay in the USA, he heard that his old nurse was dying, he returned immediately to England to see her. He wrote in his journal at the time, 'She was my favourite friend'.

'Edwardian nannies had no days off; they would not expect to go out and leave their charges to anyone else, except perhaps the nursery maid … and then only for a short while.'

Thea Thompson, *Edwardian Childhoods*

LEARNING A TRADE
A class of boys learn carpentry under the watchful eye of masters in a manual training centre. Vocational training was a much-neglected aspect of Britain's educational system. The old model of compulsory apprenticeships had fallen into disuse early in the previous century, and no comprehensive scheme for teaching young people the skills to earn a living had replaced it. For the most part youngsters either followed in their fathers' footsteps or else learned on the job in whatever trade they could find. The Education Act of 1902 placed the vocational element of schooling, like all others, under the control of local education authorities, and some took the opportunity to open facilities attached to primary schools where older pupils could learn useful, saleable job skills. Such centres were the exception rather than the rule, and most school leavers simply had to fend for themselves.

exploitation of the young on a variety of fronts. One section introduced the registration of foster parents, hoping thereby to discourage the long-established practice of baby-farming. Others prevented children from working in dangerous trades, from entering public houses and from purchasing cigarettes or fireworks.

The criminal justice system, which had previously drawn little distinction between adult and juvenile offenders, received a thorough makeover. To reduce the risk of the young being corrupted by their elders in crime, special courts were set up to handle juvenile cases. Those found guilty might be sent to reformatories, following a model already tested at a prison in Kent. Called Borstals, after the village where the prototype was situated, the new institutions were intended to emphasise education as much as punishment in a strictly regimented daily routine. One early inmate later recalled the regime with a grudging respect; there was plenty of outdoor exercise, he learned woodworking in the carpenter's shop, and was introduced to Dickens through a copy of *Oliver Twist* in the prison library.

The Children's Charter had lasting significance for the treatment of the young in Britain, but it formed only one part of the Liberal programme. The reformers also set their sights on improving the lot of working men and their families, particularly the old and the sick. The most insistent voices for change came from another political group that emerged greatly strengthened from the 1906 election – the Labour Representation Committee (LRC), soon to be renamed the Labour Party.

LABOUR ON THE RISE

For die-hard opponents of change, one of the most alarming aspects of the new intake of MPs was the return of 29 Labour members, a massive increase on the two MPs elected in the previous so-called Khaki Election of 1900. Traditionalists shook their heads in dismay. Lord Knollys, Edward VII's private secretary, privately noted that 'the old idea that the House of Commons was an assemblage of "gentlemen" has quite passed away'.

The Labour Representation Committee (LRC) was born in February 1900, at a conference in London, to provide a focus for the working-class vote that had emerged since the Reform Acts of 1867 and 1884. In the years since, the trade unions had sponsored a number of MPs, mostly from mining constituencies, who cooperated with the radical wing of the Liberal Party and were sometimes referred to at the time as Lib-Labs. Another source of support was the Independent Labour Party (ILP), founded in 1893 by Keir Hardie and others. These idealists drew on the thoughts of John Ruskin, William Morris and similar reformers.

The LRC drew less long-term support from the Marxist-oriented Social Democratic Foundation, which initially signed up to the cause but dropped out after a year. The influence of the Fabian Society was also limited. This left-wing intellectual powerhouse – under the influence, at the time, of Sidney and Beatrice Webb and the playwright George Bernard Shaw – preferred to concentrate its efforts on influencing government policy outside Parliament. In any event, in the wake of their success in the 1906 election, the LRC members decided to change their name to the Labour Party.

WORKING MAN'S VOTE

The Labour Party became a force in the Edwardian era thanks to its success in mobilising the working-class vote enfranchised by the electoral Reform Acts of 1867 and 1884. At first the Liberals had been the main beneficiaries of the Reform Acts, but the conviction gradually took hold that the working class would be best served by a political party of their own. One crucial factor was the Taff Vale decision, which in 1901 made trade unions legally liable for profits lost through strike action. Another was the economic insecurity that workers faced in an era without unemployment pay or sickness benefit. The men seen eating their lunch below – workers at the Dolcoath Mine outside Camborne in Cornwall – would have been only too aware of potential threats to their future. The mine had been worked since the early 18th century, at first for copper then primarily for tin. But by Edwardian times competition was growing from other parts of the world. Tin prices would collapse after the First World War, leading to Dolcoath's closure in 1921.

THE VOICE OF LABOUR

Keir Hardie, seen here with beard and hat, campaigning for another Labour candidate in the 1906 election. Hardie was one of the founding fathers of the British Labour movement, first elected to Parliament in 1892 as the first, independent, socialist MP. He helped to found the Independent Labour Party, becoming its first leader, and played a crucial role in setting up the Labour Representation Committee – forerunner of the Labour Party – as an autonomous, working-class political body separate from the Liberals. In 1906 he was returned to Parliament as MP for Merthyr Tydfil. In his day Hardie took some controversial stances – he was an outspoken pacifist during the Boer War, and also supported women's suffrage – that made him something of a hate figure for his political opponents; it was said of him that 'no speaker had more meetings broken up'.

The Taff Vale ruling

The biggest boost that the nascent parliamentary movement received came, ironically, from its enemies. In 1900 men working for the Taff Vale Railway Company in South Wales went on strike, unofficially at first but later, after the company hired blackleg replacements, with union backing. The management responded by bringing an action against the Amalgamated Society of Railway Servants for the losses incurred as a result of the action. The case went all the way to the Law Lords, who in 1901 decided in the company's favour, awarding damages of £23,000 and costs totalling a further £19,000 – a huge sum at the time, equivalent to around £3 million today.

The judgment had huge implications for the unions, which had previously considered themselves safe from law suits on the grounds that they were not incorporated in the manner of businesses. The Taff Vale precedent suggested that in future any kind of industrial action might be ruinously expensive. The political result was to drive much of the Labour movement into the welcoming arms of the LRC, which made it a priority to introduce legislation to reverse the judgment. In the two years that followed the Taff Vale ruling, union affiliation to the new body more than doubled, from 350,000 to 850,000.

continued on page 78

WORKSHOP OF THE WORLD

Despite fears about growing competition from Germany and the USA, Edwardian Britain remained the workshop of the world; as late as 1914 the nation had a 31 per cent share of international trade in manufactured goods, larger than that of any other country. In Lancashire and the West Riding of Yorkshire, around Birmingham, Glasgow and Tyneside, factory chimneys dominated the urban skyline as they had done for half a century and more. For the most part industry was still in the hands of family firms, but the factories themselves had grown in size as steam took over from water as the principal power source. Life was hard for the workers within them, but it was still better than the prospect of joblessness outside.

The census of 1901 showed that a third of Britain's workers laboured in manufacturing. Between them, they produced almost three-quarters of the nation's total output.

MACHINE AGE
Manufacturing in Britain remained highly localised in Edwardian times. The Potteries region of Staffordshire was famous for ceramic production, while Sheffield specialised in metalwork, particularly cutlery. Hosiery was in the East Midlands. London hosted a variety of manufactures including instrument-making and the very recent but burgeoning business of electrical engineering.

No branch of industry was more important to Britain than textiles, which accounted for almost half of all the nation's exports. It was also one of the biggest employers; the 1901 census revealed that more than 1.15 million people worked in the mills, more than half of them women. The West Riding of Yorkshire was a centre for wool and worsted, while Belfast was the hub of linen production. But the most important part of the textile trade – accounting for more than 50 per cent of total output – was cotton, largely concentrated in Lancashire, where the mills had been a driving force in mechanisation and modernisation of industry.

Many industrial towns shared a profile of large industrial buildings, factory chimneys and cramped terraced housing, as displayed by this Lancashire mill town (left). Inside the factories, conditions had improved since early Victorian days, but remained harsh. Workers in the cotton mills, like this young boy operating a giant spinning mule (right), worked long hours in almost unbearable noise levels. They often went barefoot because of the heat and slippery floors.

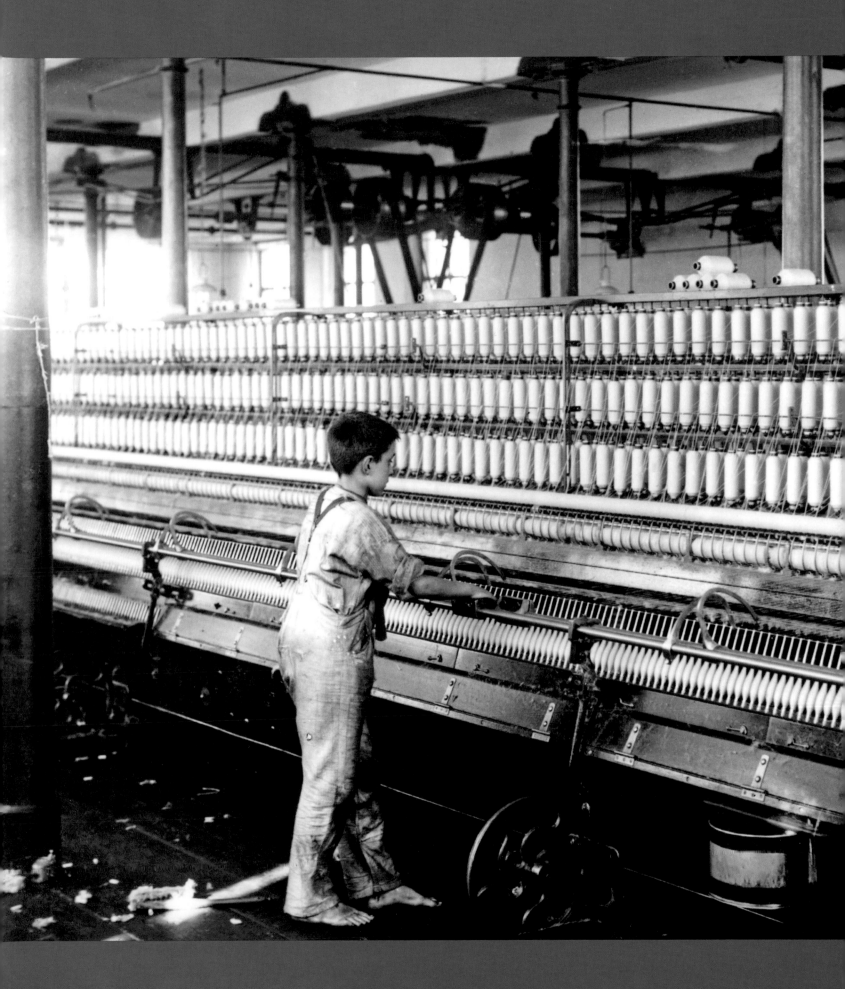

MEN'S WORK

In Edwardian days, as now, heavy industry was a male domain. Of almost 1 million people employed in the sector in 1901, just 54,000 were women. Many workers toiled in large plants, like these men in the boiler manufacturing area of the Yarrow shipyard at Poplar in London's East End (left). But there were also plenty of opportunities in smaller machine rooms, like this one (above) in a factory in Burnley. The aristocrats of the workforce were the skilled mechanics employed in workshop industries, and it was generally accepted that men were better at such work than women. This unashamedly sexist 1906 advert for Triumph boasts proudly of the fact that their bicycles were produced entirely by men, proclaiming Triumph to be 'the only Coventry cycle factory not employing female labour'.

Triumph CYCLES

MALE OR FEMALE LABOUR.

The male mechanic in the Workshop has proved himself infinitely superior to the female— he is capable of doing better, more exact, more reliable work. Morally, mixed labour does not raise the standard of either worker, and considerably lowers the standard of the work produced.

TRIUMPH Cycles are made in a factory where no female labour whatever is employed. Female labour and best work do not go together therefore let your machine be a **TRIUMPH.** "The Best Bicycle British Workmanship can produce" and made by skilled male mechanics only.

The **TRIUMPH** is the only Coventry Cycle Factory not employing female labour.

£6 14s. 9d. to £17 4s. 6d.

Gradual payments from 10/8 Monthly.

Motors from £30.

Art Catalogues Post Free. Agents Everywhere.

Triumph Cycle Co. Ltd. (Dept. G 5), Coventry. Est. 1885.

London: 4-5 Holborn Viaduct, E.C. Leeds: 4, King Edward St. Manchester: 160, Deansgate.

FACTORY WORK FOR WOMEN

In 1901 nearly a third of British women had regular jobs, with the highest proportion of female employment being concentrated in the major textile centres. The only places to rival the mill towns in the numbers of women employed were Bournemouth and Bath, which both had an unusually high demand for maids and cooks. Across the nation as a whole, domestic service was still the most common source of work, accounting for over 40 per cent of all female employment; in comparison, 14 per cent worked in the textile industry and 8 per cent in other manufacturing.

Conditions and rewards were poor by modern standards; a 1906 Board of Trade survey found that women workers in industry earned on average less than 10 shillings for a 54-hour week. Even so, that was better than the 80-hour week worked by some shop assistants at the time, some of whom, as a condition of employment, had to live in dormitories above their workplace. The result was that there was rarely a shortage of applicants for factory jobs, no matter how boring the task. The women at top left are employed as button-cutters, while the tightly packed rows of women at bottom left are hand-rolling cigarettes in a Manchester factory. Many women were employed in some sort of garment manufacture: the women at centre left are making men's caps with the aid of sewing machines. The main picture (right) shows women at work hand-crafting hats at the Sutton & Torkington factory, also in Manchester. Almost without exception the women are immaculately turned out for work, wearing clothes that they most likely sewed themselves at home.

`The first Lib-Lab pact

The next step in the Labour Party's rise came in 1903, when the LRC formed an electoral pact with the Liberals. Both parties agreed not to put up candidates against the other in constituencies where either one had a decisive advantage. Never popular with activists, the move was nonetheless effective: in the 1906 election, out of 32 of the LRC's 50 nominations who stood unopposed by Liberals, 24 won their seats. This compared with five successful candidates from the 18 who faced Liberal opponents, sometimes unofficial independents.

As Lord Knollys duly noted, the new Labour MPs did not fit preconceptions of the nation's elected representatives. All were from working-class backgrounds,

THE BACKBONE OF INDUSTRY
Smoke rises above the Wattstown Mine in the Rhondda Valley in Wales in 1905. Coal mining was a vital contributor to national prosperity, with output steadily rising to reach a peak of 290 million tons in 1913. All the traditional colliery areas were still producing, but growth was fastest in the more recently developed coalfields of Yorkshire, Wales and the East Midlands. There, as elsewhere, miners tended to live in tight-knit communities, with their own customs and a strong sense of local solidarity. The work was fairly well-paid by the standards of the day, yet few people outside the industry chose to go down the pits – the prospect of labouring long hours deep underground in dirty, dark, dangerous conditions was not an appealing one. The arduous nature of the job contributed to the passing of the Mines (Eight Hours) Act in 1908, the first piece of legislation to limit working hours for adult men.

most had trade union affiliations. There was a strong Non-conformist presence. Between them, they brought to the House first-hand knowledge of conditions in the poorer parts of Britain, giving added immediacy to the drive for reform. It was a Labour member, for instance, who introduced the free school meals measure as a private member's bill that subsequently gained government backing.

Labour MPs pushed through the Trade Disputes Act, which reversed the Taff Vale judgment and gave the unions an extraordinary degree of immunity from prosecution for peaceful picketing. At first the Liberal Cabinet preferred a less radical measure, but when Campbell-Bannerman spoke up for a stronger bill put forward by one of the trade-union sponsored MPs, the House swung behind it and it was voted into law against the advice of the government's Attorney General. Other welfare measures that the new parliamentary Labour group helped to pass into law included the Workmen's Compensation Act, which improved the benefits payable to those injured at work and provided relief in cases of industrial disease, and the Mines Act, which introduced an eight-hour working day for miners.

Challenges from left and right

Despite these successes, the Labour movement encountered many obstacles on its path to parliamentary power. Left-wing socialists objected to the compromises

DEATH IN THE MINES

Mining disasters were a regular occurrence in the Edwardian years. An explosion at East Side Pit in Senghenydd, north of Cardiff, claimed 83 lives in 1901. Four years later 119 were killed at Wattstown Mine in the Rhondda in the worst mining disaster in Wales for more than a decade. In March 1908 a fire at Hamstead Colliery (right), near Birmingham, killed 25 of the 31 miners underground at the time; the photograph shows the pithead vigil of families waiting for news. Worse was to come before the decade was out. In 1909 explosions and fire at the Burns Pit in West Stanley, Durham, killed 168 miners; the only relief for the rescuers was being able to bring out several pit ponies alive. And just before Christmas 1910, the Pretoria Pit near Westhoughton and Atherton became the scene of the worst-ever mining disaster in Lancashire, when 344 were killed. The effects of such disasters were devastating on the close-knit communities involved. Often several members of a family were killed, including boys as young as 13.

involved in working alongside the Liberals. They found a spokesman in Victor Grayson, a fiery orator from Liverpool. Nominated by the Independent Labour Party as its candidate for a by-election in Colne Valley, the 26-year-old was asked to stand down by the Labour executive in line with the Lib-Lab pact. He refused and put himself forward as an Independent Socialist. To the astonishment of the party leadership, he pipped the Liberal candidate at the post, winning by 153 votes on an 88 per cent turnout. Thereafter Grayson spent little time in the Commons, preferring to spread the socialist message at public meetings, but on one occasion when he did attend a debate he accused the House of ignoring the plight of the unemployed and rounded on the other Labour MPs, calling them traitors to their class, before being removed by the Serjeant-at-Arms.

Sharing power with the Liberals cost Labour support when the economy entered a downturn. By 1908 unemployment was a growing concern, having risen to 7.8 per cent from the average of 5 per cent that it had been for most of the decade. The slowdown was hurting the party when, in 1909, another hostile judgment was meted out by the Law Lords. The secretary of the Walthamstow branch of the Amalgamated Society of Railway Servants, one W V Osborne, was a Liberal voter who had taken exception to the fact that the union was using his dues, along with those of all its other members, to subsidise the Labour Party. He took his case to court and eventually it reached the House of Lords, where it was decided that the unions' political levy was illegal. The ruling hit the Labour MPs hard – they depended on the trade union contributions to pay their salaries. The judgment was overturned by fresh legislation in 1913, but in the intervening period the party's finances nose-dived.

Yet for all its difficulties, Labour went on to increase its share of the vote from 4.8 per cent to over 7 per cent in the January 1910 election and raised its presence in the Commons to 40 MPs. Most of the new intake could be put down to the decision of the Miners' Federation to affiliate with the party, bringing sponsored MPs who had previously stood as Lib-Labs under the Labour umbrella. A further election in December 1910 saw the Labour share of the vote drop to 6.3 per cent, but concentrated local support in industrial areas saw its number of MPs go up again to 42 seats. Overall it was an impressive showing for the young party; over the course of the decade it had seen its direct membership increase by more than half to 35,000 while the number of workers in affiliated trade unions reached 1.4 million. By 1910 Labour had established itself as a prominent feature of Britain's parliamentary democracy, even if few people could have guessed at the time that it would eclipse its Liberal partners in little more than a decade.

MOTOR CARS AND FLYING MACHINES

For all the changes the Liberal victory of 1906 set in motion, the most profound transformation at work in the first decade of the 20th century was, as H G Wells had foreseen, the transport revolution. Between 1900 and 1910 the nation entered the motor age. Automobiles were not new. The days when road locomotives had by law to be preceded by a man waving a red flag were already long gone. By 1901 there were an estimated 10,000 motor vehicles in the country, and they were allowed to power along the nation's highways at a dizzying 14mph. The new form of locomotion acquired an important ally when Edward VII came to the throne, for the King was himself a keen motorist.

To celebrate motoring's growing reliability, in April 1900 the Automobile Club of Great Britain organised the One Thousand Mile Trial, a test of stamina that saw 65 vehicles leave Hyde Park Corner in London on a tour that took in every major city in England and Scotland. All 65 managed to complete the course, although there were many tribulations on the way. One competitor negotiated the

CARS COME OF AGE
Scheduled over three weeks in April and May 1900, the One Thousand Mile Trial was a great success. Crowds turned out in all the major cities of England and Scotland to cheer on the entrants, like the cars below photographed just outside St Albans on the return leg. The front Panhard is driven by Frank Hedges Butler, a balloonist and pioneer aviator, as well as early motorist. The aim of the event was to familiarise the public with cars and to trumpet the start of the motor age, and to judge from results it was hugely successful. By the decade's end the number of vehicles on the roads had rocketed from around 10,000 to more than 80,000, and a market had grown up for motoring clothes and paraphernalia, such as the motor bonnet for ladies advertised in 1905 (below right). Although driving was still a hobby for the wealthy, like the actress Isabel Jay seen at the wheel of a Dutch-made Spyker in 1907 (right), the first mass-produced Fords would soon arrive from the USA and by the end of the decade the age of mass motoring was on the way.

last 52 miles without any steering – his passenger had to stand on the running board and kick the front wheels when the vehicle needed to change direction.

The increasing number of automobiles on the roads convinced Balfour's government of a need for fresh legislation. The Motor Car Act of 1903 made dangerous driving an offence and introduced vehicle registration, organised at the time through county councils, making it illegal for anyone but the King to drive a car without a licence plate. Drivers, too, had in future to obtain licences, although by the simple expedient of paying the council five shillings (25p).

In the years that followed the popularity of motoring continued to grow, for the most part as a recreation for the rich. The process of democratisation, opening up the roads to the middle classes, only really got under way after 1908, when the first cheap Fords were imported from the USA. In the meantime, dozens of motoring enthusiasts had set up small manufacturing plants in provincial factories and backstreet workshops, all hoping to establish a toehold in the new market. In total, 198 different makes of automobile would be offered for sale in Britain between 1900 and 1913. Most quickly failed.

Enter Rolls-Royce

One glorious exception was the Rolls-Royce company, which built its reputation on the engineering skills of Henry Royce. The son of a failed miller who had died in Henry's childhood, Royce supplemented his family's income first by selling newspapers and delivering telegrams and then by taking up an apprenticeship with

TESTING THEIR METTLE

As cars became more reliable and mechanically more sophisticated, their makers and owners sought ways of testing their capabilities to the limits, and so motor sports were born. The first Tourist Trophy (TT) races were held on the Isle of Man in 1905, the location chosen to escape the speed limits that applied on the mainland. The fourth meeting of the series, staged in 1908, has gone down in motoring history as the 'Four-Inch Race', because regulations aimed at attracting cars of Grand Prix calibre stipulated that all competing vehicles must have a four-cylinder engine with a maximum bore size of 4in. Kenelm Lee Guinness (left) failed to finish in his Hillman-Coatalen, although his brother Algernon came second; the winning Napier-Hutton averaged more than 50mph during the race. Motor trials were also popular, serving as long-distance endurance tests (right). The photograph shows a competitor in the 1906 Scottish trials negotiating the notorious Devil's Elbow, a hairpin bend on the Cairnwell Pass between Glenshee and Braemar.

the Great Northern Railway, paid for by a kindly aunt. He came to cars by way of electrical engineering, producing his first prototypes in 1904. One came to the attention of the Honourable Charles Rolls, an aristocratic automobile salesman with premises in London's West End who was looking for a new model to supplement the imported French Panhards that he already sold. The two men met in the Midland Hotel, Manchester, and agreed to form a partnership.

The rest of the story is automotive history. The first Rolls-Royce car made its debut at the Paris Motor Show in December 1904. Two years later the firm of Rolls-Royce Ltd was officially incorporated, and by the following year was winning prizes for reliability. In 1908 the firm moved to a larger factory in Derby, and a legendary British marque was up and running.

Motor racing and other developments

By that time motor transport was moving into a new era of sophistication and speed. The Royal Automobile Club, graced by Edward VII's patronage, began organising the Tourist Trophy (TT) road races on the Isle of Man in 1905. The first event was won by John S Napier at an average speed of almost 34mph; a year later the victor was Charles Rolls, always a keen tester of his firm's products. In 1907 the banked Brooklands motor-racing circuit was opened in Surrey, and by the following year cars were lapping at over 100mph, although five more years would pass before a vehicle could sustain that pace for a full 60 minutes.

By 1910 the number of cars on Britain's roads had soared to more than 83,000 and, just as significantly, the petrol engine had been adapted to many other

continued on page 88

A DAY AT THE RACES – THE BROOKLANDS STORY

When the Brooklands circuit opened near Weybridge in Surrey in 1907, it was the world's first purpose-built motor racetrack, beating the Indianapolis Speedway in the USA by over a year. Its most distinctive feature was the banking, in places almost 30ft (9m) in height, which allowed drivers to reach otherwise unattainable speeds when cornering. For reasons of economy, the track was made of concrete rather than asphalt, making for a bumpy ride in later years. Eleven days after the circuit opened, Selwyn Edge (bottom right) – an Australian entrepreneur who had won the Automobile Club's One Thousand Mile Trial in 1900 – staged a celebrated 24-hour event, leading three Napier cars in a round-the-clock endurance trial. Taking no breaks, Edge covered more than 1,580 miles at an average speed of over 65mph. Thereafter the Brooklands track became a venue for

more conventional motor races like the 1908 contest seen above, as well as for motorcycle trials. One unusual feature by present-day standards was the presence of elegantly dressed bookies (top right) offering competitive odds. In the Second World War Brooklands served as an airfield, and no further racing took place thereafter. Today, a motor-racing and aviation museum occupies part of the site.

uses. The first British motorcycles appeared at the start of the decade. In 1902 a manufacturer in Biggleswade produced the earliest commercially successful tractor, a three-wheeled model that was at first shunned by traditionalist farmers for its inability to produce manure. Motor taxis arrived in 1903 and by 1910 they were a common sight in cities, as were motor buses, supplementing the electric trams that had been part of the urban scene for a decade.

The electrification of the London Underground, begun in the 1890s, was well underway, replacing the old steam-driven locomotives and powering the new, deeper lines that were coming into use to meet the needs of the capital's growing army of commuters. The Central Line opened between Bank and Shepherd's Bush stations in 1900, and the Northern Line extension up to Hampstead opened in 1907. A comparison of journey times that year found the trip from Piccadilly Circus to Baker Street on the newly opened Bakerloo Line took 7 minutes at a cost of twopence; the omnibus cost the same but took 20 minutes; and a horse-drawn cab arrived in 15 minutes, but set the passenger back 1s 6d.

By no means everyone welcomed the noise and smells of the new motor age. The novelist E M Forster thought cars 'pestilential' and complained that, rather than liberating people, science had enslaved them to machines. The Marquis of Queensberry, famous for his eccentricities, stated on an application for a firearms licence that he needed a shotgun to shoot motorists using the roads on his estate.

MOTOR TAXI RANK
Taxis line up at a cab rank alongside London's Hyde Park in 1907. Electrically-powered vehicles, nicknamed 'Hummingbirds' for the noise they made, had been introduced experimentally in 1897, but they proved unreliable and were withdrawn three years later. The first petrol-powered cabs appeared on the capital's streets in 1903. At first they struggled to compete with the familiar horse-drawn hansoms, but that situation changed dramatically in late 1906 when the General Cab Company put 500 vehicles, made in France by Renault, onto the streets. The public quickly got the habit of using the new-fangled conveyances, and by 1910 motor cabs outnumbered their horse-drawn rivals by 6,300 to 5,000.

SPEED ON TWO WHEELS
Motorised bicycles powered by petrol
engines first began to appear as early as
the mid-1880s. By 1902 the Triumph
Company was producing machines in
Britain fitted with Belgian-made engines.
By 1907 motorcycle racing had become an
established sport, and in that year the first
TT race for bikes was held on a 15-mile
road course in the Isle of Man. The winning
machine was a Matchless, similar to the
one shown below lining up the following
year at an Essex Motor Club meeting. The
TT winner completed the 10-lap, 150-mile
race in a little over 4 hours at an average
speed of 38.21mph. Accidents were
common, with injuries to riders exacerbated
by the complete lack of safety gear; as the
photograph shows, racers did not even
wear helmets or gloves.

Opponents of combustion engines sometimes took refuge in cycling, a passion of
the old century that continued in the new. H G Wells, whose novel *The Wheels
of Chance* was subtitled 'A Bicycling Idyll', was particularly eloquent in singing
the praises of the new, low-slung safety bikes, as they opened the gates of the
countryside for urban clerks and workers who might otherwise have never had a
chance to know it. For long journeys the railways reigned supreme, and the
number of passengers grew throughout the Edwardian era. Services were reliable
and fast, with the 50-mile journey from London Victoria to Brighton, for example,
taking just 53 minutes, which compares favourably with the journey time today.

Up, up and away

The great breakthrough of the decade was the advent of powered flight. The
earliest pioneering ventures took place outside Britain, notably in the USA where
the Wright brothers first achieved lift-off in December 1903. Their exploit aroused
little interest locally at the time, with the *Daily Mail* merely noting on an inside
page the trial of what it called a 'balloonless airship'. The first flight in the UK
was not made until 1908, and then by an American, Samuel Franklin Cody, in a

continued on page 94

THE BIRTH OF FLIGHT

The concept of human flight was not new in 1900 – it had fascinated people since ancient times, and hot-air ballooning had been a vogue in France since before the French Revolution. Sir George Cayley and the German Otto Lilienthal had both had success experimenting with gliders in the 19th century. What still remained to be conquered as the 20th century dawned was powered directional flight, and the invention of the internal combustion engine in the 1880s provided the means. In 1903 Wilbur and Orville Wright achieved lift-off in a heavier-than-air machine, and the age of aviation was born. Few of the breakthrough developments took place in Britain, but it was not long before the nation was producing more than its share of talented and inventive aviators.

POWERED AIRSHIP
Aeroplanes were not the only focus of attention in the early years of flight. Inventors also sought ways of adapting hot-air balloons so they were not solely dependent on the wind for propulsion. The first airship designs were drawn up in the 18th century, and in 1852 a steam-powered model flew for 17 miles. By the turn of the 20th century engineers were scrambling to come up with new designs. The model shown here (left) was the work of Britain's Stanley Spencer; 75ft (23m) long, it was powered by a petrol motor driving a front-mounted propeller.

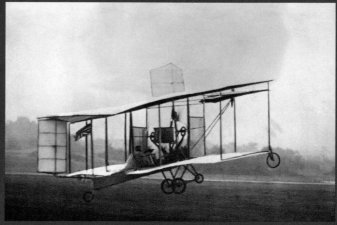

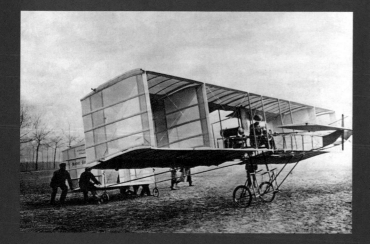

FIRST FLIGHTS

The Wright brothers' pioneering flight in 1903 set off a round of aviation records. The honour of making the first flight in Britain is usually given to the American Samuel Cody, a former Wild West Show performer who flew his Cody Aeroplane No.1 (top right) for 1,500ft (450m) at Farnborough on 16 October, 1908. A claim of first flight in Britain is sometimes made for the truly bizarre 'Venetian Blind' Multiplane (top left) built by Horatio Phillips; it briefly achieved lift-off in 1907, but the plane lacked a steering mechanism. The first British aviator to fly a steerable machine is usually credited as John Moore-Brabazon, later Lord Brabazon of Tara, who flew 450ft (140m) in a French-made Farman–Voisin box-kite biplane (bottom left) on the Isle of Sheppey in April 1909. Another contender for both firsts was Alliott Verdon Roe, who flew a short, unofficial hop in his Roe 1 biplane (centre) at Brooklands in 1907. Roe can certainly claim the first flight in an all-British-made machine – his Avro Triplane (bottom right) in July 1909.

CROSSING THE CHANNEL

The first flight across the English Channel in a heavier-than-air machine was made on Sunday 25 July, 1909, by Frenchman Louis Blériot, flying a Blériot XI of his own design (left). Trained as an engineer, the 37-year-old had already amassed a small fortune inventing and manufacturing automobile headlamps before turning his attention to flying machines. His particular interest was in monoplanes – machines with a single set of wings, rather than the twin arrangement of biplanes – and he was credited with making the first successful monoplane flight, in the Blériot V, in 1905. For his Channel hop, he took advantage of a pocket of clear weather and took off at dawn. Outstripping the French naval destroyer assigned to accompany him, he crash-landed in wind and rain outside Dover at 5.20am, having flown 23.5 miles in 36.5 minutes. The solitary witness of the historic landing was a police constable, although onlookers gathered later to view the aviator and his plane (below).

SPECTATOR SPORT

The year 1909 was something of a breakthrough year in the history of aviation. Blériot's flight received widespread publicity, following on, as it did, from a celebrated series of demonstrations by the Wright brothers in the USA and Europe. The Wrights attracted worldwide attention, which only increased when Orville crashed from a height of 100ft (30m) in September 1908, injuring himself and killing his passenger. The new interest fuelled demand for public displays. In August 1909 an international aviation meeting at Reims in France hosted 38 different machines, while in England that October Blackpool hosted a Flying Week, the first officially recognised such meeting in Britain. The picture below shows the French aviator Henri Rougier demonstrating a biplane at Blackpool.

machine he had designed for the British army. John Moore-Brabazon was the first Englishman to fly in English skies, achieving the feat in May 1909. Later that year he took a piglet up in his biplane to show that pigs could indeed fly.

By that time the *Daily Mail*'s owner, Lord Northcliffe, was an enthusiastic proponent of aviation. He announced two cash prizes: one of £1,000 for the first flight across the English Channel, the other of £10,000 for the first London-to-Manchester air journey. Both were won by Frenchmen. Louis Blériot successfully made the Channel hop in July 1909, completing the 23-mile journey in just under 37 minutes. The larger sum, not won until April 1910, went to Louis Paulhan after an epic contest with a British rival, Claude Grahame-White, both of them flying planes built by Henri Farman. Following his victory Paulhan was fêted at a victory dinner at London's Savoy Hotel, where the guests included H G Wells and Hiram Maxim, inventor of the eponymous machine-gun.

Just three months after Paulhan's success people were reminded of the continuing dangers of early flight when Charles Rolls, by now a keen flyer, was killed crash-landing his biplane at an air display in Bournemouth. His death provided a grim epitaph for British aviation's rocky beginnings.

PIONEERS OF AVIATION
Dressed in a flat cap and breeches, the French aviator Henri Farman stands between two early British flying enthusiasts, the Roe brothers – Alliott Verdon on the left and Humphrey to the right. Farman was born in Paris of British parents, his father being a newspaper correspondent, and he became a racing cyclist and motor-racing driver before taking up aviation in 1907. Soon, he was modifying plane design to improve flight control, enabling him to fly the first circuits of 1km then 2km, followed by the first cross-country flight in Europe, from Chalons-sur-Marne to Rheims. Farman would become hugely influential in the development of the aviation industry, both in France and internationally. Alliott Roe was cast in the same mould. He and his brother would found the Avro aircraft company and build biplanes in the First World War.

THE ARTS – A REFLECTION OF THEIR SOCIETY

After the 'Art for Art's Sake' aestheticism of the 1890s, writers and painters in the 1900s showed a new zest for the real world. Realism was in fact the order of the day, whether in the novels of Galsworthy, Wells and Arnold Bennett, the paintings of Walter Sickert, or the theatre of Harley Granville-Barker and George Bernard Shaw. All shared an interest in the texture of everyday life and a concern for the current, flawed condition of society.

Many of the writers and artists of the time were politically engaged, usually toward the left end of the spectrum (Rudyard Kipling being a notable exception). Some, like Shaw and, for a time, H G Wells, were deeply involved with the Fabian Society and its dream of building a socialist Britain. Others, like Galsworthy and Bennett, expressed support for Liberal social reform. Generally there was a feeling that the world could be changed – indeed, was crying out for transformation. Inequality and injustice would be uprooted and society shaped anew.

In keeping with the national mood, poetry went through something of a hiatus, with relatively little important new work appearing in the Edwardian years. In contrast, this was a great age for the novel. Henry James and Joseph Conrad were both producing important work to stand beside that of the young social realists, who were setting the tone of the day. A defining characteristic of the younger generation was an emphasis on the workaday commercial and industrial middle classes – on store owners, shop assistants and clerks, like Wells's Kipps and Mr Polly, or the protagonists of Bennett's 'Five Towns' novels. Another was the assault on Victorian hypocrisy and evasion that informed Galsworthy's *Forsyte Saga*.

E M Forster, who produced all his major works except *A Passage to India* between 1905 and 1910, made snobbery and arrogance a central theme of his writing. The victims could be foreigners, as in *Where Angels Fear to Tread*, or the self-educated as in *A Room with a View*, or the struggling bank clerk Leonard Bast in *Howard's End*. In each case they fall foul of English social exclusiveness – only the young hero of *A Room with a View* has the energy, idealism and persistence to escape its meshes and win the girl he loves in the face of her family's disapproval.

Against such closed horizons the novelists unfurled their human sympathies, producing vast panoramas of family life played out over a backdrop of passing decades. The masterpiece of the age was Arnold Bennett's *The Old Wives' Tale*, first published in 1908. It follows the lives of two sisters born in the Potteries from the cradle to the grave, spanning 70 years and arguably giving a more complete picture of the effects of the passage of time than any other British novel.

> 'Everybody got down off their stilts. Henceforward, nobody drank absinthe with their coffee. Nobody went mad. Nobody committed suicide. And nobody joined the Catholic Church.'
>
> W B Yeats, poet

A GOLDEN AGE FOR THE NOVEL

The novel was a forum for debate in Edwardian times, used by writers to assess and criticise the state of the nation. Two of the most successful authors of the day were John Galsworthy (top right) and Arnold Bennett (bottom right), who grounded their books in close observation of the workings of society. In his Forsyte novels, Galsworthy put the upper middle classes under the microscope, while Bennett's best work was rooted in the pottery towns of Staffordshire where he spent his childhood. E M Forster (top centre) shared their concern with relations between the classes, summing up his humanitarian belief in the need for

communication in the simple phrase 'Only connect ...'. G K Chesterton (bottom centre) was quite as concerned with the state of the nation as any of the others, but approached the question from his own individualistic Christian viewpoint. A flamboyant and physically imposing figure – 6ft 4in (1.93m) tall and weighing over 20 stone (130kg) – he poured his immense energy into journalism, poems and short stories as well as novels, of which the best-known was the idiosyncratic *The Man Who Was Thursday*.

Neither Joseph Conrad (top left) nor Henry James (bottom left) were British-born, but they came to be regarded among the

greatest exponents of the English novel. Conrad grew up in Poland and earned a living at sea before becoming a British citizen in 1886. His first novels appeared at the end of the 19th century; the Edwardian years would see some of his best work, including *Lord Jim*, *Nostromo* and *The Secret Agent*. American-born James had settled in London in 1876 and was already 57 when the decade began. In 1898 he moved to Rye on the south coast, where he bought the famous Lamb House, and continued to cement his literary reputation with new works, notably *The Wings of the Dove* (1902) and *The Ambassadors* (1903).

SOCIAL VISIONARY

George Bernard Shaw (right) was born in Dublin in 1856 and so was already 43 years old at the turn of the century. He came into his prime as a dramatist in the Edwardian years. Ten of his plays were staged at the Royal Court Theatre between 1904 and 1907, the first of which, *John Bull's Other Island*, made Edward VII laugh so hard he broke his chair. In 1906 Shaw and his wife moved to the house that would become known as Shaw's Corner in Ayot St Lawrence, Hertfordshire, where he lived for the rest of his life. He was a prolific writer, with more than 50 plays to his credit, and he is the only person to have won both a Nobel prize for literature and an Oscar. He was awarded – and reluctantly accepted – the Nobel prize in 1925; the Oscar came later, for the screenplay of *Pygmalion*.

Much of the Anglo-Irish playwright's boundless energy was spent on the social causes he espoused throughout his long life. He was an early member of the Fabian Society, dedicated to the cause of democratic socialism, and he wrote and edited many of the pamphlets published in its name. Shaw vigorously supported working-class representation in politics and attended the inaugural conference of the Independent Labour Party, a precursor of the Labour Party, helping Kier Hardie to write the party's programme. He campaigned vociferously for a variety of causes, ranging from equal rights for women to vegetarianism and a phonetic alphabet for the English language.

Dramatic developments

Similar social concerns were making themselves felt on stage, albeit for a minority audience. Then, as now, the great mass of theatre-goers viewed it as an excuse for a good night out, to be enjoyed after an early dinner or perhaps before a late supper *à deux*. The evening's entertainment might be a drawing-room comedy involving the complications of upper-class life, or perhaps one of the spectacular productions for which London's Drury Lane Theatre was especially famed – one play boasted not just a racetrack scene featuring six jockeys on mechanical horses, but also an on-stage train crash; another climaxed in an earthquake with houses collapsing and people (trained acrobats) leaping from windows. To see such extravaganzas fashionable London audiences paid as much as half a guinea for a seat in the stalls – roughly half a docker's weekly wage.

Such theatrical fare left the intelligentsia cold, and over the course of the decade they sought theatres prepared to stage more thought-provoking productions. One such place was London's Royal Court Theatre, where from 1904 to 1907 Harley Granville-Barker put on a ground-breaking series of plays, including no fewer than ten works by George Bernard Shaw, the most influential playwright of the age.

HOME ENTERTAINMENT
A family gathers round a piano for a sing-song, enjoying one of the home pleasures that have largely disappeared in recent times. In the days before television and computer games, people were dependent on their own resources for much of their entertainment. In particular, at a time when the only available recorded music emerged scratchily from wax cylinders, most music-making was live. Besides domestic singalongs, music-lovers could hear brass bands in city parks during the summer months, and many people also enjoyed the social recreation of singing in choirs; even medium-sized towns hosted annual performances of Handel's 'Messiah' and other oratorios. Subscription concerts were another feature of the musical scene around the country; music-lovers would pay to attend a programme of concerts, rather in the manner of season-ticket holders at present-day sporting events.

Granville-Barker wrote plays of his own that touched on similar themes of corruption beneath the façade of respectability that attracted the novelists of the day. It was the banning of his play *Waste* – the plot shockingly involved a politician's adulterous affair and a botched abortion – that helped to inspire one of the great intellectual causes of the day. Dozens of influential writers, from Shaw and James Barrie to Henry James and Thomas Hardy, lent their support to the call to do away with the right of the Lord Chamberlain's office to censor plays. In response, Henry Campbell-Bannerman's Cabinet set up a parliamentary committee to consider the matter, but despite hearing the evidence of many leading writers and thinkers in favour of change, the committee plumped for the status quo. It would be 1968 before theatrical censorship was abolished.

Prodigious musical talents

Highbrow audiences seeking less politically challenging stimulation could always head for the concert halls. In the days before effective gramophones, let alone hi-fi, CDs or MP3 players, music remained a live art, and the classical genre was experiencing an explosion of talent. The Edwardian years saw some of Britain's best-loved composers either in their prime or exhibiting extraordinary early promise. Ralph Vaughan Williams composed his first major successes in the decade – 1910 saw acclaimed première performances of his 'Sea Symphony' and 'Fantasia on a Theme by Tallis'. Cheltenham-born Gustav Holst had yet to write 'The Planets', but he was producing compositions set to Sanskrit texts, reflecting an interest in Eastern mysticism, while earning a living as musical director of St Paul's Girls' School and London's Morley College. Frederick Delius was based in France by this time, but was still producing works deeply influenced by English themes, such as 'In a Summer Garden' and 'Brigg Fair'. Folk collectors like Cecil Sharp and the Australian-born Percy Grainger were busy combing the land for the traditional songs that provided inspiration for such works.

The presiding genius of the Edwardian musical world was undoubtedly Sir Edward Elgar, whose compositions still, for many people, provide the mental soundtrack for the era. The decade began with his 'Cockaigne Overture', subtitled 'In London Town', but his most potent contribution of the time were the 'Pomp and Circumstance' marches, the first of which contained the setting for 'Land of Hope and Glory'. The march itself was an instant success: Henry Wood, who conducted the first London performance, recalled: 'The people simply rose and yelled. I had to play it again, with the same result. In fact they refused to allow me to get on with the programme.' According to Elgar, it was Edward VII who subsequently suggested that the tune be used as a setting for A C Benson's 'Coronation Ode', of which 'Land of Hope and Glory' was a part. Ironically, the composer would later claim never to have liked the words that he made into such an enduring part of the nation's heritage.

New realism in painting

In his appearance and habits, Elgar was very much an Edwardian gentleman of conservative views. As such, he provided a stark contrast with many artists of the day. The dominant personality in the world of painting was Walter Sickert, a bohemian figure whose embrace of stark realism brought him closer in spirit to the era's novelists. His unflinching portrayal of the seamier side of London life reached a peak in a sequence of paintings called 'The Camden Town Murder', which drew their inspiration from a real-life cause célèbre – the killing of a prostitute called Emily Dimmock in seedy lodgings in north London. The subject was shocking at the time, the more so for its brutal contrast with the idealised classicism of late Victorian academic art. Sickert attracted around him a group of like-minded artists, including Spencer Gore and Robert Bevan, who collectively became known as the Fitzroy Street Group after Sickert's home address – a precursor of the later Camden Town Group, formed from the same circle's ranks.

One note largely missing from the Edwardian art scene was modernism, which was beginning to attract attention on the Continent through the music of Stravinsky (his 'Firebird' was premièred in Paris in 1910) and the paintings of Matisse and the group known as *Les Fauves* (the 'wild beasts'). Some of their work finally got a showing in a pioneering exhibition staged at London's Grafton Gallery by art critic Roger Fry in 1910. Their works hung alongside paintings by Cézanne, Gauguin and Van Gogh – all virtually unknown in Britain at the time. Seeking a label to unite the various artists, Fry and his colleagues came up with 'Post-Impressionist', and the name stuck.

Fry's exhibition was controversial at the time, and many of the people who crowded in to see it came only to scoff. The poet Wilfrid Scawen Blunt called the show 'pornographic', comparing the works to graffiti on toilet walls, while a doctor-critic published an article claiming that the artists involved were clinically insane. Even so, the exhibition was a harbinger of things to come and it got people talking about the modernist trend in art as never before.

CONTRASTING ATTITUDES
The Edwardian art world spanned a spectrum ranging from the conservatism of the writer Rudyard Kipling and composer Sir Edward Elgar (above) to the raffish bohemianism of such painters as Augustus John and Jack B Yeats (below). The son of a Worcester music dealer, Elgar married the daughter of a major-general and lived the life of a country gentleman. At the time of Elgar's greatest success, Yeats – the brother of the poet W B Yeats – was working in obscurity, drawing inspiration from childhood memories of the countryside around Sligo in Ireland. He developed a highly individual Expressionist style. The playwright Samuel Beckett was an admirer, writing of him '... he brings light, as only the great dare to bring light, to the issueless predicament of existence'.

1900s

SUMMER'S
END

Within months of Campbell-Bannerman's election victory of 1906, it was all too apparent that the Prime Minister was a sick man. Before the end of the year he had the first of a series of heart attacks, and from November 1907 he was virtually an invalid. He died on 22 April, 1908, just 17 days after resigning as Prime Minister. The social reform programme that he had done so much to put into practice would forge ahead and old age pensions became a reality before the end of the decade. But there was one area where Parliament proved reluctant to act: despite growing protests, the government refused to extend the vote to women.

CHAMPION SWIMMER Henry Taylor after his victory in the 400m freestyle event at the 1908 London Olympics – one of three gold medals he won at the games.

THE PEOPLE'S BUDGET

When Henry Campbell-Bannerman resigned as Liberal Prime Minister, on 5 April, 1908, there was never much doubt as to who would succeed him. H H Asquith (his Christian names, Herbert Henry, were rarely used) had already established himself as the party's safest pair of hands.

Asquith came from a middle-class commercial background in Yorkshire, but his childhood had been complicated by his father's death when he was just 7 years old. His natural ability won him a scholarship to Balliol College, Oxford, and he subsequently embarked on a successful law career. He won the attention of the ageing Gladstone through his intelligence and eloquence, and was unexpectedly made Home Secretary in the Grand Old Man's final Cabinet when still only 39. Asquith had an impressive ability to make impromptu speeches; when asked to reveal his notes for a speech in support of the Licensing Bill of 1908, he produced a scrap of paper bearing the words 'Too many pubs'.

Asquith was Chancellor of the Exchequer when Campbell-Bannerman stepped down. The King was recuperating in Biarritz, and so the new Prime Minister had to travel to France to receive the royal assent to his promotion. He quickly gave the reform programme fresh momentum by bringing forward a policy that he himself had helped to shape as Chancellor: state pensions for the elderly poor.

The state pension and other social benefits

The business of managing the legislation to bring in the new pension devolved to David Lloyd George, Asquith's successor at the Exchequer. To replace Lloyd George as President of the Board of Trade, Asquith chose another rising talent: Winston Churchill. Between them, the two would be the drivers of a new raft of social reforms. The measures in the Pensions Act of 1908 were limited in scope, at least in the light of what was to follow. Men and women over the age of 70, with an annual income less than £31.10s, received up to 5 shillings a week for a single person or 7s 6d for married couples. Recipients had to have worked 'to their full potential' and have lived in the country for at least 20 years.

No-one doubted the long-term significance of the legislation: the state was taking on a new level of responsibility for the well-being of its least well-off citizens. Traditional Tory opinion was shocked by the move. Lord Lansdowne, who had been Foreign Secretary under Balfour, commented that public money had been better spent on the Boer War, which raised the moral fibre of the country, rather than on state pensions, which weakened it. But for the beneficiaries the money was an unalloyed blessing, providing a degree of financial security in their final years. In *Lark Rise to Candleford*, Flora Thompson recalled how recipients in her Oxfordshire village reacted: 'At first when they went to the Post Office to draw [the pension], tears of gratitude would run down the cheeks of some, and they would say as they picked up their money, "God bless that Lloyd George".'

While the Chancellor was busy with pensions, Churchill was pushing through important new measures at the Board of Trade. In 1909 he brought in labour exchanges to help unemployed workers find jobs. He also introduced minimum wages in certain 'sweated' industries, where people worked in poor conditions for

REFORMIST LEADER
H H Asquith took over as Liberal Prime Minister following Sir Henry Campbell-Bannerman's resignation. Asquith had been a successful barrister before he became a politician and he brought a clear legal mind and forensic debating skills to the Commons. He steered his party to victory in two general elections and was to hold office for eight years, the longest continuous term of any 20th-century premier until Margaret Thatcher in the 1980s. Yet his time in power was marked by confrontation and crises, first in the domestic arena and latterly with the outbreak of the First World War.

'GOD BLESS LLOYD GEORGE'

State pensions were not a novel idea in 1908; at least ten other countries had already introduced them, notably Britain's main industrial rival, Germany. British workers without financial means still faced the prospect of either dependence on their families or the workhouse in old age. That situation changed with the Pensions Act steered through by Chancellor David Lloyd George in August 1908. Even though the sums paid out were small, they brought a degree of financial security to people like these elderly London ladies, seen enjoying a day trip to Epping Forest. Soon advertisers caught on (right) and began promoting their products as an aid to longevity.

OLD AGE PENSIONERS
DARBY—"A Happy New Year, my dear. Thanks to OXO we've got the pensions and thanks to OXO we'll enjoy them another 30 Years."

low pay. Ironically, the reforms were not well received by the people they were intended to help: the Labour movement regarded them with suspicion, fearing particularly that the trade boards might cost jobs and reduce the power of the unions to maintain pay differentials between groups of workers.

Demand for Dreadnoughts

Meanwhile, the measures had to be paid for, a task complicated by demands for money from a very different source. Britain was involved in a naval armaments race with Germany, which had been sparked off by a misunderstanding in 1900 when Royal Navy seamen boarded a German mail steamer in the mistaken belief that it was carrying arms to the Boers. Although the Admiralty apologised for the incident, Kaiser Wilhelm II's government in Berlin seized upon it as the reason to set about doubling the size of the German fleet.

Britain regarded its naval supremacy as essential for the survival of its far-flung empire and felt obliged to respond in kind. The First Sea Lord, Sir John Fisher, argued vociferously for increased outlay on the Royal Navy. In particular he wanted more state-of-the-art, turbine-powered battleships like the *Dreadnought*, which was launched in 1906. The Conservative opposition in the Commons and the Northcliffe press both took up the call, coining the slogan 'We want eight and we won't wait'.

Faced with the growing clamour, the government agreed to lay down four more vessels, with a further four authorised for 1910. The decision placed an unprecedented strain on the nation's finances, already burdened by the cost of the new pensions. Casting around for new revenue sources, Lloyd George made the decision to place the burden squarely on the rich. His 'People's Budget' of 1909 increased taxes on incomes above £3,000 a year, raised death duties and the tariffs on tobacco and spirits, and, most controversially of all, introduced new taxes on land, including a 20 per cent levy on unearned rises in the value of estates.

Revolt by the Lords

Lloyd George's proposals directly targeted the land-owning classes, who not surprisingly rose in revolt against them. The Chancellor went on the attack, justifying his measures in a speech proclaiming that the 'sole function and chief pride' of his opponents was 'the stately consumption of wealth produced by others'. They responded by organising a Budget Protest League to coordinate resistance outside Parliament and the House of Lords prepared to do battle. Although by long-established convention the Lords did not vote down finance bills that had been approved by the Commons, in this case they were in no mood for compromise and made an exception. In a direct challenge to the authority of the government, the bill was rejected in the House of Lords by a majority of 225. Asquith had no alternative but to dissolve Parliament and go to the country, so the decade ended with a general election in prospect and the argument between Lords and Commons would escalate into a full-blown constitutional crisis.

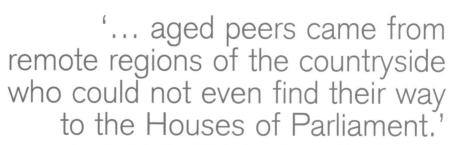

NAVAL RACE
Britain's naval rivalry with Germany was the first and perhaps the greatest of a series of costly arms races that would sap the nation's economic strength over the course of the 20th century. The race was stepped up when Sir John Fisher (above) became First Sea Lord in 1904. Condemning 150 Royal Navy ships as unfit for service, he set about replacing them with new vessels. The pride of the fleet were the Dreadnoughts, named for the eponymous turbine-powered battleship launched in 1906 (right), with guns capable of delivering a barrage of 6,800lb – more than 3 tonnes – of high explosives.

'... aged peers came from remote regions of the countryside who could not even find their way to the Houses of Parliament.'

Margot Asquith, the Prime Minister's wife, recalling the revolt in the House of Lords against Lloyd George's budget in November 1909

HOUSEHOLD NAMES

Destined to become a giant of the British high street, Marks and Spencer traces its origins to a single open-market stall in Leeds run by Michael Marks, an immigrant from Minsk in what was then imperial Russia. Marks gradually expanded the business to covered markets, like the stall above, first in Leeds and then in towns across Yorkshire and Lancashire, advertising his goods under the slogan, 'Don't Ask the Price, It's a Penny'. In 1894, needing extra capital to fund further growth, Marks went into partnership with Thomas Spencer, chief cashier for the wholesale distribution firm that provided much of his merchandise. More branches followed and by 1903, when the business became a limited company, the number had grown to over 60.

John Sainsbury had opened his first shop in 1869 in Drury Lane, London, selling fresh foods. Packaged groceries were added in 1903, when the rapidly growing business purchased a grocery store in Dalston. By the early 1920s, Sainsbury was the largest grocery chain in the country.

VOTES FOR WOMEN

By 1908 another democratic cause was making its presence felt across the nation, and it too was proving to be bitterly divisive. The women's suffrage movement had gathered momentum through the last decades of Victoria's reign, spawning a variety of organisations devoted to the cause of winning the right to vote. In an attempt to establish some sort of unity, the National Union of Women's Suffrage Societies (NUWSS) was set up in 1897 as an umbrella group to coordinate their efforts. The new body made progress through the 1900s, and by 1909 more than 200 individual groups were affiliated to it.

Yet it was another, very different group that made the newspaper headlines – the Women's Social and Political Union (WSPU), which first saw the light of day in Manchester in 1903. While the NUWSS promoted democratic decision-making by its members, the WSPU was run quite autocratically by its charismatic founder, Emmeline Pankhurst, who preferred to operate through an unelected central committee. And while most NUWSS affiliates adopted a course of patient advocacy, Mrs Pankhurst chose the path of confrontation.

Changing aspirations

Seismic changes had been going on beneath the surface of late-Victorian society and the very idea that women should be confined to the traditional roles of wife, mother, servant or governess, was increasingly under fire. Although domestic service remained the main source of employment for working-class girls, other opportunities had become available. Apart from the northern textile mills and other factories, there were also increasing numbers of so-called 'white-blouse' jobs in offices, shops and schools. Before the 1870 Education Act, for example, there had been only 14,000 teachers in the whole of England, two-thirds of them male; by 1900 there were 100,000 teachers and three-quarters of them were women. Like Hilda Lessways in Arnold Bennett's *Clayhanger*, middle-class women were gaining a degree of financial independence by putting typewriting skills and knowledge of the Pitman shorthand system to use in business.

By 1900 women's growing economic power had brought about some social and political progress. Through the education

SPREADING THE WORD

The cause of votes for women was a familiar one by 1900, but it gained huge momentum in the Edwardian years. Much of the publicity was generated by the Women's Social and Political Union, set up by Emmeline Pankhurst in 1903. From the start the WSPU adopted a confrontational approach that kept the movement in the headlines, attracting support and hostility in almost equal measure. Even among its supporters its methods were controversial. The Women's Freedom League, seen campaigning below, was a breakaway group set up by former WSPU members disillusioned with what they regarded as autocratic leadership. In particular, they took issue with the decision to cancel the annual conference and leave decision-making to a committee nominated by Mrs Pankhurst and her daughter Christabel.

provided by the board schools almost all girls were now literate and numerate, and pressure from women's groups had achieved some advances in respect of property rights within marriage. There had even been a few political gains: single or widowed rate-payers had been able to vote in local elections from as early as 1869, and the right was extended to married women in 1894. In this respect the Isle of Man was way ahead of the game, for Manx women had been given a voice in voting for the island's parliament, the House of Keys, in 1881.

In feminist eyes, such achievements paled in comparison to the work still to be done. Women may have had increasing access to the workplace, but their wages averaged barely two-thirds those of men. Despite the progress made in improving the status of wives, inequalities persisted in the divorce laws, which permitted only husbands to cite adultery as grounds for separation. Above all, British women were expected to pay taxes, while being denied any say in how those taxes were raised or spent because they were denied the right to vote.

'Never had I imagined that so many people could be gathered together to share in a political demonstration.'

Emmeline Pankhurst, writing on the Women's Sunday rally held in Hyde Park on 2 June, 1908

MASS MOVEMENT
By the latter part of the decade the suffragette cause had become a mass movement. One of the main ways of spreading the message was through public meetings and rallies like this one in Trafalgar Square (left). The speakers at such events – here a Mrs Baines from Stockport – did not always find themselves preaching to the converted; they often had to face light-hearted banter and sometimes verbal abuse or even the threat of violence. Mrs Pankhurst became renowned for the cool way in which she dealt with unwanted interruptions. When Oxford undergraduates once tried to disturb her in mid-speech by releasing a mouse onto the platform, she picked the creature up and stroked it.

By 1907 the campaign had gained a big enough following to permit Mrs Pankhurst to devote all her time to campaigning. The extent of the support became obvious the following year when the Women's Social and Political Union called a mass demonstration in Hyde Park. Held on Sunday 21 June – Women's Sunday, as the WSPU christened it – the rally attracted an estimated half a million people, brought to London from all parts of the country in specially commissioned trains. Seven separate processions, of which this is one (above right), converged on the park from different directions, and speakers made the case for the female franchise from 20 different platforms – efficient electrical amplification had not yet been invented. Mrs Pankhurst would later write: 'When I mounted my platform in Hyde Park, and surveyed the mighty throngs that waited there and the endless crowds that were still pouring into the park from all directions, I was filled with amazement not unmixed with awe.'

Emmeline Pankhurst – leading the fight

The right to vote became the focus of discontent, and Emmeline Pankhurst took up the role of suffragette standard-bearer. She inherited her dramatic flair and taste for extravagant gestures from her father, a self-made Manchester businessman who was also the city's leading amateur actor. Educated locally and at the École Normale in Paris, Emmeline married a prominent radical barrister and the two threw themselves into a variety of progressive causes. They also had five children, two of them boys who died in infancy. Of the girls, Christabel and Sylvia took a prominent part in the suffrage movement.

Following her husband's death in 1898, Emmeline was forced by economic circumstances to take a salaried job as a registrar of births and deaths. She saved most of her energy, however, for the WSPU, which was founded at a meeting in her home. The group's first act of militancy came in 1905, when a private member's bill in favour of women's suffrage was talked out in the Commons. Emmeline and others protested noisily and were duly expelled from the House. Five months later Christabel and Annie Kenney interrupted a speech by the Liberal statesman Sir Edward Grey at Manchester's Free Trade Hall; they were arrested when Christabel spat at a policeman. Refusing to pay the fines imposed, the two served short prison sentences. In the wake of the affair the *Daily Mail*, no friend of the cause, christened the WSPU militants 'suffragettes', seeking thereby to distinguish them from the more moderate 'suffragists' of the NUWSS.

The intensity of the WSPU campaign escalated. Emmeline first went to prison in 1908, when she refused to be bound over after leading a march on Parliament. That same year the largest political demonstration seen up till then in Britain took place in Hyde Park when an estimated half a million people came from all over

PRISON ORDEAL
By the end of the decade a jail term had become something of a badge of honour for militant suffragettes prepared to take direct action to achieve their goals. In 1908 Emmeline and Christabel Pankhurst (left) were sentenced to three months in London's Holloway Prison for issuing a proclamation that was considered seditious. Emmeline, who had already served a six-week term earlier that year, was disgusted by the damp, the cockroaches and the insanitary conditions in the prison, as well as by the 'hideous prison dress stamped all over with the broad arrow of disgrace'. Yet she regarded her suffering as a good way of drawing attention to the cause. She was to be arrested seven times over the next six years, telling the court on one occasion: 'We are here not because we are law-breakers; we are here in our efforts to become law-makers.' Many other militants followed her example, among them Emmeline Pethick-Lawrence, seen here (right) emerging from a 1909 prison term to the plaudits of well-wishers. At the time Pethick-Lawrence was a loyal lieutenant of the Pankhursts, serving as treasurer of the WSPU and, with her lawyer husband, running its journal, *Votes for Women*. When the couple subsequently dared to express reservations about the WSPU's adoption of violent methods, Mrs Pankhurst expelled them from the movement.

the country to attend a rally for the cause. Radical suffragettes threw stones at the windows of 10 Downing Street in the first attacks on property. In October Emmeline and Christabel were back in prison, sentenced to three months each for issuing a handbill urging their followers to 'rush the House of Commons'.

By 1909 WSPU members were regularly harassing Cabinet ministers. Some of those imprisoned went on hunger strike to draw further attention to their cause. The authorities responded by ordering the women to be force-fed, a humiliating and painful procedure that involved forcing a feeding tube up the prisoner's nose and down into the throat. Such oppressive measures stimulated responses from suffragette prisoners that sometimes bordered on extreme: one aristocratic detainee, Lady Constance Lytton, tried to tattoo the words 'Votes for Women' on her chest with a needle. By 1910 patience over the issue was wearing very thin indeed. The lack of action on the part of the government would trigger an explosion of anger from activists in the early years of the coming decade that dwarfed the confrontations of the Edwardian decade.

SPORT TURNS PROFESSIONAL

For light relief in a time of strife and economic recession the public flocked to spectator sports, which drew unprecedented crowds in the years leading up to 1910. Cricket was enjoying a golden age, bequeathing for posterity a lingering image of village greens on summer afternoons echoing to the reassuring thud of willow on leather. The decade was a great time for the amateur game, played by teams with colourful names like 'I Zingari' or the 'Free Foresters'.

Professional cricket was well established: the County Championship had been in operation since 1889, and full-time salaried players formed the backbone of the 16 sides that now took part. Up to 30,000 spectators turned out to watch Yorkshire playing at home on a sunny day. The great W G Grace retired from the game in 1900, but other giants soon came forward to take his place. Gilbert Jessop of Gloucestershire was a famous big hitter, reckoned by some authorities to have been the fastest run-scorer in cricketing history. And in the remarkable C B Fry England found the Edwardian era's successor to Grace.

A gifted popular hero

Fry was an Oxford scholar, said to have been a match for the best minds of his generation, but he is remembered for his incredible sporting prowess. He captained the England cricket team and also played in an FA Cup Final (in the Southampton team that lost to Sheffield United in 1902). He played rugby for Blackheath and the Barbarians, and in athletics was for a time the joint world record-holder in the long-jump. Legend has it that he was supple and strong enough to do a backflip from a standing position and land on a mantelpiece behind him.

For all his many sporting talents, Fry remained an amateur throughout his playing career, earning his keep first as a schoolteacher and later as the commander of a Royal Navy training vessel. He wrote several books and was persuaded by the publisher George Newnes to lend his name to *C B Fry's Magazine*, a sports and adventure monthly. In later life Fry became somewhat eccentric, suffering periods of mental instability in which he was sometimes seen running naked along Brighton beach. One of his odder ventures was a quixotic attempt in the 1930s to persuade Hitler's Germany to take up cricket to Test level. Earlier, he had been briefly sounded out as a possible candidate for the vacant Albanian throne.

The professional game

While brilliant amateurs like C B Fry continued to illuminate British sport, the way of the future lay with the professional game. That point was brought home most clearly by soccer, which benefited hugely from the increased leisure time and spending power of the working men who flocked through the turnstiles, particularly in the northern half of the country. Real wages of skilled and semi-skilled workers had risen by an estimated 30 per cent in the decades since 1870, and it was increasingly common for employees to clock off at noon on Saturdays, leaving the afternoons free for supporting the local team.

The Football League had got under way in 1888, with a Second Division added in 1892. The clubs were established as limited companies, but they rarely

UP FOR THE CUP
Dressed in their Sunday best, Everton fans in London for the 1906 FA Cup Final take a break on their way to watch the match. They would have been celebrating later that evening, for their team won by a single goal scored 13 minutes from time by their centre forward, Alex 'Sandy' Young. The result was a bitter blow for the Newcastle supporters, who had also seen their team lose the final to Aston Villa the year before. The game was played before 75,000 spectators at the Crystal Palace ground, home to FA Cup Final matches from 1895 to 1914.

made profits that were not ploughed back into the game. To keep costs down, the authorities imposed a maximum wage for players of £4 a week, about twice the sum earned by a well-paid factory worker. There was also a £10 limit on signing-on fees, but the amount paid for transfers was not capped. The most successful clubs used this loophole to attract the best players: the £1,000 barrier was first breached in 1905, when the England striker Alf Common moved from Sunderland to Middlesbrough.

The football game that the fans flocked to see was recognisably the same as the one played today, although with some noticeable differences. In the early 1900s, for example, players still wore knickerbockers reaching down to the knee rather than shorts, although the obligation to do so was removed in 1905. By that time clubs were providing gyms for their squad to work out in and were employing trainers to give them rubdowns. Supporters were quite as partisan as today, wearing club rosettes and shaking rattles, and there were lots of them: the average First Division fixture attracted a gate of 15,000, while the 1901 FA Cup Final, staged at Crystal Palace, drew a staggering attendance of 114,815. One reason for the record crowd was the fact that a London team, Tottenham Hotspur, had reached the final, a feat that before the First World War was matched by only two other London clubs. Soccer remained very much the northern game that it had been when the League was first set up with a dozen participants – none of them from further south than Derby.

A Scottish league had been established with 11 teams in 1890, and there too the game attracted passionate enthusiasm. One of the first major sporting disasters occurred at the Ibrox Park stadium in Glasgow in 1902, when part of the stand collapsed under the weight of spectators watching the annual Scotland–England international match; 26 people were killed and more than 500 were injured. Scotland also saw one of the earliest soccer riots, at Hampden Park in 1909, when a Celtic–Rangers Scottish Cup Final ended in a draw and the authorities decided to arrange a replay rather than settle the issue in extra time.

For all soccer's growing professionalism, it was still possible for the best amateur clubs to take on First Division opposition and win. Corinthians proved the point memorably in 1903 when they beat Bury 10–3 shortly after the League side had won the FA Cup without conceding a goal in the entire campaign.

The amateur–professional divide was more marked in rugby, where it caused a schism that survives to this day. In 1895 the Rugby Football Union had

TAKING THE LEAD
Harry Hampton (third from left) scores for Aston Villa after just two minutes of the 1905 Cup Final, while Newcastle United defenders look helplessly on. Villa won the match 2–0, with Hampton scoring again in the 76th minute. Teams from the Midlands and North dominated the competition through much of the Edwardian era, although Tottenham Hotspur were surprise winners in 1901, delighting a record crowd of over 114,000. The burgeoning number of spectators was an indicator of soccer's fast-growing popularity; just 2,000 fans had turned out for the first cup final, held at the Oval in 1872.

THE "SCOTTISH TEAMS" SERIES.

THIRD LANARK

GROUND -
NEW CATHKIN PA
GLASGOW.

Hi, Hi, Hi.

THIRD L[RY]

STAYING COMPETITIVE
One sign of the growing professionalism of soccer was the development of the league game, which by the turn of the century was well established in Scotland as well as England. Queen's Park, Scotland's oldest football club, agreed to join the Scottish League in 1900, having previously objected to the fact that players could be paid for their services. The Glasgow team Third Lanark (above) was a founder member of the Scottish League. They were champions in 1904 and remained top-level competitors until the 1960s, before collapsing into bankruptcy in 1967.

determined to retain the amateur principle and clubs that paid their players or charged entrance fees to spectators were banned from Union membership. But the Northern Union needed the gate money to support the working men who made up most of its teams, and so it broke away. The split between rugby union and rugby league became permanently entrenched in the 1900s as rule changes drove an enduring wedge between the two traditions. In 1906 rugby league teams were reduced in size from 15 to 13 players and a new rule permitted players who were brought down while holding the ball to retain possession by back-heeling it to another member of the side. The aim was to reduce the number of loose rucks and mauls and so encourage a more open, mobile game that would entertain the watching crowds.

The split that opened up in rugby football's ranks in a sense epitomised the north–south divide that continued to mark the country as a whole, just as it had throughout Queen Victoria's reign. Yet there was one sport that was not only truly national in its scope but also managed to appeal across the social classes. This was horseracing, which thoroughly earned its nickname of the Sport of Kings from the patronage it received over the years from Edward VII. The horse of the decade was the filly Sceptre, which as a three-year-old in 1902 won the Grand Slam of the St Leger, the Oaks, and the 1000 and 2000 Guineas. She is still the only horse ever to win four British classics outright in one season.

BRITAIN'S PLACE IN THE WORLD

As the first decade of the 20th century drew to a close, one man put his mind to taking stock of the years since Victoria's passing. Charles Masterman, a progressive Liberal MP and grand-nephew of the prison reformer Elizabeth Fry, published *The Condition of England* in 1909. A major area of concern, for Masterman and others, was the fear that Britain was being outpaced both industrially and technologically by its overseas competitors.

The decade had seen aviation pioneered in the USA and France, while Germany had come to the fore in motor engineering – at least until Henry Ford developed the techniques of mass production that would establish US dominance for much of the century. Even in shipbuilding, long one of Britain's great strengths, the Germans were making rapid advances; ocean liners built in German shipyards won the prestigious Blue Riband for the fastest Atlantic crossing in three successive years, from 1904 to 1906. Only in 1907 did the turbine-powered *Lusitania* re-establish Britain's hold. British industry had success stories – chemicals were thriving, and by 1911 mechanical and electrical engineering were employing twice as many workers as iron and steel – but these were too often outshone by the progress being made in other countries.

Like many of his contemporaries, Masterman was also concerned that Britain was falling demographically behind its main rival, Germany. 'The headlong collapse of the birth rate of this country – a fall greater than in any other nation in Europe – is a phenomenon to which all the classes, save the very poorest, are probable contributors', he wrote. The decline was only comparative, for the population of the mainland in fact grew by almost 4 million over the course of the decade to a total of 40.5 million. But the rate of increase was down, and this fact combined with a decline in the number of deaths to signal an ageing population.

The effects were particularly marked in the countryside, where the continuing drift to the cities contributed to a sense of decay. By the end of the decade only 8 per cent of the workforce earned a living from the land, and people were increasingly aware that Britain had become an urban nation. In Masterman's words: 'The little red-roofed towns and hamlets, the labourer in the fields at noontide or evening, the old English service in the old English village church, now stand but as the historical survival of a once great and splendid past.' The Britain of 1910 belonged more and more to the middle classes of the cities and suburbs, who were challenging the right of the landed aristocracy to run the country.

Red-brick rise

One reason for the rise of the middle classes lay in the educational revolution that had begun in 1870 and gathered pace since Balfour's Education Act of 1902. The Edwardian years saw rapid expansion of higher education. Birmingham University got its royal charter in 1900, and existing colleges in Sheffield and Bristol acquired full university status in 1905 and 1909 respectively. This initial roll call of what became known as the 'red-brick' universities was completed by the conferral of independent status on the three constituent parts of the existing Victoria University, respectively as the universities of Manchester, Liverpool and Leeds.

Architecturally the decade was more marked by private residences, built by the likes of Edwin Lutyens and Charles Rennie Mackintosh, than by large-scale public commissions. Masterman deplored the shortage of the latter, claiming they were limited to 'a Byzantine cathedral at Westminster, a Gothic cathedral at Liverpool, a few town halls and libraries of sober solidity [and] the white buildings which today line Whitehall'. House-building was a recurrent theme in literature, whether in the shape of Forsyte's new Surrey mansion in Galsworthy's *Man of Property*, the Howard's End of E M Foster's novel of that name, or the new family home that plays a central part in Arnold Bennett's *Clayhanger*. The house represented more than a bricks-and-mortar statement of social status: it stood for a way of putting down roots in a society increasingly in flux.

For Britain was changing fast throughout Edward's reign. On the surface the upper classes maintained the formality and decorum of the previous century, as though to proclaim that life in the capital of empire was rolling on majestically as it had always done. If anything, the Edwardian upper classes added a touch of showiness to the older traditions and a flaunting of new wealth. Yet fresh forces were making themselves felt, whether in the fierce rhetoric of the suffragettes demanding rights for women or the intellectual 'anything-goes' of the emergent Bloomsbury Group, who would come to the fore in the following decade. And if the middle classes were finding their voice politically, then so too were the workers, whose political vehicle, the Labour Party, would eclipse the reformist Liberals before a dozen years were out. In retrospect the Edwardian decade would come to seem like a golden summer, but all too soon the glow would fade through a brief, troubled autumn into the savage winter of the First World War.

WHITE CITY WONDERLAND
The Franco-British Exhibition that ended up hosting the 1908 Olympic Games was a lavish monument to the spirit of friendship between the two nations in the wake of the Entente Cordiale. It was the largest such event since the Great Exhibition of 1851, occupying a 140-acre (57-hectare) site at Shepherds Bush that would thereafter be known as White City from the colour of the exhibition buildings. The attractions on display included the Flip-Flap (top right), a precursor of the London Eye offering panoramic views over the city, and the Court of Honour, where visitors could admire the Indian-style architecture from pedal-powered Swan Boats (bottom right) or from electric launches. After dark the Court of Honour was lit up by 160,000 lightbulbs in a spectacular demonstration of the power of electricity.

Among the other highlights of the exhibition were the Irish and Senegalese villages, designed to illustrate life in different corners of the empire. The Irish village was staffed by 150 'colleens' demonstrating handicrafts. The exhibition ran from mid-May until the end of October, attracting more than 8 million paying spectators, with the Olympic Games taking place in July. The site on which the exhibition stood is now occupied by the BBC Television Centre and the Westfield shopping precinct.

LONDON'S FIRST OLYMPICS

The 1908 Olympics were not originally destined for London. They had been assigned to Rome, but an eruption of Mount Vesuvius in 1906 required such a costly relief effort that the Italian government pulled out on financial grounds. With just two years in which to prepare, the organisers took advantage of a major event already planned for 1908: the Franco-British Exhibition. Happy to draw extra spectators, the exhibition authorities agreed to build a 66,000-seater stadium on their site at White City in West London. All the work was completed on time and, with the City toastmaster (right) in attendance to make announcements, the Games were ready to begin.

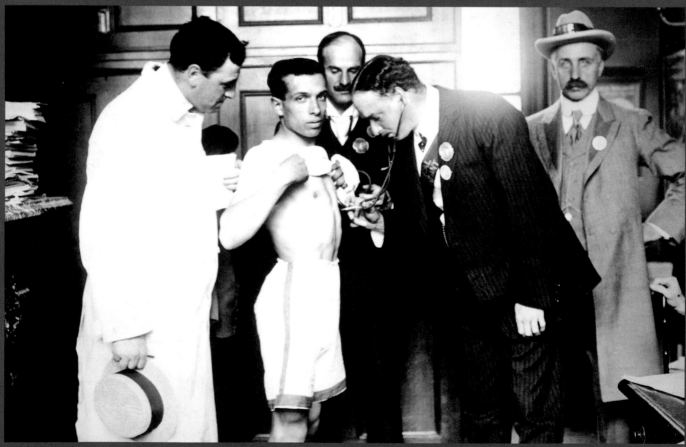

ON WITH THE SHOW

From the start the 1908 Games were dogged by controversy. The organisers failed to display the US flag in the stadium, and in response the flagbearer of the US team refused to dip the Stars and Stripes, as custom demanded, when marching past the royal box. The bad feeling continued when a US runner was judged to have deliberately impeded the British favourite in the 400m final. The race was declared void and the offender disqualified, but then the other two finalists, both from the USA, refused to take part in the re-run, so the British athlete

became the only person ever to win Olympic gold by a walkover.

Despite such niggles and the rainy July weather, the Games soon got the nation's attention. The Marathon was a highlight, run from Windsor Castle to White City. It was the first time the length of the race was set at 26 miles 385 yards, the original route having been lengthened to avoid tramlines and cobbles, and to include a final section in the stadium to give spectators a view of the contestants. Competitors had to provide a certificate of fitness and were examined by the Games' own doctors (left).

The Italian Dorando Pietri was leading on entering the stadium, but was in the final stages of exhaustion; after collapsing several times, he was helped to the finish line by sympathetic officials. As a result he was disqualified, but he had so impressed the crowd that he was awarded a special cup by Queen Alexandra.

Britain came out overall winners with 146 medals, well ahead of second-placed USA with 47. The British cycling pursuit team (above) won gold, while Walter Tysall from Birmingham (right) took silver in the individual gymnastics.

CROWD PLEASERS

The Games featured several events that were later dropped from the Olympic schedule. One such was the tug-of-war (top left), contested from 1900 to 1920. Participation was open to clubs rather than national teams, meaning that several teams from one country could enter; in 1908 all three medals went to British police outfits, including the Liverpool squad shown here, which won silver.

Archery was dropped in 1920, but was reinstated in 1972 and is still regularly contested. The women's event in 1908 (bottom left) attracted only home entrants, ensuring that British competitors swept the medals. The victor was 53-year-old Sybil 'Queenie' Newall from Rochdale, the oldest woman ever to win Olympic gold.

Fears that the Games might not be a success soon proved unfounded, although not before the poor weather caused some initial qualms. To stimulate interest, celebrities were invited to attend – the biggest draw was Maud Allan, an exotic dancer whose daring performance of the Dance of the Seven Veils from Oscar Wilde's play *Salome* was the hit of the London season. Thereafter, the stadium was regularly filled to capacity. These spectators (right) are celebrating the victory of 19-year-old Reggie Walker of South Africa in the 100m final; he beat three North American rivals to take gold.

In all, 2,008 athletes from 22 nations participated in 110 events. Only 37 of the competitors were women, competing in archery, ice-skating and tennis .

1910s

1910s
THE END OF A WORLD

It was a tumultuous start to a momentous decade. Within the space of a year, two bitter general elections were fought to decide whether peers or people governed the nation. In between them, King Edward VII died and the fleeting Edwardian Summer came to an end. The Conservatives fought relentlessly to stop the Liberal government granting Home Rule to Ireland – especially after the Parliament Act removed the power of the House of Lords to veto legislation from the Commons. Labour unrest was rife as strikes reached record-breaking levels, while suffragettes were prepared to go to prison to win the right to vote. Then, in faraway Sarajevo, Archduke Franz Ferdinand of Austria was assassinated. Within weeks, Britain was embroiled in the First World War.

HEADING SOUTH The *Terra Nova*, the ship that carried Captain Robert Scott and his ill-fated expedition to the Antarctic, forces her way through the pack ice: it took three weeks to regain open water.

PEERS VERSUS PEOPLE

It was nothing less than a battle over who ruled. The Liberals had secured an overwhelming majority in the House of Commons in the general election of 1906, but the Conservatives – or Unionists as they then preferred to be known – were masters of the House of Lords. Some 475 of the 602 peers were Unionists; less than 90 were Liberals. Arthur Balfour, the defeated Unionist leader, was quick to capitalise on the situation. It was everyone's duty, he thundered in Nottingham, just four days after losing his parliamentary seat in Manchester, to ensure that 'the great Unionist Party should still control, whether in power or whether in opposition, the destinies of this great Empire'. Egged on by Balfour, the Lords proceeded to slaughter many cherished Liberal measures, either by amending them out of all recognition or rejecting them outright.

The Education Bill was the peers' first victim, followed by the Plural Voting Bill, then the Lords forced the government to postpone its Licensing Bill; when this did reach them, in November 1908, they showed little mercy. They allowed the Old Age Pensions Bill to go through that same month, even though many of them heartily disliked the measure, but the following year they fought tooth and nail against David Lloyd George's controversial budget. When the budget reached the House of Lords, in November 1909, Lord Lansdowne, leader of the Unionist peers, denounced it as 'a monument of reckless and improvident finance'. It was

YOUNG LIBERALS
Schoolboy supporters – all, bar the driver of the wagon, not yet old enough to vote – parade in support of Sir Stephen Collins, the Liberal candidate for the Lambeth Kennington constituency, in the first of the two General Elections held in 1910. Collins had entered the House of Commons in the Liberal landslide victory of 1906; he held his seat until 1918, when – like many Liberals who supported Asquith, the party leader – he was defeated by a Coalition candidate in the election that followed the end of the First World War. Collins was one of many Liberal backbenchers who supported the administration in pressing to force Lloyd George's radical 1909 budget through the Lords. There was growing determination among government MPs to curb the power of the House of Lords to veto legislation that the Commons wished to become law.

AWAY FROM IT ALL

Herbert Asquith, who succeeded Sir Henry Campbell-Bannerman as Prime Minister of the Liberal government in 1908, is pictured here (above, second from right) taking a country break from the cares of office with some of his supporters. Asquith needed all his wits about him as the new decade dawned. Though the House of Lords eventually let David Lloyd George's budget through, Asquith faced a constitutional crisis. The Liberals were determined to strip the peers of their power of veto; the Opposition was determined to resist the move at all costs. Tempers boiled over in the House of Commons on 24 July, 1910, when Asquith was howled down by Unionist backbenchers as soon as he rose to speak. For 30 minutes, he tried in vain to make himself heard. 'It was', Winston Churchill, the Home Secretary, reported to the King, 'a squalid, frigid, organised attempt to insult the Prime Minister.'

rejected by an overwhelming 350 votes to 75. The government responded immediately by dissolving Parliament and calling a General Election.

The build-up to the election of January 1910 saw a bitter contest. Herbert Asquith, the Liberal Prime Minister, told his East Fife constituents that the Lords had 'violated the constitution' by rejecting the budget, in a 'proceeding without precedent'. The pugnacious Lloyd George had warned peers of the consequences if they rejected his budget – 'they are forcing a revolution and they will get it', he told a cheering audience in Limehouse. He claimed that the wishes of the vast majority of ordinary folk across the land were being thwarted by 'five hundred men, chosen accidentally from among the unemployed'. Winston Churchill, the Home Secretary, was as scathing as the Chancellor, calling for 'a smashing blow from the electors to finish it off forever'.

'… a played-out, obsolete, anachronistic assembly, a survival of a feudal arrangement utterly passed out of its original meaning, a force long since passed away …'

Winston Churchill, on the House of Lords

At 86.6 per cent, the turnout for the election of January 1910 was the highest in British electoral history. The Liberals saw their great 1906 majority melt away into a hung parliament. They still dominated in Scotland and Wales, but the Unionists – the Conservatives with their Liberal Unionist allies – won the largest share of the vote, becoming the majority party in England with a net gain of 116 seats. Overall the two were evenly balanced with the Liberals on 275 seats and the Unionists on 273. The government held on to power with the support of the 82 Irish Nationalists and a growing band of 40 Labour MPs.

Though the House of Lords was now grudgingly prepared to let the budget through, the Liberals were still determined to curb the legislative powers of the upper house. But the premier had a problem. Edward VII's private secretary, Lord Knollys, had warned Asquith that the King 'would not be justified in creating new peers until after a second General Election'. Without the new peers to override the Conservative majority – or a meaningful threat that they would be created – there was no chance of passing legislation of the kind the Liberals had in mind.

Carefully drafted resolutions, setting out the government's plan, were laid before the House of Commons in April 1910. The Parliament Bill was to follow. Not only did Conservative diehards detest the planned legislation, they also knew that if it became law, Home Rule for Ireland would almost certainly follow – a move they were determined to prevent. The country was on the brink of the greatest constitutional crisis it had faced for centuries. Then something happened that no one had foreseen. The King collapsed and died.

RADICAL PARTNERSHIP
Chancellor of the Exchequer David Lloyd George with his wife Margaret on his right, Winston Churchill – newly promoted to Home Secretary – on his left and William Clarke (carrying the briefcase), his private secretary, in Parliament Square. The Chancellor was on his way to introduce the 1910 budget. Lloyd George and Churchill were close friends and usually supported each other in Cabinet debates. Newspaper proprietor Sir George Riddell wrote 'they act in the closest co-operation and are obviously impressed with each other's powers.' Some Liberals – including Margot Asquith, the Prime Minister's wife – were not happy about the relationship. After the January 1910 election, she actually wrote to Churchill warning him against copying Lloyd George's style of language. 'Believe me, cheap scores, hen-roost phrases & oratorical want of dignity is out of date.' Margaret Lloyd George disliked Churchill intensely. It made no difference. The two men remained firm political partners.

THE DEATH OF THE KING

Edward VII had been ailing for some time. That April, at the insistence of his doctors, he went to Biarritz for a much-needed holiday, but he returned looking almost as exhausted as before. He then suffered an acute attack of bronchitis, but despite being desperately ill, he insisted on continuing to work. Queen Alexandra was called back early from a Mediterranean cruise, but even she could not persuade Edward to take it easy.

When it came, the end was sudden. On 6 May, after toying with a light luncheon in his bedroom at Buckingham Palace, the King decided to play with his canaries, whose cage stood by the window curtains. As he tried to cross the room, he fell to the floor. It was clear that he was suffering a series of heart attacks, but he refused to be helped to bed. Instead, he sat in a chair, protesting: 'No, I shall not give in; I shall go on; I shall work to the end.'

After a brief examination, Edward's doctors agreed that there was no hope. They administered morphia for the pain and the Archbishop of Canterbury was summoned. While the Archbishop waited in an antechamber, the Prince of Wales told his father that one of his racehorses had won the 4.15 at Kempton Park. 'I am very glad', the King murmured in reply. They were the last coherent words he spoke. He lapsed into a coma, which allowed his nurses to undress him and put him to bed. Shortly before midnight, with the Archbishop and Alexandra at his bedside, Edward VII passed away peacefully. The Prince of Wales, now George V, wrote: 'I have lost my best friend and the best of fathers.'

CLOSE TO DEATH
Concerned members of the public crowd respectfully against the railings outside Buckingham Palace to read the latest medical bulletin detailing the King's condition. The news of Edward VII's sudden collapse stunned the capital. 'London tonight,' the *New York Times* reported, 'is a despairing city … Even the physiognomy of the streets showed a sudden change. Thoroughfares which are normally scenes of life, bustle and gaiety resemble the streets of a city through which the shadow of death has stalked.' Shortly before midnight on 6 May, 1910, it was all over. The much-loved King was dead and a grieving nation mourned.

ROYAL FUNERAL

On the day of the Edward VII's funeral, 20 May, the country came to a standstill. In Sussex, Rudyard Kipling recorded how, apart from the birds singing, there was not a sound to be heard. All rail traffic had been halted as a mark of respect. The funeral procession was imposing. The new king, George V, rode behind the gun-carriage bearing his father's coffin, with his cousin Kaiser Wilhelm II of Germany beside him. Then followed the kings of Belgium, Bulgaria, Denmark, Greece, Norway, Portugal and Spain. Other royals present included Archduke Franz Ferdinand, heir to the Austro-Hungarian throne, and Marie Feodorovna, sister of Queen Alexandra and Dowager Empress of Russia. Theodore Roosevelt, a former US president, represented the USA. Edward's favourite charger – with his riding boots reversed in the stirrups – took part in the procession, here (left) seen arriving at Paddington Station. He is followed by little Caesar, the King's favourite fox terrier, walking disconsolately with a Highland servant, perhaps the most poignant sight of all. Edward's coffin was loaded reverently onto a special train to Windsor and his remains were buried in St George's Chapel.

The nation was totally distraught. There was, said Lord Morley, the Secretary of State for India, a 'sense of personal loss in a way deeper and keener than when Queen Victoria died'. One of the dying King's last visitors, with the consent of his wife Alexandra, was Alice Keppel, Edward's last mistress. Her husband Colonel Keppel told one of his daughters: 'Nothing will ever be quite the same again.' The Prime Minister received the news by wireless on board the Admiralty yacht *Enchantress* as it steamed homewards from Gibraltar through the Bay of Biscay. Asquith later recorded: 'I went up on deck, and I remember well that the first sight that met my eyes in the twilight before dawn was Halley's comet blazing in the sky … I felt bewildered and indeed stunned.'

It was a sentiment that millions shared. Edward's body lay in state in Westminster Hall from 17 to 19 May, and some 250,000 people filed silently past to pay their last respects. Hundreds of thousands lined the streets the next day to watch the funeral procession pass. Many thousands more lined the railway tracks to Windsor as the funeral train puffed slowly by.

Once Edward's funeral was over, life began to return to normal. Many expected the Royal Ascot race-meeting to be cancelled, but George V declared it should go ahead – given Edward's love of racing, this seemed fitting. Gazing down from the stands above the racecourse, Elizabeth, Countess of Fingall, noticed the large black feathered hats worn by every woman in the crowd. It made it look, she thought, as if 'an enormous flight of crows had just settled'.

A CONSTITUTIONAL CRISIS

The social season may have resumed, but Parliament had reached an impasse. Asquith was reluctant to press an inexperienced ruler, at the very start of his reign, to create the new peers needed to force the Parliament Act through the House of Lords. Instead, supported by his Cabinet colleagues, Asquith said he was prepared to explore a compromise. Even parts of the Tory press supported his point of view. James Garvin, the influential editor of *The Observer*, led the way by calling for a political truce and an inter-party conference. It was the duty of the Unionist leaders, Garvin stated, to spare the new sovereign the 'fiercest of partisan fights'. The Unionists agreed to take part.

Conference failure

The so-called Constitutional Conference began on 17 June, 1910, and met a dozen times before the summer holidays, then reconvened in the autumn, but still failed to reach agreement. Predictably, the sticking point was Home Rule. The Liberals – represented by Asquith, Lloyd George, Lord Crewe (leader of the House of Lords) and Augustine Birrell (Chief Secretary for Ireland) – refused to accede to the Unionist demand that any Home Rule Bill be exempt from the operation of the Parliament Act. Instead, they proposed that if such a bill were rejected twice by the Lords, it should be put to the people in a national referendum. The Unionists, for their part, rejected Lloyd George's call for the formation of a coalition government with an agreed programme on all the main issues of the day.

HEIR AND SUCCESSOR
A curious portrait of George V (above), taken around 1910 shortly before his succession, in the act of lighting a cigarette. A passion for the habit was one of the things that father and son had in common. George was more reserved than his fun-loving father, but perhaps that was appropriate to the times. Just three years after George rode with his cousin, Willhelm II of Germany, behind Edward's coffin, their two nations would be on the brink of war.

Asquith had no choice but to call another election and ask the King for a promise to create the new Liberal peers he required. Like his father before him, George was unwilling to agree, but in the end he gave way. 'After a long talk,' he recorded in his diary, 'I agreed most reluctantly to give the Cabinet a secret understanding that, in the event of the Government being returned with a majority ... I should use my Prerogative to make peers if asked for.'

With this pledge in his pocket, Asquith went to the country in December 1910 confident of victory, but the result was almost a re-run of the previous election. The voters were bored with the endless constitutional struggle. They wanted the politicians to resolve it with no more appeals to the country.

The siege of Sidney Street

What was really gripping public attention in the bitter cold January of 1911 was an armed clash in a street in Stepney in the East End of London, where two Latvian anarchists had taken refuge. Previously, in 1909, the pair had been part of a violent gang involved in an attempted robbery in Tottenham; a policeman had been shot trying to stop them stealing the weekly wages being delivered to a local rubber factory. One of the gang killed himself and 27 bystanders were injured. 'Who are these fiends in human shape?' the *Daily Mirror* cried, before going on to answer its own question. 'The answer is they are foreign anarchists, men who have been expelled from Russia for their crimes; whose political creed and religion is that human life is of no value at all.'

Special Branch believed that Christian Jalmish, a young Latvian otherwise known as Jacob Fogel, was the leader of the gang in the 'Tottenham Outrages' as they were christened by the press. His followers included Peter Piatkow, swiftly dubbed 'Peter the Painter', who in December 1910 was caught with some other Latvians in the act of tunnelling into a jeweller's shop in Houndsditch. They promptly opened fire, killing three police officers and injuring two more in what still ranks as the worst peacetime incident for British police. The gang fled back up the tunnel and escaped, but almost three weeks later, two of the men were tracked to a house in Sidney Street where they barricaded themselves in.

The anarchists were well armed and the police sent an urgent request for reinforcements to Winston Churchill, the Home Secretary. A detachment of Scots Guards was immediately sent to the scene, and a battery of horse artillery was also ordered up, though in the event the latter did not go into action. Churchill hurried to Sidney Street to take personal charge of operations. The anarchists chose to die, rather than surrender: seeing that their position was untenable, they set fire to the house. When the police and troops finally managed to break in after some seven hours of shooting, they found two charred bodies in the ruins.

UNDER FIRE

A line of police holds back a crowd of onlookers struggling to see what is going on in Sidney Street, as soldiers of the Scots Guards prepare to fire on 3 January, 1911. The Guards had been rushed to the scene by Home Secretary Winston Churchill to support the police in their attempt to apprehend some Latvian anarchists suspected of being involved in the shooting of five policemen, three of whom died, in Houndsditch the previous month. A massive manhunt tracked some of the men to a lodging house in Sidney Street, where Churchill was quick to take personal charge of the situation. During the lengthy shoot-out that followed, the building was set on fire, but the anarchists refused to surrender; they even shot at the Fire Brigade when firemen tried to save the building. Two anarchists died in the siege, but the body of 'Peter the Painter' was not found.

THE CORONATION SUMMER

There was one event in particular that people looked forward to in the summer of 1911: the coronation of George V and Queen Mary. It went ahead on schedule on 22 June. As the King noted that morning, the weather was 'overcast and cloudy', but that did not deter spectators cramming into the crimson stands that lined the processional route from Buckingham Palace to Westminster Abbey.

The Abbey slowly filled up with notables invited to attend the ceremony. Among them were Rudyard Kipling and his wife, who had made an early start from their Sussex home to drive up to London by motor car. Kipling spotted Richard Haldane, the Secretary of State for War, scurrying up the aisle with his peer's robes askew, resembling, Kipling thought, 'a Toby dog strayed from a Punch and Judy Show'. Queen Mary arrived looking 'pale and strained', according to the Master of Elibank, the Liberal Chief Whip. Finally, the King entered the Abbey.

The climax of the long service came when the Archbishop of Canterbury placed the crown on the King's head. The young Prince of Wales then approached the throne, doffed his coronet and on bended knee pledged allegiance, before rising to kiss his father on both cheeks. Queen Mary's crowning followed. It was an occasion, and a spectacle, that no one who witnessed it would ever forget.

After the King and Queen had departed, the Abbey slowly emptied and the cleaners moved in to sweep up. They found three ropes of pearls, 20 brooches, half a dozen bracelets, 20 golden balls that had fallen off coronets and three-quarters of a diamond necklace. All jewels were safely returned to their owners. Queen Mary was greatly relieved that it had all gone so well. Writing to her Aunt Augusta in Germany she commented: 'You may imagine what an immense relief it is to us that the great and solemn ceremony of Thursday is now over …'

WINDOW WITNESSES
A postcard commemorating the coronation of George V and Queen Mary in June 1911 (left). Workers lucky enough to be on the route to the Abbey – like these female factory workers (above) – stopped to watch the procession go by, no doubt with the blessing of the factory owners. The day of the coronation started off grey and clammy, but this did not deter the thousands who

lined the streets along the processional route. The Abbey filled up quickly with guests. Some, like Lady Huntingdon, had set off as early as six o'clock that morning to make sure of being in their seats in good time. Six thousand stools and chairs, carved of fine mahogany and emblazoned with a coronet, were specially made for the ceremony. Each one had the name of its intended occupant inscribed on the back.

'... the ceremony ... was an awful ordeal for us both.'

Queen Mary, in a letter to her Aunt Augusta

HEAT WAVE
Children enjoy a paddle in a man-made seaside playground in Fulham in July 1910. If that summer was hot, the following one – the Coronation summer – was even hotter. After a cold April, the temperature rose inexorably. Those who could afford it went to the coast. The Churchills – Winston had married Clementine Hozier, grand-daughter of the 10th Earl of Airlie, in September 1908 – took a house in Broadstairs in Kent. A visitor, Neville Lytton, described Clementine as coming forth 'like the reincarnation of Venus re-entering the sea'.

The Coronation day had been peaceful – the police reported not one arrest. And the festivities continued. The Wimbledon tennis championships began on 26 June, and true to form the weather on the opening day was unsettled. The *Daily Telegraph* noted 'the familiar spectacle of sodden courts and idling players'. That evening, the King and Queen attended a gala ballet performance given in their honour by Russian impresario Sergei Diaghilev's Ballets Russes. The Russian dancers were the sensation of the season. Leonard Woolf, then a young civil servant just back from Ceylon, wrote that he had 'never seen anything more perfect, nor more exciting on any stage'. The actress Ellen Terry declared that the art of dance had been restored to its 'primal nobility'.

On 7 July, George V and Queen Mary left the capital for a coronation tour. Their first task was to preside over the investiture of Edward, their eldest son, as Prince of Wales. A 10,000-strong crowd watched the event in the ruins of Caernarfon Castle, transformed, so one onlooker recorded, into 'a medieval tilting gallery' for the occasion. Next to the Royal Family, Lloyd George, himself a proud Welshman, was the star of the show. He had coached the 17-year-old Edward in the Welsh language and both prince and politician were greeted with tremendous cheers. For Lloyd George, this was a far cry from Coronation Day, when he had been booed by some in the aristocratic stands. Winston Churchill, as Home Secretary, proclaimed the long list of titles with which Edward had just been invested. After getting through it without a single slip, he later told the Prince that he had practised for hours, reciting the list on the golf course.

Crisis in the Lords

Back in London, where the weather had turned scorching, trouble was looming as the political temperature rose even further. The Parliament Bill had been returned to the Commons, but the Lords' amendments had rendered it toothless. The government now asked the King to allow them to make public his promise to create peers. The King agreed. Accordingly, Asquith wrote to Balfour and Lord Lansdowne, telling them that 'should the necessity arise, the Government will advise the King to exercise his Prerogative to secure the passing into Law of the Bill in substantially the same form in which it left the House of Commons.' Asquith left them in no doubt, concluding: 'His Majesty has been pleased to signify that he will consider it his duty to accept, and act, on that advice.'

By this time, the Unionist peers had split into two factions. There were the diehards, the so-called 'Ditchers', led by Lord Halsbury, who were ready to defy the House of Commons regardless of the consequences, and the 'Hedgers' who were prepared to vote with the government or at least abstain. The vote took place late in the evening of 10 August. By 131 votes (81 Liberals, 13 Bishops and 37 Unionists) to 114 diehards, the Lords resolved not to insist on their amendments to the Parliament Act. It was law at last. The King wrote in his diary: 'So the Halsburyites, thank God, were beaten and I am spared any further humiliation.'

Trouble from abroad – show-down at Agadir

Sir Edward Grey, the Foreign Secretary, had other worries on his mind. A major international crisis was brewing following the arrival of the *Panther*, a German gunboat, off the port of Agadir in Morocco. The French regarded North Africa as their own particular sphere of influence, but Germany now demanded territorial concessions. The big question was which side would Britain support?

Thanks largely to the diplomacy of Edward VII, Britain's relations with France had vastly improved in recent years, leading to the cultivation of an *entente cordiale* between the two nations. Meanwhile, despite close royal connections, relations with Germany had deteriorated. Kaiser Wilhelm II was not a popular figure in Britain. His determination to create a High Seas Fleet big enough to challenge the Royal Navy had resulted in a hugely expensive naval race, with both countries building more and bigger warships.

The tensions found their way into novels and dramas of the day. William Le Queux had a bestseller with a gripping thriller called *The Great Invasion* of 1910, which imagined a full-scale German landing in Britain. The novel's success was due in part to serialisation of the book by the *Daily Mail*, which hired a troupe of out-of-work actors to goose-step though the West End dressed in Prussian uniform. On stage, Guy du Maurier's *An Englishman's Home* played to packed houses with its depiction of an unsuccessful invasion by thinly disguised 'Norlanders'. The patriotic fervour displayed by the audiences at du Maurier's play inspired the War Office to set up a recruiting booth for the new Territorial Army in the theatre's foyer; some 20,000 volunteers came forward in the first seven weeks of the production.

ATTACKING JEWS IN BRITAIN
Britain was not immune to anti-Semitism. This Jewish couple are in the doorway of their shop in South Wales, damaged in anti-Semitic riots in the summer of 1911. What caused the riots remains unclear. They lasted a week and Home Secretary Winston Churchill sent in troops from the Worcester Regiment to suppress what he tersely labelled 'a pogrom'. The rioting started at Tredegar, where many had suffered as a result of the previous year's coal strike. According to one observer, some '200 young fellows' took to the streets to attack Jewish shops while 'singing several favourite Welsh hymn tunes'. The trouble then spread to the neighbouring Gwent valley towns of Ebbw Vale, Rhymney, Cwm, Abertysswg, Brymawr and Senghennydd, where two Jewish-owned stores were burned to the ground. Some speculated that the rioting resulted from the shops putting prices up, others that Jewish landlords had increased rents. Understandably, commentators in the *Jewish World* condemned the rioters as criminals, but *The Times* reported that the attackers were 'respectable people to all appearances.'

No one was prepared to put up with any more bombast from the Kaiser. It was Lloyd George – up until then considered by many to be a pacifist, given his outspoken opposition to the Boer War – who made Britain's position crystal clear. In a speech at the Mansion House he warned: 'If a situation were to be forced on us in which peace could only be preserved ... by allowing Britain to be treated ... as if she was of no consequence in the Cabinet of nations, then I say emphatically that peace at that price would be a humiliation intolerable for a great country like ours to endure.' In the event, Germany and France came to terms over Morocco and war was averted – for now.

INDUSTRIAL AND SOCIAL STRIFE

The North African crisis was not the only emergency. The Cabinet had to address a major dock strike and a still more threatening railway dispute. Both were part of an industrial upheaval that contemporaries called the 'Great Labour Unrest'. The unrest had started in autumn 1910, when miners in South Wales went on strike after colliery owners locked out the union members at some of the pits. Riots broke out in Tonypandy and Home Secretary Winston Churchill, ordered in police reinforcements and troops – the latter were kept in reserve. By the time calm was restored, one striker had been killed and more than 500 injured.

Things did not get any better the following year. Seamen went on strike at the time of the Coronation, followed by dockers in London, Liverpool, Hull, Bristol and Southampton. Riots in Liverpool led to 2,500 troops being dispatched to the city; a cruiser, anchored off Birkenhead, trained its guns on the shore. At 30 hours' notice, four railway unions declared they were ready to call their members out. Despite a last-minute plea by the Prime Minister, the strike went ahead, paralysing the North and Midlands and partially affecting the south of the country.

Lloyd George was given the task of persuading the railwaymen back to work. In just 48 hours he succeeded and Asquith was quick to congratulate him: 'It is the latest, but by no means the least, of the loyal and invaluable services which you have rendered.' Yet the unrest continued. In January 1912 the Miner's Federation threatened a national strike to force a guaranteed minimum wage. When the mine-owners refused point-blank, the men came out. Eventually, the government was forced to impose compulsory wage machinery on the industry, but true to its laissez-faire beliefs, it refused to lay down what the new minimum rates should be. The London dockers struck again, but this time the employers held out for victory; the strike collapsed in July as impoverished dockers began to drift back to work.

Railwaymen, miners and dockers were by no means the only people to resort to strike action. Middle-class doctors threatened to strike in protest against rules imposed on them by Lloyd George's reforming National Insurance Act. In 1911 even schoolchildren came out on strike in 62 towns and villages up and down the country demanding longer lunch breaks and an end to corporal punishment.

'WAKE UP ENGLAND'
A scene from *An Englishman's Home*, Guy du Maurier's hit play which opened to critical as well as public acclaim in London's West End in January 1909 and was still playing to packed houses more than a year later. Du Maurier, an uncle of the famous novelist Daphne du Maurier, was a serving officer in the Royal Fusiliers concerned by the unpreparedness of the country to deal with a determined foreign invasion. His theme echoed the fears of many notables of the day, including Lord Roberts – a former commander-in-chief of the army who, in retirement, became the president of the National Service League – who was calling for the urgent introduction of peacetime conscription.

continued on page 144

STRIKES AND LOCKOUTS

Contemporaries called it the 'Great Labour Unrest'. In 1909 some 2,690,000 working days were lost in strikes. Year on year that number rose relentlessly: to 9,870,000 in 1910; 10,160,000 in 1911; then, in 1912, a staggering 40,890,000 working days lost. The actual number of strikes was relatively small, but they were in huge vital industries – such as the pits, railways and docks – and on a national scale. It was little wonder that some feared revolution might be just around the corner.

STRIKERS AND SCABS
Members of the National Union of Clerks, wearing masks to conceal their faces, march to Hyde Park (below) to demand better pay and conditions. They were not alone in staging protests. Footballers went on strike, albeit briefly, and strike action also threw the music halls into confusion. Some employers responded by locking strikers out and bringing in blackleg labour – strikers called them scabs. These stokers (right) were among workers recruited by colliery owners in South Wales to try to keep one of the pits at Tonypandy running; in an attempt to drive down wages, the owners had locked the miners out in autumn 1910. Rioting broke out as strikers tried to shut the colliery down. On 7 November, hundreds of striking miners marched on the pit. Trouble flared that evening when the strikers threw stones at policemen guarding the power station. The rioting swiftly spread to the town square, where it resumed the following day. By the time it ended, 500 miners – one of whom later died – and 80 policemen had been injured. Home Secretary Winston Churchill ordered in troops and police reinforcements to keep order, a move never forgotten in the Welsh coalmines.

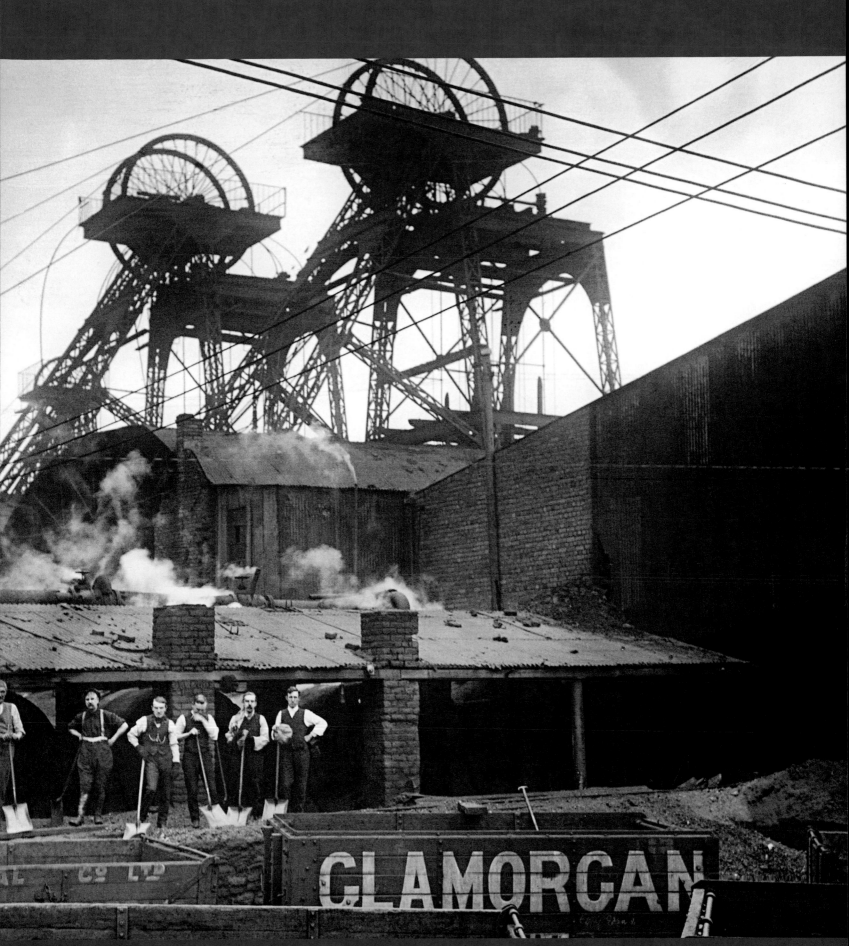

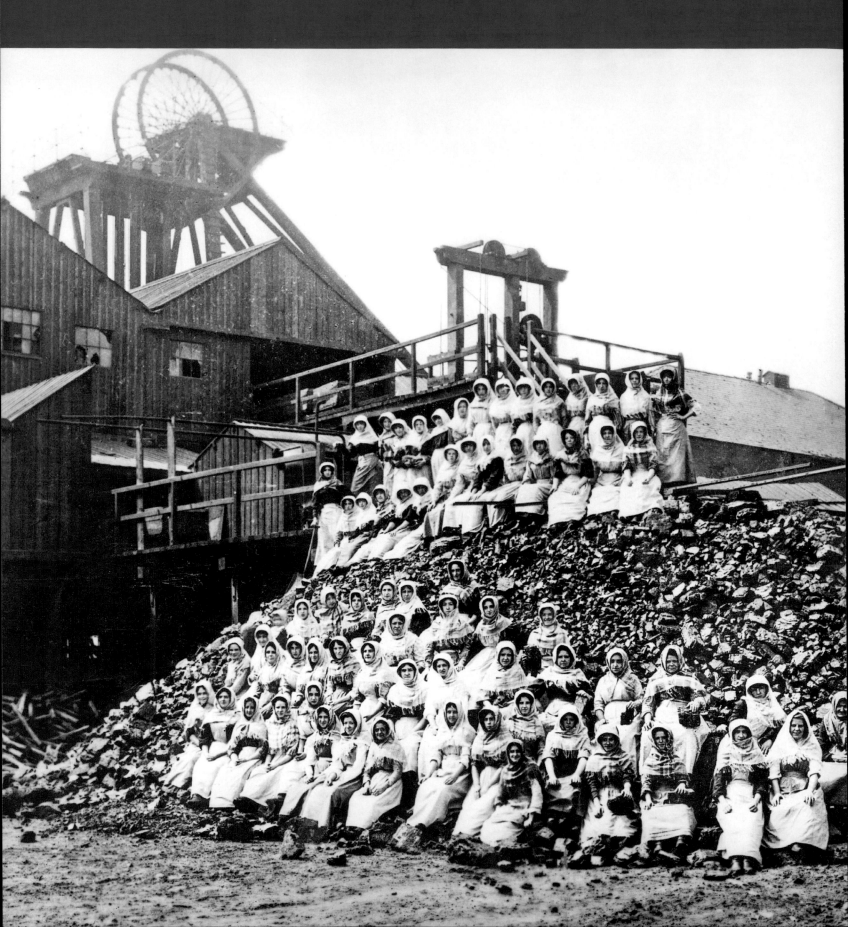

WOMEN AND CHILDREN

Women mineworkers in Wigan, Lancashire, photographed on a pile of coal during the 1912 national coal strike. Not all strike scenes were as peaceful. In South Wales, women joined with their striking husbands in fighting police and soldiers when renewed rioting broke out in Tonypandy on 22 November, 1910. A sympathetic local newspaper reported how the women 'joined with the men in the unequal combat and displayed a total disregard of personal danger which was as admirable as it was foolhardy'. They were swiftly dubbed 'the Amazons of the coalfield'. As the strikes went on, times became harder and harder for the strikers. Women and children were forced to resort to scavenging coal from local slag heaps near the closed mines to try to keep their homes warm. There was suffering in London's East End, too, when the dockers went on all-out strike in July 1911. These children (below) are waiting for charity food hand-outs. Lord Davenport, chairman of the London Port Authority and leader of the employers' side, declared publicly that he would starve the dockers back to work. He succeeded. After staying out for a fortnight, the men were forced back to work on Davenport's terms.

'We will not allow the ordinary civil operations of strikers, of men on strike, to be hampered and interfered with by a needless display of force.'

Ramsay MacDonald, Labour leader, speaking in the House of Commons in 1911

Votes for women

Women were on the march with a simple demand: to be granted the right to vote. Suffragette tactics differed, but it was the militant WSPU – led by Emmeline Pankhurst and her daughter Christabel – who stole the headlines. They heckled politicians at public meetings, demonstrated outside Parliament, smashed shop windows and chained themselves to railings. Many were prepared to go to prison. Parliament – like the public as a whole – was divided as to whether women should have the vote. Most Liberals were broadly in favour, but Prime Minister Asquith was opposed. Most Unionist-Conservative MPs were against, but Arthur Balfour and his successor as Unionist leader, Andrew Bonar Law, were prepared to see women get the vote. F E Smith, Tory politician and later Lord Chancellor, spoke for the 'no' camp when he told the Commons of his 'implacable resistance'.

The government allowed a free vote on two women's suffrage bills introduced by backbenchers, but refused to give up the necessary parliamentary time to them. There was a certain amount of political expedience behind this reluctance. To win Unionist support and to give the impression of moderation, the bills proposed that only a limited number of women – property owners aged over 30 – be granted the vote. But Liberal leaders quickly saw that such legislation would add a substantial number of Unionist voters to the electoral roll. Put to the vote in May 1912, the bill failed to get a second reading.

Asquith now offered a significant compromise. The Reform Bill that the government was about to introduce would be amended to put women on the same voting basis as men. The amendment was due to be debated in January 1913, but before it came up the Speaker of the House ruled the proposal constitutionally unacceptable. Such an amendment, he declared, was so fundamental that the Reform Bill itself would have to be withdrawn and reintroduced. To the suffragettes' fury, the government dropped it, offering to allow time for another private member's bill instead, but when the time came it, too, was rejected.

In February 1913 suffragettes smashed up the orchid house at Kew, set fire to post boxes and railway carriages, and even attempted to plant a bomb to destroy Lloyd George's country retreat. Then, in June, Emily Davison threw herself in front of the King's horse in the Derby. It was all to no avail. In February 1914, Lloyd George bluntly told a women's deputation that the position was 'quite hopeless as far as this Parliament is concerned'. Adding insult to injury, he blamed the suffragettes themselves, declaring that 'militant members have made it almost impossible for those Liberal leaders who are in favour of women's suffrage to address meetings in support of it'.

DYING FOR THE CAUSE
The funeral of Emily Wilding Davison (right), who died of head injuries four days after throwing herself in front of the King's horse, Anmer, in the Epsom Derby. Both horse and jockey were unscathed. The coffin, adorned with a simple wreath and the banner of the Women's Social and Political Union, was escorted by a suffragette guard of honour from London's Victoria to King's Cross Station then on to Morpeth, Davison's home in Northumberland, where she was buried.

The suffragette motto 'Deeds not Words' is carved on her tombstone. Emily Davison had joined the movement in 1906 and had already been jailed several times before her fatal action at the 1913 Epsom Derby. Some said that her dramatic gesture was a publicity stunt gone horribly wrong, but Mrs Pankhurst wrote that 'Emily Davison clung to her conviction that one great tragedy, the deliberate throwing into the breach of a human life, would put an end to the intolerable torture of women.'

MURDER AND DISASTER

There was plenty of other news to keep newspaper readers occupied. In October 1910, Dr Hawley Harvey Crippen – the first criminal in history to be arrested with the aid of radio transmission – went on trial at the Old Bailey for the murder of his wife. He was caught after a dramatic chase that took pursuing Scotland Yard detective, Chief Inspector Walter Dew, across the Atlantic to Canada. Back in Britain, the jury took just 27 minutes to find Crippen guilty. He was executed at Pentonville prison on 23 November that year. Ethel le Neve, his mistress who had fled with him disguised as a boy, was acquitted of being an accessory to the crime.

TRANSATLANTIC PURSUIT
Face swathed in a scarf, Dr Hawley Harvey Crippen (left) is escorted down the gangplank by Chief Inspector Dew. Crippen was accused of murdering his wife, Cora, who was also known by her stage name of Belle Elmore. The remains of a poisoned, dismembered body had been found in the cellar of the couple's London home at 39 Hilldrop Crescent. Though the sex of the body was not certain, it was assumed to be Cora, who had disappeared, and a manhunt for Crippen was launched. Meanwhile, in Antwerp, he boarded the SS *Montrose* bound for Canada with his mistress Ethel le Neve (above), posing as a merchant and his 16-year-old son. The captain was suspicious and radioed to the ship's owners that he thought he had 'Crippen London cellar murderer and accomplice' on board. Dew promptly followed on a faster ship, reaching the St Lawrence River before them, where he boarded the *Montrose* and made his arrests before they could disembark.

Tragedy in the Antarctic

Just over a year later, events unfolded in the remotest part of the globe that proved even more gripping. In January 1912, Captain Robert Falcon Scott and four fellow explorers were in a race against time in the Antarctic wilderness. The venture had begun as an attempt to become the first men to reach the South Pole. They achieved their objective on 17 January, but found a Norwegian flag already planted there. An expedition led by Roald Amundsen had beaten them to it by more than a month.

For Scott and his companions, the return journey became a desperate and heroic battle for survival. Petty Officer Edgar Evans was the first to die, followed by Captain Titus Oates. Crippled by frostbite and conscious that he was holding the others back, Oates calmly left the tent where he and his companions were sheltering and went out into the teeth of a howling, freezing blizzard. His famous

SINKING THE UNSINKABLE

The White Star liner RMS *Titanic* (above) steams slowly out of Queenstown harbour, Ireland, for her maiden voyage to New York in April 1912. The ship was a gigantic floating palace, the most luxurious liner in the world, pronounced by *The Shipbuilder* to be 'practically unsinkable'. Just before midnight on 14 April, the ship was steaming at high speed when she struck an iceberg. If she had hit the iceberg head on, some believe, she might have survived. Instead the crew attempted to manoeuvre out of the way and the iceberg gouged a 90m slash along *Titanic*'s starboard side. She sank at 2.20am on 15 April, less than three hours after hitting the iceberg. Only 706 people survived the night; more than 1,500 passengers and crew were drowned in the freezing waters of the North Atlantic – the ship did not carry enough lifeboats for everyone on board. Thomas Andrews, the naval architect who had designed the vessel, and Captain Edward Smith, in command for the ill-fated voyage, were among those who went down with the ship. Another was Benjamin Guggenheim, the American multi-millionaire. While others queued for lifeboats, he retired below decks with his valet to change into evening dress, telling a steward: 'If we have to die, we will die like gentlemen.'

last words were: 'I am just going outside and may be some time.' The end came on 29 March, 1912, just 11 miles from their supply depot. Scott and his two remaining companions, Lieutenant Henry Bowes and Dr Edward Wilson, were trapped in their tent by yet another blizzard. With fuel and food exhausted, they rapidly grew weaker. In his final diary entry, Scott wrote: 'It seems a pity, but I do not think I can write more. For God's sake, look after our people.' The bodies of the three explorers were found by a search party in November.

THE IRISH IMBROGLIO

As 1914 dawned, the government was facing yet another crisis. With the Parliament Act now in operation limiting the power of the Lords, the Liberals had kept their promise to the Irish Nationalists and introduced a third Home Rule Bill. Though the House of Lords still had the power to reject it twice, on its third submission the Bill would automatically become law.

But Ulster Loyalists were in no mood to accept any sort of devolution of power to Dublin. They pledged that, should the Home Rule Bill become law, they would set up a provisional government of their own to take over the province.

BIRTHDAY CELEBRATION
Captain Scott (left, at the head of the table) celebrating his birthday on 6 June, 1911, with members of his expedition. By November – the start of the brief Antarctic 'summer' – he was ready to set off for the South Pole with a hand-picked team of four men. Unlike Amundsen, his Norwegian rival, who was equipped with sleds pulled by huskies, Scott's expedition relied on human muscle power: the newfangled motorised sledges they had taken with them proved a disaster, while the back-up Siberian ponies were quite unequal to the freezing conditions. The weather, too, was against them. 'Our luck in weather is preposterous', Scott wrote in his diary. 'The conditions are simply horrible.' Nevertheless, he and his companions struggled doggedly on. Eventually, on 17 January, 1912, they made it to the Pole, but the remains of Amundsen's camp with a Norwegian flag tied to part of an abandoned sledge told the story. 'The Norwegians … are first at the Pole,' Scott wrote, 'I'm afraid the return journey is going to be dreadfully tiring.' But he and his four companions all perished as they attempted it.

> ## 'I can imagine no length of resistance to which Ulster can go in which I should not be prepared to support them …'
>
> Andrew Bonar Law, at a rally of 15,000 Unionist stalwarts at Blenheim

Hundreds of thousands of Ulstermen – 471,444, it was claimed – signed a Solemn League and Covenant, binding themselves to fight Home Rule to their last breath. Back across the Irish Sea, Bonar Law and the other Unionist leaders encouraged the Ulster Loyalists in their defiance, convinced that they would 'be supported by the overwhelming majority of the British people.'

In response to pleas from King George, the two party leaders met secretly to seek a compromise. Asquith proposed that Ulster be given the chance to opt out of Home Rule for a number of years, but Bonar Law demanded indefinite exclusion. Neither could agree on how much of the province should be excluded.

Mounting tension

The situation got worse when a decision to send troop reinforcements to Ulster provoked a mutiny. Brigadier-General Hubert Gough and 60 officers of the 3rd Cavalry Brigade, stationed at the Curragh outside Dublin, announced that they would resign their commissions rather than take part in any military operation in Ulster. They demanded that the government give a promise, in writing, that the army would not be used to quell opposition to Home Rule. John Seely, the incautious Secretary of State for War, duly gave them the assurance they sought. Asquith reacted immediately. Seely, together with General Sir John French and Sir John Ewart, the adjutant general, who had both agreed with Seely's unfortunate letter, were all forced to resign. The Prime Minister then took control of the War Office himself.

On 26 July, 1914, British troops opened fire on a stone-throwing crowd near Dublin. Three Irish Nationalists were killed and 38 wounded. That same month, George V convened a last-ditch conference at Buckingham Palace. The Speaker of the Commons took the chair, with Nationalist and Loyalist representatives from north and south participating, as well as the Liberal and Unionist leaders. The key issue, it transpired, was the future of two northern counties, Fermanagh and Tyrone. But neither side would give them up and as a result the conference collapsed in failure.

War in Europe looms

What might have happened next is a matter of conjecture, for other events intervened. The government intended to press on, but the Unionist leader Bonar Law persuaded Asquith to postpone legislation, arguing that 'to advertise our domestic dissensions at this time would weaken our influence for peace'.

On 28 June, 1914, while on a visit to Sarajevo in Bosnia-Herzegovina, Archduke Franz Ferdinand, the heir to the Austro-Hungarian throne, and his wife Sophie had been assassinated by a Bosnian-Serb nationalist. The Austrians, suspecting the hand of Serbia behind the murders, despatched an ultimatum to Serbia and began to mobilise their forces. Russia, France and Germany followed, lining up on different sides according to alliances. A European war was looking inevitable. The big question was what would Britain do? If negotiations to resolve the crisis failed, would she remain neutral or would she rally to the support of France and Russia?

ALL OVER BY CHRISTMAS

When Britain went to war with Germany on 4 August, 1914, virtually no one anticipated that four years of devastating conflict were to follow. 'It will all be over by Christmas', was the popular refrain. David Lloyd George, Chancellor at the time, declared it would be 'business as usual'. The Treasury's official view was that the war would have to end in 1915 as by then all the combatants would have run out of money. One man begged to differ. Lord Kitchener, the newly appointed Secretary of State for War, told disbelieving colleagues that the war would last for at least three years and that to fight it Britain would need to raise a mass army for the first time in its history. He called for a million volunteers.

FOND FAREWELL A British Tommy says goodbye to his family before joining his unit to embark for France. Mobilisation followed meticulous plans laid out in the so-called War Book, compiled to provide a blueprint for action.

THE GREAT WAR BEGINS

E ven as Europe lurched towards war, Britain's position was still far from clear. As late as 31 July, 1914, Asquith told Randall Davidson, the Archbishop of Canterbury, that in the event of war in Europe Britain would not be dragged in. The next day, George V wrote in his diary that 'public opinion' was 'dead against our joining in the war'. Half the Cabinet favoured maintaining neutrality. Prime Minister Asquith and Sir Edward Grey, the Foreign Secretary, had to threaten to resign to force Cabinet to agree to honour its pre-war undertaking to France to safeguard shipping in the Channel. According to Asquith, Lloyd George in particular was 'against any kind of intervention in any event'.

Then, on 3 August, Germany invaded Belgium. When the news reached London, the mood changed in an instant. Germany and Britain had signed a treaty guaranteeing Belgian neutrality. German violation of this pledge triggered the despatch of an ultimatum to Berlin, calling for immediate German withdrawal. Unless the Kaiser and his government acquiesced to the British demand by 11pm on 4 August, the two countries would be at war. Theobald Bethmann-Hollweg, the German Chancellor, was incredulous. 'Just for a scrap of paper', he exclaimed to Sir Edward Goschen, the British ambassador, Britain was prepared to go to war.

Even before this, vast crowds had started to gather in London – notably outside Buckingham Palace, where they called for the King and Queen to appear on the balcony. 'One could hear the distant roaring as late as 1.00 or 1.30 in the morning', noted the Prime Minister in Downing Street. Everyone, it appeared, was

ON OUR WAY TO WAR
The front page of the *Daily Express* on Wednesday, 5 August, 1914 (above). The evening before, Trafalgar Square had been packed with crowds (right), awaiting the expiry of the British ultimatum to the Kaiser. In Downing Street, a sombre Prime Minister sat waiting for a reply from Berlin that never came. Many years later, his wife Margot recorded the scene in her autobiography. 'I looked at the children asleep after dinner', she wrote, 'before joining Henry in the Cabinet room. Lord Crewe and Sir Edward Grey were already there and we sat smoking cigarettes in silence; some went out; others came in; nothing was said. The clock on the mantelpiece hammered out the hour. We were at War.' Asquith believed that, in the absence of German withdrawal from Belgium, involvement in the conflict was inevitable, but he did not – like some of his colleagues – relish the prospect. Earlier that day he had written: 'We are on the eve of horrible things.'

now a patriot. Strolling around Trafalgar Square, the philosopher and pacifist Bertrand Russell discovered to his astonishment that 'average men and women were delighted at the prospect of war'. In stark contrast to Russell, the journalist F S Oliver was delighted at what he saw as the resurgence of true national spirit. 'I had not conceived it possible that a nation could be born again so quickly,' he wrote. 'This war even now has undone the evils of a generation.'

Mobilising for war

At Waterloo, crowds gathered to cheer the sailors who were being rushed to Portsmouth to reinforce the fleet. Loud choruses of 'All the Nice Girls Love a Sailor' and 'Rule Britannia!' rang out as the special trains slowly puffed out of the great station, heading south.

The Navy was already prepared for action. Months previously, it had been decided that, to save money, the summer naval exercises should be combined with a test mobilisation. Some 20,000 reservists had been recalled; every battle squadron and shore establishment was at full strength. The manoeuvres were

scheduled to end on 27 July, after which the fleet would normally have dispersed, but Winston Churchill, now First Lord of the Admiralty, and Prince Louis of Battenberg, the First Sea Lord, decided that the international situation was so threatening it would be best to keep the fleet concentrated together. Instead of being sent to their home ports, the ships were ordered north to Scapa Flow, ready to take up battle stations if the unthinkable happened and the nation found itself at war. They had only nine days to wait. At 11.01 pm on 4 August, 1914, a signal was radioed from the Admiralty to all British naval vessels wherever they were in the world. It read simply: 'Commence hostilities against Germany.'

The army, too, had a carefully worked-out plan. It had started with the initiation of what was termed the 'Precautionary Period' on the Wednesday before war broke out, when a signal flashed from the War Office to army commands throughout Britain and Ireland, putting them on the alert for war. Mobilisation followed on 3 August; the fateful war telegrams were despatched the following day. Time was tight. In little more than a week, the 80,000-man British Expeditionary Force (BEF) – with artillery, munitions, horses and supplies – had

FORCED TO RESIGN
Prince Louis of Battenberg, the First Sea Lord when war broke out, inspects naval cadets on a training ship. He had played a key part in preparing the fleet for war, but a venomous press campaign against him on account of his German birth led to his resignation on 27 October, 1914. Many thought that he had been treated unfairly. J H Thomas, a prominent Labour MP and trade union leader, wrote to *The Times* to 'express my extreme regret at the announcement that Prince Louis of Battenberg has, by his resignation, pandered to the most mean and contemptible slander I have ever known.'

to be shipped across the Channel to France in accordance with plans drawn up by the General Staff and agreed with its French counterparts some years before.

All over the country, troops were mustering. The Rifle Brigade was one of the first units ready to go. As its 1st Battalion marched through Felixstowe en route to Colchester, Bandsman H V Shawyer noted how he and his comrades were acclaimed by an enthusiastic crowd. 'The place was full of holidaymakers lining the pavement to see us go', he recorded. 'Most of the people couldn't do enough for us, and they were pretty loud in the doing of it, cheering, shouting, singing, waving their handkerchiefs and showering us with sweets and packets of cigarettes. Some of the young girls were even pelting us with flowers as if we were blooming Spaniards or something.'

TO THE FRONT
British troops, newly arrived in France, wait for a troop train that will carry them north to the Belgian border. The journey was long and uncomfortable. Each train – the aim was to despatch one every 10 minutes – consisted of 49 box-cars, which could carry 80 horses and more than 1,000 men; the officers travelled in carriages tacked on at the end. Once a train was on the move, progress was by no means plain sailing. Even when the going was good, a strict speed limit meant that trains could not travel at more than 20mph. In fact, few reached even half that speed and there were long halts and delays. Some Tommies learned that they could jump down onto the tracks, sprint to the front of the train and fill a mess tin with hot water from the steam engine, then rejoin their comrades waiting to brew up mugs of tea.

Boulogne, Rouen and Le Havre were the BEF's chosen destination ports. There, the welcome the troops got was even more rapturous. In Boulogne, the entire town appeared to have taken to the streets to greet the Tommies. The harbour wall was packed with cheering crowds. As the first troopship inched slowly towards its berth, the enthusiasm reached such a pitch that one over-excited elderly Frenchman fell in. He was quickly fished out, none the worse for wear.

INTO ACTION

It was no small achievement to ship the entire BEF across the Channel without incurring a single casualty. All the soldiers were kitted out with rifles, bandoliers and pouches for their small-arms ammunition, and supplied with iron rations – emergency food consisting of a tin of corned 'bully' beef, a few biscuits, tea and sugar – to keep them going until they reached camp in France. Kitchener had penned a final message to the men, which they all carried in their pay books as a reminder of their mission: 'You are ordered abroad as a soldier of the King to help our French comrades against the invasion of a common enemy…'. The message ended with the simple but stirring injunction to 'Do your duty bravely, Fear God, Honour the King.'

No sooner had the BEF assembled in France than it was rushed north to take up positions on the left of the French Fifth Army, close to the Franco-Belgian frontier. By 24 August, it was ready for action – which came sooner than anyone had anticipated. In accordance with Germany's Schlieffen Plan, the bulk of the German armies were surging westwards through Belgium, aiming to sweep round the British and French and on into the heart of France. General Joffre, the French commander-in-chief, reacted by ordering a general advance on his left flank to rebuff the German hordes.

It all sounded straightforward enough, but the reality on the ground was very different. Forming up for battle in and around the gloomy Belgian mining town of Mons, the BEF discovered that, far from advancing, the French were actually being forced back: the gap between them and the British was widening by the hour. General Sir John French, the British commander-in-chief, promptly issued new orders. He would fight on to maintain his positions along the Mons Canal and hold the advancing Germans in check to cover the French retirement. Little did he realise that his troops were outnumbered by more than three to one – or that the Germans would throw their whole weight into an attack the very next day.

Once the battle began, the British hung on grimly in the face of overwhelming German artillery fire. They repulsed attack after attack, before falling back to new

'They think we cannot beat them. It will not be easy. It will be a long job; it will be a terrible war; but in the end we shall march through terror to triumph.'

David Lloyd George, from a speech made at the Queen's Hall, September 1914

FIGHTING AT MONS
British Tommies silhouetted along a ridge during the battle of Mons, close to the Franco-Belgian frontier. Starting on 23 August, it was the first major clash between the British and the Germans on the Western Front and it ended with the BEF in a fighting retreat. Desperately outnumbered and outgunned, they nevertheless managed to check the German attack for a vital day, inflicting heavy casualties. Such was the speed and accuracy of the BEF's rifle fire – the men were trained to fire a steady 15 rounds a minute – the Germans believed they were up against machine guns. At home, some attributed the BEF's survival to divine intervention. The patriotic postcard (left) depicts angels that had, so people said, descended from heaven at the height of the battle to help the beleaguered British. Within weeks, the story had passed into popular folklore.

positions to the west of Mons. Then General French issued a new order for a general retreat: it was vital to keep in touch with the French. The BEF obediently fell back, fighting every step of the way – perhaps most notably at Le Cateau, where General Sir Horace Smith-Dorrien, commanding the Second Corps, ordered his exhausted men to stand and check the German advance, giving the rest of the BEF more time to withdraw.

At bay on the Marne

Mile after weary mile, the retreat continued for 13 days, until the BEF finally halted on the River Marne. At General Joffre's urging – though it took the personal intervention of Kitchener to persuade Sir John French to agree to the plan – it was decided that the British and French would now turn on the advancing Germans, who had left their right flank dangerously exposed. And so, on 4 September, another great battle began. By the time it ended a few days later, the Germans were in full retreat. The weary but victorious Allies called it 'the miracle of the Marne.'

The Germans retreated as far as the River Aisne, where they stopped and dug in on a chalk ridge that rose 500 feet (150m) above the far bank of the river. The Allies pursued them across, but were forced back. They tried attacking again two days later, but were repulsed once more, after which they, too, began to dig in.

The war of movement was almost over. Though no one realised it at the time, the trench warfare that would dominate tactics on the Western Front was about to begin. In fact, in certain sectors of the front, digging in had started even before the battle of the Marne. The tactical stalemate that followed was to prove virtually unbreakable; the deadlock would last until 1918.

The race to the sea

Before the stalemate developed, the Germans had one last card to play: they tried to outflank the Allies to the left. Bitter fighting flared along the open flank

DIGGING IN
British soldiers in a communication trench, probably near Ypres, in late October 1914. Digging in, as it was termed, was the order of the day as both sides feverishly dug trenches in a line from the Channel through France to the Swiss border. Trenches were never straight. Instead, they had a series of bays facing the enemy with traverses at an angle to the bays. The intention was to lessen the effect of a shell bursting in a trench and to make it harder for enemy attackers to fight along it.

between the River Marne and the Channel, spreading through Picardy and Artois and on into Flanders. It was, so both sides proclaimed, a 'race to the sea'. The BEF, which that October was transported from the River Aisne up to Flanders, was in the thick of the fighting. It was centred on the Flemish city of Ypres.

By the time the fighting came to an end that autumn, with both sides settling into trenches for the winter, the BEF that had shipped out to France in August had been virtually wiped out. The Kaiser had dismissed it as 'a contemptible little army', and yet Britain's comparatively small force of highly experienced regular soldiers had played a vital part in stopping the German advance. The terrible cost was that most men of the BEF had been killed or wounded in action.

On the baskets/shelves: ARTILLERY · 5TH INFANTRY · A S CORPS 6.27TH INFANTRY · CAVALRY 7&28 INFANTRY · ENGINEERS 8.29TH INFANTRY · BLIND TERRITORIAL · 3RD INF. (BASKET IN FRONT) · 1ST & 2ND · R.A.M.C. (BASKET IN FRONT)

THE HOME FRONT

At home, war fever mounted. The news that the BEF had suffered two serious reverses in the space of three days did not reach the public until 30 August, a whole week after the battle of Mons had been fought. Kitchener would rather not have released the news at all. All the newspapers had to go on were official army communiqués, which often concealed more than they revealed. In the absence of hard news, they turned to speculation. There was an abundance of atrocity stories to tut-tut over at the breakfast table, largely gleaned from tales told by the growing flood of Belgian refugees. Many gave credence to the rumour that a band of angels had descended from Heaven to save the BEF from destruction at Mons.

Everyone seemed to have an opinion as to how best to be useful. Holiday-makers were urged to put aside their golf and tennis and 'enquire in any rural village whether help is required with the harvest'. Some called for theatres, music halls and cinemas to be closed. Later, places of entertainment were ordered to close

KEEPING IN TOUCH
Sorting the post to the BEF at the Military Post Office in London (above). Letters were eagerly awaited, as were parcels of food, cigarettes and other items – many sent by strangers. A Company Quartermaster in the King's Liverpool Regiment recorded typical consignments: 'Yesterday I drew a lot of cigarettes presented by somebody, and a pipe per man sent by the Glasgow tramway men, as well as some peppermint sweets from the manufacturers. Today again there was a supply of cigarettes and tobacco as well as a lot of tinned salmon given by the government of British Columbia. We have also socks from Princess Mary, gloves from the Archduke Michael, razors from a man in Sheffield ... surely no army has ever before been so well looked after.'

not later than 10.30pm, a measure christened the 'beauty sleep order.' Everybody preached the twin virtues of self-sacrifice and economy. There were suggestions that breweries and distilleries should be shut and the grain diverted to food production. Suttons, the seed merchants, advertised 'the desirability of sowing and planting every spare piece of land with such food crops as there might still be time to sow before the autumn.' Many took their advice.

The government ordered the banks to remain closed for three days after the August Bank Holiday to prevent a financial panic and to give time for £1 and 10 shilling notes to be printed and distributed. These were to take the place of sovereign and half-sovereign coins, the minting of which was suspended for the duration of the war. It was clear that the country would need its gold. The new notes, Lloyd George assured the nation, would be as safe as the Bank of England, for 'the whole credit of the British Empire' lay behind them. They were nicknamed 'Bradburys' after Sir John Bradbury, the Secretary to the Treasury, whose signature appeared on every note. On 8 August, the Defence of the Realm Act, 'Dora', was passed into law, giving the government sweeping new powers to assist it in putting the entire country on a war footing.

'Your King and Country Need You'

Men from all walks of life flocked to join up. By the end of August 1914, nearly 300,000 had volunteered. Old men dyed their hair to fool the recruiting sergeants; boys barely out of school lied about their age. All were in a hurry to get into the fight. Godfrey Buxton, a Cambridge undergraduate, recorded how he and his fellow volunteers 'were quite clear that Germany would be defeated by 7 October when we would go back to Cambridge'. They were to be disappointed. It took months to equip and train them. Marjorie Llewellyn, a Sheffield schoolgirl, recalled how, to their chagrin, the young men who had rushed to volunteer had been 'sent home and then sent down to the Bramall Lane football ground and to Norfolk Park, where they were drilled and learned to dig trenches'.

> '**My pals were going, chaps I had kicked about with in the street, kicking cans or a football … When you went to the pictures you'd be shown crowds of young men drilling in Hyde Park … or a band playing "Tipperary". The whole thing was exciting.**'
>
> F B Vaughan, a steelmaker from Sheffield and volunteer

Joining up with Pals

Many volunteers joined the so-called Pals battalions, units linked to a locality, business or industry. Exactly who had the idea is unclear – some give the credit to Lord Derby, the biggest landowner in Lancashire and now Director of Recruitment at the War Office – but whoever thought of it was inspired. The first battalion, the 'Stockbrokers' of the Royal Fusiliers, began recruiting on 21 August. It was soon joined by others, including the Accrington Pals, Grimsby Chums, Glasgow Corporation Tramways, University and Public School Brigade, Tyneside Scottish, Tyneside Irish, Cotton Association and many more. Derby raised four battalions of his own, so winning the title of 'England's best recruiting sergeant.' The locals on his Knowsley estate knew them as the Derby Comrades Brigade.

continued on page 168

FORMAL PORTRAITS

POSED FOR POSTERITY

Photographers had never been so busy as they were in August 1914. First, there were the weddings (above), as men under orders to embark for France hastened to pop the question to their sweethearts. Jewellers were gratified by the run on engagement and wedding rings. Even the Archbishop of Canterbury did his bit for romance by giving special permission for ecclesiastical offices to stay open round the clock to issue special marriage licences. He also allowed clergymen to perform marriages after the legal hour of 12 noon.

Everyone wanted their own pictorial memento in the event of the worst happening and a beloved son, brother or husband being killed, wounded or taken prisoner. The pictures here (right) are all the work of Henry Mayson, a photographer working in Keswick in the Lake District. The soldier and his wife (top) look calm, collected and ready for anything, while the boy soldier (centre) looks far too young to have been sent overseas. The two Tommies in full field uniform (bottom) are both NCOs; the one seated is a lance corporal, while the other carries an NCO's swagger stick.

FLOCKING TO THE COLOURS

They came forward in their thousands from all walks of life. Between August 1914 and December 1915, a staggering 2,466,719 men enlisted, creating the largest volunteer army in history. Many believed that the war would be short and even be fun. The poet Julian Grenfell, a regular officer and son of Lord and Lady Desborough, wrote: 'I adore war, it's like a big picnic without the directlessness'. He died of wounds in May 1915.

SMILES ALL ROUND
A crowd of happy men queue to join up at Southwark Hall, south London (left), in response to the national recruiting campaign. A patriotic song to rally the crowd would have blared out from the gramophone at this mobile recruiting station in Trafalgar Square (below), encouraging eager volunteers to register. The rush to sign up took the War Office by surprise. Lord Kitchener, the newly appointed Secretary of State for War, had appealed for 100,000 men of military age to come forward in the first instance, but in the first month of war alone, 300,000 volunteers flocked to the recruiting stations – 33,000 of them on just one day. Many men joined the new 'Pals' battalions, units linked to a specific locality or to a particular business or industry. They formed the core of Kitchener's New Army, which took to the field in 1915. By that time, with casualty lists mounting, the number of men coming forward had started to dwindle and mounting pressure was put on all eligible civilians to volunteer. Posters everywhere drove home the message and music hall stars took a leading part in the campaign. Marie Lloyd sang 'I didn't like you much before you joined the army', while Vesta Tilley chorused 'The army of today's all right'. If that was not enough, there was always the risk of being handed a white feather in the street by some woman passer-by.

THE PRESSURE TO JOIN UP
By the end of 1914 the rate of recruitment had slowed, but men were still coming forward, like these Belfast shipyard workers (above right), lined up in rows behind pipers and ready to sign up for the cause. The smartly dressed civilians (top right) had just joined the London Scottish Regiment. Some in high places called for the immediate introduction of compulsory conscription, but the government resisted such a move. Instead, a Parliamentary Recruiting Committee organised 12,000 meetings, 20,000 speeches and an estimated 54 million posters, leaflets and other publications to promote the cause. Lord Kitchener (above left), already a national hero, spearheaded the recruitment campaign calling for men of military age to come forward to serve their country if required. It was only when this recruitment drive began to fail that the introduction of conscription became politically practical. Even men who had good reason to stay behind – because of their age, for example, or on medical grounds – were urged to enrol for civilian national service (top left) in order to release fit young men for fighting at the front.

GETTING READY

Recruits to the London Scottish Regiment get acquainted with their rifles under the watchful eye of a Regular Staff Sergeant-Major (above). They were lucky to be issued with guns; they were still waiting for uniforms, which, like weapons, were in short supply. The empire rallied to the mother country. Canada, Australia, New Zealand and South Africa all sent men to the Western Front. Detachments from the Indian Army, too, were pressed into service. These Indian soldiers (right) are about to board a troop train in Paris to take them to Flanders and the front. As the German generals prepared to attack at Ypres in autumn 1914, they told their troops that they would quickly 'finish with the British, Indian, Canadian, Moroccans and other trashy, feeble adversaries …'. Despite the cold and the unfamiliar conditions, Indian troops like these men bravely proved those generals wrong.

NO WAR!

Not everyone was in favour of the war. Organisations like the Union of Democratic Control, founded in August 1914, argued for peace by negotiation. The No Conscription Fellowship, formed in December 1914, opposed attempts to introduce conscription; by November 1915, it had 61 branches across the country. The men depicted here (above) are attending its National Convention. The authorities were determined to clamp down on all such movements, regarding them as potentially seditious. Bertrand Russell, the leading philosopher of the day, was among those prosecuted for expressing pacifist views. In June 1916, after conscription had become law and the first conscientious objectors were being hauled before military tribunals, Russell was fined £100 for his anti-conscription activities. Trinity College, Cambridge, deprived him of his lectureship following his conviction.

'We Don't Want to Lose You'

Those unwilling to volunteer came under increasing pressure. Derby himself set the tone. 'When the war is over', he declared, 'I intend, as far as I possibly can, to employ nobody except men who have taken their duty at the front.' A London firm of stockbrokers told its employees that 'the firm expects that all unmarried staff under 35 years of age will join Earl Kitchener's army at once, and also urges those who are married and eligible to take the same course.'

Many women played an active part in shaming men into volunteering. Penrose Fitzgerald, a retired admiral, advised women to hand out white feathers to any able-bodied young men not in uniform. Mrs Montague Barstow, better known to posterity as Baroness Orczy, author of *The Scarlet Pimpernel*, founded the Active Service League, whose members pledged 'never to be seen in public with any man who being in every way fit and free for service has refused to respond to his country's call'. Norman Demuth, who enlisted in the London Rifle Brigade, recalled being 'given a white feather when I was 16, just after I had left school … I had been trying to persuade the doctors and recruiting officers that I was 19 and I thought, well … I must look the part, and so I went round to the recruiting offices with renewed zeal.' A letter-writer to *The Times* wondered if 'the feather-brained Ladies' would not 'be better advised to learn to nurse the wounded and thus become useful instead of offending nuisances to the community?'

THE FIRST CHRISTMAS

As the year drew to a close, people at home became more subdued; it was becoming obvious that the war would not be 'over by Christmas'. In London, though the Lord Mayor's customary Juvenile Fancy Dress Party went ahead as usual, this year the children came costumed as sailors, nurses and soldiers shouldering toy rifles. There was even a six-year-old admiral, wearing a small cocked hat and proudly sporting a little sword. Gamages, a leading London store, offered miniature field service uniforms for sale. They were complete in every detail but scaled down to fit children aged between six and 12.

Most people's minds were on their menfolk in the trenches. The great autumn battles, culminating in the first battle of Ypres, had finally brought the Germans to a standstill, but the casualty lists made grim reading. The armies now faced each other in a long line of trenches snaking from the sand dunes of the Belgian coast right across France to within sight of the Swiss Alps. What was left of the BEF had gone to ground in the chill Flanders wastelands. Not much fighting was going on; an ammunition shortage meant that bullets and shells were too precious to waste. Nor was the weather conducive to offensive action, as blinding rain turned to hail and then snow. Though the generals, safe and warm behind the lines, might be debating when and where to launch the 'big push' that would end the war, the minds of most of the Tommies were simply on survival. Private Clifford Lane of the Hertfordshire Regiment recalled eating 'what the English newspapers called Christmas Dinner ... cold bully beef and a cold lump of Christmas pudding'.

Christmas, at least, brought some cheer from home. Every soldier in the BEF received a handy metal box – a present from Princess Mary, the King's daughter – with cigarettes, pipe tobacco or, for the few non-smokers, chocolate. Not to be outdone, the Kaiser sent his troops cigars, ten per man, labelled in their boxes 'Weinachten im Feld, 1914' – Christmas in the Field, 1914. For the British there was chocolate from Cadbury, butterscotch from Callard & Bowser and a mountain of homemade cakes and sweetmeats. Knitting for the troops was a national obsession and vast quantities of socks, mufflers and other homely garments were sent across the Channel. Sometimes, recipients were less than grateful. Captain John Liddell of the Argyll and Sutherland Highlanders, writing home to his family, remarked on some of the oddities that he and his men received, especially 'the atrocity known as the heeless sock'.

The Christmas truce

As Christmas dawned, the singing of carols was heard on both sides of the barbed wire that festooned the trenches. It may have been this that triggered one of the most extraordinary events of the war. Along parts of the front an impromptu truce broke out, which in some places lasted for several days. Britons and Germans cautiously emerged from their dug-outs, crossed into no man's land and swapped greetings and gifts. Captain Stockwell of the Royal Welch Fusiliers recalled how the Saxon troops presented him and his men with a barrel of beer. The Royal Welch gave the Saxons some of their plum puddings in return. Troops on both sides took advantage of the unexpected peace to mend and straighten barbed wire, lay duckboards, pump out water from the trenches and bury the dead.

The truce was not universal. Nor could it last. As Sergeant George Ashurst of the Lancashire Fusiliers recalled, 'the generals behind must have seen it ... so they gave orders for a battery of guns behind us to open fire and a machine-gun to open out, and our officers to fire their revolvers at the Germans. That started the war again.' Sir John French was not disposed to show the officers who had condoned the proceedings any seasonal goodwill. He reminded them that it was not their job to allow their men to strike up friendships with the enemy. Their task was to foster the offensive spirit and to win the war in 1915.

BRAVE LITTLE SOLDIER
A youngster dressed in uniform – a replica of that worn by British officers at the front – salutes smartly for the camera (below). The uniform may well have been his Christmas present. One woman wrote to *The Times* to offer her two-year-old as a mascot to any regiment that would have him, bemoaning that her 'great misfortune was to have no sons of military age'. Children featured in advertisements designed to shame men into volunteering. One celebrated recruiting poster depicted a humiliated father being asked by his children 'Daddy, what did you do in the Great War?'

1910s

BOGGED
DOWN

The new year, 1915, began with the generals waiting for better weather and for the reinforcements they had been promised. Once Kitchener's New Army was ready, they would break through the German lines and win the war. At least that was the plan. In the event, the appalling losses suffered at Aubers Ridge, Loos, Neuve Chapelle and Ypres proved the generals wrong. Sir John French was replaced as commander-in-chief by Sir Douglas Haig, but the Somme offensive that Haig launched in 1916 was even more costly than its predecessors. It was the bloodiest battle of the entire war – and was still inconclusive.

WALKING WOUNDED Two wounded British soldiers make their way towards a dressing station with a German prisoner, also wounded and walking with the aid of a stick.

IN IT TOGETHER

While some Tommies in Flanders celebrated Christmas 1914 by making friends with their foes in no man's land, at home Prime Minister Asquith spent the holidays reviewing the future conduct of the war. Despite the confidence of the generals, a swift victory in France looked increasingly in doubt. Within the Cabinet, there was growing pressure for the adoption of an alternative strategy, rather than simply shipping more and more men to the Western Front to try to break the stalemate.

Winston Churchill was the first to suggest something new. He and Lord Fisher, the First Sea Lord, had dreamed up a scheme to force entry into the Baltic Sea and land an expeditionary force on its shores, just 90 miles north of Berlin. He suggested combining this with an assault on the Dardanelles in the eastern Mediterranean to open a way through the straits into the Black Sea. Churchill believed that such a blow might force Turkey, Germany's ally since October 1914, out of the war altogether. It would also open a direct supply route to Russia, Britain's other ally. Either scheme, he wrote to Asquith, would be preferable to sending more men 'to chew barbed wire in Flanders'.

Lloyd George also favoured opening up a new theatre of war, but he argued for landing troops in Salonika in Greece. He was deeply critical of Kitchener and the War Office, which he felt had failed to get a grip on the manufacture of munitions. 'Had I not been a witness of their deplorable lack of provision', he wrote to the Prime Minister, 'I should not have thought it possible that men so responsibly placed could have displayed so little foresight.'

'I am uneasy about the prospects of the war … I can see no signs anywhere that our military leaders and guides are considering any plans for extracting us from our present unsatisfactory position.'

David Lloyd George, in a letter to Asquith, December 1914

THE WESTERN FRONT
British Tommies and French troops march together along the main street of a small village not far behind the front line. The casual attitude of the British seems to indicate they are on the way down from the line. The troops got on well enough, despite the occasional disagreements of their leaders. Marshal Joffre, the French commander, wanted to launch a major French offensive to break through the lines and force the German armies into headlong retreat. In his opinion, the BEF would be best employed in keeping the Germans pinned down, while the French armies bore the brunt of the battle. Sir John French, the British commander-in-chief, disagreed and went ahead with plans for his own offensive. The battle of Neuve Chapelle was the result.

COVERING FIRE

Sweating shirt-sleeved artillerymen finally get their guns into action at Gallipoli, after dragging them to the cliff top above Cape Helles. On paper, it had looked easy enough, but as General Sir Iain Hamilton, in command of the expedition, ruefully wrote home to Lord Kitchener, 'Gallipoli looks a much tougher nut to crack than it did over the map in your office'. This was hardly surprising, for the whole scheme had been prepared in haste. It was little wonder that, after a promising start, Hamilton's troops were forced to dig in around their beachheads.

ORDERING EVACUATION

In November, after months of stalemate and the failure of a further landing at Suvla Bay in August, Kitchener went out to Gallipoli to see the situation for himself. Until then, he had vehemently opposed any proposal for abandoning the campaign. 'I absolutely refuse to sign an order for evacuation', he had telegraphed, 'which I think would be the greatest disaster and would condemn a large percentage of our men to death or imprisonment.' The visit changed his mind. Convinced by General Sir Charles Munro, who had replaced Sir Iain Hamilton, and the other commanders on the spot that there was no viable alternative, he recommended pulling out. In stark contrast to the actual campaign, the evacuation was carried out skilfully and with minimal casualties.

BOTCHED LANDING

In August 1915, General Hamilton tried to break the stalemate by landing more troops at Suvla Bay. These men (left) are British troops of IX Corps. Unfortunately, he was given the wrong man for the job. General Sir Charles Stopford was not only old and not in the best of health, but he had never commanded an army in the field. Instead of following his instructions to 'push on rapidly', Stopford delayed his advance even though, at least initially, he met with little opposition. The delay gave the Turks the time they needed to bring reinforcements to the scene.

'Those damned Dardanelles'

As was his custom, Asquith did not take sides. Instead, he brokered a compromise. A fleet was to be sent to bombard the fortifications of the Dardanelles, the gateway to Constantinople (Istanbul); troops would follow, if required. The action started at the end of February, reaching a climax on 18 March, when the ships involved steamed to within a few miles of the Narrows, shelling the Turkish positions heavily as they advanced.

The Turks waited apprehensively for the attack to be renewed. It never happened. Instead, Admiral John de Robeck, shaken by the losses he had incurred, decided to wait until the expeditionary force, under the command of General Sir Iain Hamilton, was ready to make a simultaneous landing. Their objective was to capture the Gallipoli peninsula and silence the Turkish guns. When Churchill tried to overrule de Robeck, Fisher supported his admiral.

The expeditionary force was not ready to disembark until 25 April, when troops from Australia and New Zealand – the ANZACs – were put ashore at what would later become known as Anzac Cove. British and French forces landed at Cape Helles. They expected a quick and easy victory, but were soon disillusioned. The Turks had used the respite they had been given well. Instead of storming ashore and advancing swiftly inland, the Allied expeditionary force found itself pinned down in the face of newly erected Turkish defences. Trenches were swiftly dug around the beachheads. It was the Western Front all over again.

Life back in Blighty

People at home had precious little to cheer. The first cracks in the industrial truce that had been agreed at the start of the war were starting to appear, as ordinary folk realised that, though they were being forced to scrimp and save, war

profiteers seemed to be doing very nicely. Prices were rising as the cost of living rose inexorably. By the beginning of 1915, food prices were 20 per cent higher than they had been just six months earlier. Staples like potatoes, milk and butter doubled in price – 'the true patriot who can afford it will eat asparagus, not potatoes', the government advised – while the cost of sugar rose by a staggering 163 per cent, largely because it had to be imported.

The General Federation of Trade Unions complained that 'pallid and unappetising brisket' was now selling at 9d a pound, twice as much as before the war. Fish shot up in price – so much so that the Roman Catholic Archbishop of Westminster gave his flock permission to eat meat on fast days. The authorities preached the virtues of so-called 'meatless days' and urged people to substitute margarine for expensive butter. The King set an example by ordering the flowerbeds at Buckingham Palace to be dug up and growing his own vegetables. He also took what became known as 'the King's pledge' and gave up drinking alcohol for the duration of the war. Food manufacturers chimed in with their own suggestions. 'Everyone has less money to spend on food', ran one advertisement. 'The wise ones make nourishing Quaker Oats the stand-by ... Your family won't miss expensive bacon and eggs if you serve delicious Quaker Oats.'

FEEDING THE NATION
A young boy helps his father dig up their crop of potatoes on an allotment in Dulwich, south London (above). With food getting more expensive, the government began by appealing for voluntary restraint and encouraging people to eat less. Following a poor wheat harvest in North America in 1916, bread in particular was in short supply. It was not until April 1917, when Lord Rhondda became Minister of Food, that bread supplies were regulated and the price of a loaf controlled. All sorts of other controls followed. By the end of the war, 85 per cent of all the food consumed by the nation was bought and sold by firms controlled by the government and 94 per cent was subject to price control.

Tax is good!

Not to be outdone, the manufacturers of Bovril, the celebrated beef-extract drink, proclaimed that taking just a teaspoonful of the beverage before every meal would reduce daily food consumption by a fifth. People certainly needed to economise as taxes and duties were increased on everything from beer, spirits and tobacco to sugar, coffee, cocoa and matches. An advertisement for Murray's Mellow Mixture tobacco encouraged people to pay up and keep on smoking: 'Don't stop smoking because tax on tobacco has increased. It is your duty to the State to keep on smoking. The Chancellor increased the duty on tobacco to give smokers an opportunity of contributing towards the successful issue of the war.' In 1915, income tax went up and the tax threshold was lowered to £130 a year.

Even though wages were rising, many found it harder and harder to make ends meet. Rents soared, particularly around the rapidly burgeoning munitions factories, where an influx of thousands of new workers led to housing shortages. In November 1915 around 20,000 tenants on Clydeside started a rent strike. For once, the government was forced into direct intervention, rushing a Rent Restriction Bill into law which stabilised the rents for working-class housing at pre-war levels. But over-crowding continued, while the growing shortage of building materials meant that many houses grew increasingly dilapidated.

HOME FRONT UNDER FIRE

For some, the actual war was coming terrifyingly close to home. For the first time in many centuries, Britain came under direct attack by a foreign foe. On 16 December, 1914, five battle cruisers and a light cruiser of the German Imperial High Seas Fleet steamed through the dawn mists and proceeded to bombard Hartlepool, Scarborough and Whitby on the North Sea coast. In the space of just 30 minutes, more than 1,500 shells were fired and 127 civilians killed. The victims in Scarborough included a 14-month-old baby boy. In Hartlepool, the first reported casualty was Hilda Herseley, a 17-year-old seamstress who was caught by the bombardment on her way to work.

Some people were lucky to escape with their lives. The *Scarborough Pictorial* recorded how one visiting commercial traveller, having been woken by the sound of the shelling, 'hurriedly dressed and gathered his bags together, and had just got outside the door when a shell came through the wall and blew to fragments the bed which he had vacated only a few minutes before.'

> 'Just around our house, hundreds of windows were smashed and two houses were blown to nothing next door to us.'.
> Wright Bottomley, Scarborough resident, December 1914

To add insult to injury, the raiders slipped back into the mists and got away. Though the Admiralty assured people that any military damage the Germans had inflicted was 'insignificant', a howl of protest arose at the inability of the Navy to bring the enemy vessels to battle. It transpired that neither the Grand Fleet, stationed at Scapa Flow, nor the battle cruiser fleet at Rosyth had been able to steam south fast enough to engage the enemy.

Attack from the air

People began wondering what else might be coming their way. In early January 1915 Thomas Livingstone, a bookkeeper from Glasgow, wrote in his diary: 'German plans for smashing up Britain are made. They will do it with Zeppelins and submarines, end of the month, so they say.' Sure enough, on 19 January, the first-ever air raid on Britain took place. Two Zeppelins – the LZ-2 and LZ-3 – bombed Great Yarmouth and King's Lynn in Norfolk, killing two people and injuring 16. Livingstone described it as a 'German "murder" raid', adding 'of course the airship got away'.

The next month, in response to the British naval blockade, Germany declared the waters around Britain to be a war zone. All shipping in British waters now ran the risk of surprise U-boat attack. The British objected that refusing to give a warning before launching an attack was a clear breach of international law.

BOMBARDED FROM THE SEA …
A Scarborough shop (left) shows the
scars of war after German battle-cruisers
bombarded the seaside town on
16 December, 1914. It was one of a series
of hit-and-run raids that the German
Imperial High Seas Fleet launched against
towns on Britain's North Sea coast. Not
only Scarborough but also Whitby, Great
Yarmouth, Lowestoft and Hartlepool all
came under fire. Sylvia Pankhurst,
daughter of the redoubtable Emmeline,
was one of 10,000 people who poured
into Scarborough to see the damage.
She recorded how 'the big amusement
"palaces" on the front were scarred and
battered by shell-fire, iron columns twisted
and broken, brickwork crumbling, windows
gone. Yawning breaches disclosed the
pictures and furnishings, riddled and rent
by the firing, dimmed and discoloured by
blustering winds and spray.'

… AND BOMBED FROM THE AIR
Passers-by inspect the damage inflicted
by attacking German Zeppelins in
Bartholomew Close, in Central London,
while workmen clear the debris and repair
the sewers. Airship attacks began in
January 1915, striking first at Great
Yarmouth and King's Lynn. The first attack
on London came on 31 May, and Zeppelins
returned whenever flying conditions were
right. On 13 October, four airships set off
from their base in Belgium to bomb the
capital in what was their most successful
raid to date. LZ-15 dropped a string of
bombs along the Strand, damaging the
Lyceum and Strand theatres; 21 people
were killed and 16 injured. The airship's
commander, Kapitan-Leutnant Joachim
Breithaupt, recorded how easy it was to
spot landmarks like Regent's Park, the
Serpentine and Waterloo Bridge from the
air, despite a primitive black-out being in
place. LZ-24, carrying 30 high explosive
and 10 incendiary bombs, struck at
Woolwich – the arsenal there was a prime
target – Croydon, Battersea and Clapham.

So too, they said, were the Zeppelin raids which, though sporadic, grew in frequency over the next months. People started to look out for what they termed 'Zeppelin weather' – dark but fine, calm nights – suitable for staging attacks.

On 31 May, London was raided for the first time. The Kaiser had been persuaded to lift his ban on air attacks on the British capital, though he insisted that they must be confined to the districts east of the Tower of London. Two airships – the LZ-37 and LZ-38 – dropped 90 incendiaries and 30 small high explosive bombs as they strafed the area between Stoke Newington and Leytonstone. Nine people were killed and 32 injured. Rioting followed, as people of supposed German origin were targeted by the mob. People were outraged by the bombings, especially since there seemed to be no effective means of defence. It was not until September the following year that a German airship was finally brought down in flames by a British fighter plane. The pilot, Lieutenant William Leefe Robinson, was promptly awarded the Victoria Cross for gallantry. Another airship was downed the following month.

The Zeppelins returned time and again, spreading their attacks to other parts of the country. They got as far north as Edinburgh and as far west as Liverpool. Some people demanded that savage reprisals against their crews. No less a

'... something should be done to wrest from the Germans the supremacy of the air which at the present time they seem to enjoy.'

Lord Oranmore and Browne, House of Lords, 1916

personage than churchman Henry Wace, the Dean of Canterbury, demanded 'an authoritative statement that we shall make it an indispensible condition of peace that representatives of the persons responsible for Zeppelin raids should be delivered up to our Government for public execution.'

A SHELL SCANDAL

Nor were things going any better in France, where the BEF went into action at Neuve Chapelle on 10 March, 1915. Initially, the Germans were taken by surprise, but then the attack bogged down. This was largely the fault of a breakdown in communication between the troops in the front line, the reserves, the commanders in the rear and the supporting artillery. But Generals French and Haig, commander of the First Army which carried out the attack, and their subordinate generals quickly found another scapegoat: the munitions workers. Sir John French bombarded the War Office with complaints about lack of ammunition. Haig railed against the munitions workers at home, blaming shortages on their fondness for

MAKING DO
By the end of 1914, the BEF was running short of ammunition and the artillery to fire it. Sir John French noted in his diary: 'There is more delay in sending these new 9.2 guns. It is said to be caused by the Christmas holidays which the men in the factories insisted on having.' Whatever the cause, in the trenches improvisation became the order of the day. The soldiers here are filling empty jam tins with nails, tamped down with gun cotton, to make primitive bombs to be hurled at the enemy. The same tins served as ammunition for an equally makeshift trench mortar, made by ingenious engineers from a length of drainpipe soldered up at one end with a touchhole bored above it.

DEPENDING ON WOMEN

A government poster (above) appeals to women to come forward to join the ranks of the munitionettes, as they were called. These two women (above right) are at work in the Vickers factory in Newcastle-upon-Tyne, fitting interior tubing inside empty shell cases, ready to be filled with explosives. As 1915 dawned, the manufacture of guns and shells was lagging far behind demand. One reason for this was that thousands of skilled engineers had rushed to join up; another was the stubborn refusal by the trade unions to allow unskilled labour into the armaments factories. At home, recruits to Kitchener's New Army had to drill with imitation wooden rifles, but in France the situation was far worse. Sir John French constantly complained to the War Office that his reserves of ammunition were falling below danger level. Eventually, after witnessing an abortive attack, the exasperated French leaked his complaints to *The Times*. The resulting scandal was a major factor in bringing down Asquith's Liberal government; it was replaced by a coalition, with Asquith still at its head.

holidays and drink. 'The best thing, in my opinion, is to punish some of the chief offenders', he wrote to Leopold de Rothschild. 'Take and shoot two or three of them, and the "Drink habit" would cease I feel sure.' It sounds extraordinarily harsh today, but at the time even Lloyd George thought he had a point. 'We are fighting Germans, Austrians and Drink', said the Chancellor, 'and so far as I can see the greatest of these deadly foes is Drink.'

The role of the press

Lord Northcliffe, the great press baron, blamed Kitchener. 'Lord Kitchener', he stormed in the *Daily Mail*, 'has starved the army in France of high-explosive shells.' But he immediately found out that Kitchener was sacrosanct. Overnight, the paper's circulation plummeted from 1,386,000 to just 238,000 copies. In London, 1,500 indignant stockbrokers held a protest meeting to condemn 'the venomous attacks of the Harmsworth Press' on their idol, ending by burning copies of the offending newspaper on the floor of the Stock Exchange.

But Lloyd George and Asquith were becoming disenchanted with the War Minister. Based on Kitchener's assurance that the ammunition supply was more than adequate, the Prime Minister had publicly congratulated armament workers in Newcastle-upon-Tyne for the efforts they had made, refuting the charge that they had let the country down. Yet French continued his protests, eventually going public. 'I could see', he later wrote, 'the absence of sufficient artillery support was doubling and trebling our losses in men. I therefore determined on taking the most drastic measures to destroy the apathy of a Government which had brought the Empire to the brink of disaster.' He told his side of the story to Colonel Charles Repington, the military correspondent of *The Times*.

Six days later, Repington broke the news. He pulled no punches, reporting that: 'British soldiers died last week on Aubers Ridge because the British army is short of shells.' Meanwhile, French sent two of his staff officers to London, carrying a secret memorandum outlining his complaints, with copies of all the correspondence that had passed between himself and the War Office over the preceding months. French instructed them to show everything to Lloyd George, Arthur Balfour and Bonar Law, the former and present leaders of the Unionist Party. French hoped that this would be enough to bring the government down.

A NEW COALITION GOVERNMENT

In the event it was not French's revelations, damaging though they were, that led to the fall of the Liberal government. The crisis that forced Asquith into a coalition with the Unionists was sparked off by the sudden decision of Lord Fisher to resign as First Sea Lord. Tension between the Admiral and Churchill over the navy's commitments in the Dardanelles had been growing for months. About the only thing they agreed on was to try to blame William Turner, the luckless captain of the transatlantic liner *Lusitania*, for the loss of his ship. She was torpedoed by a U-boat off the coast of Ireland on 7 May, 1915, and sank in just 18 minutes. Only 761 people were saved; 1,198 passengers and crew perished. Early in the morning of 14 May, Fisher left the Admiralty intent on resignation.

As news of Fisher's departure began to leak, Bonar Law visited Lloyd George at the Treasury and warned that he could no longer keep his restless backbenchers in check. It was more than likely, he said, that they would insist on ending the party truce to launch an all-out attack on the government over the conduct of the war, focusing on Churchill's alleged maladministration of the Admiralty. Lloyd George immediately saw the gravity of the situation and went to the Prime

LOSS OF THE *LUSITANIA*

Survivors of the *Lusitania* disaster make their way along a street in Cork in shock from the experience (below left). Some of the victims were buried in a mass grave in County Cork (right). The sinking was greeted with outrage in Britain and the USA; the front page headline below is from the *New York Herald*. The USA was not yet a combatant in the war, yet many of those who lost their lives were American citizens. The Cunard transatlantic liner had sailed despite an official warning from the German Embassy in Washington that the ship would be entering a war zone and that passengers embarked at their own risk. She was torpedoed by a German U-boat off the Irish coast early in the afternoon of 7 May, 1915, and in just 18 minutes vanished beneath the waves taking 1,198 souls with her.

The last minutes on the vessel were confused to say the least. Fannie Morecroft, a stewardess, recalled the passengers 'running around like a bunch of wild mice'. She escaped in the last lifeboat launched. Captain William Turner also survived to report that he believed a second torpedo had sunk his ship. Kapitan-Leutnant Schweiger on the U-boat put the explosion down to 'boilers, coal or powder'. The inquest jury in Ireland declared a verdict of wilful murder against the crew of the submarine and the German government.

Minister. In 'less than a quarter of an hour', they agreed that a coalition with the Unionists was the only way forward. That same evening Asquith informed Lord Stamfordham, the King's private secretary. 'After much reflection & consultation today with Lloyd George and Bonar Law', he wrote, 'I have come decidedly to the conclusion that, for the successful prosecution of the war, the Govt. must be reconstructed on a broad and non-party basis.'

With the agreement of his Shadow Cabinet, which he called together the following day, Bonar Law accepted Asquith's offer, but he made two provisos. First, Churchill would have to leave the Admiralty. And second, Lord Haldane, the Lord Chancellor, would also have to go: the Unionists had not forgiven Haldane for stating before the war that he regarded Germany as his 'spiritual home'. Despite fervent pleadings to be allowed to stay on at the Admiralty, Churchill was fobbed off with the sinecure position of Chancellor of the Duchy of Lancaster. Balfour replaced him at the Admiralty, while Bonar Law became Colonial Secretary. Haldane retired to the backbenches. Lloyd George was appointed head of a newly created Ministry of Munitions. Arthur Henderson, the Labour leader, became President of the Board of Education. John Redmond, leader of the Irish Nationalists, refused to serve, but Sir Edward Carson, leader of the Ulster loyalists, became Attorney-General. In all, there were 12 Liberals, eight Unionists and one Labour representative in the coalition Cabinet, plus Kitchener, who stayed on as Secretary of State for War.

Churchill did not stay in his new position for long. That autumn, when he learned that he would not be part of the new War Council, he resigned and went to command a battalion of Royal Scots Fusiliers on the Western Front. Major Jock McDavid witnessed the former minister's arrival in the trenches. 'Out of the first car', he recollected, 'came this well-known figure dressed in a long, fine-textured waterproof, wearing a poilu helmet and a Sam Browne belt holster with a revolver stuck well into it … the second car … was piled high with luggage of every description. To my horrified amazement, on the very top of all … was a full-length tin bath. What the hell he was going to do with all this I couldn't think.'

Forging the guns

The most demanding of the challenges that the new government faced fell to Lloyd George at the Ministry of Munitions. Speaking to the House of Commons in June 1915, he was in no doubt of the importance of the task: 'I would say that ultimate

OUT, OUT, OUT!
A sign chalked up in London's East End assures passers-by that the shop is Russian-owned (below). Following the sinking of the *Lusitania*, angry mobs attacked many suspected German-owned premises. At least seven people were killed in riots in the East End. In Liverpool, the *Lusitania*'s home port, housewife Ada McGuire of Wallasey recorded: 'There have been dreadful riots in Liverpool & Seacombe against the Germans. The Scotland Road women I believe were just like the women of the French Revolution, so I was told by an eye-witness … Of course, they will be punished, but I think we all feel the same only we are more restrained.' Everyone with a foreign-sounding name, it seemed, was suspected of being a potential spy.

victory or defeat in this War depends on the supply of munitions which the rival countries can produce and with which they can equip their armies in the field.' He started off with just two secretaries in a tiny office equipped with two tables and a single chair. By the end of the war, the ministry's headquarters staff alone numbered more than 25,000, managing around 20,000 'controlled establishments' as well as 15 giant National Projectile Factories, 15 National Filling Factories and four National Cartridge Factories that Lloyd George had ordered to be built from scratch. He let nothing stand in the way of boosting the armaments supply by the fastest possible means. The Munitions of War Act, passed in July 1915, gave him the power to do anything he thought necessary to expand armaments production. His ministry had absolute priority over supplies of fuel, power and transport, and over land for building new factories. He could order existing factories to produce for the government and, if necessary, bring them under state control.

The task faced by Lloyd George was daunting. The army was not just lacking guns, mortars, shells and machine guns – the War Office had ordered 26,000, but only 5,500 had been supplied – it also needed 70,000 hand grenades a day, of which it was receiving just 2,500. To fortify a single mile of the Western Front required 900 miles of barbed wire, 6 million sandbags, 1 million cubic feet of timber and 360,000 square feet of corrugated iron. The response to the challenge was magnificent. By the time Lloyd George took over the War Office in July 1916, the number one priority of industry had at last become the mass-manufacture of weapons to enable the army to beat the Germans in the field. It was a far cry from the business-as-usual attitude that had hitherto prevailed.

Labour unrest

Before the formation of the coalition, ministers had brokered an industrial truce in an attempt to put an end to strikes and labour disputes for the duration of the war. Most importantly, trade unions agreed to allow the unskilled to do the work of the

NEW COALITION MEMBERS
Unionist leaders Sir Edward Carson (above left) and Andrew Bonar Law (above right) cross Whitehall on their way to the House of Commons in August 1915. Both became ministers when Prime Minister Asquith formed a Coalition government, Bonar Law serving as Colonial Secretary and Carson as Attorney-General. Carson's tenure of office was short-lived. He resigned in October in protest at the failure of the Allies to send military assistance to help Serbia. The following year, he played a pivotal role in bringing about Asquith's resignation.

skilled, to abandon restrictive practices and to accept compulsory arbitration to settle disputes. The proviso was that things would return to normal after the war. As a quid pro quo, an excess profits tax, designed to stop employers making too much money out of supplying war materials, was eventually introduced. But there remained some legal, if nefarious, ways of mitigating the tax, as many canny businessmen discovered.

It looked well enough on paper, but not everyone toiling at the coalface, in the shipyards and in the engineering works was prepared to go along with the deal. In February 1915, the first serious strike of the war broke out on the Clyde when 5,000 engineers downed tools in protest at some American workers being taken on at higher rates of pay. That July, 200,000 miners in South Wales downed tools in protest against the attempt to impose a national pay settlement on them. In December, with the Clydeside engineers again threatening trouble, Lloyd George rushed north to appeal personally to their shop stewards not to take industrial action. In a mass-meeting on Christmas Day, attended by 3,000 men, he was howled down. The ruffled minister returned to London in a rage. Frances Stevenson, Lloyd George's secretary and mistress, recorded in her diary: 'D says that the men up there are ripe for revolution … He is convinced there is German money up there.' Though the dispute was eventually settled – the government assured the militants that their jobs were secure and that their traditional privileges would be restored after the war – there were more strikes to come.

WOMEN AT WORK

Many women were eager to do their bit and take the place of the hundreds of thousands of men who had volunteered to join the fighting forces, but things were slow to get off the ground. In March 1915 the government launched a registration scheme for women prepared to work for the war effort. Almost 79,000 women immediately came forward, but only 1,800 of them found jobs.

Many felt that this was simply not good enough. That July, Mrs Pankhurst and her fellow suffragette Millicent Fawcett organised a massive 'Women's Right to Serve' rally. Some 30,000 demonstrated in Hyde Park in London, carrying banners emblazoned with slogans such as 'We Demand the Right to Work', 'Shells Made by a Wife May Save a Husband's Life' and 'Women's Scissors Will Cut The Red Tape'. They were pushing at an open door. The nation was ready for change.

Many women, primarily from the upper and middle classes, went into nursing. The number of military nurses rose from 2,600 in 1914 to more than 18,000 by

STEPPING UP
Before the war, women were most commonly employed in domestic service. Now, they stepped forward to fill the shoes of the hundreds of thousands of men away at the war. Women took over from men in all sorts of jobs and surprised many by their abilities and strength – like this young woman delivering coal (left) who seems well up to the physical demands of the job. By the end of the war, the number of women in paid employment had increased from 5.9 to 7.3 million. They were not paid as much as the men they replaced and some of them faced considerable male hostility. One Lancashire tram conductress recalled how male passengers sometimes simply refused to show her their tickets.

HANDLE WITH CARE
Women in an armaments factory gently steer loaded shells from the factory floor. From the time the government set up the Ministry of Munitions, the number of women working in the munitions industry steadily increased. In June 1915 the Woolwich Arsenal employed only 195 women; by July 1916 the figure had risen to 11,000, then to more than 250,000 a year later. Though reasonably well-paid, working conditions were hazardous. In addition to the risk of accidental explosions, many women contracted TNT poisoning in which the chemicals in the explosive attacked the red corpuscles in the blood and vulnerable body organs, such as the liver. Toxic jaundice was another hazard and the faces of women suffering from it turned bright yellow.

the end of the war, with a further 74,000 serving in VADs (Voluntary Aid Detachments). The society beauty Lady Diana Manners was one of them. After training as a VAD at Guy's, she persuaded her parents, the Duke and Duchess of Rutland, to turn part of Arlington House, their palatial London home, into a hospital for the wounded. Agatha Christie, another VAD, became a dispenser in a hospital pharmacy. She put the knowledge she gained of poisons to good use when she turned detective writer after the war.

Women took over from men in offices, on the trams, buses and railways, in shipyards and engineering plants and on the factory floor. Many found work in the rapidly expanding armaments industry, filling shells with high explosives and shrapnel. They were swiftly dubbed 'munitionettes'. Lord Selborne, the President of the Board of Agriculture, set up the Women's Land Service Corps, which eventually became the Women's Land Army. *The Times* gave a cautious blessing to such changes, while heralding the possible impact. 'Even if many of the posts formerly held by men which women are now filling are for the duration of the war only, and will have to be yielded up should their original holder return safe and sound, they will have tested women's capacity in a way that may have a lasting effect on women's work in the future.'

It was not all plain sailing. Some women met resistance from male co-workers, who resented their arrival in the workplace. And with so many cooks, maids and housekeepers leaving domestic service for better-paid war work, many middle and upper-class women struggled to run their homes. 'Neither my Mother, sister or myself had ever done any serious housework or cooking of any kind, so it was an entirely new experience to be confronted with meals to cook and rooms to clean', one officer's wife recalled. 'It required an entirely new mental adjustment.'

THE WOMEN'S LAND ARMY
By September 1916, the Board of Agriculture calculated that 57,497 women had registered to join the Women's Land Army, although only 28,767 of them were employed at that time. These two photographs show some of the ones who were – a young women handling a horse and cart on a farm in Surrey, and a group of foresty girls enjoying a laugh during their lunch break in Epping Forest. Ploughing, milking, hoeing and harrowing competitions were organised to show farmers what women could do. After one competition in Hertfordshire in July 1917, *The Times* wrote of 'the land women, bronzed, freckled and splendidly healthy' clearing ditches, loading carts with manure and harnessing horses. On average, land volunteers earned 3d to 4d an hour for an eight-hour day – less than an unskilled farm labourer, but with board and lodging provided.

The coming of conscription

Manpower and how best to mobilise it was one of the most critical problems facing the coalition government. As voluntary recruitment slowed and casualty lists grew, military demands for more men constantly increased. In the spring of 1915 Kitchener had committed the country to creating a 70-division army on the Western Front, but as the months went by it seemed less and less likely that the target could ever be met without compulsory military service. The politicians were divided. Many Unionists and some Liberals – most notably Churchill and Lloyd George – favoured conscription. So, too, did King George who wrote to Asquith that, though he trusted 'we shall not be obliged to come to compulsion', he was 'interested to see it has been advocated in the H of C this evening by one of your late whips, who has been at the front for ten months!!!'. Many Liberals fervently opposed it, some on conscientious grounds and others, including Reginald McKenna, who had succeeded Lloyd George as Chancellor, because they doubted whether the country could afford it.

The Prime Minister prevaricated, but eventually the failure of the BEF's offensive at Loos in September 1915 – during the battle, the British, following the German example, employed poison gas for the first time – persuaded Asquith to change the commander-in-chief in France. He replaced French with Sir Douglas Haig, and he also took away some powers from the over-extended Kitchener by bringing General Sir William Robertson (who had been French's Chief of Staff) back to the War Office as head of the Imperial General Staff. Now, Asquith was facing demands from the army for 35,000 new recruits a week.

At first, true to form, Asquith compromised. Lord Derby devised a scheme under which all men of military age were urged to attest that, if called upon to join the colours, they would do so. Out of 2.2 million eligible single men, about 840,000 came forward; around 1.35 million married men also attested, trusting Asquith's promise that single men would be called up before them. But pressure continued to mount on the beleaguered premier until universal conscription was made law in two Military Service Acts in 1916 – one in March covering single men, the other in May extending the call-up to married men.

THE EASTER RISING

It was while the controversy over conscription was reaching its climax that the government found itself facing another major crisis. On Easter Monday, 1916, some 2,000 Irish National Volunteers, abetted by members of the Irish Citizen Army, rose in armed rebellion in Dublin and proclaimed an Irish Republic. They took over the General Post Office in Sackville Street as their headquarters, where they were promptly besieged.

Though British intelligence had warned that a rising was likely, Asquith and his colleagues seemed taken by surprise. Duff Cooper, a young civil servant in the Foreign Office, recorded in his diary how they got the news. 'During the morning they brought us over a telegram which Birrell [the Irish Chief Secretary] had received from Ireland and which he hadn't been able to decode because his

THE IRISH REBELLION
British regulars snipe at Nationalist rebels from behind a hastily erected barricade of beer casks near the Dublin quayside (right). The British administration was initially taken by surprise, but troops were rushed to the scene to nip the uprising in the bud. The Nationalists were outnumbered and outgunned; they had hoped for German aid, but the promised arms never came. Michael Collins (top), seen here in the uniform of a general in the Irish Volunteers, and Eamon de Valera (above) were two of the rebel leaders who lived to fight again. Others were not so fortunate and were executed by British firing squads.

THE RISING CRUSHED

Dubliners view the remains of buildings destroyed by British artillery fire during the Easter Rising (left). After the rebellion had been suppressed, the government authorised a policy of savage repression. Fifteen of Sinn Fein's leaders were court-martialled and shot, while martial law was imposed throughout the south of Ireland. Sir Roger Casement (right), who had gone to Germany to plead for help for the Irish Nationalist cause, returned to Ireland on the eve of rebellion and was arrested soon after. He was imprisoned in the Tower of London, tried for treason at the Old Bailey and hanged in Pentonville Prison. He is seen here on his way to the gallows. Asquith deputed Lloyd George to try to broker an Irish settlement, but despite his most persuasive efforts, the 'Welsh wizard' failed to reconcile the two sides. When Lady Scott, widow of the celebrated explorer and a confidante of the Prime Minister, asked what else could be proposed, Asquith replied: 'They have nothing to suggest but despair.'

secretary was away and no one else knew where the cipher was!' Cooper concluded acerbically: 'It really seems amazing that when things of this kind are going on in Ireland Birrell should be unable to decipher his own telegrams ...'.

Reinforcements were despatched to crush the rebellion, which itself had got off to an inauspicious start. The ship the rebels were counting on to supply them with arms had been sunk off the coast of Kerry a few days before, while Sir Roger Casement, a former British diplomat who had made his way to Germany to plead the Irish cause, had been arrested soon after being landed back in Ireland from a German U-boat. Nevertheless, it still took the British six days and much bitter fighting to force the insurgents to surrender. Some 450 Irish were killed and 3,614 wounded; the death toll on the other side was 116 British soldiers and 16 members of the Royal Irish Constabulary.

Reprisals were immediate and savage: 15 of the ringleaders were summarily executed by firing squad. Among them were Patrick Pease, the Republic's provisional president, and the wounded James Connolly, who had to be propped up on a chair to be shot. Some 3,000 rebels and supposed sympathisers were arrested, 1,867 of them ending up in prison. Casement was hung for treason. British rule in Ireland continued for the rest of the war.

THE BIG PUSH ON THE SOMME

The Irish rebellion was a most unwelcome distraction, for the attention of the government – and ultimately of the nation – was fixed on the great offensive that General Haig was preparing to launch on the River Somme, along a 20-mile stretch of the Western Front. It was the long-awaited 'big push' and this time, the government was assured, it would achieve the big breakthrough.

Originally, Haig had planned the battle with Marshall Joffre as a joint Franco-British effort, which was why the Somme had been chosen rather than Flanders, which Haig would have preferred. The plan was for the two Allied armies to launch an all-out assault on the German positions on the Somme, with the British attacking to the north and the French to the south of the river. But in February 1916 the Germans began a massive and sustained attack on the French positions at Verdun. Months of intensive fighting had drawn off most of the troops that Joffre had intended for the Somme: by the time battle was joined, only six French divisions were free to fight with the British.

Haig was not too worried by the reduction in the French contribution. He wanted to win a decisive British victory. The BEF had been massively reinforced by Kitchener's New Army, which was finally, so it was felt, ready to take to the field. Haig was in command of nearly a million men and had more guns than ever before. An awesome artillery bombardment would precede the initial assault, ceasing only when the troops were ready to go over the top. The attacking foot-soldiers were told that the sheer fury of the barrage would obliterate any defences confronting them, annihilate the enemy artillery and smash to smithereens the machine gun nests that festooned the German lines.

Over the top

The 'big push' began on 1 July, 1916. Promptly at 7.30am the sound of officers' whistles rang along the trenches as thousands upon thousands of men started to scale the assault ladders. Private Albert Andrews, serving in the Manchester Regiment, recorded the countdown: 'The orders came down: "Half an hour to go!" "Quarter of an hour to go!" "Ten minutes to go!" "Three minutes to go!" I lit a cigarette and up the ladder I went.'

They began moving forward into no-man's-land, advancing in line and at a steady pace, precisely as instructed. John Andrews, another private in the Manchester Regiment, recorded that he carried with him 'a rifle and bayonet with

BIG GUNS
The 39th Siege Battery artillery in action during the battle of the Somme (right). In the week before the battle, more than a million shells were fired on German positions in a preliminary bombardment. The rolling rumble of the guns could be heard across the Channel. And yet this massive bombardment failed in both of its primary objectives, which were to cut the barbed wire entanglements protecting the German trenches and to destroy the machine-gun nests that formed the backbone of the enemy defence. When Britain's Tommies went over the top, they found both were still intact.

INTO THE STORM
British soldiers go over the top during the battle of the Somme (below), which began on 1 July, 1916. On the first day they were cut down in their thousands by German machine-gun fire. Half of the first wave were killed within 30 minutes of going over the top. By evening, the BEF had suffered 57,470 casualties; of 13 villages targeted, just three had been taken in an advance of less than a mile. On 14 July a second attack further south along the river met with some initial success, but a third thrust at the end of the month was a total failure. Worsening weather eventually forced Haig to call a halt on 19 November. The British had advanced just seven miles and lost 419,654 men, of whom 131,000 had died on the battlefield.

'The first line all lay down and I thought they'd had different orders because we'd all been told to walk. It appears they lay down because they'd been shot and either killed or wounded. They were just mown down like corn.'

Private Reginald Glenn, York and Lancaster Regiment, 1916

a pair of wire cutters attached; a shovel fastened on my back ... haversack containing one day's iron rations and two Mills bombs; 150 rounds of ammunition; two extra bandoliers containing 60 rounds each, one over each shoulder; a bag of ten bombs.' Troops weighed down by loads like this probably would not have been able to move faster even if they had tried.

It soon became clear that the preliminary bombardment, the first part of Haig's plan, had failed in its objectives. In many places, both the barbed wire protecting the German trenches and the German machine guns were still intact, and the latter were firing on the advancing British to murderous effect. Then the German artillery opened fire. By the end of that first day, the BEF had suffered 57,470 casualties, of whom 19,240 had been killed or died of their wounds.

Senseless slaughter

There was to be no breakthrough. Instead, the battle just went on and on, with Haig launching attack after attack until, with the coming of the autumn rains, the slaughter was finally brought to an end on 19 November. The troops were once again bogged down in mud to face the winter. In four-and-a-half months of fighting, the longed-for great advance had been limited to just seven miles.

At home, the casualty lists made heartbreaking reading. Marjorie Llewellyn, a Sheffield schoolgirl, recorded that 'there were sheets and sheets in the paper of dead and wounded ... It was a very, very sad time – practically everybody was in

GAS ATTACK!
Soldiers of the Machine Gun Corps man their Vickers weapon wearing gas-masks during the battle of the Somme in July 1916. By this stage in the war, gas-masks were standard equipment for every soldier, but when the Germans first used gas, at Ypres in spring 1915, it took the British completely by surprise. The War Office immediately appealed to the public to make half a million gas masks at home. Harrods set up a special counter to sell the gauze, cotton wool and tape required and its staff gave demonstrations of how to put a mask together. The government aimed to send 100,000 of these homemade masks to the front within a week. Meanwhile, soldiers were told to improvise by wetting a piece of cloth – handkerchiefs and socks were favourites – to tie over the mouth and nose until the gas clouds passed. Before long the British retaliated in kind and used gas against the Germans.

COPING WITH THE WOUNDED
A dressing station on the Somme packed with wounded awaiting treatment. No one had foreseen the number of casualties. Lieutenant Lawrence Gameson, a young medical officer, recalled how he 'worked for hours on end without respite; at the crude dressing tables, at men grounded on stretchers, at men squatting or sitting'. The walking wounded were the most fortunate; the seriously injured had to face agonising journeys in unsprung ambulances jolting over the endlessly shelled roads back to hospitals behind the lines. Sergeant Tom Price remembered how he and six other wounded men were 'put on a Ford ambulance van with rubber tyres, hard wheels. I don't know which of the six of us screamed the most on that journey down over the rutted, shell-holed roads.'

mourning … The city was really shrouded in gloom … and nothing seemed to matter anymore.' Asquith himself was closely affected. Raymond, his eldest son who was in the Grenadier Guards, was killed leading his men over the top.

Battle in the North Sea

Nor was there any other good news to cheer people up. On 31 May, the two great fleets had finally clashed in the North Sea at the battle of Jutland, but far from winning a Nelsonic victory, as everyone had expected, the Royal Navy ended up losing more ships than the Imperial High Seas Fleet. Before turning tail and making for home, the Germans managed to sink three British battle cruisers, four armoured cruisers and eight destroyers. The Germans lost one battle cruiser, an old pre-Dreadnought battleship, four light cruisers and five destroyers. 'Heavy and Unaccountable British Losses', ran the headline in the *Daily Express*, echoing Admiral Sir David Beatty's comment as two of his battle cruisers were blown up in quick succession. 'Chatfield', he said to one of his officers, 'there seems to be something wrong with our bloody ships today.'

ASQUITH FALLS

The coalition government began to crumble. In June, Lloyd George had pressured the Prime Minister into appointing him Secretary of State for War in place of Kitchener, who had drowned while on a diplomatic voyage to Russia when the ship he was travelling on, HMS *Hampshire,* struck a mine. At the time Margot Asquith wrote presciently in her diary: 'We are out: It can only be a question of time now when we shall have to leave Downing Street.'

Meanwhile, Lloyd George had found that he was unable to exert much power over the generals – Sir William Robertson, as Chief of the Imperial General Staff, had supreme strategic authority – and grumbled that he was little more than a butcher's boy, rounding up men to be slaughtered. With Unionist support, Lloyd George urged Asquith to set up a new, small War Committee to take over much of the responsibility for running the war. He would be its chairman. Asquith demanded that it be made clear that he retained 'supreme and effective control of War policy', and the two men agreed that they could live with the compromise. But then something happened that made the arrangement unworkable.

For months the press, particularly *The Times* and *Daily Mail*, had been almost unremittingly critical of Asquith. Now *The Times* returned to the attack. Someone – possibly Lloyd George himself – leaked the terms of their agreement. In December 1916 Asquith wrote to Lloyd George demanding that he, not Lloyd George, be chairman of the War Committee: 'Unless the impression is at once corrected that I am being relegated to the position of an irresponsible spectator of the War, I cannot possibly go on.' He had already announced his intention of reconstructing the government. Lloyd George now made it clear that he would not serve in an administration on Asquith's terms, and the Unionists – some more reluctantly than others – backed him. With the Unionists against him and his own party divided, Asquith lacked the support to carry on. He resigned.

The King called the party leaders to a conference, chaired by Arthur Balfour, who was accepted as being impartial. Balfour's conclusion was that it was impossible for Asquith to form a new government. Bonar Law was ready to try, if Asquith was prepared to serve under him. If not, Lloyd George should be given the chance. After consulting Liberal colleagues, Asquith declined. Accordingly the King summoned Lloyd George to Buckingham Palace. Within 24 hours, he formed a new coalition government and Asquith was gone – for good. The country ended the year with a new leader. One thing, though, was certain. The war would go on. It would be fought, said Lloyd George, to 'a knock-out blow.'

THE OVERTHROWN PRIME MINISTER
Herbert Henry Asquith (above), pictured in 1916 shortly before his enforced resignation as Prime Minister. He had led the Liberal government brilliantly since 1908, but the 64-year-old premier was no longer at the height of his powers. As the war news went from bad to worse, his seemingly laid-back conduct of affairs was considered by many to be dilatory. The Coalition government was unsettled and unstable; he also faced constant criticism in the press. As the political crisis around Asquith's premiership neared its climax, Lord Northcliffe was deterred only at the last minute from running a *Daily Mail* leading article headed 'Asquith: A National Danger'. After his resignation, Asquith wrote to a close friend: 'I have been through the hell of a time for the best part of a month, and almost for the first time I begin to feel older. In the end, there was nothing else to be done, though it is hateful to give even the semblance of a score to our blackguardly Press.' He never held office again.

> '**I saw that I could not go on without dishonour or impotence, or both; and nothing could have been worse for the country and the war.**'
>
> H H Asquith, in a letter to a friend shortly after his resignation

IN THE TRENCHES

The men of the BEF had hastily dug themselves into trenches for some sort of protection during the war's first autumn and winter, but by 1918 the trench system had become much more sophisticated. There was a lightly held Forward Zone, the main Battle Zone and a Rear Zone. With everyone expecting a major German attack, Haig ordered the British forces to defend their positions in depth. The question was whether there would be enough time to prepare the defences fully.

WAITING AND WATCHING British and French troops share a dug-out in a trench on the Western Front during a lull in the fighting in early 1915 (below). The BEF was to launch its first major offensive later that spring. Three years later men were still in the trenches. Here (right), in mid-March 1918, one man keeps watch while his colleagues from the 7th King's Liverpool Regiment stand to at a strong point in the Forward Zone. The photograph was taken shortly before the Germans launched their own all-out offensive that their commanders confidently expected would win the war, before the Americans had time to arrive in strength. The attack was expected, but after Britain's serious losses of the previous year – and Lloyd George's refusal to sanction the despatch of replacements – Haig and his generals were short of men to repel it when it came. Sir Hubert Gough, commanding the Fifth Army on the Somme, where the first blows fell, was aware of what was coming: 'We knew we were going to be attacked in overwhelming force.' The onslaught started on 21 March, 1918. Aided by the cover of a thick morning mist, the Germans soon broke through the Fifth Army's defences.

SEEING IT THROUGH
Men of the Duke of
Wellington's Regiment show
the ability to sleep anywhere,
as they take shelter in a shell
hole after a successful
advance into no-man's-land
(left). Back on the BEF's front
line, some Tommies brew up
a hot stew on a so-called
Tommy cooker (top), while
others snatch a nap in a

cramped dugout (above).
What the Tommies called
all-in stew was a favourite, as
were porridge and pea soup.
Some trenches were far
superior to others, as the
23rd Brigade discovered
when it took over a section
from the French on the River
Aisne in May 1910. In the
words of Lieutenant Walter
Harris, detached from the

Rifle Brigade to command a
trench mortar battery, they
were: 'The best system of
corridors and dugouts I had
ever seen – it must have
been a great effort by the
French to make such a fine
underground headquarters.'
Captain Philip Ledward was
also impressed: 'The
trenches and dugouts were
in wonderful condition.'

1910s

BRITAIN BATTLES ON

The year 1917 was the bleakest of the entire First World War. In an attempt to starve Britain into submission, Germany resumed unrestricted submarine warfare: in April alone, half a million tons of British shipping were lost. As supplies at home began to run short, the Ministry of Food urged Britons to cut back on what they ate. Food queues grew longer and prices soared. Nevertheless, most Britons remained ready to see things through. The Admiralty adopted a convoy system in an attempt to defend merchant shipping against U-boat attack. Then the United States of America joined the war on the Allied side: things must surely get better.

THE YANKS ARE HERE Two US soldiers fire at a German machine-gun nest in September 1918, as infantry advance through what remains of the Argonne Forest in northeast France. By this time, the final German attempt to win the war had failed and they were in full retreat.

EAT LESS FOOD

On 10 January, 1917, Thomas Livingstone, still keeping his diary in Glasgow, recorded that 'the War Loaf is official'. To save grain, the amount of white flour in bread was reduced and substituted with other grain or potato flour. People complained about the 'Government Bread' – but they still ate it. In an attempt to reduce bread consumption, the new Ministry of Food urged Britons to heed the advice of a character called Mr Slice O' Bread. Cutting out 'waste crusts', the poster advised, would save 48 million slices of bread a day; the Ministry also calculated that if every person in the land saved a teaspoon of breadcrumbs a day, the total saving would amount to 40,000 tons a year. Following the King's example, loyal citizens were urged to take what was christened the Householder's Pledge to reduce bread consumption voluntarily by a quarter and to 'abstain from the use of flour in pastry'. The campaign even had a badge – a purple ribbon with the slogan 'I eat less bread' – while schoolchildren throughout the land were encouraged to learn the campaign song.

The problem was that bread was the staple food for most ordinary folk, especially since meat was becoming far too costly except for special occasions. In April, *The Observer* reported that queues for bread and potatoes in Edmonton, north London, were so long that the police had to be called to regulate them. By December, according to *The Times*, queues of a thousand people or more were commonplace. Small wonder that there was a resurgence of industrial unrest. In March 1917, many munition workers went on strike, followed by engineers at Rochdale. By May, unrest had spread to 48 towns, with 200,000 workers idle.

In 1918 Lord Rhondda, who had succeeded Lord Devonport as Minister of Food, finally brought in official rationing. The scheme was piloted in London and the Home Counties before being rolled-out nationally in July. The new rations were enforced by police. One man from Mitcham in south London, charged with illegally shooting a deer, pleaded in mitigation: 'It's a job to live on these meat rations. I must have something for my children.' He was heavily fined, as was a woman from Dover, who fed bread and milk to her 14 dogs.

Disaster in Silvertown

The arrival of the 'War Loaf' was not the only bad news to report. Glaswegian Thomas Livingstone recorded in his diary that there had been a 'great munitions factory disaster near London'. The catastrophe happened on 19 January, 1918,

SAVING FOOD AND RATIONING
As the German U-boat campaign against British merchant shipping created growing shortages, government posters like this one (above) delivered a direct appeal to the nation to save bread. In February 1917 Lord Davenport, the newly appointed Minister of Food, urged people to restrict themselves voluntarily to no more than four pounds of bread, two-and-a-half pounds of meat and 12 ounces of sugar per week. In April, Davenport was replaced by Lord Rhondda, who in February 1918 instituted an official rationing system. It was tested out in London and the Home Counties, then rolled out across the country in July. Each household had to register with a retailer, who was supplied according to the needs of his customers. The weekly allowances per person were 1½lbs of meat, 4oz of butter or margarine and 8oz of sugar. Women were allowed 4lbs of bread a week; men got 7lbs. Children aged less than six got half the meat ration, though adolescent boys and men involved in heavy labour got extra. The number of customers in restaurants was restricted and all had to hand over coupons with their orders.

'We've no unpatriotic joints,
No sugar and no bread.
Eat nothing sweet, no rolls, no meat,
The Food Controller said.'

Aelfrida Tillyard, *Invitation Au Festin*, 1917

FRESH FROM THE OVEN

Army bakers in France (right) display freshly baked loaves from a mobile bread oven. At home, people were encouraged to cut down on bread consumption so that troops at the front had sufficient, and by early 1917 food shortages were starting to bite: this queue of women and children (below) is at a South London soup kitchen. The German U-boat campaign to starve Britain into submission was reaching its height. Eventually, the government set up National Kitchens to provide cheap meals for the needy. The first was opened by Queen Mary in May 1917. The Queen herself served the first meals, but one elderly customer did not realise who had served him. 'The fact that it was the Queen must have been pointed out to him by the crowd outside', an observer reported, 'for shortly afterwards he returned, edged his way back to the serving-counter, and solemnly waved his hat three times at her.'

in Silvertown in the East End. As firemen tried to douse a fire in a chemical plant, 50 tons of TNT, an extremely powerful explosive, suddenly detonated. A large part of the factory was instantly destroyed, together with many buildings in nearby streets. It was the biggest single explosion ever recorded in the capital. In all, some 70,000 homes were damaged, 73 people were killed – 69 instantly and four later in hospital – and more than 400 were injured. The bodies of those closest to the explosion were never found. The noise resounded right across the capital, and damage was seen miles away. Elizabeth Fernside, a housewife in Fulham, reported: 'The noise was so terrific that I thought the Huns had dropped a surprise packet. There are … great cracks and gaps in the roads, people three miles off were blown out of their houses and were running about, seeking a place to shelter.' Contrary to popular rumour, an official enquiry concluded that the Silvertown explosion was accidental and was not caused by a German bomb.

DEATH FROM THE SKIES

At the end of May, the enemy returned to the skies over Britain for real and this time, rather than Zeppelins, they were flying new, twin-engined Gotha G-4 bombers capable of carrying a 1,000-pound payload. Flying out of bases at Ghent in Belgium, they struck first at Folkestone in Kent, dropping 23 bombs and killing 95 people, a number of whom had been waiting in a food queue outside a shop.

Pilots, observers and ground crew of No.1 Squadron, Royal Flying Corps (RFC), pose for the camera. One pilot (right foreground) is holding a beagle – the squadron's mascot. By the time of the battle of Arras in April 1917, RFC pilots had shot down some 200 enemy aircraft. Everyone, from Lloyd George downwards, admired the airmen greatly; the premier dubbed them 'the knighthood of the war, without fear and without reproach'. They were certainly brave. For one thing, they were not equipped with parachutes when they flew – officially, the reason was that the parachutes of the day were too bulky to fit into a fighter's cockpit, but a secret report of the Air Board revealed another reason: 'It is the opinion of the Air Board that the presence of such an apparatus might impair the fighting spirit of pilots and cause them to abandon machines which might otherwise be capable of returning to base for repair.'

The bombers moved on to London, which quickly became their main target. The city was raided by day and by night. The first raid, on 13 June, 1917, resulted in 162 deaths and 432 injuries, mainly in the area around Liverpool Street Station. Another daylight raid that same month killed 158, including 18 children at a school in Poplar, and caused near panic throughout the East End.

The government was quick to take action. An iron ring of anti-aircraft guns and searchlights was thrown around the capital, while Royal Flying Corps fighters were recalled from France to bolster the defences. Nevertheless, bombers still got through. Maroons – a type of firework – were fired to raise the alarm as bombers approached, and people rushed to take refuge in cellars, under railway arches, in foot tunnels beneath the Thames and in the London Underground. All waited anxiously for the sound of bugles being blown by Boy Scouts and Boys' Brigades to signal the 'All Clear'. The upsurge of public outrage at the continued attacks led George V to change the name of the Royal dynasty from the German-sounding Saxe-Coburg-Gotha to plain patriotic Windsor.

A perilous balance

Lloyd George's mind was not on the air offensive. It was focused on what was going on in France, where Haig was advocating the launch of another all-out offensive. Britain's two main allies were in a parlous state. Russia was heading

TAKING SHELTER

Two volunteers (left), clutching mugs for tea, stand in the exit of a YMCA dugout, erected as an air raid shelter in a London street. Government policy did not stretch to providing individual family shelters, but some, like this family in south London (right), built their own. Most people took shelter as best they could under railway arches, in church basements and crypts, and in the cellars of private and public buildings; in Knightsbridge, for example, Harrods threw open the vast man-made caverns under the store to people seeking safety. Thousands of Londoners sheltered in the Underground. At the height of the air attacks, in autumn 1917, up to 300,000 people a night were taking refuge in Underground stations. When the air raid alarm was raised, the crowds were at times prone to panic. One St John's Ambulance Brigade Officer noted: 'Everyone runs at once ... People arrive in a state of excitement which changes to hysteria when the guns begin to fire.' By the time the Germans called off their bombing campaign in 1918, due to mounting losses, they had flown 397 missions; 24 Gothas had been shot down and 37 lost through accidents.

inexorably towards revolution, while in France the failure of General Robert Nivelle's assault on the Chemin des Dames ridge in April 1917 had led to widespread mutiny among the French troops. Nivelle, a hero of Verdun, had replaced General Joffre as commander-in-chief of the French armies in December 1916. Now it was Nivelle's turn to go. In May 1917 the French government called upon the more cautious General Philippe Petain, the other great hero of Verdun, to take overall command and restore order among the ranks.

For Britain and France, there was one thing above all that gave cause for hope: in April 1917 the USA had joined the war on the Allied side. But it would be many months before American troops could play a significant part. Petain placated his war-weary troops with a promise that there would be no more futile, costly offensives. 'We must wait', he said, 'for the Americans and the tanks.'

British success at Messines

In June 1917, after a year of careful preparation, 19 enormous mines literally blew a hole through the German defences at Messines and the Second Army, under General Herbert Plumer, inflicted impressive carnage on the Germans. Captain Martin Greener, a company commander in the Royal Engineers, recorded how 'the earth seemed to open and rise up to the sky. It was all shot with flame. The dust and smoke was terrific.' Rifleman Tom Cantlon, of the King's Royal Rifles, recalled 'None of us had ever seen anything like it. It was just one mass of flames. The whole world seemed to go up in the air.' *The Times* reported the attack as a 'brilliant British success'. The King was quick to congratulate the troops. 'Tell General Plumer and the Second Army', he wrote to Haig, 'how proud we are of his achievement, by which in a few hours the enemy was driven out of strong entrenched positions held by him for two-and-a-half years.'

Flushed with this success, Haig argued that his forces were more than capable of breaking out of the Ypres salient, advancing into open country and forcing the Germans into full-scale retreat. He proposed to launch a new war-winning

RUINED BY WAR
A British convoy passes through what remains of the ancient city of Ypres in January 1917, soon to be the scene of renewed fighting in the horrific Battle of Passchendaele. Before the war, Ypres had been one of the jewels of Flanders. Now it was a ghost town. Not a leaf grew on a single tree. From the battered ramparts, the eye swept across a wilderness of rubble to low-lying swampy country beyond. Only the jagged ruins of St Martin's Church and the medieval Cloth Hall bore witness to the fact that a community had ever flourished there.

offensive in Flanders, centred on the tiny village of Passchendaele near Ypres. Lloyd George was not convinced. The new offensive, he believed, could easily turn into another Somme. Summoning the commander-in-chief before the War Cabinet, he told Haig bluntly that incurring heavy casualties in yet another inconclusive battle would have 'disastrous effects on public opinion'. It would be preferable to wait for the Americans and for the French armies to recover from their own failed offensive, or to send troops to support the Italians in their bitter struggle against the Austrians. Anything would be better than gambling with hundreds of thousands of lives 'merely because those directing the war can think of nothing better to do with the men under their command'. But eventually Haig got his way. The War Cabinet, albeit reluctantly, authorised preparations for his attack.

PASSCHENDAELE

Over the next month, reinforcements moved inexorably towards the jumping-off points for the attack, taking full advantage of the cafés in places like Poporinghe along the way. Night after night, the Tommies crowded into them, consuming mountains of eggs and chips and drinking gallons of cheap white wine. It cost just a franc a bottle. Then, on 16 July, Haig started the preliminary bombardment. He had mustered no fewer than 2,299 guns – one to every five yards of the front – to smash the German defences. During the two weeks the barrage lasted, the British artillery fired four times as many shells as it had during the prelude to the Somme.

The constant drumming of the distant guns could just be heard in London, 120 miles away, where the War Cabinet met over dinner. It decided, somewhat late in the day, to allow the offensive to start, but with a major proviso. According to Sir Maurice Hankey, the Secretary to the War Cabinet, it was not to be allowed to 'degenerate into a drawn-out, indecisive battle of the Somme type'. If that happened, 'it was to be stopped and the plan for an attack on the Italian front would be tried'. But nothing could stop the offensive now.

Over the top once more
On 31 July, at 3.50am, the soldiers of the Fifth Army, commanded by General Sir Hubert Gough, went over the top. It all started deceptively well – but ended badly. By the end of the first day of battle, the attack had stalled on the German defences. Then it started to rain and the downpour continued without let-up.

The month of August 1917 was to be the wettest in Flanders in living memory. The ground that the troops were expected to advance over rapidly turned into a

swamp. Every stream turned into a torrent, every ditch into a watercourse and the trenches filled with water faster than the Tommies could bail them out. The massive artillery barrage had not helped as the shellfire had destroyed the intricate local drainage system, so helping to create a muddy morass.

The conditions were indescribable, particularly for the wounded waiting to be rescued from the battlefield. Sister Calder, a nurse at a casualty clearing station, recalled how the 'boys', as she and the other nurses referred to them, 'were in a shocking state, because so many of them had been lying out in the mud before they could be picked up by the first-aid orderlies. Their clothes were simply filthy. They didn't look like clothes at all. We had to cut them off and do what we could.'

Bogged down in mud

Undeterred, Haig ordered the attack to continue. On 16 August, Gough's men went over the top again, but although they succeeded in taking the village of Langemarck, fierce German counter-attacks – and the rain – prevented further gains. The Fifth Army had now lost 3,420 officers and 64,586 other ranks since

FIGHTING FROM SHELL HOLES
Canadian troops in a quagmire of mud slowly advance up the ridge above Passchendaele in the teeth of determined enemy resistance. Haig had thrown the Canadian Corps, under General Sir Arthur Currie, into the battle in a last-ditch attempt to take the village and the high ground above it, but the Germans were ready for them. Private Jim Pickard of the Winnipeg Grenadiers recorded his experience of one abortive attack: 'The shells were falling thick and fast, and by some sort of capillary action the holes they made filled up with water as you looked at them – or as you lay in them, for the only way we could move was to dodge from one hole to another, hoping that lightning really didn't strike twice in the same place.'

31 July. Gough appealed to Haig to call off the offensive, but the commander-in-chief was confident that his strategy was correct. General John Charteris, Haig's Chief of Intelligence, assured him that he was killing Germans faster than his own men were being killed. Haig was also told that, once his troops managed to get onto the ridge above the little village of Passchendaele, they would find it 'as dry as a bone'. He turned to General Plumer to get him there.

Plumer was not ready to renew the attack until 20 September, when another massive artillery barrage signalled the start of yet another assault, as the Second Army men fought for control of the ridge above the Menin road. To an extent the attack succeeded – in places, the British line moved forward by up to a mile – but it did not achieve the breakthrough that Haig still believed was possible. Plumer attacked again at Polygon Wood and Broodseinde. The casualty lists grew longer. By the end of September, British losses amounted to 88,790 killed and wounded.

One more time

Haig called for one last all-out effort. The British attacked again – this time, without a preliminary bombardment in the hope that they would take the Germans by surprise. But the advancing British ran headlong into the Germans, who had been preparing to launch their own counter-attack. And the weather worsened again into the bargain. Both Plumer and Gough now appealed to Haig to halt further attacks, but he responded by throwing the Australians and then the Canadians into the battle.

At last, on 10 November, the Canadian Corps, supported by the Anzacs on their right and the Royal Naval Division on their left, succeeded in taking the ridge and the village of Passchendaele. The cost had been terrible – in the words of Corporal Baker of the 28th North-West Battalion: 'My impression was that we had won the ridge and lost the battalion.' Haig finally decided to bring the battle to a close. He had captured a barren wilderness. After nearly three-and-a-half months of fighting, the BEF had advanced just a few miles. Indeed, it had failed to secure all of the objectives that Haig had confidently predicted would be taken during the first day of the battle. It was worse, some said, than the Somme. Lieutenant Guy Chapman, serving in the Royal Fusiliers, recorded being told, as his unit moved up to the front, that the earlier battle was a 'picnic' compared to Passchendaele.

> ## 'Good God, did we really send men to fight in that?'
>
> General Sir Launcelot Kiggell, General Haig's Chief of Staff, on seeing conditions on the battlefield

False triumph at Cambrai

Haig, now a Field Marshal, told a frankly disbelieving Lloyd George that he had come close to breaking the morale of the German army, thanks to the vast number of casualties that had been inflicted on it. In fact, the losses were probably about equal on both sides at Passchendaele. Nevertheless, the commander-in-chief had one final card to play. Even while the battle was coming to a close, he authorised General Sir Julian Byng, commander of the Third Army, to launch yet another attack on the Germans – this time to the south at Cambrai.

Earlier in 1917, Byng had been in command of the Canadian Army Corps and won a major victory at Vimy Ridge. He planned his new assault equally carefully. There was to be no preliminary artillery barrage to alert the enemy that his troops were about to go over the top. Instead, his men would go into action led by more

THE WOUNDED AND THE DEAD

Stretcher-bearers wade knee-deep through much to recover casualties from the battlefield of Passchendaele near Ypres (left). For the wounded, this was just the start of a long journey. With the help of a specially laid railway (below), a workhorse hauls casualties from a field dressing station to the base hospital; from there the wounded were put on hospital trains and shipped back to Blighty. By August 1917 packed hospital trains were pulling into Charing Cross Station every hour.

Then there were the dead to be buried. Paddy King, a young Lieutenant in the East Lancashire Regiment, recalled how he and his fellow subalterns were each ordered to take out a section of men to perform this gruesome task: 'It was an appalling job. Some had been lying there for months and the bodies were in an advanced state of decomposition and some were so shattered that there was not much left.'

WONDER WEAPON
Soldiers ride on a Mark IV tank during an exercise. In 1917 the British launched their first mass tank attack at Cambrai, quickly punching through the enemy defences. Corporal Jack Dillon of the Tank Corps recalled: 'We got through all four German lines without any serious opposition. The tanks reached their objective quickly and when I caught up with them I found the crews sitting down drinking mugs of tea.' It was a great victory and the church bells in England were rung to celebrate, but there were no reserves available to follow up the attack and the Germans soon recovered the lost ground.

than 300 tanks – some equipped with fascines (bundles of brushwood) to bridge the German trenches. The attack did take the Germans by surprise and the tanks breached the much-vaunted Hindenburg Line in several places. Behind them, the Third Army advanced nearly four-and-a-half miles, losing just 5,000 men. For the Western Front, this was astonishing progress. It was a clear-cut victory. At home, the government ordered the church bells to be rung in celebration.

But the bells rang out too soon. With no reserves on hand to take advantage of the initial success, the British could not make their gains secure. Many of the tanks proved mechanically unreliable and broke down. Then a fierce German counter-attack drove the British back, retaking all the lost ground. By the time the fighting ended on 7 December, the BEF had suffered another 45,000 casualties. Haig's claims that enemy morale was at rock bottom had been shown to be false.

Better news from the Middle East

As 1917 drew to a close, there was little good news from the various war fronts to cheer up the folk back home. The one encouraging development was the British army's success in Palestine. On 9 December, General Sir Edmund Allenby's forces marched into Jerusalem, liberating the city from the Turks and bringing four centuries of Ottoman rule to an inglorious end. It was an ideal Christmas present for the war-weary nation. The government particularly welcomed the news, since the previous month it had authorised Arthur Balfour, now Foreign Secretary, to

BEHIND BARBED WIRE
German prisoners-of-war in a holding cage at Saint-Hilaire-au-Temple on the Marne (left). Haig was convinced that his attacks were wearing down the enemy. When Lloyd George visited him in August 1917, Haig arranged for the premier to be taken to visit a prisoner-of-war camp, where, he insisted, the Prime Minister would see for himself how the prisoners were exhibiting a marked 'deterioration in physique'. But before Lloyd George arrived at the camp, the prisoners were carefully sorted so that he was shown only the oldest, the most unfit and the most unprepossessing. Despite such precautions, Sir Maurice Hankey, the War Cabinet secretary who accompanied the Prime Minister on his inspection, recorded how the prisoners 'still sprang to attention as though under review by the Kaiser'.

INSPIRATIONAL HERO
Colonel T E Lawrence, better known to posterity as Lawrence of Arabia, poses with American newspaperman Lowell Thomas (on the right), who was to make Lawrence famous by publicising his exploits during the Arab revolt against the Turks. It was Thomas who was responsible for dubbing Lawrence 'the uncrowned king of Arabia'. A shy Oxford academic before the war, Lawrence became military liaison officer to the so-called Northern Arab Army, which successfully employed guerrilla tactics to pin down some 25,000 Turks in Transjordan and laid siege to Medina and its 4,000-strong garrison. With Sharif Hussein, Lawrence led the Arabs on a dramatic raid to take the coastal town of Aqaba.

write what was to become one of the most famous letters in history. The Balfour Declaration, as it became known, pledged Britain to 'view with favour the establishment in Palestine of a national home for the Jewish people'. It was the first official recognition of Zionist ambitions by a major power.

FLANDERS WINTER
A group of Tommies (left) huddle round an open fire by the roadside near Ypres. Winter in Flanders could be freezing. Sub-Lieutenant William Benham of the Royal Naval Division arrived in France in late 1917. He recorded how 'there was snow all over the Western Front. There had been a very severe frost and there were lots of frozen corpses that couldn't be moved or buried.' Despite the cold, many felt that it was better than what had gone before – the wettest autumn in living memory. Bombardier Palmer of the Royal Field Artillery recalled that 'it was mud, mud, everywhere; mud in the trenches, mud in front of the trenches, mud behind the trenches. Every shell-hole was a sea of filthy, oozing mud.'

ON THE DEFENSIVE

For the first time, some of the press began to turn against Haig. *The Times*, one of his staunchest supporters, now called for his replacement. Lloyd George would have been happy to oblige, but Haig still had powerful friends. He survived. In February 1918 the Prime Minister engineered General Sir William Robertson's removal by promoting him to be the chief military representative on the new Allied Supreme War Council at Versailles. When Robertson refused the post – and also declined the chance to stay in his current position but with reduced powers – he was packed off to take charge of Eastern Command. General Sir Henry Wilson, no friend of Haig's, took Robertson's place as head of the Imperial General Staff.

If Lloyd George could not sack Haig, he could at least clip his wings. 'Haig does not care how many men he loses,' the premier confided to close colleagues. 'He just squanders the lives of these boys.' Rather than give the commander-in-chief the replacements he was seeking, the Prime Minister kept as many men as he could away from the Western Front. In any event, the nation's manpower reserves were fast being exhausted. The government gave priority to the navy and the air force, followed by ship-building, airplane and tank manufacture, then food and timber production. The army was bottom of the list.

To make more recruits eligible, the age limit for conscripts was raised at the top end to 50 – 55 in the case of doctors – and lowered at the other end to 17 years 6 months. The newspapers launched a virulent campaign against the retention of men of military age in the Civil Service, labelling government departments 'the funkholes of Whitehall'. Duff Cooper, chafing at the bit in the Foreign Office, abandoned his London life for the rigours of an officers' training battalion. Eventually, he was commissioned into the Grenadier Guards. Not everyone was keen to see their sons going off to serve King and country. On the last day of embarkation leave before sailing for France, Private Reginald Backhurst of the Royal West Kent Regiment recalled that his mother 'followed me around the house until it was time for me to go. I got to the front door and she was crying and holding me round my knees – I was forced to drag her to the front gate.'

Looking for light relief

Yet life went on and people tried to make the best of it, even if the imposition of an entertainments tax had driven up the price of theatre, music hall and cinema tickets. Gramophone records were selling faster than ever. People in their thousands flocked to chuckle at the latest madcap silent exploits of Charlie Chaplin. In London, musicals like *Chu Chin Chow* and *The Maid of the Mountain* and revues like *The Bing Boys are Here* – with its hit song 'If You Were the Only Girl in the World' – played nightly to packed houses.

Music halls, dance halls and night clubs – a new social phenomenon – were all crowded. In London's Soho district, more than 150 night clubs flourished, despite raids by the police, who were urged to crack down on after-hours drinking. People also managed to go on holiday, even though the trains were overcrowded and often late. Sports lovers were not so fortunate, as some golfers in Eastbourne found in February 1918, when they were heavily fined for illegally using petrol to get to the golf course. Professional football had not been played since 1915, when the Football Association gave in to newspaper calls for its suspension. With the exception of the annual Newmarket meeting, horse-racing ceased as well. Even the annual Oxford and Cambridge boat race was abandoned.

GAS VICTIMS
Temporarily blinded by German mustard gas, casualties wait to be treated at an advanced dressing station near Bethune, during the battle of the Lys in April 1917. The photograph inspired the American painter John Singer Sargent, then serving as an official war artist, to paint his celebrated picture 'Gassed'. By 1918 both sides had built up deadly arsenals of shells employing various types of gas. So-called Green Cross shells contained phosgene, a lung irritant that was 16 times more lethal than the chlorine used when gas made its first appearance on the Western Front in 1915. Yellow Cross shells contained mustard gas, which severely burned the skin and had a terrible effect on the eyes. Soon, its victims were blind, helpless and in agonising pain. Furthermore, this insidious gas took up to ten days to disperse.

GERMANY'S FINAL THROW

In France, for the first time since 1915, Haig and the BEF were preparing for defence. In part this was due to shortages of fighting men, but the main reason was that, following the Russian Revolution in October 1917, Russia's new rulers had negotiated their own truce with Germany. Haig and the other Allied generals on the Western Front were all too aware that with Russia out of the war, thousands of German troops on the Eastern Front had been freed up to reinforce the German

armies in the West. The German High Command had come to a momentous decision. It would gamble everything on a final bid for victory before the Americans arrived in strength.

By March 1918, the Germans had amassed 191 divisions on the Western Front, faced by 178 on the Allied side. The big question for the British was where and when would they strike. The answer came on 21 March. The Fifth Army, under the command of General Sir Hubert Gough, was holding a long stretch of the line between Cambrai, St-Quentin and La Fere. Now Ludendorff, the German Quarter-Master General, and Hindenburg, the German army's supreme commander, unleashed their all-out effort along 50-miles of this front. Supported by more than 6,000 guns, the Germans attacked at 9.40am. Vastly outnumbered, Gough's men buckled under the ferocity of the onslaught. By the end of the day, the Germans had advanced up to eight miles and Gough had ordered a general retreat. This opened up a gap between his forces and the Third Army, on the British left under General Sir Julian Byng. The Germans were quick to take advantage of the opportunity. By 23 March, they had punched a 40-mile-wide hole in the British lines and were pouring forward into open country.

'With our backs to the wall'

As Gough fell back, Haig conferred anxiously with Petain. The German aim seemed clear: to drive the British and French apart and then advance up both banks of the River Somme, forcing the BEF back to the sea. Haig appealed for support, but Petain expected to be attacked at any moment in Champagne and had instructions from his government to protect Paris at all costs. He would give Haig what help he could, he said, but must follow his orders, even if that meant losing contact with the battered British armies. Haig was thunderstruck. He noted after the meeting that Petain struck him 'as very much upset, almost unbalanced'. When they heard what Petain had proposed, so were the British and French governments. For a while, it seemed to some as if the Kaiser might win the war after all.

At a hastily convened meeting at Doullens on 26 March, it was agreed that the situation was so desperate it required emergency action. The pugnacious Marshal Ferdinand Foch would be appointed to supreme command of the Allied armies. Meanwhile, the fighting raged on. The German thrust was eventually halted just short of Amiens, but they were by no means finished. Ludendorff turned on the British in Flanders, driving them back to the gates of Ypres. It was, Haig thought, the supreme crisis of the war. On 11 April, he issued a special order of the day to the BEF. 'There is no other course open to us but to fight it out', he exhorted his weary men.

There was no denying that the British had suffered terribly in the German onslaughts. Some were near the end of their tether. Lieutenant Frank Warren, of

> ## 'With our backs to the wall and believing in the justice of our cause each one of us must fight on to the end. The safety of our homes and the freedom of mankind alike depend on the conduct of each one of us at this critical moment.'
>
> **Field Marshall Douglas Haig, in a special order of the day to the BEF on 11 April, 1918**

TEMPORARY HALT
As they retreat through Flanders in spring 1918, British soldiers man a makeshift barricade in Bailleul in a vain attempt to check the advancing Germans. The town fell a few hours later to the German Sixth and Fourth Armies. Haig's troops finally managed to stop the enemy advance, but not before General Herbert Plumer's Second Army had been forced to withdraw from Passchendaele, the scene of so much sacrifice less than a year before. At home, the setbacks rekindled national determination. *The Times* advised: 'Be cheerful, face facts and work; attend volunteer drills regularly; cultivate your allotments; don't exceed your rations; don't repeat foolish gossip; don't listen to idle rumours and don't think you know better than Haig.'

the King's Rifle Corps, recorded how the troops under him were 'gaunt and weary, unwashed and with eight days' growth of beard … they obey orders mechanically, but sink fast asleep when opportunity offers.' Captain Thomas Westmacott, marshalling traffic across a vital bridge over the Somme, agreed. 'Towards midnight, about 500 men passed me on the bridge, deadbeat and hardly able to walk', he recalled. 'I shouted out "What battalion is that?" and a man I knew answered out of the darkness "It is what is left of the 17th Brigade".'

THE TIDE TURNS

Though the exhausted British Tommies could not know it, the tide of battle was starting to turn against Ludendorff. Further attacks on the BEF were repulsed as all along the line the troops managed to stand firm, resisting German attempts to exploit their initial successes. The advancing enemy was finally running out of steam. Ludendorff had failed to take Amiens. He had failed in Flanders, where Plumer had managed to blunt the German attack. Now, like a floundering whale, he threw his troops against the French in an attempt to break through to Paris. They came within 40 miles of the French capital, before being halted again on the Marne. Then, on 7 July, the French turned and counter-attacked, aided by the

Americans, who were now arriving in France at the rate of 250,000 a month. Ludendorff cancelled a projected offensive in Flanders. By 7 August, the Germans had been forced back almost to where they had started.

At home, the nation had rallied round the government, recognising that this was a time of national peril. Strikes practically ceased and productivity soared as the factories and munitions plants worked around the clock to churn out shells, guns and tanks to make up the British losses. Reinforcements were rushed to France. In Parliament, Lloyd George triumphantly trounced Asquith as the former premier attempted to censure him for misleading the House about the BEF's strength at the start of the offensive. Asquith also had to face some outrageous accusations in an extraordinary libel case brought by a celebrated dancer of the day, Maud Allen, against Pemberton Billing, an eccentric right-wing Independent MP. In making his defence against Allen's suit, Billing alleged that Asquith and his wife Margot were among 47,000 sexual 'perverts' listed in a German 'Black Book' and that they were being blackmailed into sabotaging the British war effort. It was all obvious nonsense, but the jury acquitted Billing in just half an hour.

Forward to victory

Haig judged that the moment had come to strike. The pessimists at home – Sir Henry Wilson, chief of the Imperial General Staff, and Winston Churchill, whom Lloyd George had brought back into the Cabinet as Minister for Munitions, were

VICTORS AND VANQUISHED
Brigadier-General Campbell, commander of the 137th Brigade, addresses his troops from the bridge over the St-Quentin canal at Riqueval (left), which they captured from the Germans on 29 September, 1918. The 137th Brigade was part of the 46th Division, which by the end of the day had taken 70 guns, more than 1,000 machine-guns and 4,200 prisoners. The demoralised Germans were by now surrendering en masse. Arthur Pick, a captain in the Leicestershire Regiment, recorded how he and his men entered an enemy trench and 'found the occupants unarmed, all their belongings packed up and ready to be marched back'. This British soldier (above) is offering a captured German a drink of water from his canteen, as other dispirited prisoners of war look on.

among them – might believe that the war would drag on into 1919 or even 1920. The commander-in-chief knew better – and this time he was right.

On 8 August, the BEF smashed through the German lines at Amiens, advancing eight miles and taking 15,000 prisoners. 'It was', said Ludendorff, 'the black day of the German army.' Between 21 August and 25 September, the British repeatedly attacked all along the Somme and as one victory succeeded another, the Germans fell back in disorder, their resistance crumbling with each new blow. Ludendorff hoped that his battered troops would be able to regroup behind the fortified Hindenburg Line and hold on for the winter, but on 29 September Haig's troops stormed across the Canal du Nord and broke through the German defences into open country. The day before, Ludendorff had told the Kaiser that Germany had reached the limit of its resources and that the war must be ended.

The Allied offensive continued, the French and Americans joining in along their sectors. Back in Germany, largely due to the Royal Navy's relentless blockade, people were starving. Revolution threatened as anti-war rioters took to the streets and the Imperial High Seas Fleet mutinied. Germany's allies – Austria-Hungary, Turkey and Bulgaria – were on the point of capitulation. On 9 November, the Kaiser was forced to abdicate. He fled to neutral Holland. Two days later, a new republican government in Berlin requested an armistice.

THE WAR IS OVER

The terms the Allies insisted on were harsh. Matthias Erzberger, the Centre Party politician charged with negotiating with Marshal Foch, failed to secure anything but the most trivial of concessions. Early in the morning of 11 November, 1918, as he signed the armistice document, he warned that 'a people of 70 million are suffering, but they are not dead'. Foch pointedly ignored him.

At the eleventh hour of the eleventh day of the eleventh month, the armies ceased fighting along the entire Western Front. Captain Cecil Gray, serving with the Canadian Machine Gun Corps, recorded how his troops took the news. 'Every man had a grin from ear to ear on his face. Nobody yelled or showed uncontained enthusiasm – everybody just grinned – and I think the cause was that the men couldn't find words to express themselves.' As the guns fell silent, birdsong was heard in no man's land, some said for the first time in four years. At long last, the Great War – the 'war to end all wars' – was over.

VICTORY AT LAST
British troops cheer as an officer reads the news that the armistice has been signed. Sergeant-Major Richard Tobin of the Royal Naval Division recorded how he felt: 'The Armistice came, the day we had dreamed of. The guns stopped, the fighting stopped. Four years of noise and bangs ended in silence … We were stunned … I should have been happy. I was sad. I thought of the slaughter, the hardships, the waste and the friends I had lost.' Lieutenant John Nettleton of the Rifle Brigade wrote: 'We were told that this was "the war to end war" and some of us at least believed it … All the mud, blood and bestiality only made sense on the assumption that it was the last time civilised man would ever have to suffer it.'

SOMETHING TO CELEBRATE

In the end, it was all over dramatically suddenly. Lieutenant Richard Dixon of the Royal Garrison Artillery was on leave on board a boat steaming into Folkestone harbour as the armistice came into effect. 'Every craft in there possessing a siren began to let it off', he recalled. 'We on board that leave boat were at first astounded by the noise – what was all the fuss about? But, as it went on and on and we steamed slowly and majestically to our appointed berth and beheld the crews of several ships cheering and waving at us, we tumbled to it. "Dickie", said Captain Brown, "The bloody war's over! It's over!" And it was.'

In London, five minutes before the war officially ceased, Lloyd George appeared in Downing Street, setting out for the Commons to announce the end of hostilities. 'At eleven o'clock', he told the cheering crowd, 'this war will be over. We have won a great victory and we are entitled to a bit of shouting.' He was the hero of the hour. He was cheered to the echo as he led peers and MPs from Parliament to St Margaret's Church, Westminster, to 'give thanks to Almighty God' for the nation's triumph.

Return of Big Ben

When Big Ben, which had been silent since August 1914, tolled out the hour, people erupted in spontaneous celebration. They flocked to Buckingham Palace, chanting 'We want the King!' George V duly obliged, appearing on the balcony with Queen Mary to wave to the vast crowd. Once back inside, he marked the occasion by breaking open a bottle of vintage brandy, his first alcohol since 1915. It had been laid down by the Prince Regent to celebrate Wellington's victory at Waterloo and tasted, the King noted, 'very musty'.

All across the land, alerted by the ringing of the church bells, people poured into the streets. It was one massive party. Everyone was kissing everyone else. Perched on top of a bus trapped by the crowds between the Royal Exchange and the Mansion House in the City of London, Florence Baker, a VAD at Bethnal Green Military Hospital, had a bird's eye view. 'Well, if everywhere else is like London', she wrote to her mother, 'then all England must be mad!' Indeed, the celebrations were universal. Lieutenant John Nettleton, who was home from the front on leave, went down to the promenade in normally sedate Cheltenham, where he saw 'the people milling about the streets, singing and dancing'.

IT'S PEACE AT LAST
A crowd in London celebrates (right) as news of the armistice spread in various ways. Fireworks known as maroons – used during the war as air-raid warnings – were set off now to alert people to the good news. Boy Scouts cycled around the city blowing the 'All Clear' on their bugles, and Big Ben struck the hour for the first time in more than four years. Just as they had on the day that war broke out, huge crowds gathered outside Buckingham Palace, calling for the King and Queen. The royal couple came out onto the balcony, Queen Mary carrying a small flag, which according to one observer she waved 'violently'. Another recalled how the 'buses had to cease running for the soldiers seized the [sign] boards from the sides and front to help make a big bonfire in Trafalgar Square'. People were celebrating everywhere. In Brackley, Northamptonshire, they hung effigies of the Kaiser and his son, the German Crown Prince, in the street. In Glasgow, Thomas Livingstone 'took Agnes and Tommy [his wife and young son] into town to see the sights'. It was, he recorded in his diary, 'the greatest day in the history of the world'.

'… it was impossible to drive through Trafalgar Square … the crowd danced under lights turned up for the first time for four years – danced so thickly that the heads, the faces, were like a field of golden corn moving in a dark wind … They revolved and whirled … with a kind of religious fervour, as if it were a duty.'

Osbert Sitwell, writer and cartoonist, recalling Armistice night in London, November 1918

Mourning the fallen

But not everyone felt like celebrating. Duff Cooper, who was also home on leave, felt 'unable to take part in the enthusiasm. This was the moment to which I had looked forward for four years and, now it had arrived, I was overcome by melancholy. Amid the dancing, the cheering, the waving of flags, I could only think of my friends who were dead.' His mood may have been affected by the fact that he was suffering from the first symptoms of influenza. Around 228,000 were to die in the influenza pandemic that swept the country over the following months. He was one of the lucky ones who lived through the flu as well as the war.

Many others had mixed feelings, too. Victoria Smith, a schoolgirl at the time, recalled how she and her classmates were let out of school as the church bells pealed. She saw 'the geography mistress, head in hands, quietly crying. She had been widowed by the war.' The author Vera Brittain – who had lost her fiancé, brother and two close friends to the war – shared the same emotions. Peace, she wrote, 'had come too late for me. All those with whom I had been really intimate were gone: not one remained to share with me the heights and depths of my memories.' In Shropshire, the mother of the war poet Wilfred Owen had particular reason to grieve. An hour after the armistice, a War Office telegram arrived informing her that her son had been killed a week earlier, mown down by German machine guns as he attempted to lead his men across the River Sambre.

Bring the boys home!

As for the men at the front, some did not know how to react at first. Many had presumed that they would not live to see the end of the war. Now, the thoughts of most turned to home – they wanted to get out of khaki and back into civilian life as quickly as possible. Demobilisation, though, turned out to be a cumbersome process. It did not start until 9 December and the slowness with which it was carried out – at least initially – fostered active discontent among the now reluctant

HOME TO STAY

Soldiers back from France and on their way to be demobilised queue to change their francs for pounds at a bureau de change in Waterloo Station. Many protested that the whole process of getting them home was taking too long. The *Daily Herald* called on the government to 'send the boys home'. The article continued: 'The war is not officially "over", but everyone knows that in fact it is over. Munition-making has stopped; motorists can joy ride; the King has a drink; society has had its victory ball.' It concluded: 'Danger of too rapid demobilisation? Bunkum!' Thousands felt the same.

soldiery. Many wanted to avoid the risk of being posted to Germany, as part of the forces which were to be sent to occupy Cologne and the western part of the Rhineland. Still more dreaded the prospect of being despatched to Russia to support the so-called White Russians in their attempt to suppress the revolution.

Trouble started in January 1919, when 10,000 soldiers at Folkestone refused to board the ships standing ready to take them back to France. Protests followed at Dover and Brighton. Soldiers picketed government officers in Whitehall, carrying placards with slogans such as 'No more red tape' and 'We want civvie suits'. The most serious incident took place at Calais, when thousands of troops rioted, took over their transit camp and refused to return to their units. Haig, convinced that the rioters were being 'led astray by Bolshevik agitators', actually proposed that the ringleaders be shot. Government action was needed. Winston Churchill, now Secretary of State for War and Air Minister, came up with a new scheme to speed up demobilisation. Soon, according to him, men were being released 'at the enormous rate of 13,000 or 14,000 daily'. By the end of 1919, only 125,000 men eligible for release from the army were still waiting.

Putting women back in their place

At home, women were being demobilised with little ceremony. Women workers on government contracts received two weeks pay in lieu of notice, a free rail pass and an 'out of work donation'. This was set at 20s a week for the first 13 weeks of unemployment and 15s for the next 13 weeks. After that, it stopped. Some were not sorry to see the women go. The *Leeds Mercury* welcomed the dismissal of the city's female bus conductors. 'Their record of duty well done is seriously blemished by their habitual and aggressive incivility … Their shrewish behaviour will remain one of the unpleasant memories of the war's vicissitudes.' The only areas in which women were really successful in keeping their wartime jobs were in shops and offices. Many were forced back into domestic service.

FIGHTING SPANISH FLU

A masked cleaner sprays the top of a bus with disinfectant during the great influenza pandemic of 1918-19. 'Spanish flu', as it was termed, killed more than 200,000 in Britain and an estimated 50 million worldwide – far more than had been killed on all sides in the entire war. The first wave of the pandemic struck in the summer of 1918, the second that autumn and winter and the third in early 1919. Unlike other pandemics, in which children and the old had been the main victims, this time it was largely young adults who were most at risk. Everyone was terrified of contracting the disease. *The Times* labelled it 'the great plague of influenza'. In Ireland, Molly Deery, a Donegal resident, recalled that 'people were told to keep to one side of the road if someone in a house had it' The *Dungannon Democrat* reported that 'it can be seen that this is no ordinary influenza but some form of disease which … baffles the best skill of medical men'.

ADJUSTING TO PEACETIME

In a general election held in December 1918, Lloyd George and the Coalition were swept back to power with a staggering 478 seats in the Commons – 335 Unionists, 133 Coalition Liberals and 10 Coalition Labour MPs. Non-Coalition Labour held 63 seats, but the official Liberals were reduced to a rump of 28: Asquith lost his seat in East Fife to a Coalition candidate. It was the first election in which women were allowed to vote. No one doubted that they had earned the right through their efforts in the war, though the franchise was limited to women over 30 and they also had to be ratepayers or married to ratepayers.

The Irish Nationalist Party was also decimated, winning just seven seats. Sinn Fein, with its demand for immediate Irish independence, took 73 seats. The Sinn Feiners – including Countess Markowitz, the first woman to be elected as an MP – refused to take their seats in Westminster. The following year, 29 of them met in Dublin, proclaiming a republic. War with Britain was the inevitable result.

'Homes fit for heroes'

Lloyd George looked impregnable and set for a long term of office – even Andrew Bonar Law, the Unionist leader, commented that he 'can be Prime Minister for life, if he likes'. But in practice, his difficulties were mounting. The Unionist MPs, on whom the government depended, wanted a speedy return to pre-war normality. This meant swiftly dismantling state controls, allowing private enterprise to operate freely once more, the reduction of taxes and abandonment of what they regarded as wasteful welfare schemes. Amid much grumbling, the school leaving age was raised from 12 to 14, but the ambitious housing programme of 'homes fit for heroes' that Lloyd George had promised – the aim was to build 500,000 new homes in three years – was an early casualty of the drive for economic austerity.

'Make Germany pay!'

Britain emerged from the conflict as a debtor nation. In order to pay for the war, it had sold 25 per cent of its overseas investments. It had also borrowed prodigiously and now owed more than £1,350 million – most of it to the USA. The question was how would this staggering debt ever be repaid? The hard-faced Unionists massed on the back benches believed they had the answer – 'Make Germany pay!' Sir Eric Geddes, First Lord of the Admiralty, told voters: 'We will get everything out of Germany that you can squeeze out of a lemon and a bit more. I will squeeze her until the pips squeak.' At first, Lloyd George seemed inclined to go along with him. At a meeting in Bristol, he declared 'we propose to recover the entire cost of the war from Germany'. It was a popular rallying cry, but like another of his pledges – to bring the Kaiser to trial – it was one he came to regret.

Luckily for Lloyd George, the plan to put the Kaiser in the dock came to nothing when the Dutch refused to give him up for trial. But the pledge to make the Germans pay the bill for the war would not go away. It bedevilled the peacemakers when they met in Paris, in January 1919, to discuss the terms to be imposed on their defeated enemy. President Wilson, anxious to gain support for his cherished idea of a League of Nations, had sailed from the USA to be among

SIGNING THE VERSAILLES TREATY
Allied officers and diplomats stand on chairs and tables in the antechamber to the Hall of Mirrors at Versailles, trying to get a glimpse of the peace treaty being signed inside on 28 June, 1919. Two days later Lloyd George made a formal announcement to the House of Commons that the treaty had been concluded. He received a standing ovation, but even before he spoke nearly every MP had risen to cheer him and to sing 'God Save the King'. In the debate that followed, the Prime Minister described the terms of the treaty as 'stern but just'. Its aim, he told MPs, was to 'compel Germany, in so far as it is in her power, to restore, to repair and redress'. But there were some who doubted even then the wisdom of the treaty's severity. The writer Harold Nicolson, a promising young diplomat, wrote that 'the real crime is the reparations and indemnity chapter, which is immoral and senseless'.

STREET PARTY
A children's street party in full swing on the Isle of Dogs in London's East End. It was held to mark Peace Day – 19 July, 1919 – though the Treaty of Versailles, which officially brought the war to an end, was signed on 28 June. The centrepiece of the occasion was a great military parade through the heart of the capital. Thousands gathered in the streets to cheer. The only moment of quiet came when the troops marched down Whitehall past the temporary Cenotaph that Sir Edwin Lutyens had designed for the occasion. 'The memorial was most impressive', reported the *Sunday Times*, 'with its summit crowned by a great laurel wreath, holding in place a Union Jack that was draped loosely above the monument. On the steps were a number of tiny home-made wreaths and humble garden flowers, placed there by loving hands.' The temporary structure was replaced the following year by a permanent one, officially unveiled on the second anniversary of Armistice Day.

MINISTERING ANGELS
Nurses and soldiers honour war heroine Edith Cavell as her coffin returns to Dover in May 1919 (left), shortly to be reburied at Norwich Cathedral. Cavell had been arrested by the Germans in Brussels for helping prisoners to escape. She was tried by a military tribunal, found guilty and shot in October 1915. The night before her execution, she told the chaplain who visited her in her cell that 'Standing as I do in view of God and Eternity, I realise that patriotism is not enough. I must have no hatred or bitterness for anyone.' She wanted to be remembered, she said, simply as 'a nurse who tried to do her duty'. Many thousands of women volunteered to serve as nurses, including Vera Brittain (above), who became a VAD after the deaths of her brother and fiancé at the front. She later wrote *Testament of Youth*, in which she condemned the futility of the war but took some consolation from the opportunities for emancipation which came to women as a result.

them. Wilson, Georges Clemenceau (the French premier) and Lloyd George wrangled over many points, one of them being the question of reparations. Lloyd George now argued for reducing the amount that Germany would be forced to pay, but the French refused to budge. The consequences would be catastrophic.

The peace treaty was signed at Versailles at the end of June and the severity of its financial clauses were swiftly denounced by John Maynard Keynes, a brilliant young Cambridge economist. His *Economic Consequences of the Peace* became a best-seller. But others attacked the treaty for not being harsh enough. Marshall Foch, who boycotted the signing ceremony in protest, spoke for the diehards when he grumbled: 'This is not peace. It is an armistice for 20 years.'

An uncertain future

Despite the pessimists, the British were in no doubt that they had won a remarkable victory. General Smuts, premier of South Africa and a member of Lloyd George's War Cabinet, told his fellow colonial leaders that the empire had 'emerged from the war quite the greatest power in the world, and it is only unwisdom or unsound policy that could rob her of that great position'. With the acquisition of League of Nations mandates over Palestine, Tanganyika and Iraq as part of the peace settlement, the British Empire reached its greatest territorial

ALCOCK AND BROWN – NON-STOP ACROSS THE ATLANTIC

Intrepid aviators John Alcock (on the left) and Arthur Brown (right) were both military pilots during the war. They achieved lasting fame by becoming the first to fly non-stop across the Atlantic Ocean. They made their historic flight in a converted Vickers Vimy IV bomber, powered by twin Rolls-Royce engines, and are seen here enjoying a celebratory breakfast after the event. They took off from Newfoundland early in the afternoon of 14 June, 1919, getting into the air before their rivals, who were still test-flying their Handley-Page aircraft. The flight was cold and arduous; more than once they flew upside down in dense freezing fog, while Brown crawled out onto the wings to chip off ice. After sixteen-and-a-half hours of flying, they reached their destination – Ireland. The landing, in a bog, was less than perfect (below). People on the ground had tried to warn them and direct them to a nearby airstrip, but Alcock and Brown just thought they were being greeted and waved cheerfully back. Their rewards were national acclaim, a £10,000 prize put up by the *Daily Mail* and knighthoods from the King.

extent. The great victory parade in London in July 1919 seemed to bear Smuts out. For hour after hour, the crowds watched the participants pass by – stalwart blue-jackets from the greatest navy in the world and soldiers from the largest army the British had ever raised. Australians, New Zealanders, Canadians, Indians and representatives from all the colonies took part. The guns that had deluged the enemy with millions of shells trundled by, as well as tanks, the new war-winning weapon pioneered by British inventiveness. The Royal Air Force staged a fly-past. With more than 20,000 aircraft it, too, was the biggest in the world.

The celebrations would be short-lived as peace brought its own problems. A brief post-war boom soon turned to bust and thousands of ex-servicemen found themselves on the dole. Lloyd George's famous promise of 'a land fit for heroes to live in' would come back to haunt him, and he and his government had other worries. Bolshevism seemed to be spreading westward from Russia, while in Ireland civil war loomed. Britain faced an uncertain future. In winning its great victory, had it sowed the seeds of its own decay and decline?

GRIM REALITY

A demobilised NCO wears his discharge
medals on a threadbare suit (right), while
two disabled veterans make paper flowers
for the Ypres League at a workshop in
London's Old Kent Road (left). Roughly a
quarter of the men who returned home
from the war were suffering some degree
of physical disability; lost limbs were
common. The government eventually
agreed to pay pensions, but the rates were
mean and set on a sliding scale. A fully
disabled man got £1 5s a week, with an
extra 2s 6d for each child. It was not until
1921 that the Pensions Act raised disability
pensions to a semi-respectable level. Even
for the fully fit, jobs were hard to come by,
especially after the brief post-war boom
fizzled out. George Coppard, who had
served as a machine-gunner, remembered
bitterly 'Lloyd George and company had
been full of talk about making the country
fit for heroes to live in, but it was just so
much hot air. No practical steps were taken
to rehabilitate the broad mass of demobbed
men ... there were no jobs for the "heroes"
who haunted the billiard halls as I did.'

1920s

1920s

A LAND FIT FOR HEROES?

Britain at the dawn of the Twenties was a nation lost in grief and confusion. Barely a year had passed since the Armistice had brought the Great War to an end and the after-echoes of the guns still hung in the air. Bereavement was an almost universal reality. Everybody had lost a friend or a brother, a father or a son in the war. Each family's sorrow was a private affair, but Britain as a whole had yet to grasp the cataclysm that had overtaken it. Life could not return to something resembling normality until the country came to terms with its monstrous loss.

SOLEMN OCCASION The coffin of the unknown soldier is escorted to Westminster Abbey by Field Marshal Douglas Haig, who had commanded the British Expeditionary Force during the war. In the Twenties, Haig devoted himself to the welfare of ex-servicemen.

A DAY OF REMEMBRANCE

The British people had a need to mourn as never before and out of their longing grew an idea for a monument, a collective headstone, for the nation's many dead. That yearning found a focus when the architect Edwin Lutyens was commissioned to build a temporary structure on Whitehall as part of the victory parade held to mark the completion of the Versailles Treaty. His Cenotaph or 'empty tomb' was designed and built of wood and plaster in just two weeks. On Peace Day – 19 July, 1919 – the serried ranks of Allied troops marched past and saluted, and through that act of homage Lutyen's piece of stage scenery unexpectedly took on a well-nigh magical significance. 'Near the memorial there were moments of silence when the dead seemed very near', wrote the correspondent of the *Morning Post*, 'when one almost heard the passage of countless wings. Were not the fallen gathering in their hosts to receive their comrades' salute and take their share in the triumph they had died to win?'

In the days that followed, people came in their thousands to the Cenotaph and placed wreaths upon it, as if it were a place of burial. The austere design of the memorial was quickly acknowledged as a perfect expression of the national feeling. 'Simple, grave and beautiful', said *The Times*, 'it has been universally recognised as a just and fitting memorial of those who have made the greatest sacrifice. And the flowers which have daily been laid upon it since the march show the strength of its appeal to the imagination.'

A permanent memorial

By the end of the month the government had decreed that a permanent stone Cenotaph should be built and unveiled on the second anniversary of the Armistice: 11 November, 1920. As the plans were being laid another proposal emerged, the brainchild of an army chaplain named David Railton who had served at the front. Railton wrote of how he first conceived the idea one evening in 1916: 'I came back from the line at dusk. We had just laid to rest the mortal remains of a comrade. I went to a billet near Armentières. At the back of the billet was a small garden, and in the garden a grave. At the head of the grave there stood a rough cross of white wood. On the cross was written in deep black-pencilled letters, "An Unknown British Soldier" … I remember how still it was. Even the guns seemed to be resting. How that grave caused me to think. Later on I wrote to Sir Douglas Haig to ask if the body of an "unknown" comrade might be sent home.'

Railton received no reply, but the thought stayed with him. In August 1920 he sent his proposal to Bishop Ryle, the Dean of Westminster, who passed the letter on to the King and the Prime Minister, David Lloyd George. The King thought the suggestion somewhat superfluous, but Lloyd George saw the genius in it: here was a chance to create a rite that would have national and personal significance for all British citizens and perhaps go some little way to healing the wounds of war.

In October the proposal to re-inter one anonymous soldier in Westminster Abbey was approved and the process of selecting his remains was set in motion. On 7 November, 1920, four work parties in France were sent out into the main British battlefields of the war – the Aisne, Somme, Arras and Ypres. Each party

GUARD OF HONOUR
The body of Britain's unknown soldier at the Channel port of Boulogne in France, with a combined guard of honour drawn from both British and French forces.

Marshal Ferdinand Foch, head of the French army and (from March 1918 to the end of the war) supreme commander of the Allied armies, came to the quayside to pay his last respects. He can be seen, standing with head bowed, just behind the two French soldiers at the rear of the carriage. Following a brief ceremony, the coffin was carried on board HMS *Verdun* for the short sea voyage to England.

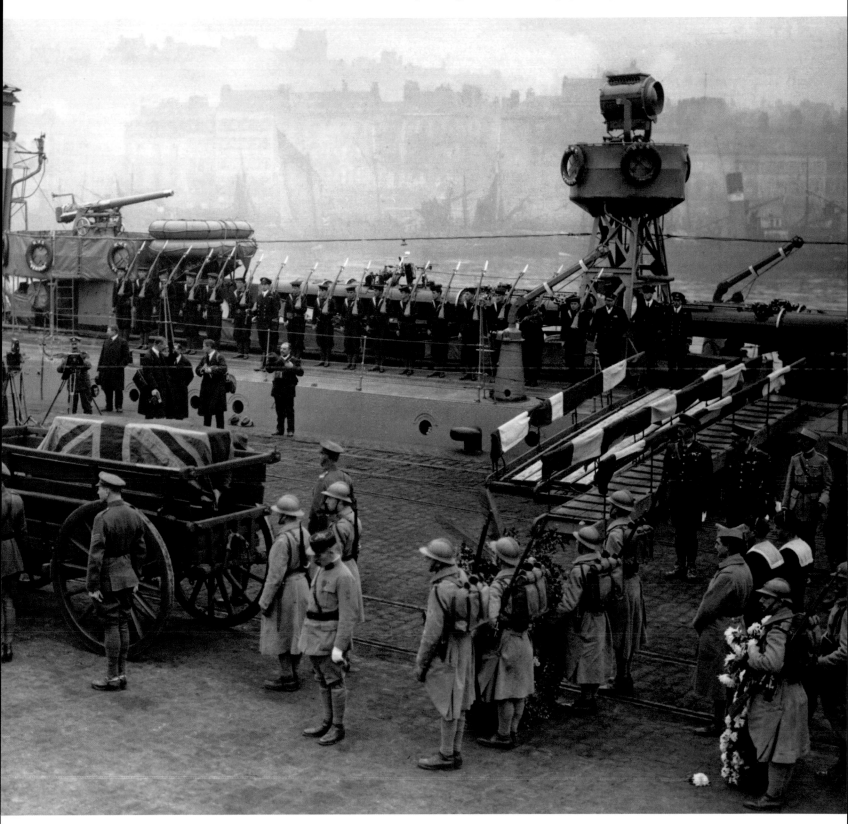

exhumed a body, which was examined to make sure that it was unidentifiable but definitely British. The four bodies were laid in plain deal coffins and placed in the chapel at St Pol. At the stroke of midnight, Brigadier General L J Wyatt, then commander of British forces in France, entered the chapel and laid a hand on one of the four coffins. That coffin was sent to Boulogne, where it was placed inside a beautifully crafted sarcophagus, made from an oak that had grown in the park of Hampton Court Palace. The oak casket was sealed with heavy iron bands, which also held in place a crusader sword from the personal collection of George V, who by now had warmed to the idea. The body of the unknown soldier was carried back to Britain on a destroyer, where it was met with a 19-gun salute from the battlements of Dover Castle. On 10 November the coffin was conveyed by train to London. All along the way people thronged the stations, standing in silence, heads bared, to pay their respects as the funeral train passed by.

Laying the 'Unknown Soldier' to rest

The next day, Sunday 11 November, 1920, two solemn ceremonies took place. Early in the morning, at Victoria Station, the coffin of the unknown soldier was set on a gun carriage harnessed to six black horses, and draped in a Union Jack that had been carried through the war and was literally 'dyed with the blood of British soldiers'. An ordinary soldier's tin helmet was placed on top and the coffin then began its long procession through the huge crowds towards Westminster Abbey.

THE EMPTY TOMB
The giant Union Jacks fall away from the Cenotaph in the moment of unveiling on the second national Remembrance Day, Sunday 11 November, 1920. The word cenotaph comes from the Greek meaning 'empty tomb'. When the body of the deceased was lost, the ancient Greeks would sometimes perform a symbolic funeral and bury an empty sarcophagus. After the Great War, when so many thousands of men had died and been lost without trace, the form of the cenotaph seemed singularly appropriate. Lutyens' monument was much praised for the classic simplicity of its design, though some critics thought its symbolism inappropriately unchristian.

The Times recorded that it was a 'perfect late autumn day … with a touch of frost in the air, a veiled blue sky, and sun that would soon break through in full splendour.' The procession took nearly two hours to reach Whitehall, where it was met by George V. As Big Ben struck the eleventh hour, the King pressed a button and the flags that covered the Cenotaph fell away to reveal the monument 'clean and wonderful in its naked beauty. Big Ben ceased, and the very pulse of Time stood still. In silence, broken only by a nearby sob, the great multitude bowed its head. Over all the Empire and the world's seas, men's hands had dropped from their toil and voices were hushed, and cities and peoples stood frozen.'

The King fell in behind the coffin, which proceeded the short distance to the Abbey. A thousand war widows waited inside, along with a hundred recipients of the Victoria Cross. There were no foreign dignitaries in the congregation. The coffin was borne to a grave at the west end of the nave and lowered gently into the ground. The King scattered some French soil on top, and the pit was later filled with earth – 100 sandbags' full – brought from the battlefields of Flanders. The ceremony was over by noon, but for the rest of the day and for many days after people queued to file down Whitehall to Lutyen's empty tomb, then on to the fresh grave in the Abbey. The stream of mourners still flowed in the middle of the next week, by which time the Cenotaph was practically obscured by the many thousands of wreaths and bouquets.

MOUNTAIN OF FLOWERS
The unveiling of the permanent Cenotaph on Sunday 11 November, 1920, was followed by a mass pilgrimage of mourners. All that day, throughout the night and the whole of the next day, the queue to file past never disappeared. It was at its shortest in the small hours of Monday morning, but by midday the line of people stretched all the way up Whitehall to Trafalgar Square and back again. By midweek, the monument was almost buried beneath the thousands of fading bouquets.

LEST WE FORGET

Memorials to the war dead sprung up all over Britain in the course of the Twenties. Some of the most poignant and impressive memorials were not on British soil, but were erected across the Channel in Flanders, where half a generation of British youth had met its death. One such monument is the Menin Gate (top), on the outskirts of Ypres in Belgium. The names of Commonwealth soldiers who were lost and have no grave were to be carved on the walls of its vast Hall of Memory, but on completion it was found that there was not nearly enough space. Although 55 thousand men are commemorated here, the names of another 34 thousand were inscribed on the Tyne Cot memorial near Passchendaele.

War memorials in Britain tended to be local, and so were on a much smaller scale. Some, like the main memorial in the London borough of Southwark (centre), took the form of statuary: a determined Tommy wading through the mud, or a grim-faced sentry in a cape, his head bowed in sorrow. The most modest forms of war memorial were also the most common: a Celtic cross in a churchyard, as in the Bodmin Police Memorial (bottom), a plaque in a railway station or town hall, or a simple obelisk on a village green. And always a sad list of names, perhaps accompanied by a biblical verse: 'Their name liveth for evermore'.

'It can be said of each one: "He is not missing; he is here."'

Field Marshal Lord Plumer, at the unveiling of the Menin Gate, 1927

SHORT BOOM, LONG SLUMP

That Remembrance Day in 1920 was perhaps the last moment of true national unity in what was to be a decade of political turmoil and industrial strife. In the election campaign of 1918, Lloyd George had said: 'We have just emerged from a great peril. And now what is our task? To make Britain a fit country for heroes to live in. Don't let us waste this victory merely in ringing joybells.' He intended his remark as a call to arms for a time of peace, a statement of the challenge that lay ahead. But what people grabbed hold of was the undertaking – slightly misremembered then and ever since – to create a 'land fit for heroes'.

For a time it seemed that the government was keeping its word. For two years after the war, the country enjoyed an economic boom. Factories of all sorts had been kept busy for years by government contracts, and had turned a good profit for their owners. Now that the fighting was over, industry switched to producing consumer goods for the masses. Many families had seen their incomes swell to twice the size or more during the years that the womenfolk were engaged in paid work for the war effort and the men's pay packets – earned in the trenches – piled up at home. Some soldiers came back with gratuities of up to £40, at a time when the average weekly wage was about £2. The time had come to spend, and the shops were piled high with things to buy.

From promises to reality

The boom was short-lived, an illusion that brought no lasting good. It would take more than a post-war spending spree to turn the country into a land for returning heroes. For one thing, the main beneficiaries of the cash-rich years were not the returning officers and enlisted men, but the people who had never gone away. For the veterans of Flanders, Lloyd George's words had seemed to promise two things: a place to live and a job to earn a living by. As it turned out, neither was forthcoming. In the year up to March 1920 only 715 new homes were built in England and Wales, even though the government estimated that 600,000 were needed. Some ex-soldiers camped out in abandoned railway carriages or hastily constructed canvas huts, barely larger than a shed and no warmer or drier than a tent. There were even some instances – literally echoing the words of Viscount Long – in which ex-soldiers did end up making their homes in disused pigsties.

> 'To let them [demobbed men] come back from the horrible waterlogged trenches to something little better than a pigsty here would be criminal, a negation of all that has been said.'
>
> Viscount Walter Long

The search for work

The crisis in housing was matched by an equally acute and disappointing shortage of jobs. The disillusion over employment prospects was eloquently expressed by one ex-battery commander, writing in February 1920: 'During the War, all those who put on the King's uniform had a great access of friends. We were heroes in

WITHIN THESE WALLS

As late as 1926 this woman and her five children were living in a cell in Worcester's disused prison. They were among the many victims of the chronic shortage of homes. The loss of skilled builders during the war, combined with the slow demobilisation of those who did survive, contributed to the housing crisis after the war. Yet local authorities had an obligation to house the destitute – hence the strange turn of events that led to this family and others going to a jail, albeit one with an unlocked door.

LOOKING FOR A LIVING

Returning servicemen, young and old, often found that they were all but unemployable. Former officers could be in financial straits almost as dire as those faced by the working-class soldiers who had served under them. These two officers (right), both with families to support, were also making a political point as they operated a hurdy-gurdy on Whitehall. Some ex-officers made a living by hiring themselves out as dancing partners at swish London venues. And it was said in jest that you could not get a job as a West End chorus boy unless you were the holder of the Military Cross. Some took work as street peddlers, reduced to a role at the very bottom of the retail hierarchy. Old soldiers often wore their campaign medals on their coats, hoping that sympathy might elicit more sales from the public. It was little short of begging. Matches were one of the most widely sold commodities – everyone needed matches to light the stove or their cigarettes.

those days … When at last we came home, were demobilised and doffed our uniforms, we realised how much our welcome had depended on the glamour of our clothes, with all that they implied. In mufti we were no longer heroes, we were simply "unemployed" … I know there is no "right to work" in the economic sense, but the community owes a debt which it can and ought to pay … Are you going to withhold payment until it is too late?' The dismay of many ex-soldiers turned to anger as unemployment began to rise. The jobless count passed a million in 1921, never again to dip below that point at any time during the decade.

'A man who is frankly seeking a job is not a welcome guest.'

Ex-battery commander writing in February 1920

Men in paid work were in a barely less precarious position than their workless fellow. As the country and its economy returned to peacetime rhythms, employers in the heavy industries – the coalmines in particular – assumed that they could reimpose the Victorian conditions that had existed before the war. In particular, the mine-owners wanted to go back to the system where wages varied from one mine to another, depending on the varying overhead costs of extracting coal. The unions saw this as an attempt to divide and rule, and were determined to resist. In the spring of 1921, a 'Triple Alliance' of miners, railwaymen and transport workers downed tools. A general strike loomed and the government declared a state of emergency as political rallies turned into pitched battles between strikers and the massed ranks of police. Armed soldiers

were posted on the streets of many big cities. In the event, the nationwide stoppage did not materialise, but even so a staggering 89 million working days were lost to industrial action in the course of the year.

Time for a British revolution?

In their comfortable suburban homes, shopkeepers and bank managers quietly worried that a revolution was brewing, that a hard core of British Bolsheviks were waiting for their moment to stage a coup, just as their Russian comrades had done four years before. There was certainly enough rumour and circumstantial evidence of a 'Red Peril' to frighten the jittery bourgeoisie. For example, when Remembrance Day came round again on 11 November, 1921, one wreath laid at the monument bore the bitter inscription 'To the dead victims of Capitalism, from the living victims of Capitalism' – it was deemed offensive and removed by police. One decorated soldier marched down Whitehall wearing not his medals, but the paper tickets he had got in exchange when he was forced to pawn them.

WORKERS OF THE WORLD
The British Communist Party was founded in 1920. One of its most effective agitators was Wal Hannington, seen here addressing a crowd of the unemployed in Trafalgar Square in 1922 (above). Though still in his early twenties, Hannington was a leading light in the National Unemployed Workers' Movement, which organised many of the hunger marches that took place in the early Twenties. He was arrested in 1925 under the 1797 Incitement to Mutiny Act, and sentenced to a year's imprisonment.

AT THE END OF THE ROAD
David Lloyd George (right) was described by the economist John Maynard Keynes as 'this extraordinary figure of our time, this siren, this goat-footed bard, this half-human visitor to our age from the hag-ridden magic and enchanted woods of Celtic antiquity'. Perhaps this strangely overwrought description was merely a hostile way of saying that Lloyd George was a charismatic Welshman in a position of authority over Englishmen. Winston Churchill, who knew Lloyd George well, said more generously that he was 'the greatest master of getting things done and putting things through that I ever knew'. But by the end of his premiership, that practical talent for achieving results had deserted Lloyd George. As a statesman, he failed to persuade the great nations to sort out the international chaos left at the end of the war. As Prime Minister, he could not mitigate the effects of the economic crisis that engulfed the country. By the time this photograph of him was taken, in September 1923, he had been out of power for almost a year.

CHILDREN OF THE MINES
The life of a child in the mining villages of the north was always tough, made tougher in times of strikes and disasters. Children as young as this girl in Wigan – photographed during the miners' strike of 1921 – were often expected not only to look after younger brothers and sisters, but also to bring lunch to the pithead. In the evenings they were often turfed out onto the street so that their fathers had the space and privacy to fill a tub and wash off the grime of the pit.

IDLE HANDS

Striking miners in Wigan take the children to hear a little backstreet oratory. In March 1921 Britain's mine owners decided they could no longer sustain the relatively high wages that had been paid during the war. Unilaterally, they cut miners' wages and locked the gates to any workers who did not agree to their new terms. The miners' union called its members out on strike, fully expecting the dockers and railway workers to come out in sympathy. But not for the last time the miners had to go it alone.

Close to the Cenotaph, members of the newly minted British Communist Party distributed newspapers to individuals in the unhappy crowds.

The year 1922 saw the first of the hunger marches that would later become such a feature of the 1930s. But the spectacle of long columns of men marching on London could easily be interpreted as a threat to law and order. The marchers were desperate, hungry men asking for help; but with their grim, pinched faces and red banners they looked worryingly like the vanguard of the proletariat, flexing its revolutionary muscle. It certainly appeared that way to Prime Minister Lloyd George, who remarked darkly that his government 'could not take risks with labour. If we did, we should at once create an enemy within our own borders, and one which would be better provided with dangerous weapons than Germany.'

WORK AND PLAY

'Hopping' was an annual holiday for poor urban children, and a chance for their mothers to do some paid work. As many as a quarter of a million people migrated to Kent at the end of August for the hop-picking season. About a third of them came from the East End of London. Families were generally accommodated in communal huts made of corrugated iron. But the regiments of hoppers spent much of their leisure time as well as their working hours in the open air – resting, eating food cooked on an open fire and giving the children a scrub with a soapy wet flannel.

The fall of Lloyd George

In the end it was not the workers who brought down the government, but the Conservative members of Lloyd George's parliamentary coalition. The Tories had never liked or trusted the 'Welsh wizard' – he was a Liberal, after all – but they had allied themselves to him at a time when his claim to be 'the man who won the war' still rang true. Four years on, he was looking like the man who had lost the peace. In the summer of 1922, it became known that Lloyd George had amassed huge political funds by selling honours to anyone who could afford them: knighthoods could be had for £12,000, baronetcies for £30,000. In October the parliamentary Conservative party voted to cut their links with the Prime Minister. It was the end of the line for Lloyd George – and also for the Liberal Party, which has not headed a government in Britain since.

THE HIGH TIDE OF EMPIRE

The war had changed the balance of power in the world, and at the beginning of the decade it appeared that Britain and her Empire had benefited. Certainly, Britain emerged from the war with no rivals for world supremacy among the former powers of Europe. The Austro-Hungarian Empire had fallen apart and in its place there had arisen a jigsaw of independent nations with exotic and barely pronounceable names, such as Czechoslovakia and Yugoslavia. The Ottoman Empire had melted away like a snowfall in spring, and here too a new nation was taking shape: the secular republic of Turkey. Russia, under its new Bolshevist rulers, was at war with itself and out of the geopolitical game for the time being.

Germany was laid low. Her imperial assets in Africa had been added to Britain's formidable portfolio, giving the British Empire in the immediate post-war years a greater geographical extent than ever before. This fact alone was proof, if any were needed, that Britons were the world's pre-eminent nationality. To ensure that the upcoming generation shared in that assurance, every classroom in the land was decorated with a map on which the places ruled by Britain were coloured red. What schoolroom maps did not show was how fragile and uncertain was Britain's hold on some of those overseas territories.

There was not, as yet, any strong movement for independence in dominions such as Australia, Canada and New Zealand, although even there the horrific cost of the war in terms of young men's lives led some to question the ultimate authority of the 'Mother Country'. But elsewhere, independence movements were gathering momentum. And nowhere was the demand for freedom more insistent than in Ireland, the most volatile corner of the whole empire.

'Without the Empire we should be tossed like a cork in the cross-current of world politics. It is at once our sword and our shield.'

William Morris Hughes, British-born prime minister of Australia, speaking in 1926

Ireland on the brink of war

Ireland had been part of the United Kingdom since 1801, with elected Irish MPs sitting in the Westminster Parliament. But then, in the general election of December 1918, Sinn Fein swept to victory with 73 of Ireland's 105 seats. Instead of becoming MPs in Westminster, they set up their own Irish parliament in Dublin – the Dáil. The day that the Dáil met for the first time, on 21 January, 1919, Irish 'volunteers' killed two members of the Royal Irish Constabulary (RIC) in Tipperary. The shots that killed those two policemen were the opening salvo in the Irish War of Independence (also known as the Anglo-Irish War) that lasted for more than two years. They were also the beginning of a guerilla strategy in which Irish police and British soldiers – 43,000 troops were stationed in Ireland – were targeted as 'agents of a foreign power'.

The Black and Tans

Prime Minister Lloyd George responded to the terrorist tactics of the Irish volunteers by declaring Sinn Fein illegal and having the party leaders arrested. This action was swiftly followed by a recruitment campaign in mainland Britain to

WAR ZONE

On December 11, 1920, Cork city centre was burned to the ground (below). Cork was a focus of resistance to the British presence in Ireland, and the burning of the city was the culmination of reprisals there by the Black and Tans. The immediate catalyst was an IRA ambush in which a British soldier was killed. That night, fires broke out in and around Patrick Street. The superintendent of Cork fire brigade saw 'forty or fifty men walking in a body in the centre of Patrick Street, coming towards us in very mixed dress – some with khaki coats, some with khaki trousers, and some wore glengarry caps'. Among the buildings burned that night were the City Hall (with all its municipal records) and the Carnegie Library. At first, the authorities denied that British soldiers were involved – then later blamed the arson on renegade auxiliaries.

bolster the ranks of the demoralised RIC. Seven thousand men signed up, many of them ex-soldiers grateful to have the chance of some paid work. There were not enough green RIC uniforms for the new recruits, so they were kitted out in military khaki and black belts, giving rise to the name by which they would become notorious – the dreaded Black and Tans.

The methods of the Black and Tans were brutal and attracted growing criticism not just in Ireland but also in mainland Britain. The main tactic was to answer every attack on the forces of law and order in Ireland with a bloody reprisal. They kicked in doors, smashed up houses, sacked villages and burned the centre of Cork to the ground – they shot at Irish firemen who turned out to try to douse the flames. They viciously maltreated anyone suspected of being a 'shinner' and terrorised the civilian population on the assumption (broadly true) that practically everyone in southern Ireland was a Sinn Fein sympathiser. On a particularly infamous occasion – Bloody Sunday, 21 November, 1920 – they opened fire on the players and spectators at a gaelic football game being played in Croke Park, Dublin, killing 14 people including the captain of the Tipperary team, Michael Hogan.

THE FIRST BLOODY SUNDAY

Covert operations were a feature of the Anglo-Irish War as both sides used spies and infiltrators to gather intelligence. The Cairo Gang (right) was a group of British agents working in Dublin in 1920. Their mission was to prepare a 'hit list' of republicans and IRA members – in effect, a list of candidates for assassination – for the British military authorities. But the IRA's Intelligence Department had an informant in the Dublin police force who gave the IRA the names and addresses of the entire Cairo Gang.

On Sunday, 21 November, 1920, in a coordinated operation planned by Michael Collins, IRA men burst into the hotels and guesthouses where individual members of the gang were boarding. Some of the British spies died fighting; most were summarily executed on the spot. One of the gang, Lieutenant Donald Maclean, asked not to be shot in front of his wife; his attackers granted his request and took him up to the roof to kill him there. In all, 14 British agents were shot dead that morning, but the bloodshed had only begun. Later that same day, detachments of Black and Tans burst into a gaelic football match being played in Croke Park, Dublin, supposedly on the trail of some of the gunmen. They opened fire on spectators and players, killing 14 unarmed Irish civilians, including the captain of the Tipperary team; six more people were wounded. The final act of Bloody Sunday came that evening, when three IRA prisoners held at Dublin Castle were 'shot trying to escape'.

The separation of Ireland

Inevitably, the outrages of the Black and Tans stoked the fires of hatred. Droves of young Irishmen rushed to join the ranks of the Irish volunteers, now increasingly known as the Irish Republican Army (IRA). The change of name made sense, because the Irish were now fighting the British in an all-out war of independence.

Yet even as the shootings and ambushes were going on, the Government of Ireland Act was making its way through Parliament in Westminster. The Act made provision for six counties of Ulster to remain part of the UK, in line with the wishes of their largely Protestant population, but proposed that the rest of the country become an 'Irish Free State' with dominion status, like Canada and Australia. The two Irelands came into being in 1922. It was not the end of the violence, but the greater part of Ireland was now on its way to independence.

Agitation in India – and massacre at Amritsar

Irish independence was a shocking event for many English people, who considered Ireland an unalienable part of Britain, but even more unthinkable was the idea that India should ever be anything but a British colonial possession. Yet far away on the subcontinent an independence movement was gathering momentum.

As in Ireland, the post-war chapter began in blood and violence. In April 1919 three Europeans were killed in Amritsar during anti-British rioting and an English lady, a missionary, was dragged off her bicycle and beaten by the mob. Three days later, a large but peaceful crowd of Indians gathered in a walled garden near the centre of the city. They were ordered to disperse by the local British commander, General Reginald Dyer, but they remained seated on the ground. So the general ordered his troops – Gurkhas and Sikh auxiliaries – to fire into the crowd and to keep firing 'until their ammunition was exhausted'. Nearly 400 people were

continued on page 263

THE ARCHITECTS OF IRISH INDEPENDENCE

Among the most talented advocates of Irish independence was Arthur Griffith (above left), who had founded the Sinn Fein political party in 1905. Griffith was a theorist as well as an activist; he argued that the union of the British and Irish crowns in 1801 was illegal and that Ireland still constituted a separate monarchy. He suggested that Ireland might become an autonomous state under the British monarch, but this idea was unpalatable to out-and-out republicans. Michael Collins, the 'big fellow' (above right), was a brilliant military commander who master-minded the guerrilla war against the British in Ireland. Both men took part in the Anglo-Irish Treaty talks in London, having been appointed to the delegation by Eamon de Valera, seen here (right) in dark hat and overcoat, taking the salute of an IRA division in County Clare in 1921. De Valera was president of Sinn Fein throughout the Anglo-Irish War, but spent most of the time in the USA raising funds. Astutely, he avoided taking part in the talks in London and so, unlike Griffith and Collins, was not tainted by signing the Anglo-Irish Treaty in December 1921. De Valera went on to found Fianna Fail (Warriors of Destiny), which under his leadership ruled Ireland from 1932 to 1948. Neither Griffith nor Collins survived the fateful year of 1922. Griffith died of a haemorrhage, aged 50, on 12 August, 1922. Ten days later, Collins was ambushed and shot dead by former colleagues near Bandon in County Cork.

'Early this morning, I signed my death warrant.'

Michael Collins, speaking to his friend John O'Kane
after signing the Anglo-Irish Treaty on 6 December, 1921

A DISUNITED REPUBLIC

The Anglo-Irish Treaty, signed in 1921, caused a split in Sinn Fein and in its armed wing, the IRA. Most of those in the higher ranks of the IRA were in favour of the treaty, and agreed with Michael Collins' tactical assessment that the IRA was not strong enough to continue the fight against the British. But the rank-and-file was split. A majority of Irish volunteers objected to the treaty because it did not bring total independence for all of Ireland, and because they believed that they could defeat the British army on Irish soil.

After the declaration of the Irish Free State in 1922, the British government washed its hands of southern Ireland. The Black and Tans were withdrawn and disbanded. But many Irish republicans were not satisfied with the terms of the treaty between Britain and the Free State. In particular, they objected to the symbolic oath of allegiance to the King that Irish parliamentarians were expected to swear. Fighting now broke out and escalated between the two factions – on the one hand the pro-treaty republicans, who had taken over power from the departed British, and on the other the anti-treaty hardliners. As a result, the Anglo-Irish War of Independence segued almost seamlessly into an Irish Civil War that cost the lives of many hundreds more Irishmen. In Dublin, Michael Collins was forced to order his troops (left) to shell the anti-treaty republican army, which had established its headquarters in the Four Courts.

killed and more than a thousand wounded. In the days that followed, the unrepentant Dyer ordered that all Indians on the street where the English lady had been attacked should crawl its entire length on their bellies.

The news of the Amritsar massacre unleashed a fresh wave of agitation for independence. During this upswell of anti-British feeling a new leader emerged, an Indian lawyer recently returned from South Africa. His name was Mohandas Gandhi. He was steeped in the ancient philosophies of his native land, and he had also been deeply influenced by his reading of the Sermon on the Mount. His thinking had brought him to the conclusion that non-violent resistance to British rule was the only moral way to win independence, and so he formulated a strategy that he called *satyagraha* – the force of truth. It involved Indians boycotting British goods – everyone was encouraged to weave cloth for their own clothes – refusing to use British services such as the bus network and declining to work in British institutions such as law courts, schools and the armed forces.

Not everyone understood or agreed with Gandhi's revolutionary peaceful idea. The political turmoil in India saw frequent outbreaks of violence between the Hindu majority and the Muslim minority. In 1922 insurgent Hindu peasants attacked a police station and killed 22 officers inside. Gandhi was held to be somehow responsible and imprisoned by the British. He was released two years later, and carried on the campaign to get the British to go home.

Squeezing Germany

In the 1920s, the uprisings inside the Empire looked like aftershocks of the war. Back in Europe the German state had been disarmed and German cities occupied by troops of the victorious nations. Under the terms of the Versailles Treaty the German state was to be made to reimburse the Allies for all 'loss and damage' incurred in the war: the total monetary value was later set at 269 billion gold marks. Quite how Germany was supposed to find this money was not clear.

The harsh treatment of Germany was already backfiring. In Bavaria, paramilitary organisations grew strong on the resentment that ordinary Germans felt against the perceived unfairness of the Versailles Treaty. In 1923 *The Times* correspondent in Munich reported on one of these organisations, the Bavarian National Socialist Workers party: 'The so-called Bavarian *fascisti* continue to hold frequent rallies. Bands of troops march about in strictly military formation. They wear grey uniforms somewhat after the Italian fashion [and] have been equipped with steel helmets of the regulation Government pattern … The reactionary press announced that the proceedings had been of a purely social and sporting character … [but] it is difficult to believe that steel helmets, tight-fitting military uniforms, and machine gun slings are necessary for a day's sport in Bavaria.'

The report went on to say that the excitable leader of the organisation was prepared to grant interviews to British journalists for a fee of £5, but *The Times*' man did not think the scoop was worth the outlay. Instead he offered this sketch of the man: 'Adolf Hitler has been described recently as one of the three most dangerous men in Germany. This is probably rather a flattering estimate of the little Austrian sign painter. By many he is regarded as a useful tool, to be discarded in the case of success and disowned in the event of failure.' Sure enough, Hitler the rabble-rouser was in a Munich prison by the end of the year, having botched an attempt to overthrow the Bavarian government. The readers of *The Times* were free to assume that they had heard the first and the last of him.

BRITISH EMPIRE EXHIBITION – 1924

The Empire Exhibition at Wembley was a celebration of the great global family over which Britain ruled. Almost every imperial possession was represented by its own exotic pavilion, displaying the wares and achievements of that country. In the Ceylon pavilion the air was thick with spices; the Canadian pavilion displayed a life-size representation of the Prince of Wales carved from refrigerated butter. The Exhibition opened for business on St George's Day, 1924. To mark the occasion, George V made a speech that was broadcast live across the land and Edward Elgar conducted an orchestra playing his best-known composition, 'Land of Hope and Glory'. Queen Mary (left) was one of the first visitors, accompanied by a posse of courtiers, police officers and African tribesmen. These last were some of the hundreds of colonial subjects shipped to the mother country as living exhibits: in the course of a day you could encounter Australian sheep-shearers, Ashanti weavers, Malay basketweavers – and many others, all hard at work. It fell to the Duke of York, later George VI, to sample the helter-skelter (bottom) in what was as much a vast amusement park as a trade fair. The architectural centrepiece of the exhibition was the Empire Stadium, which was saved from demolition when the rest of the pavilions and amusements were dismantled in 1925. Later renamed Wembley Stadium, it became the home of English football. The first event staged there, just four days after completion, was the FA Cup Final in 1923.

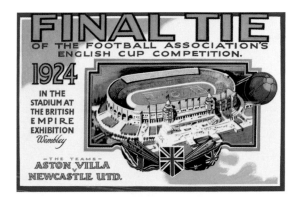

1920s

A WOMAN'S WORLD

On the day that the Armistice was declared bringing the war to an end in November 1918, the novelist Florie Annie Steel sat down to pen an article for the *Daily Mail*. 'The world is fresh and new for womanhood', she wrote. 'It is not possible for us to go back to what we were before the flame of war tried us as in a fire. And why should we?' It was already clear to Steel, as it was to millions of other women across Britain, that the post-war world was going to be very different.

POOL PARTY The latest bathing suits on display in 1928. It is not just the fashions that are thoroughly modern; before the war, the unabashed smoking of cigarettes and application of makeup would have been very shocking things to do in public.

KEEP YOUNG AND BEAUTIFUL

One spectacular change for women had come about in the hastily organised 'khaki election' of December 1918, when for the first time women were allowed to take part – both as voters and as candidates. For the suffragettes of the pre-war years, the women who had fought to win electoral rights, this was a moment to savour, but there was still more to be done. Only women over 30 were granted the privilege of voting (though, oddly, a woman could stand for election as an MP at 21). All the same, the attainment of a degree of female suffrage was a huge step towards formal equality with men.

Genuine electoral parity came at the end of the 1920s, when the voting age for women was lowered to 21 – the same as for men. In the ten years between those two milestones women strove for equality with men in all sorts of spheres of life. Huge changes were wrought by the women of the 1920s in work and leisure, dress and decorum, sex and marriage. But unlike the serious-minded suffragists of the Edwardian era, this younger generation had a great deal of unabashed fun while forging their revolution.

Hairstyles and hemlines

The flapper was the dominant female archetype of the 1920s, the 'thoroughly modern miss' who was out to forget the war and have a good time. Not every woman was a flapper, of course, but most young women aspired at least to have something of the flapper look, which was, in the first instance, a spirited and determined rejection of the time-consuming and physically restrictive fashions of the pre-war era. Out went stiff whalebone corsetry and in came light clothes that allowed women to move, to bend, to play tennis and, above all, to dance. Out went long hair that took hours to arrange; in came, the short, stylish and far more manageable 'bob'.

Hairstyling was no longer something that a lady had done by a servant in her private boudoir. It was now a social activity that women paid for in the public arena of a beauty salon. It followed that short hair was somehow more democratic, more egalitarian, than long hair. To cut one's hair was to demonstrate solidarity with other emancipated women. Short hair was the very cipher of modernity, and the fringed bob was just the starting point. The classic bob framed the face with two neat 'wings', à la Louise Brooks. It looked good in combination with the bell-shaped cloche hat, which became universal at the start of the Twenties and endured for a good ten years. If you wanted to wear a cloche (and everyone did), then you had to have a bob: it was impossible to pile an elaborate, old-style Grecian coiffure inside one.

The standard bob eventually gave way to the shingle, in which the back of the head was shaved. This development led to much merriment and consternation in the popular press. *Punch* ran a cartoon in which a confused young fellow was told

> '[There was] an almost complete rupture with pre-war ideas … an entirely new code for conduct and thought.'
>
> **Edith, Marchioness of Londonderry, on the new relations between the sexes**

to 'grow your hair, man, you look like a girl'. In the 'Eton crop', which arrived in 1926, the whole head of hair was cut extremely close and slicked down to reveal the contours of the skull. Some of the most bohemian wearers of the Eton crop went the whole hog and sported dinner suits and monocles, the logical extreme of the striving for a 'boyish' appearance that was the height of Twenties chic.

A practical statement

In some ways, the new fashions were a stylish continuation of the practical dress worn by the young women who had done war work. Long hair was a dangerous liability for women toiling over machines in arms factories, and you could not bend to milk a cow in a corset. Once the war was over, the commonsense changes in the outward appearance of women took on unavoidably political implications. There was a link between women's social freedoms and the clothes that women actually wanted to wear. 'We are expected to walk the broad earth in that?', exclaimed one outraged young woman in response to a newspaper article that mooted a return to the long, tight, hobbling skirts that typified the curvaceous 'Gibson Girl' look from before the war. 'Land girls, who have known the comfort of breeches, will you consent to be pinioned in this way? Munitionettes, fellow

SUMMER HOLIDAYS
The war's end, and the brief period of affluence and optimism that followed, presented Britain's women with some new-found freedoms. For young working-class women, like these bathers having fun in Herne Bay (above), not only was there the time and leisure for a seaside holiday, but also the freedom to lark about in a relatively skimpy bathing costume.

war workers, all who have learned to out-distance men in the fierce race for the omnibus, will you fall back into unequal contest?' The answer to her rhetorical questions was, of course, 'no'. But despite its obvious practicality, the flapper style seemed to some to be a deliberate denial of natural femininity. Bosoms were bound tight to create the flat-chested look and the feminine contours of the figure were disguised by lowered waistlines. The effect was variously described as 'lath-like' or 'tubular'. One fashion magazine characterised voguish women in general as 'such enchanting, sexless, bosomless, hipless, thighless creatures'.

Some people tried to account for the new look by pointing to the wartime shortage of fats and sugars, as if the privation of rationing had turned an entire generation into scrawny stick insects. Some disapproving, overwhelmingly male, commentators saw the denial of hips and breasts as a symbolic and unpatriotic refusal on the part of women to embrace the maternal side of their natures. It was surely a woman's duty, went the argument, to knuckle down to the business of

ANYTHING MEN CAN DO
One of the themes of female emancipation in the 1920s was the constant striving on the part of women to do things that were thought of as exclusively male activities. The world of sport provided many opportunities for women to demonstrate that they were just as capable as men. These confident motorcyclists were taking part in the 1925 Six Days Reliability Trials at Brooklands.

bearing and rearing sons to replace those who had been killed and – though this was not explicitly stated – to provide a new crop of cannon fodder for the next war when it came. It was even seriously suggested by some doctors that the unnatural act of walking in shoes with high heels could displace a woman's uterus and so render the daughters of the Empire infertile.

None of this impressed the flappers, many of whom had lost fathers or brothers in Flanders and knew well enough what the war had cost. 'The reason my generation bobbed and shingled their hair, flattened their bosoms, and lowered their waists, was not that they wanted to be masculine, but that we didn't want to be emotional', wrote Barbara Cartland, a flapper in her youth. 'War widows, many of them still wearing crepe and widows' weeds in the Victorian tradition, had full bosoms, full skirts, and fluffed-out hair. To shingle was to cut loose from the maternal pattern; it was an anti-sentiment symbol, not an anti-feminine one.'

At the time, the main objection to the new women's fashion was the perceived lack of femininity. From the point of view of men, modern girls looked wilfully unsexy. But not everyone thought so. The aesthetic eye of Cecil Beaton, just beginning to make a name for himself as a photographer, clearly saw the attraction of the new. 'To me the fashions of the Twenties are infinitely alluring', he later wrote. 'One is above all struck by the simplicity of line … those longer-than-life ladies … symbolised the visual aspect of the period … The 1914 war preceded an utter revolution in the concept of femininity, a revolution which, with its planes, straight lines, flattening out of bosoms and silhouettes, is more than superficially related to cubism in art, and to the tubular world of Fernand Léger.'

'Bobbed hair is a state of mind … I consider getting rid of our long hair one of the many little shackles that women have cast aside in their passage to freedom.'

Mary Garden, opera singer, writing in 1927

Legs and lingerie

Without doubt, there were exciting elements in the flapper style that mitigated the androgynous effect. There was the fact that dresses grew shorter in the first half of the 1920s, thereby eroticising women's legs. Pre-war dresses had encased women down to the ankle, making them look like tottering mermaids. Now, as hemlines rose, more and more leg was on show and usually it was displayed to best advantage in flesh-coloured 'artsilk' – that is 'artificial silk', the newly invented rayon. A garter worn just above the knee made for a titillating finishing touch. 'They were delicious concoctions of ribbon and rosebuds and lace', wrote Ethel Mannin, 'sometimes with a dashing touch of feather or marabout, excitingly glimpsed when the knees were crossed, and worn for no other purpose, it would seem, since our lovely shiny silk stockings were supported by suspenders.'

More alluring still was the new underwear necessitated by 1920s styles. Although not generally on show, thanks to the cinema and stage everybody knew what went on beneath that cylindrical exterior. In a play entitled *The Garden of Eden*, the American actress Tallulah Bankhead – who represented the outrageous extreme of post-war womanhood – sensationally ripped off her wedding dress to

continued on page 278

FASHION AND STYLE

The 1920s were the first decade in which fashion became the property of the young. Styles, especially for women, changed dramatically, bewildering and sometimes outraging the older generation – which, of course, was part of the point. There was a deliberate break with sartorial conventions of the past and with the buttoned-up, tight-laced attitudes that had so constricted the people of Victorian and Edwardian Britain. In the post-war world, clothes became as loose, free and frivolous as the morals (it was widely assumed) of those who wore them.

THE NEW LOOK

The change in women's clothes from before the Great War to the decade that followed it is probably the greatest ever seen in the history of fashion. In the 1920s, as in most ages, women's fashions evolved more rapidly than men's. When Cecil Beaton (far left) went to watch cricket at Lord's with his father and two sisters in 1927, the simple shift-style dresses worn by his sisters were very much of the season – they could not have been worn a decade before. In contrast, apart from the cut of Cecil's waistcoat and rakish angle of his top hat, the men's morning suits were pretty much unchanged in two generations. Women's hemlines were not quite as upwardly mobile as is often supposed.

The knees were on display briefly in mid-decade, but generally were kept out of sight. Cloche hats, low waists and straight dresses were a consistent theme. Walking sticks (below left) seem to have been a brief affectation. The practical woollen two-piece worn over a hip-length jumper (below) was a popular style, typical of the era.

'The camiknicker evolved from the camisole, which was a deep bodice which preceded the brassiere. They were fussily pretty, with a good deal of lace, and threaded with narrow ribbon, in pink or blue, called "baby ribbon".'

Ethel Edith Mannin, novelist, travel writer and 'Bright Young Thing', from *Young in the Twenties*, published in 1971

FUNDAMENTAL CHANGES

The new flapper fashions required a totally new approach to underwear. Boned corsets were out: sales declined by two-thirds over the course of the decade, and those who did buy them were invariably of the older generation. Younger women's undergarments, meanwhile, were reinvented almost from scratch. The most popular item was the 'camiknicker' (far left), a stitched-together word for a stitched-together combination of camisole and knickers. It was designed to be comfortable, to sit invisibly below a sleeveless, knee-length dress and to promote the bustless, hipless, almost boyish shape that was the goal of 1920s womanhood. It was often made of artificial silk, a recently invented man-made material perfectly suited to the new style since it was light, convenient and somehow heralded the future. In the 1920s women's underwear, no less than hairstyles, were an almost political statement. Camiknickers, like Eton crops and cloche hats, sent out the message that women were entitled to dress and live as they pleased. The popularity of the camiknicker inevitably led to variations on the theme, such as this combination of camisole and knee-length bloomer (left). It would not have worked so well under a short dress, and was probably designed first and foremost as a stage costume: ladies in their underwear were a stock element of light theatre in the 1920s – one of the attractions of the genre.

HAPPY FEET

In the Edwardian era, ladies' feet and therefore shoes were not meant to be seen. But in the fashion revolution of the 1920s, when hemlines rose from the floor and legs came into view, shoes acquired a new importance in the fashion world. This also happened to be the decade in which shoes began to be mass-produced, so suddenly there was a choice of affordable, attractive footwear to be had. A penchant lasted throughout the decade for straps fastened across the instep, and also for the elegantly curving contours of a Louis heel (top and above right). A striking piece of jewellery (above left) was one way of drawing attention to that highly prized attribute, a 'well turned ankle'. Beaded stockings, a brief vogue in 1923, achieved the same effect, but were difficult to keep straight. The knee-length 'highland puttees', tied with straps under the shoe, would help to keep out the cold in draughty country houses.

HEADS UP

Hats were an essential item of dress for women in the 1920s – and the cloche was the almost universal style. Most women had several: a change of hat was an easy and relatively cheap way to adjust one's look, particularly since most women kept their hats on when they were out in public – even in a restaurant or cinema. The vogue for hats was good news for the milliners (above), who thrived even as other businesses struggled. In Luton, the hatmaking capital of Britain, the local paper claimed that the popularity of the cloche had 'banished unemployment'. Cloches, like dresses, were subject to the fluctuations of fashion. The brim was wider some years than others; occasionally it was turned up and worn flattened against the forehead. Sometimes cloches were worn plain – in which case they bore an alarming resemblance to the scuttle helmets of the German armed forces. But they could also be adorned with a sprig of fake flowers (far left) or a jewelled brooch. Geometric Art Deco motifs were occasionally seen in ribbons and hatbands (left).

BOBS AND SHINGLES

Almost every young woman cut her hair short, but there was still room to express one's own style. The actress Jessie Matthews (top) looked fabulous with her 'raven's wing' bob. The three chorus girls (top right) display the decade's predominant styles: a bob or shingle, a 'permanent wave' and a waved shingle. The new hair salons were equipped with new-fangled machines such as electric dryers (above). Hairdressing became a lucrative industry in the decade and society coiffeurs such as Antoine Cierplikowski (right) grew rich and famous.

reveal the flimsy one-piece combination undergarment known as the camiknicker. Anny Ondra wore a similar garment in the first British talkie, *Blackmail*, directed by Alfred Hitchcock. In a celebrated scene Ondra, the murderer, stalked her victim dressed only in a short cami and armed with a large kitchen knife.

For ordinary women, the main advantage of the camiknicker over anything that had gone before was that it was comfortable to wear. Gone were restrictive whale-bone corsets and starched cottons. Instead, women could choose from light, silky undergarments, prettily trimmed in different colours. The writer Ethel Mannin recalled: 'The most popular shade for lingerie, as we genteelly called underclothes, was pink. The term was "prostitute pink" – but we liked it.'

LOVE AND MARRIAGE

Flappers and their male consorts soon got a reputation for immorality. It was widely assumed that the flamboyant and scandalous Tallulah Bankhead was not joking when she made remarks such as 'I've tried several varieties of sex. The conventional position makes me claustrophobic. And the others give me either a stiff neck or lockjaw.' The older generation feared and suspected that women who liked to charleston the nights away were also more than likely inclined to be sexually promiscuous, and that the licentious behaviour of the privileged few was

HERE COMES
THE BRIDE

Marriage was still the normal route to security and happiness for women of all classes. This young bride (above) on the way to her wedding is Lady Elizabeth Bowes Lyon, the future Queen Mother. When she married the Duke of York in 1923, the affection of the nation followed in her train. The confetti-covered groom with top-hat in hand (right) is Alfred Hitchcock – the very English formality of his wedding in 1926 contains no hint of the talent to terrify and shock that was just beginning to emerge in his cinema work. Shorter hemlines soon featured even on bridal gowns, as worn by this beaming bride (left). The groom was a fireman and the guard of honour was provided by his colleages.

ALL IN THE FAMILY
The almost annual round of childbirth took a heavy toll on working-class women. Charities helped in poor communities, but many, like this Catholic nun (left), were from organisations adamantly opposed to any form of family planning. Few people were prepared even to discuss the issue of birth control, let alone tackle it. One exception was Marie Stopes. In her campaign to promote birth control, she quoted a letter she had received from one barely literate woman: 'What I would like to know is how I can save having any more children as I think I have done my duty to my Country having had 13 children, 9 boys and 4 girls.'

somehow seeping out and influencing the morals of society as a whole. Certainly, sex outside marriage – or more likely, in anticipation of marriage – became more common in the Twenties than it had been in the preceding decades. This was surely one effect of the war. What was the point of waiting for marriage, when you knew that your betrothed would go away and might never return?

Everybody had been aware that the death toll in the war was creating a shortage of men and a corresponding surplus of women. Some far-sighted individuals had also seen that this imbalance was likely to have damaging social and emotional consequences. As early as 1916, the feminist and suffragist Helena Swanwick declared in a speech that 'when this devastating war is over there will be more young women than young men to mate with them. Are the older people who made the war and sent the young men to give their lives in it going to wash their hands of the consequences to the mateless maidens, to talk outrageously of them as "waste products of civilisation", and to offer nothing but lifelong repression?'

People worried about the demographic consequences of a female 'surplus' in the population, and certainly the carnage in France deprived many individual women of the chance of marriage. But it was a myth that the imbalance between the sexes put the fruitfulness of the nation as a whole in jeopardy. Statistics show that, while the incidence of marriage decreased in the 1920s, the dip was shallow. Among younger age groups, the number of marriages actually increased. At the same time, people's vision of what a marriage should be started to shift from the Victorian ideal, in which the husband was the undisputed patriarch and ruler of the household, to something more balanced and companionable. In matters of sex, there was a dawning realisation among both middle and working classes that women had rights in the bedroom – not least, to information about sex – just as they did at the ballot box.

Pioneering family planning

Many came to this knowledge through the pioneering work of Marie Stopes, who made it her life's mission to tackle the profound sexual ignorance of the British people, and of British women in particular. She published two books that were widely read in the Twenties. The first of them, *Married Love*, set out to describe the mechanics of intimacy between husband and wife (it was always husband and wife – Stopes deeply disapproved of sex outside marriage). Her aim was to instruct and to strip away the layers of shame that had accrued to the subject over the decades. Her language was lyrical and sometimes confusingly obscure, as when she set out to describe an orgasm: 'The half-swooning sense of flux which overtakes the spirit in that eternal moment at the apex of rapture sweeps into its flaming tides the whole essence of the man and woman, and, as it were, the heat of the contact vapourises their consciousness so that it fills the whole of cosmic space …' But her readers seemed to understand what she was driving at and got the gist of the message – that sexual desire was normal, that most sexual problems were solvable and that sex itself was not shameful. Many men engaged to be married wrote to her to say that they had given their fiancée a copy of her book.

Stopes's other book, *Wise Parenthood*, was about birth control. She believed that contraception was necessary to ensure that the racial stock of the imperial British remained strong and pure and, more compassionately, to prevent suffering to women – poor women, above all. The section of society that knew least about family planning was the one least able to afford to raise large families. Stopes routinely recommended that women use the 'Dutch cap', a device just then becoming widely available. But she fought a losing battle against men's unwillingness to take any responsibility for birth control. One man described the use of so-called 'male appliances' as 'like having a bath with top hat and spurs on'.

In 1921 Stopes opened Britain's first family planning clinic in Holloway, North London. For the first time, women – married women, at least – had a place to go for practical help and advice on birth control. Professional doctors – all of them men, of course – were practically useless in this regard. One woman complained that doctors were constantly telling her to have no more children, but when she asked them how to achieve this 'they just smile'. Stopes's charitable undertaking brought much criticism from churchmen – especially from Catholic ones. She sued (and lost) when a Catholic doctor accused her of 'experimenting on the poor'. But it was the gentle, sensible thoughts expressed in *Married Love* that prompted this vitriolic response from one male reader: 'Is it a desire to put bank notes into your pocket that you wrote such stuff? Do you really think that my wife and I are sadly in need of such dirty advice as you offer? Some of the things you propose in your book might have emanated from the brain of a Kaffir woman.'

WORKING WOMEN

A FORCE FOR CHANGE
Dr Marie Stopes (above), remembered today as a pioneering campaigner for birth control, was also a brilliant scholar, a palaeontologist and a passionate believer in women's suffrage. She is pictured here with her second husband, Humphrey Verdon Roe, outside the Royal Academy in London in 1926. Although her first marriage had ended in annulment, Stopes remained an advocate for the married state and disapproved of sex between unmarried couples.

Many of the men who wrote to Marie Stopes expressed concerns that it might not be proper to allow their wives to continue working after marriage. This concern was part of a wider national debate about the role of women in the workplace. There was a widespread belief that it was a bride's duty as a woman and a citizen to put aside her work to stay at home and raise children. Some skilled women workers – teachers, nurses, even sorely needed doctors – found that the decision to work or not to work was taken out of their hands by employers, many of whom sacked female employees as a matter of policy as soon as they married. Right through the decade and beyond, Establishment figures occasionally voiced the opinion that such measures constituted the obvious answer to the evil of male unemployment. As late as 1933, Sir Herbert Austin, owner of the car firm and a Birmingham MP, declared that all employed women in Britain should be sacked and their positions given to jobless men.

Such views, like so many of the attitudes and prejudices of the Twenties, were rooted in the war years. While the fight was on, women were showered with praise for rolling up their sleeves and labouring in factories, driving trams, taking the place of engineers and mechanics, as well as office workers. The resilience and know-how exhibited by the female half of the population came as a surprise to

'We know now, as we never knew before, what women can do.'

George Birmingham, novelist, writing in 1919 in praise of working women

many, and seemed to suggest that a new economic and social order might be one of the fruits of victory. 'Women themselves are conscious, as they never were before, of their own powers', wrote the novelist George Birmingham in 1919. 'We have everything to hope for and very little to fear from the new activities, the new powers of those who in time of trial have shown themselves noble-hearted, devoted and capable.' On the other hand, men recently returned from the front began to complain that 'the girls were clinging to their jobs, would not let go of the pocket-money which they had spent on frocks'. What had been seen as

GOOD MORNING, MISS

It was said ruefully in the 1920s that 'men must be educated, and women must do it'. Then, as now, women constituted a large proportion of the teaching staff in primary schools. Many of those teachers belonged to the National Union of Women Teachers, which broke away from the NUT in 1920 to campaign for equal pay with men. The NUWT addressed feminist issues such as the marriage bar and maternity rights, as well as purely educational matters such as corporal punishment, class sizes and the school leaving age.

selfless toil by women while the war was on turned into selfish money-grabbing in the cash-strapped peace. Female civil servants in particular were viewed with disdain. 'While there are a quarter of a million ex-soldiers who cannot get work', commented Field Marshal Sir William Robertson, 'the retention of one woman in the War Office is a monstrous injustice.'

Longstanding suffragists such as Eleanor Rathbone, president of the National Union of Societies for Equal Citizenship, saw this kind of talk as a dangerous attack on women's rights. 'The popular outcry against the employment of women is arousing very bitter feeling', she wrote to *The Times*. 'To judge from these many utterances, one would imagine that women were aliens [foreigners], instead of citizens who pay their full share of taxation and have the same right as other citizens to take whatever part in the industry of the country their abilities have won for them. To shut these women out from the opportunity of earning their living is unjust to them and not, in the long run, in the interests of the country.' And yet, perhaps surprisingly, Field Marshal Robertson's viewpoint was shared by some women, who put a noble gloss on redundancy by seeing it as a form of sacrifice. 'The present is not the time for women to press their claim to any work that can be considered a man's job', wrote one female civil servant. 'It seems to me that it would be a national service if women should now practise a kind of self-denying ordinance and tacitly decide that for this generation they will call a halt to their efforts to increase the number of women in masculine jobs.'

Women's work

All parties in the debate made an exception for 'charwomen, shorthand typists and typists', whose work was regarded as 'non-substitutional', that is, beneath the dignity of a self-respecting war veteran. In the end it was through this kind of work, non-skilled or humbly administrative drudgery, that women began to gain a foothold in male-dominated workplaces. Clerical jobs, in particular, were a kind of Trojan horse that got women inside office buildings and made them an acceptable presence among the regiments of 'black-coated workers'.

At the bottom of the employment ladder, the fact that women doing factory or manual work were paid less than men may have kept them their jobs later in the decade, when new waves of economic crises swept the country. Higher-paid men were often the first to be given their cards, while cheaper female labour was kept on. In working-class communities, this pattern tended to raise the status of women within the family, as often the young women of the household brought home a wage long after their brothers and fathers had been laid off. In this way, the women of the Twenties gradually took possession of what the writer Vera Brittain described in 1927 as 'the twentieth century's greatest gift to women. It is dignified work', she wrote, 'which puts her on the same level as men.' Brittain was perhaps

FLOWER GIRLS

In the economy of the 1920s there were many jobs that only women were willing to do. These workers are gathering in the daffodil harvest in Cornwall. West Country farmers could make good money growing daffodils, which bloomed early in the southwest due to the mild climate. Regiments of women would cut the flowers and tie them into bundles, which were then freighted by train to market in London. Luxury items such as cut flowers would have been impossible to supply without a ready pool of cheap female labour. This springtide source of work dried up later in the century, when it became possible to import flowers earlier and even more cheaply from overseas.

overstating her case, because women were still a long way from achieving equality in the workplace, but the Sex Disqualification (Removal) Act, passed in 1919, had been a step in the right direction. It stated that: 'A person shall not be disqualified by sex or marriage from the exercise of any public function, or from being appointed to or holding any civil or judicial office or post, or from entering or assuming or carrying on any civil profession or vocation ...'. This meant that the professions were legally obliged to let women in if they were suitably qualified.

The new law impacted most strongly on the legal profession itself. In 1921 Ivy Williams made history by becoming the first women called to the Bar in England. In fact, she had passed all her law examinations by 1903, but had to wait for the change in the law before she was allowed to practise. She then chose not to do so, and so the honour of being the first working female barrister fell to Helena Normanton in 1922. Normanton was subsequently one of the first two women to be appointed King's Counsel, and has the small distinction of being the first woman ever to be issued a British passport in her maiden name.

A long list of female firsts

One curious consequence of the Sex Disqualification Act was that Britain became obsessed with female pioneers. It was always news when a woman did something that a woman had never done before. The first female 'stable lad' made her

A DESK OF ONE'S OWN
Training as a nurse (right) was already a time-honoured career path for women. It required intelligence, as well as the feminine virtue of compassion, and so commanded respect. Office work was a newer option; the young woman above is at her desk in the Topical Press Agency in 1924. Women clerks were not always treated seriously. According to the *Daily Mail* in 1927, they 'kept their position partly, if not chiefly, by their appearance'. *Miss Modern*, a magazine aimed at female office workers, explained to its readers exactly why their looks were so important: 'A pretty, charmingly turned-out secretary is a great asset to a busy man. Being pretty she has confidence in herself, and so is more self-reliant than a plain girl. Also she adds brightness to an office and helps give it a cheerful atmosphere.'

YOU SHALL GO TO THE BALLOT
Women had plenty of opportunities to exercise their newly acquired right to vote: there were no fewer than four general elections over the course of the decade. But the political parties were unsure of how to appeal to women – and in any case it was widely assumed that wives would dutifully vote the same way as their husbands. Politicians could not help describing female voters condescendingly as 'domestic chancellors' whenever the economy was under discussion. The voting age for women was lowered to 21 in 1928, and some commentators predicted unseemly dizziness at the ballot box. But according to the *Daily Express*, in the 'flapper election' of 1929 'the women went about the business of voting solemnly, responsibly and thoroughly'.

debut with much media fanfare in 1919, shortly followed by the first women jurors and the first female boxers. Lady Mary Bailey set the world altitude record for light aeroplanes, climbing to 18,000 feet in a flimsy de Havilland Moth; nobody, of either sex, had flown that high. She had earned her pilot's certificate the year before, having taken lessons in secret from her husband as a way to 'get away from prams'. She cemented her reputation as a pioneering pilot – or 'aviatrix', as the newspapers called women flyers – by flying solo from England to South Africa. She was equipped with a small map taken from a travel agent's advertisement, and a revolver in case she ran into trouble with 'tribesmen'.

A less spectacular but more significant achievement belongs to Margaret Bondfield. Her appointment as Minister of Labour in Ramsay MacDonald's Cabinet in 1929 made her the first female member of government. On the day she and her male colleagues took the train to Windsor to be sworn in by the King 'there were crowds all along the line cheering, and engine drivers blowing whistles as our trains came through'. Margaret Bondfield had been an MP since 1923 – she was one of the first women to win a seat for the Labour Party – and was an eloquent parliamentary spokeswoman for women's rights.

One of Bondfield's colleagues was Ellen Wilkinson, known as 'Red Ellen' both for her radical politics and her auburn hair. Looking back on the decade from the start of the Thirties, Wilkinson noted that 'women doing startling new things fill the papers until one begins to wonder if men are doing anything at all. They beat flying records, carry off the architectural prize of the year, apparently beating men at their own games all along the line. The impression gets about that all England's women are barristers, or aeronauts, or crack Channel swimmers.' She went on: 'Of course, it is not like that really.' But it was not entirely unlike that either. Individually and collectively women achieved great things in the Twenties – far more than the pre-war generation could have hoped for or expected. All in all, not bad going for a bunch of dizzy flappers.

1920s

RICH AND POOR

For countless generations, to be wealthy meant to own land – to own the agricultural products of the land, to be lord over the people who lived on the land and to have the right to exploit the coal and minerals that lay beneath the soil. For some, like the left-wing political thinker Sidney Webb, this was a situation in desperate need of change. 'Nine-tenths of all the accumulated wealth belongs to one-tenth of the population', he wrote in 1920. 'The continued existence of the functionless rich, of persons who deliberately live by owning instead of by working, adds insult to injury.'

PUPPIES FROM HEAVEN The Honourable Mrs Chesterman enjoys a day out at a Northampton Aero Club meeting in 1929. She is holding aloft two stuffed toy dogs, dropped by parachute as part of the display; the dog on the lead is real.

INHERITED WEALTH

The kind of privileged people that Webb had in mind included families such as the Londonderrys who owned 50,000 acres of land across England, Ireland and Wales, and were proprietors of coalfields in County Durham that employed 10,000 men. Lady Londonderry, granddaughter of the Duke of Sutherland and wife of the seventh marquess of Londonderry, used her immense wealth to gain access to political power. She held a grand reception to mark each new session of Parliament, which the prime minister of the day attended with all his Cabinet. These occasions were as much a part of the political system as the Budget or the King's Speech. Even Ramsay MacDonald – who, as a socialist, might have been expected to shun such upper-class ostentation – was charmed by Lady Londonderry. During his time as Prime Minister, she was a close friend and confidante. For many Labour supporters, it was less Lady Londonderry's unearned eminence that rankled than MacDonald's apparent readiness to cosy up to her.

Taxing the land

Lady Londonderry was a fixture of political life well into the 1930s. Yet in 1920, the year that Sidney Webb published *A Constitution for the Socialist Commonwealth of Great Britain*, the wealth and power of the landed gentry was already on the wane. But the changes in fortune that took place over the decade were due not so much to the rise of socialism, as to the vagaries of capitalism. In particular, the aristocracy were under siege from a relatively new tax on inherited wealth. In 1908 death duties – or estate duty, as it was then known – were raised from a fairly negligible rate to 8 per cent on any inheritance worth a million pounds or more. The introduction of expensive social policies – and the even costlier war – led governments to hike up estate duty at every turn. By 1918 the rate stood at 30 per cent.

Most of that taxable wealth was tied up in the land itself and the elder sons of the aristocracy, bequeathed their estates by their fathers, often had to sell some of their land in order to keep the rest of it. Some of those sons and heirs were killed in the war and the economic effects of the premature death of an eldest son could be crippling; if he had already inherited the estate, it would mean paying death duties twice in one generation. This was often enough to sever the long-standing connections between noble families and their ancestral lands.

KING COAL
King Alfonso XIII of Spain, flanked by Lord and Lady Londonderry, on a visit to a new colliery in Seaham, County Durham, in about 1925 (bottom left). Lord Londonderry refused to compromise with his workers on pay and conditions. Around the time that this picture was taken, he remarked: 'I am proposing to devote a great deal of my time to defeating the socialist menace in one of the reddest portions of the kingdom' – his own coalfields in the northeast.

'There is still an Upper Class ... [who] wield a certain influence behind the scenes'

Lady Londonderry, writing in 1938

At the same time, the value of agricultural land was falling – a process that had been ongoing since Victorian times. After the war, a point was reached where the interest earned on money in the bank was giving a better return than could be had from the rents and produce of the land. Consequently many families sold the houses and lands that they had owned for generations, and bought into bonds, stocks and equities – a strategy that some would bitterly regret at the end of the

LADY OF THE HOUSE
The Astor family at home. Lady Nancy Astor became the first woman to take a seat in the House of Commons, after being elected as MP for Plymouth Sutton in 1919. She was the only female MP in that Parliament. Her pioneering achievement made her an eminent public figure throughout the 1920s, but unlike many of the earliest women MPs, she had not earned her spurs in the suffrage movement. An American by birth, she was independently wealthy and led the life of an upper-class socialite. Significantly, the parliamentary seat that she won had just been vacated by her husband, Waldorf Astor, who had been elevated to the Lords.

A competitor leads his prize bull at the Royal Counties Agricultural Show in Guildford, Surrey, in 1922. The three young ladies on the right, from the East Anglian Institute of Agriculture, have their hands full with young charges for sale at the Essex Pig Show in Chelmsford in 1927. Although most land was in the hands of large landowners, a large proportion of the rural population were not so much farmers as smallholders – people who eked out a living from a few acres of rented land. Much of the smallholding would be devoted to growing vegetables, but there might also be a small apple orchard and a chicken run. Most smallholders would invest in a pig in spring, to be killed in the autumn and provide a valuable source of protein through the winter. Pigs were cheap to rear, because they could be fed on scraps and windfall apples. Other necessities could be had by barter, but for most families, some sort of extra paid work would be necessary to avoid dire poverty. Those that owned cows could let them graze freely on the roadside verges – a practice that became more hazardous, and so less common, with the rise of the motor car.

decade, when the global stock market crumbled. For a short while, there was no shortage of buyers for country estates. The new breed of industrialists – some of them MPs described by Stanley Baldwin, before becoming Prime Minister, as 'hard-faced men who look as if they had done very well out of the war' – were only too keen to acquire the prestige of a stately pile. Many of them already had the requisite title – or soon would, thanks to Lloyd George's dubious policy of selling peerages for cash. The result of all these trends was a massive shift in ownership of the countryside. It has been said that more land changed hands in the Twenties and Thirties than at any time since the Norman Conquest.

This process entailed a parallel social upheaval for the English aristocracy. One way to keep the old estates together was to marry money rather than sell to it. That meant admitting the nouveaux riches to aristocratic society, and ultimately, perhaps, into one's own family and bloodline. Some of the most influential hostesses and sought-after heiresses of the Twenties were Americans who had grown wealthy through business – families such as the Astors, the Cunards and the Vanderbilts. They were not just super-rich, they were also a breath of fresh air. They carried the heady scent of the Jazz Age with them like pollen on a bee. And their accents, being foreign, did not bring with them the taint of less than impeccable class origins.

> '**The bottom's coming up, my dear, and the top's coming down.'**
>
> Overheard remark of an anonymous aristocratic lady

POOR MAN, BEGGAR MAN

Beyond the large imposing doors of Berkeley or Eaton Square, on the streets of every city, there were destitute and damaged ex-servicemen looking for odd jobs, or standing in the gutters singing patriotic songs with a cap at their feet. Even before the slump set in in 1921, the slogan 'Homes For Heroes' sounded hollow. A good proportion of heroes' homes were in fact slums of almost unbelievable squalor. 'Here we have a population of some 30,000 packed into a fetid atmosphere arising from the excrementary deposits outside their larder windows of all this pitiful population', wrote one Northumberland man in a letter to Marie Stopes in the early Twenties.

Matters were barely better in the countryside. Overcrowding was a fact of life – partly because farm work, being casual and seasonal, required a mobile army of manual labourers. 'Families with insufficient room for themselves are under great pressure to take in lodgers', wrote a correspondent of *John Bull* magazine in 1925, 'generally young or middle-aged men who have work in the village but have no chance of getting a cottage or even a single room to themselves. Instances are legion in which these lodgers sleep in the same room with various members of the family, more or less independent of considerations of age and sex. It would serve no purpose to give details of the indecencies, not to say scandals, that result.'

BAREFOOT ON THE COBBLES
This cheerful group of children were
photographed outside their homes in
Belfast in 1926. Unlike impoverished rural
families, the urban poor had to find the
cash to buy everything they needed – every
scrap of food that they ate, every item of
clothing they wore. During the week many
children subsisted on bread and margarine,
or bread and dripping (bread was usually
home-baked, in a brick oven, because that
was cheaper than buying it from a shop).
Protein came in the form of a slice of
saveloy or the occasional egg. In many
cities, communities were bound by family
ties, with grandparents, cousins, aunts and
in-laws all living within a street or two of
each other. In other words, city slums were
often urban villages, as close-knit and
inward-looking as any rustic hamlet.

Making ends meet

Part of the problem in the countryside was that the long-term depression in
agriculture was producing a trickle-down reduction in wages. An agricultural
labourer who earned £2 a week in 1918 could only hope to take home 25 shillings
(£1.25p) in 1923. This ought to have benefited the employers – the farmers who
needed to employ extra hands in the busy summer months. But arable crops
simply could not be made to pay. Some farmers switched to dairy in the hope that
there was more money in milk than wheat. Others sat tight and hoped to ride out
the economic downturn.

One farmer's wife, a Mrs Crabtree, recalled some of the desperate measures
they were forced to adopt: 'Our worst experience of the depression was when we
were faced with two months and no money coming in whatsoever. We were
employing five men and they needed their wages on the Friday night, and to us
those men were friends as well as our workers. My husband had in those days
two beautiful Cleveland bay horses; they were the first to go, and we lived on the
proceeds of them and paid our wages for the first month. Then came the second
month … My husband said to me: "I can't pay the wages; what are we to do?"
And I suddenly remembered we had up in the attic quite a lot of silver which
had been given to us as wedding presents. We filled the back of our old Wolseley
car and, believe me, it was the hardest day's work I've ever done to sell that
silver to raise the wages …'

FAREWELL TO THE ISLES

In 1923 and 1924 a catastrophic triple economic crisis struck the islands of the Hebrides. First, there was a failure of the potato crop; then the very wet summer prevented the peat harvest from taking place; and finally the normally rich herring-fishing industry was badly hit by the loss of German and Russian markets. As a consequence, according to an article published in 1924 in *Press & Journal*, a local Hebridean newspaper, 'There is absolutely no employment of any kind for the thousands of men who are involuntarily idle.' In the midst of these dire times Canadian agents came to the islands to encourage people to emigrate to 'a land of prosperous communities, with boundless opportunites for youth and ambition'. Many families, like these sad but determined-looking women (right), decided that their best chance was to grasp the opportunity and leave.

MIDDLE-CLASS SPREAD

Between the extremes of rich and poor stood the vast bulwark of the middle classes. Then, as now, the term covered a broad range of attitudes, occupations and circumstances. At the bottom end of the scale it encompassed teenage clerks and female typists, first-generation members of the urban bourgeoisie, doing newly invented jobs, and using their wits to escape a life of servant drudgery or manual labour. At the upper end were well-off professionals – bankers, lawyers, diplomats, civil servants. Ranged between were country doctors, teachers, skilled tradesmen, graduates, down-at-heel former officers and myriad small businessmen.

Within this disparity there were many gradations of status, which is what George Orwell was referring to when he jokingly described his own background as 'lower upper middle class'. One thing – perhaps the only thing – that all middle-class people had in common was aspiration: they were all striving to be better off than their parents and to make sure that their children did better still.

The march of suburbia

The middle-class home was the expression of a family's status and their social hopes and fears. In the Twenties, a new kind of dwelling burst forth in large numbers, like daffodils in spring. This was the semi-detached house, two conjoined mirror-image homes, two storeys high, designed to be bought and lived in by people who, to echo Orwell, might have been termed 'middle middle middle class'. Newly constructed semis were more affordable than a free-standing house and easier to manage without servants.

Aesthetically, with their false half-timbered gables and private lawned rear gardens, they represented a backward-looking architecture that was easily mocked. Osbert Lancaster described them as 'a glorified version of Anne Hathaway's cottage with such modifications as were necessary to conform to transatlantic standards of plumbing'. But the attraction of these 'olde-worlde' new-builds, quite apart from mod cons such as hot water and electricity, was that they placed the owner mid-way between town and country, just as the owner's fiscal status put him at the mid-point between wealth and poverty. The new houses were neither too cheap nor too expensive, neither grimly urban nor inconveniently rustic. And therein lay their appeal: they were middling in every way.

These Tudorbethan houses – the term was coined in the Thirties after John Betjeman's invention of 'Jacobethan' – were built in their thousands on the fringes of London and other cities, and throughout the home counties. For better or worse, they became the archetypal suburban style of the 20th century. But the kind

NEW ROADS AND HOUSES

Two proud roadbuilders, foreman F H Atkins and workmen's representative W H Goring, wait to be presented to the Prince of Wales at the opening of the new Dartford bypass (below). New roads brought with them new housing, as speculative builders threw up middle-class homes along the highways into the big cities. The roads made it easy to get into town by car, and the proliferation of cars led in turn to the construction of more roads, then still more homes. The biggest

project of all was the 'cottage estate' built over a period of ten years at Becontree near Dagenham (right, under construction). The Becontree estate, built on land compulsorily purchased from market gardeners and farmers in Essex, was paid for by London County Council. Some 25,000 small family houses were built, and more than 100,000 people – most from London's East End – moved into them. It was a hugely ambitious project and even today Becontree remains the largest housing estate in Europe.

of speculative building that created the suburbs turned uglier as it stretched far out into the countryside, giving rise to 'ribbon development'. Throughout the Twenties and into the Thirties, speculators bought up land along highways leading into cities. They would then build a string of semis or low-lying pebble-dashed bungalows on either side of the road as far as they could afford. Such houses were immensely convenient for car-owners and they were also extremely desirable, because at the back they afforded views over open country. Here again was that perfect synthesis of easy access to the city combined with the rural idyll, but an unfortunate effect was to cut travellers off from the very country through which they were moving. For mile after mile, there was little to see but neatly clipped hedges.

The dangers of uncontrolled speculative building had been noted by the end of the decade: 'It is no exaggeration to say that in fifty years, at the rate so-called improvements are being made, the destruction of all the beauty and charm with which our ancestors enhanced their towns and villages will be complete.' This was no snobbish architect speaking, but Prime Minister Stanley Baldwin in 1928. Some professionals believed that Baldwin's nightmare vision was already coming true. 'Take Peacehaven or Waterlooville or Bournemouth', wrote architect Clough Williams-Ellis, also in 1928. 'There was no attempt at intelligent general layout plan; all was cut-throat grab, exploitation and waste – a mad game of beggar-my-neighbour between a host of greedy little sneak-builders and speculators, supplying the demand for homes meanly and usuriously.' He was equally scornful of the houses: 'There they are – caught all higgledy-piggledy and looking thoroughly lost and foolish, indeed not knowing which way to look.'

A NEWER LOOK

The style of the 1920s was Art Deco, which by the end of the decade was as ubiquitous as the cloche hat. Art Deco worked best in new settings – in new apartments and cube-like houses with flat façades, clean lines and plain interior walls that functioned like a blank canvas. Done well, it was sophisticated and witty, but it could just as easily be conspicuously garish. It worked particularly well in public buildings, where there was room for a bold architectural statement. Many of the picture palaces built in the late 1920s used Deco design to superb effect.

Modern moments

Occasionally, in the midst of the kinds of houses that Williams-Ellis so plainly detested, a visitor might encounter something uncompromisingly Modernist, a 20th-century house built for a 20th-century lifestyle. It is questionable how far these chic Art Deco white boxes, with their metal-framed windows and flat roofs, were suited to the English climate – which is one reason why they were often sited on the sunny south coast. To many, they were more of an eyesore than the ubiquitous semi-detached, but to others they were the concrete expression of the Twenties spirit. And if you could not have an Art Deco exterior, you could create the look indoors, as Ethel Mannin wrote of her quaint country cottage: 'Furniture and clocks and fireplaces were all cubistic, angular, and carpets and cushions and lampshades patterned with zigzag, jazz designs. Curves were out and angles were in. There were orange cushion covers with black cats appliqued to them; there were orange and yellow artificial chrysanthemums and bright blue lupins, ideal for standing in a tall papier-mâché vase in a corner of the dance room.'

Sunday drivers

Conformists and Bohemians alike took to the private motor car, a social and technological development without which modern living would not have been possible. It was the urban network of trains that made it viable for developers to sell homes in suburbs and ribbon developments, but it was the car that carried city and suburb-dwellers on their weekend voyages of exploration. In the Twenties middle-class motoring, like middle-class housing, was a way of integrating urban life with the rustic idyll. Car manufacturers understood this, and the lure of the countryside was often the central plank of their sales pitch. 'Every weekend a holiday', ran one newspaper advertisement. 'Where shall it be this week? Through highways to old-world towns and villages or byways to the woods and fields; a quick straight run to the silvery sea or a dawdle amid hills and dales. Each weekend a new scene – that is what this Standard Light car means to the family.'

That Standard car cost £235 in 1924, and most family motors – the Austin Sevens, the American Fords, the Talbots and the Morrises – cost about the same. By 1929 a brand-new Morris Cowley could be had for as little as £195. Such prices put a car well within the means of a professional man. Whereas before the war a motor vehicle was exclusively a rich man's toy, by the end of the Twenties most middle-class families had a car in the garage, as surely as they had a wireless in the sitting room and roses in the back garden.

A private car was more than a means of transport, it was an all-consuming hobby. Just mastering the controls involved a considerable commitment of time and effort. Every gear change required the driver to 'double de-clutch', judging the engine speed to get the timing right. And drivers needed to be reasonable mechanics – at the very least, they had to know how to change a wheel or deal with an overheated radiator (a common problem on long uphill stretches). They also had to be strong enough to crank the engine into life with the starting handle. Unsurprisingly, independent women drivers were a rare breed.

But drivers in general were becoming ever more common. By 1929 there were four times as many petrol-driven vehicles in London as horse-drawn ones. The change in the composition of traffic was certainly a result of the affordability of cars, but it also had something to do with the fact that cars were an exhilarating symbol of the age. The Twenties were a decade when for many excitement and freedom were what life was about. A new world of pleasure was there to be had. If you wanted it, and could afford it, all you had to do was reach out and grasp it.

> 'Two years ago the lowest-price Morris sold at £465. Today we are marketing a better car at £225 complete.'
>
> William Morris, car manufacturer, 1922

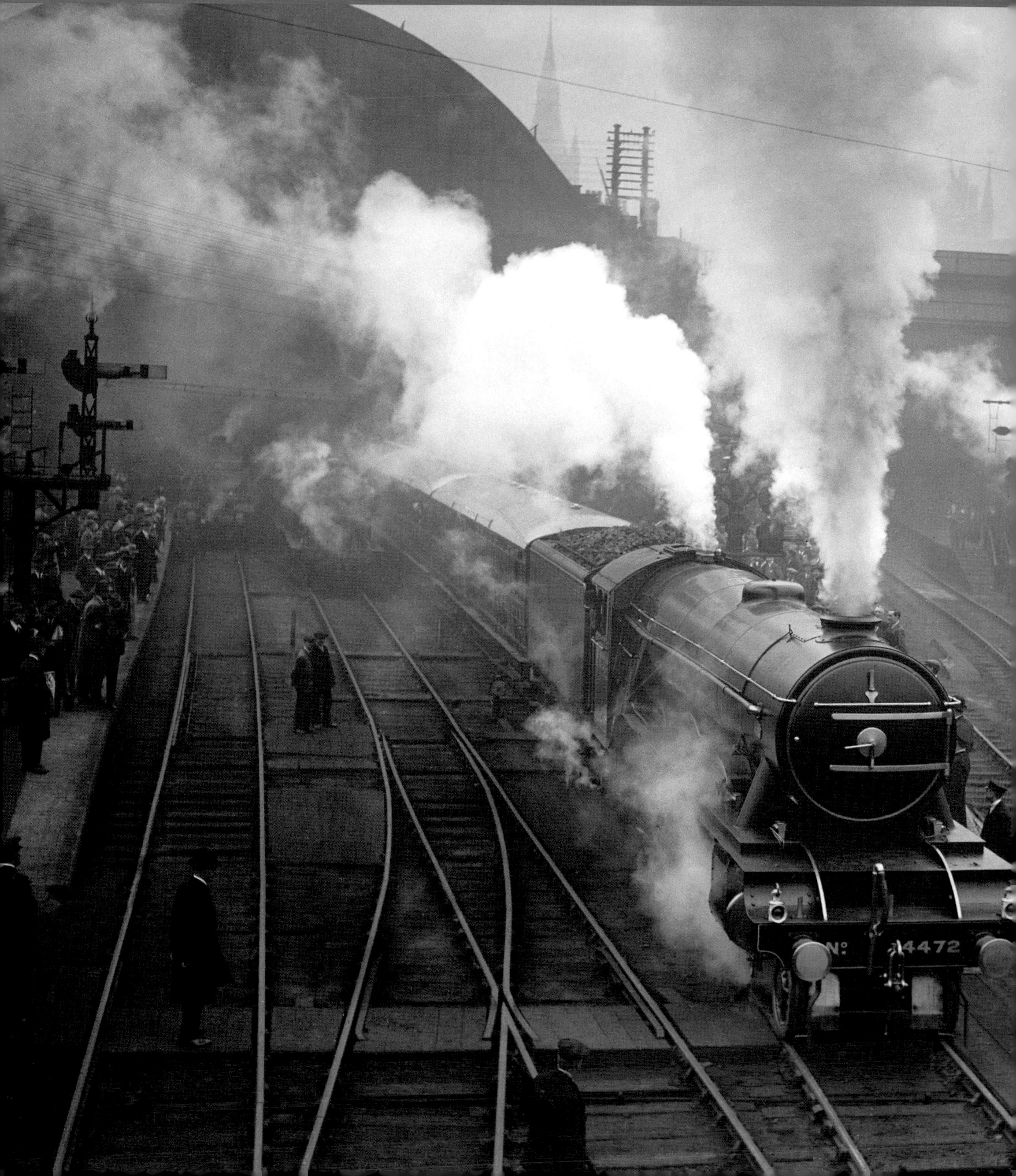
Nº 4472

TRANSPORT

In the 1920s the business of getting from one place to another became not just more democratic but also more glamorous. Personal means of transport, such as the car and the motorcycle, were now within the grasp of middle-class professionals and working-class wage-earners. Meanwhile, long-distance forms of transport – trains, ships and aircraft – aimed to offer well-to-do passengers a touch of luxury. It was, in many ways, the golden decade of travel.

STYLE AND SPEED
The Flying Scotsman (left) on its first non-stop run from London to Edinburgh on 11 May, 1928. The famous steam train started service on the 392-mile route in 1923. By 1928 technical improvements to the engine made it possible for the train to cover the distance on one tender of coal and arrive in Edinburgh shortly after six in the evening. A corridor was installed in the tender so that the crew could be relieved half-way without stopping the train. Steam trains were a stylish mode of travel – this one had a cocktail bar and hairdressing salon on board – but motorbikes were also chic in their way. They were a symbol of independence for flappers and the perfect way to arrive at a tennis party.

BY AIR AND BY SEA

There was an obsession in the 1920s with setting new records for speed and endurance in various forms. Aeroplanes – still very much a new-fangled invention – provided plenty of scope for pioneers to test themselves and their machines. In 1926 a British aviator named Alan Cobham flew to Australia and back. Here he is (top left) in the final seconds of his journey, stopping the traffic on Westminster Bridge as he comes in to land on the Thames. In 1928, in a novel test of speed, an Imperial Airways bi-plane named 'The City of Glasgow' raced the Flying Scotsman from London to Edinburgh. The plane is seen here (bottom left) crossing the river at Berwick-upon-Tweed, but the train on the viaduct is not, in fact, the Flying Scotsman, but the Junior Scotsman.

Intercontinental travel was still the realm of ocean liners, such as the *Laconia* (above), seen here leaving Liverpool for New York in 1922. For a while it seemed that airships might become viable rivals to seaborne carriers. The dining room of the R100 (right), which made its maiden flight in 1929, was as sumptuous as that of any ocean liner and the airship was capable of crossing the Atlantic. But in 1930 its sister ship, the R101, crashed in bad weather in northern France, bursting into flames and killing most of those on board. The development of airships in Britain thus came to an abrupt end.

ENGINE OF PROGRESS
By the end of the 1920s, cars were big business and trade car shows were a regular event at Olympia in London; this one (above) took place in 1929. The most successful British manufacturer was William Morris, a brilliant entrepreneur who got into the motorcar business as early as 1910, and exhibited his first model – the Morris Oxford – in 1912. He produced cars in large volumes on a production line at his factory at Cowley in Oxford (bottom right). Models such as the Morris Cowley led the way in affordability, forcing other car manufacturers to lower their prices, too. In many ways, Morris was the Henry Ford of the British automobile industry. Over the decade the country was opened up to motorists. The two ladies admiring Crummock Water in the Lake District (top right), may have been taking a chance on the reliability of their machine when they drove to such a remote spot, but by 1929 – when this photograph was taken – the risk was small and the stunning views were well worth it.

'How swift and yet how safe! How easily they thread the traffic, how tenaciously they take the corners, how effortlessly they top the rise!'

From a newspaper advertisement for Riley cars

THE BRIGHT YOUNG THINGS

For some, the Twenties was a time of more or less unrestrained hedonism and this image of the decade has stuck. Having fun was a good way to forget and for a short while the British went out of their way to dance, drink and be merry, for yesterday so many had died. Pleasure in all its forms seemed a life-affirming pursuit, and many people began the decade with the means to pursue it. 'For a time officers and men who had taken their war gratuities had money to burn', wrote war correspondent Philip Gibbs. 'They burned it in nightclubs and dance-halls, which sprang up like mushrooms ... It was a kind of feverish gaiety which burned high and burned low. Those who went in search of joy found often an intolerable boredom. In the wild Twenties there was, now and then, an underlying depression.' At the time few heard that note of sad despair: it was drowned out by the brassy beat of the Jazz Age.

> '**The feeling, which lasted over several years, was to forget all unpleasant things and to get as much fun out of life as possible. People didn't want to see the social troubles in our midst ...** '
>
> C B Cochran, West End impresario

At the vanguard of the pleasure-seeking masses was a small coterie of the super-rich, well-connected men and women who became known as the Bright Young Things (BYTs). Their raison d'être was to be outrageous, and their antics, as reported in the papers, provided thrills of amusement or disapproval for readers. While the country reeled from crisis to crisis, they drank cocktails with names such as 'Strike's Off', a coinage that says it all about their humour and the depth of their political awareness.

Non-stop party

There was, wrote Cecil Beaton, 'scarcely a night without some impromptu gathering. Quite often fancy dress taxed one's resourcefulness, but added to the fun'. Beaton's talent was just beginning to be noticed, and it gave him an entrée into the charmed circle of BYTs. He recalled that 'Loelia Ponsonby, Zita, Baby and others of the Guinness contingent, organised "stunt" parties, paper chases, find-the-hidden-clue races, bogus impressionist exhibitions and bizarre entertainments based on the fashions of the latest Diaghilev ballets. Loelia, enjoyed devising ingenious ways of eking out her income while living at a spanking pace. She was the first to give parties at which the guests were bidden to make a contribution ... providing something high in the gastronomic scale such as oysters, a croute of fois gras, or a bottle of champagne.'

The stunt parties involved such wheezes as storming Selfridges en masse and dancing on the polished counters. Young men went haring round London's streets in sports cars on a mission to acquire objects such as a policeman's helmet or a spider in a matchbox. On one notorious occasion, 300 people received an invitation which read: 'We are having a party with Romps from ten o'clock to bedtime. So write and say you'll come, and we'd love to have Nanny too. Pram park provided. Dress: anything from birth to school age.' Men turned up in

PARTY TIME
Revellers on their way to the 'motor carnival ball', one of them mounted on a sidecar apparently disguised as a giant cocktail shaker. All in all, a typically risqué 1920s combination of girls, fun, silly fancy dress costumes and motorised transport.

rompers or sailor suits, dummies in their mouths. Everyone drank martinis and manhattans from nursery mugs, and once they were thoroughly tipsy they raced each other in perambulators. The baby party was denounced as an insult to the innocence of childhood, more shocking somehow than the party that ended with gallons of petrol being poured into the Thames and set alight.

The BYTs had an influence out of all proportion to their numbers or their usefulness, partly because many of them were from old aristocratic families – they were the celebrities of their day. Lady Diana Cooper managed to span the divide between the British nobility and the emerging aristocracy of film and stage by being both a viscountess and an actress. It helped that she was quite beautiful. The exclusive attitudes of this elite were expressed in an idiom all their own. Men with beards, those Victorian representatives of all that was old and stuffy, were called

FANCY DRESSERS

The 'bright young things' had a rather childish fondness for dressing up. The icily beautiful Lady Castlerosse (left) wore this elaborate constellation of stars on her head for the Galaxy Ball Pageant in 1929, while the coterie of upper-class clowns (right) are enjoying the Chelsea Arts Ball from the vantage point of a box at the Royal Albert Hall. The high-pitched excitement of such occasions was captured by the socialite Duff Cooper, when he described a party at Lady Curzon's residence: 'Everyone was in the highest spirits, everyone was in fancy dress and several wore one or two different ones during the course of the evening. The stately rooms of Carlton House Terrace looked more like a Montmartre restaurant, littered with confetti, masks, streamers, celluloid balls etc. I wore first a skeleton mask in which nobody recognised me and I had the greatest fun. When I finally had to take it off to drink I later put on another different one and again escaped recognition for a long time. All the women looked beautiful, or so I thought.'

But even amid the pranks and gaiety, there was a strict social code. 'Our morals might be nowhere, but when it came to fashion and etiquette we conformed', observed Ethel Mannin. 'There were various small niceties, too – we always offered both Turkish and Virginian cigarettes when we entertained, we served finger-bowls with warm water and a slice of lemon, our coffee sugar was coloured crystals, and we put out coloured matches for those who wished to smoke … Long cigarette holders became fashionable … and the ladies, of course, all smoked conscientiously, as the outward and visible sign of sex equality.'

'beavers'. The term was taken up as a taunt by boys and hurled at bearded men in the street. The characteristic Twenties term 'flapper', in its lighthearted modern sense, emanated from these same privileged circles. In earlier generations the word had been a low dialect term for a very young prostitute, a usage that was a metaphorical extension of its original sense: a fledgling duck.

A few years after the radiance of the bright young things had dimmed, Archibald Lyall wrote this of the language they used: 'The archetypal upper-class flapper lived, moved and had their hyperbolic being in a world where everything was "quite too thrilling" or "too, too marvellous". And where, instead of being mildly annoyed or amused, one was "purple with rage", "mad with passion", "speechless with laughter", or "quite hysterical", such descriptions being generally reinforced by the most inapposite adverb in the language, "literally".' But when

such jargon and mannerisms were adopted by outsiders, who were neither bright nor young, all the glamour somehow began to look rather tawdry and old-hat. Beaton, as a middle-class interloper in this circle, saw it more clearly than most: 'Under Loelia's baton, the Bright Young Things were not only bright but talented. The name, however, when taken up by the gossips, soon acquired a stigma. A "bottle party" became synonymous with drunkenness and squalor, and no longer had any connection with its charter members long before a not very "bright" middle-aged woman shot someone under a piano.'

Noël Coward, the wry poet laureate of the Gay Decade, saw it too. His song 'Poor Little Rich Girl', written in 1925, contains the wistful, forward-looking lines: 'In lives of leisure / The craze for pleasure / Steadily grows. / Cocktails and laughter / But what comes after / Nobody knows …' The fact that the brightest young things were from the highest echelons of society made their outrageous escapades seem almost acceptable. Or at least, their look and their tastes appeared to those lower down the social scale to be enviable and worthy of imitation. 'This is the Age of Luxury', wrote the *Manchester Guardian* in 1926. 'Before the war and in the uneasy years which immediately followed it, luxury was mainly a matter of means. Now any young typist from Manchester or Kensington can keep her hair trimmed and waved, and her busy feet in fine silk stockings and pale kid shoes.' The mention of busy feet is a reference to the hypothetical typist's leisure hours, which typically would have been spent dancing.

PRESENT LAUGHTER
Noël Coward (above, second from left), with theatre producer Charles Cochran, Cochran's wife and three dancers, on board ship bound from New York to Southampton. Plays such as *Blithe Spirit*, *The Vortex* and *Hay Fever* made Coward rich and famous as a dramatist, but he is perhaps best known as a writer of comic revues and witty romantic songs such as 'Room With A View'. Coward managed to satirise upper class life in the Twenties, while at the same time revelling in it. His works are far more than mere period pieces, because they say something about the general maladies of 20th-century life – the barely disguised shallowness, the brittle vanity, the aimless pursuit of pleasure. Not that there was anything wrong *per se* in pursuing pleasure: these four ladies in a punt on the Thames during the Henley Regatta (right) seem to be having a perfectly nice, uncomplicated day out.

GET UP AND DANCE

Dance – frenetic, joyful, vivacious dance – was an obsession in the Twenties. Ethel Mannin, a precocious young novelist and member of the Bohemian fringe, spent many evenings dancing at a little nightclub called the Ham Bone in Soho. She also attended 'tea dances and dinner dances and the late-night restaurants with "floor shows" … the Hammersmith Palais de Danse, Prince's in Piccadilly, the Criterion Roof, Romano's in the Strand, the Savoy. It was very smart to dance at the Savoy after the theatre, between the courses of supper.'

There was an ever-changing succession of dances to be mastered – and then discarded like spent matches the moment they became unfashionable. The shimmy, the lindy hop (named in honour of transatlantic aviator Charles Lindbergh), the turkey trot and the camel walk all came and went. The black bottom involved stretching out the arms, 'like a man balancing on a tightrope', then making a

DINNER DANCE
No sizeable restaurant or hotel could afford to be without a band, a cabaret and a dance floor. Middle-class diners wanted to be serenaded as they ate, and then be able to get up and dance the rest of the night away.

For most of the decade, that constituted the be-all and end-all of a night out – in London, at least, where venues such as the Palm Beach Café on the Thames (left, in 1926) and the Criterion roof garden (above, in 1922) were places to be seen.

series of stamping movements while wiggling the hips. If performed poorly the black bottom was inelegant to say the least, which may be one reason why the fad did not last.

The American influence

America, of course, was the source of all the new dances flooding into Britain. By far the most popular was the charleston, which was introduced by two exhibition dancers, Robert Sielle and his partner Annette Mills (sister of the actor John Mills and later the presenter of BBC's *Muffin the Mule*). The pair were known as the 'English Astaires', even though Sielle was American. They performed the charleston at the Kit Cat Club in 1925, and from there it spread like an epidemic. A dance floor filled with enthusiastic charlestoners was a spectacular sight to behold – and a hazardous place to be: all bobbing heads and flailing limbs, oscillating rapidly like a mass of pendulums and metronomes in a dizzying, syncopated pattern.

The charleston was wonderfully boisterous fun, and that was why people loved it – or hated it. Office managers complained that employees, in the grip of charleston mania, sat twitching at their desks in an echo of the previous night's revelries, or in anticipation of the next. The *Daily Mail* wrinkled its prim editorial nose and pronounced that the charleston was 'reminiscent only of negro orgies', even though the dance was actually about as sexually provocative as running on the spot. A vicar in Bristol preached against it from his pulpit, saying 'It is neurotic! It is rotten! It stinks! Phew, open the windows!' But once it became known that the dashing Prince of Wales enjoyed the charleston – and did it well, too – then everyone felt that when they danced, they did so by royal appointment.

It was chic to dance at home to music played on a gramophone. Furniture would be moved back, the carpet rolled up and the box wound up so the music could begin. Imported American recordings were flooding into British music stores, so the latest music was easy to get hold of. The HMV company produced records with different coloured labels corresponding to genre: red for classical (not at all the thing for parties), magenta for light music. A label called Zonophone offered variety and music-hall acts. But it was dance music that drove gramophone sales. The number of shellac discs produced annually in Britain went up over the decade from 22 million to nearly 72 million.

But just as often, people went out to a club or dance hall to dance. In many of these establishments men were supposed to keep their gloves on – which seems a strange point of decorum until one realises that it was a response to the fashion for low-backed dresses and was intended to prevent men touching the bare backs of their dance partners. The West End of London was crammed with louche nightclubs where one could bunny hop to the music of a 'negro band' and drink – illegally – out of hours. If the place was raided by police, well for the richest and best-connected revellers that was all part of the fun. Many a Bright Young Thing rounded off a night out with an early morning court appearance – followed by a brief encounter, still in evening dress, with the gentlemen of the popular press.

Dancing was a pastime that recognised no social boundaries. 'Today dancing as an active recreation appeals to many people of all classes', stated the *New Survey of London Life and Labour*, a kind of anthropological study of

'The hours flew away, I hardly remember whom I danced with … It was half past four when I got home."

Duff Cooper, diary entry, February 1924

TAPPERS AND KICKERS

In a generation that lived to dance, what could be more glamorous than to be a dancing girl? People enoyed watching dance almost as much as – sometimes more than – doing it themselves, and there was a great vogue for high-kicking chorus girls. The undisputed queens of 'precision dancing' were the Tiller Girls (bottom right), a troupe that had been founded in the last days of the Victorian era, and so had a professional headstart over the rest. They were masters, so to speak, of the synchronised technique known as 'tap and kick'. They had many imitators, including the cabaret girls of the Piccadilly Hotel, shown here in musically themed frocks (top right). Most people loved a pretty chorus line, but for one cultural commentator, the German sociologist Siegfried Kracauer, the Tiller Girls were not so much dance artists as expressions of the new machine age: 'When they raised their legs with mathematical precision, they joyfully affirmed the progress of rationalisation', he wrote. 'When they continually repeated the same manoeuvre, never breaking ranks, one had the vision of an unbroken chain of automobiles gliding out of the factory.'

working-class tribes in the capital, written in 1928. 'The dance-halls are within the range of nearly everybody's purse, and typists, shop assistants and factory girls rub shoulders in them. People drop into a palais after work or on Saturday evenings as casually as they go to a cinema.' The dance-hall owners were of course delighted that their venues were filled to the brim. 'The younger generation ... have come to love the jazz step, as it typifies pep, energy, push, advancement, the love of living, and the things that go with an up-to-date modern world', wrote an anonymous contributor to the monthly *Hammersmith Palais Dancing News*.

In the north of England, where dancing was called 'jigging', the nightly ritual of the dance halls had a complex social etiquette all of its own. Inside the great barn-like interiors, young men would gather in the half-light on one side of the hall, while the women arraigned themselves like rows of trinkets in a jeweller's shop window on the other. One by one the men would cross the floor and choose a partner. The girls left standing would resignedly dance with each other, hoping that their moves, if not their looks, would catch the attention of a male dancing partner. In many such dance halls, the proceedings were overseen by a master of ceremonies, who was something of a cross between a headmaster and a chaperone. 'Our major domo stood five feet one – a pocket Valentino in evening dress', wrote Robert Roberts, who grew up in Salford between the wars. 'He had a fearsome reputation as a Don Juan ... [but] in his way our MC was a stickler for decorum. He came down heavily on any males gyrating as they smoked, or with their hats on. That, he felt, lowered the tone.'

THE FLICKS AND TALKIES

In the darkness of the picture house, ordinary people entered another world inhabited by silent smouldering 'vamps' like Theda Bara. The studio promotional material claimed that she had been born in Egypt and that her name was two anagrams: Theda was death rearranged (terribly daring) and Bara was the reverse of Arab, a byword for the exotic. In fact, she was the daughter of a Jewish tailor from Poland and Theda was her childhood nickname, shortened from her real name, Theodosia, while Bara came from her maternal grandfather's name, Baranger. The audiences for films such as Bara's *Unchastened Woman* consisted overwhelmingly of young wage-earners with money to spare. Young working girls, in particular, spent their money on going to the pictures two or three times a week. Well into the Thirties, there were cheap 'flea-pits' that charged just a penny a ticket to watch a film. Up-market picture houses were a more expensive outing, but a fellow could easily treat his girl to the cinema for less than a couple of shillings and – if she was agreeable – spend a couple of cosy hours entwined on the double seats that many establishments provided at the back of the auditorium.

Disapproving voices
Some people objected to the cinema precisely because it provided a place outside the home for courtship. The chief constable of Guildford felt constrained to point out that picture houses were places 'where young men and women attend together not for the purpose of following the pictures, but to be spoony', as if 'spooniness'

continued on page 324

PICTURE PALACES

The Tooting Electric Pavilion was a typical old-style cinema, built in 1914 when film was still in its infancy. By the mid-1920s it was rather run-down, its appearance not helped by the line of washing, which some bright spark had decided was a good way to promote the Mary Pickford film *Suds*. As films became more sophisticated, so too did the buildings in which they were shown. The next generation of cinemas was more like the New Gallery, Regent Street, which in the mid-1920s was given a brightly illuminated canopy – and a uniformed doorman to add a note of exclusivity. Inside was a spectacular, 256-foot long Greek frieze and one of London's finest Wurlitzers. In the 1930s, the New Gallery became well-known as the theatre in which Disney's feature cartoons were premiered. The Tooting Electric also went up in the world: its façade was remodelled in Art Deco style in 1933 and it was renamed the Astoria. It was demolished in the 1970s, but the interior of the New Gallery still survives.

FILM STARS

It was in the 1920s that movie stars became household names. Charlie Chaplin had blazed the trail – he was famous before the Great War – but in the 1920s cinema-goers began to feel somehow personally acquainted with the people up on the screen. They could see them up close, by the end of the decade they could hear their voices, and through the gossip columns and fan magazines they gained a delicious peek at their private lives.

KINGS OF COMEDY
Both Stan Laurel and Oliver Hardy – seen here (left) taking a break from filming *The Finishing Touch* – served a long comic apprenticeship. Laurel (on the right) was born in Ulverston, Lancashire. He worked in music hall and was understudy to Charlie Chaplin before emigrating to the USA in 1912. Hardy was a singer who became a silent film performer. He made more than 250 films before pairing up with Laurel in their hugely successful double act in the mid-20s. But for many film fans, Buster Keaton was the finest visual comedian of them all. Despite his mournful face – seen below in *Sherlock Junior* made in 1928 – he was less mawkish, more inventive and in the end simply funnier than Chaplin.

BEHIND THE MASKS

Charlie Chaplin, seen here in 1929 (left), contemplating a mannequin of his on-screen persona. Chaplin was the first global superstar, his worldwide fame made possible by the universal language of silent film. The 1920s were the first decade of international celebrity. Theda Bara (above) made a name for herself with a darkly sexy persona that was every bit as manufactured and fictional as Chaplin's little hobo. Ronald Colman (above right) was the genuine article: a handsome veteran of the Western Front who did his own stunts despite a serious war wound to his leg. In the silent era Colman was often paired with the Hungarian actress Vilma Banky; they are seen here in a publicity shot for *Night of Love*. Romance was a staple of silent cinema, and no-one did wordless passion better than Greta Garbo. In *The Temptress* (bottom right), she was paired with Antonio Moreno, but she smouldered best in the embrace of John Gilbert – 'the great lover' – with whom she had a very public affair.

Chaplin, Colman and Garbo all survived the transition to dialogue-led movies, heralded in 1927 by Al Jolson's groundbreaking talkie *The Jazz Singer* (centre right). Theda Bara, already past her prime, faded away in the middle of the decade.

'A tramp, a gentleman, a poet, a dreamer, a lonely fellow, always hopeful of romance and adventure.'

Charlie Chaplin, describing his down-at-heel on-screen alter ego

were an arrestable offence. An attempt to link the flicks to crime – and one which has had echoes through the years – was made by Lilian Russell, wife of Charles Russell, the Chief Inspector of Reformatory and Industrial Schools, who tried to drag teenagers out of the flea-pits and into the wholesome embrace of the Lads' Clubs over which she presided. 'The cinema-play', she wrote, 'though not exactly vicious, is often very low in tone, giving young people who frequent it an altogether false and vulgar, foolishly sentimental, and in the worst sense, Americanised view of life. We have seen not a few weak-willed young fellows in prison who have been convicted for thefts committed, as they confessed, to get money to "buy some tabs [cigarettes] and go to the pictures".'

> ## 'It is not the single talkie drama that does the harm, but the cumulative effect of many which affect the impressionable mind.'
> **Lilian Russell, determined critic of the social effects of the cinema**

The content of the 'cinema-plays' was not nearly so deleterious as Mrs Russell believed. The British Board of Film Censors banned a long list of subjects, including: 'the modus operandi of criminals … indecorous dancing … scenes in which the king and officers in uniform are seen in an odious light … vitriol throwing … women fighting with knives … salacious wit … drunken scenes carried to excess … surgical operations … outrageous and irreverent sub-titles … commitment of crime by children … criminal poisoning by the dissemination of germs … realistic horrors of war.' While many of the interdictions are laughable or unfathomable, the prohibition placed on 'insistence on the inferiority of coloured races' was ahead of its time.

The coming of talkies

The allure of the cinema was barely affected by detractors. In fact, its magical pull grew stronger year by year. Cinemas became more attractive as out-dated Edwardian venues were replaced and reinvented as splendid 'picture palaces' in the form of Egyptian temples, Roman villas and Moorish citadels. Art Deco was a popular style. Then the first talkie, *The Jazz Singer*, arrived: the first spoken sentence consisted of four words captured by accident as Al Jolson was about to break into song. They were, appropriately enough, 'Ma, listen to this'.

That summons spelled the end for the silent movie, but not everyone realised it at the time. Though talkies were a technological step forward, they were viewed by highbrow commentators – the kind of people who said *k*inema rather than *s*inema – as an inferior art form. The *New Statesman* denigrated talkies as 'squawkies'. *Punch*, usually good-humoured and good at spotting a trend, said in its review of *The Jazz Singer* that 'the silent film is not seriously threatened'. The following year an article in *Punch* vilified cinema audiences: 'The film public is a doped public. They sit in a stupor, hypnotised by the organ and the comfy seats … swallowing without protest things which, if they saw them in the theatre, would cause them to rise up, boo, and go out.' But the public didn't care two hoots for the snobbish opinions of journalists. In 1930 the silent-versus-talkie debate was settled once and for all by a new film, *The Kiss*, starring Greta Garbo. It was advertised with huge posters stating simply 'GARBO TALKS'. People flocked to the picture palaces to hear the husky, sexy tones of the Swedish ice-maiden: 'Gimme a visky, ginger ale on the side. And don't be stinchy, baby …'

OPENING UP THE AIRWAVES

RIDING THE CREST OF THE WAVES
Wireless technology developed in tandem with the programme content. As the decade progressed, receivers became simpler to operate and began to look less like the contents of an electrician's workshop, more like polished mahogany vanity cases. At the same time, the transmission of popular light music became the main function of the new devices. Although they do not know it, these serious fellows, photographed in 1922 (above) are on the very cusp of that transformation, as they link their valve radios in series in order to channel a musical programme through a loudspeaker.

At the start of the decade, 'wireless telephony' was still a rather dull technical hobby. All wireless users were required to apply to the Postmaster General for a licence, which gave permission for 'the installation and use of a station for receiving wireless signals for experimental purposes'. The crystal receivers came in kit form and had to be assembled. There were no programmes broadcast at all, so the sport consisted of seeing if one could pick up a signal. Hobbyists donned headphones and tuned in to an engineer of the Marconi Company in Chelmsford reciting nursery rhymes or lists of railway stations. Real enthusiasts would attempt to pick up signals from Paris, Luxembourg or Berlin. So the wireless habit was a bit like aural angling, fishing for distant signals. When the Prince of Wales visited Mill Hill School he congratulated the boys on having managed to 'wireless the Atlantic' and pick up a signal from America. For most people it was quite baffling. In 1923, when the wireless was demonstrated to the Archbishop of Canterbury, he asked if he ought not open the window to let the signal in.

In 1920 the Marconi engineers, bored of chanting nonsense into a microphone, invited two local singers – a Mrs Winifred Sayer and a Mr Edward Cooper, a tenor with a day job in the Marconi factory – to sing a few pieces on their 'experimental' wavelength. These two amateurs thus became the first artistes ever to showcase their talents on the radio in Britain. Later the same year, Dame Nellie Melba was persuaded to go to Chelmsford to give a recital which, it was said incredulously, could be heard 'within a radius of a thousand miles'.

Birth of the BBC

At this stage the audience was still tiny and the Marconi Company decided to discontinue its broadcasts. But the protests of enthusiasts were so voluble that the largest manufacturers of crystal sets became convinced they could sell large numbers if there were interesting broadcasts to be received. In 1922 they set up the British Broadcasting Company Ltd to make programmes and their private venture became a huge success. The opportunity to have entertainment piped into one's home was something people were prepared to pay for. It was still only possible to listen on headphones, but that did not seem to matter.

Music dominated the early broadcasts – dance band music by the likes of Jack Payne and also light orchestral pieces, brass ensembles and classical. The provision of enjoyable content was to transform the wireless from a potting-shed pastime into the single most powerful mass medium in the country. In the four years after the BBC was incorporated, the number of wireless licensees rose from 6,000 to 2 million, and the cartel of wireless manufacturers was growing rich from sales of equipment.

For the government, the monopoly of the airwaves was too precious to remain in private hands. So in 1927 the shareholders of the British Broadcasting Company were bought out with state funds and the organisation was nationalised. The Company was renamed the British Broadcasting Corporation, which preserved the three initials by which it was already known. The new BBC's main broadcasting station was moved to Borough Hill near Daventry in Northamptonshire, a high and geographically central point from which to broadcast to the entire island. 'Daventry calling …' would later become the signature of the BBC Empire Service, recognised and revered by Anglophiles and British expats around the globe.

The impact on British life of the creation of the BBC is hard to overstate. It allowed the wireless to develop as a public service, independent of commercial or political pressures. The Corporation, under the terms of its Royal Charter, did not belong to government. If it belonged to anyone, that person was John Reith, its general manager. Reith was committed to a formula which he himself devised: that the BBC's mission was to 'educate, inform and entertain'. He never allowed the politicians to use the organisation as a mouthpiece, not even in times of crisis such as the General Strike of 1926 – in fact, especially at such times. National leaders, when they spoke on the wireless, were merely borrowing the airwaves to put their case to the nation. It added up to a unique and democratic use of the new technology. The wireless raised social and political awareness, it was a source of knowledge and ideas, it spoke across social barriers, and so worked as a positive force for change in an already rapidly changing world.

LISTEN WITH PALMER
It was a requirement of presenters on the BBC that they be smartly dressed, even though they could not be seen by listeners. This dapper looking chap in spats and bow tie is Rex Palmer (above), a veteran of the Royal Flying Corps and one of the founders of the Corporation. Much of the output in the early years was created on the hoof. Palmer was known to thousands of children as 'Uncle Rex', as he was one of the BBC staffers who took it upon themselves to display their talents in *Children's Hour*, a 'nightly romp' filled with childish misbehaviour. 'Uncle-ing' became a kind of semi-professional hobby for Palmer and several other BBC executives, who received sacks of fan mail from children. Palmer also happened to be a fine baritone and sang 'Abide With Me' to the nation at the close of programmes every Sunday.

WORKING ON THE BOX

In the middle of the decade, as wireless sets were becoming a fixture in every home, a Scottish engineer named John Logie Baird – right and below, with fellow-Scot and actor Jack Buchanan (seated) – was working on transmitting moving pictures. The story goes that in 1925, in an upstairs lab in Soho, he succeeded in broadcasting the image of a ventriloquist's dummy's head from his transmitter to a receiver in the next room. Soon after he did the same with a live head, that of an office boy called William Taynton, who thus went down in history as the first person ever seen on the screen of a 'televisor', as Baird called his set. In 1929, Baird persuaded the BBC to take an interest in his invention. But his system depended on mechanical revolving discs inside both the transmitter and receiver – as seen in his stripped-down prototype (right) – and this turned out to be a technological dead end. The form of television that eventually caught on exploited an entirely different principle, based on the cathode ray tube.

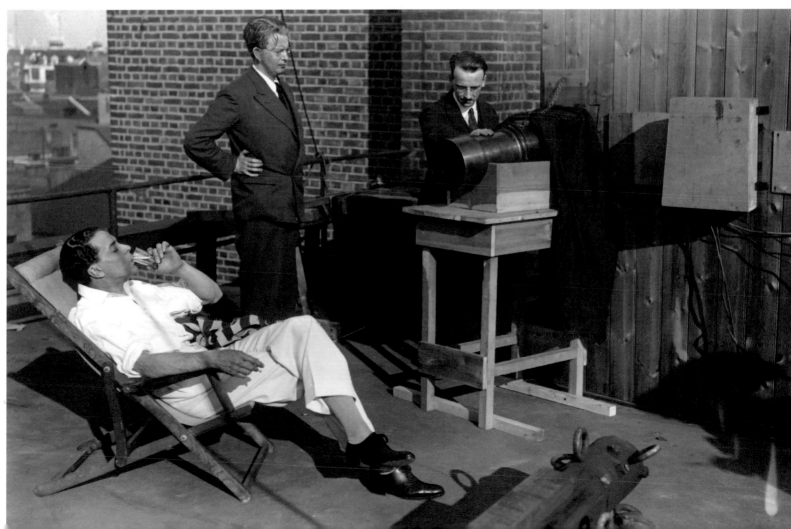

1920s

SUNNY SIDE OF THE STREET?

Most working people in Britain felt insecure in their jobs as the Twenties wore on, but possibly no-one more so than the Prime Minister. Running the country was a precarious business – the occupant of 10 Downing Street changed no fewer than six times over the course of the decade, but from 1923 the same two figures – Stanley Baldwin and Ramsay MacDonald – kept coming round, like the wooden toys on a Swiss clock. Ramsay MacDonald became, briefly, the first Labour Prime Minister in January 1924. The General Strike of 1926 was on Baldwin's watch and though the strikers failed in their immediate aims, the event was a defining moment in the decade.

HORSE AND GROOM Workmen cleaning the Quadriga on top of the Wellington Arch, high above Hyde Park Corner, in an era when attitudes to 'health and safety' were very different from today.

MINISTERS OF THE CROWN

Broadly speaking, the frequent changes of leadership in the 1920s were a symptom of the economic sickness that was rapidly spreading through the land, but in the case of Andrew Bonar Law – who succeeded David Lloyd George as Prime Minister in 1922 – it was illness that made his time in office so brief. Soon after taking office he was diagnosed with terminal throat cancer. He resigned in May 1923, by which time the condition had made it impossible for him to speak in Parliament. His tenure was 209 days in all, which was too little time to make much of a mark, other than giving him the distinction of serving the shortest term of any Prime Minister in British history. He died six months after leaving office. At his funeral in Westminster Abbey, Lord Asquith remarked that they were burying the Unknown Prime Minister next to the Unknown Soldier. The jibe became Bonar Law's unofficial epitaph – unfairly, because he had a long and distinguished career in Parliament and public life. It was cruel, too, because Bonar Law had lost two sons in the war. For all anyone knew, he was being laid to rest beside one of his own boys.

The mantle of leadership was picked up by Bonar Law's chancellor, Stanley Baldwin, who saw himself as the pipe-smoking kindly uncle of the people – an image that he projected rather well. He was the first party leader and Prime Minister to master the medium of the new-fangled wireless and harness its power to put a message across directly to the public. His broadcasts took the form of self-deprecating 'fireside chats', but his tone was old-fashioned and rather noble. 'I am just one of yourselves, who has been called to special work for the country', he told the listening public. 'I have but one idea, which was an idea that I inherited … service to the people of this country. All my life I believed from my heart the words of Browning: "All service ranks the same with God". It makes very little difference whether a man is driving a tramcar or sweeping streets or being prime minister, if he only brings to that service everything that is in him and performs it for the sake of mankind.'

Baldwin's solution for the nation's economic troubles was, in one word, protectionism. He proposed to safeguard British jobs and British products by placing a high tax on foreign goods, with only a slightly lower one on imports from the Empire. Big business was delighted, but most people were appalled by the prospect of paying more for their food. The policy was particularly unpopular

HOT NEWS
An 'electometer' set up by a Fleet Street newspaper – a novel way to bring the public up-to-the minute news about election results. Britain's political climate changed radically in the 1920s. The Liberal Party, a major force for generations, went into rapid decline. The Labour Party enjoyed a corresponding rise and socialist ideas created a new ideological environment in the country. The Conservative Party had to find strategies to deal with the changed conditions – and with a different primary opponent. Much of the civil strife in the 1920s was a struggle between the reds and the blues, between the aggrieved working classes on the one hand and the stout bourgeoisie on the other.

CONSERVATIVE LEADERS

Andrew Bonar Law (right), photographed while inspecting a troop of boys at Kew in southwest London, is little remembered as Prime Minister today, partly because he did not have time to prove himself in office, but also because in the course of his career he was often outshone by more ebullient personalities, such as David Lloyd George. He was modest about his own political gifts; he is said to have remarked of Asquith that 'he can make a better speech drunk than the rest of us can sober'.

Bonar Law's resignation due to illness opened the way for his successor Stanley Baldwin (below). Baldwin's manner was self-confident, his style might now be termed 'presidential'. A born delegator, he left his ministries to look after themselves. He did the minimum of paperwork, preferring to issue orders and make his views known through speaking personally to the right individual. He drank champagne to 'buoy himself up', and left the office promptly at 5pm on a Friday.

THE POWER AND THE GLORY
It was an historic moment when Ramsay MacDonald (above, standing) became the first Labour Prime Minister in January 1924. He led a minority government, so it is no surprise that his tenure turned out to be shortlived, lasting only 10 months. When he called another election in October 1924, MacDonald asked the British people to give him the executive might of a Prime Minister, in addition to the mere job title. But for the time being the public remained unconvinced by the socialist experiment and power passed back to the Tories.

with the recently enfranchised female section of the electorate, since they were generally the ones who had to manage the household budget. Baldwin called a general election in order to get the people's mandate for his high-tariff policy – but he did not get the result he wanted. The outcome was a hung parliament, in which the Conservatives won 258 seats, the Liberals 159 and the Labour Party – suddenly a political force to be reckoned with – won 191.

The Liberal Party declined to support the Conservatives, so in January 1924 the government resigned. King George V then called on the Labour leader, Ramsay MacDonald, to form a government. 'They have different ideas to ours as they are all socialists', he confided to his royal diary. 'But they ought to be given a chance and treated fairly.' MacDonald accepted the King's call and the first Labour government in British history came into being.

LABOUR IN POWER

The prospect of MacDonald and his newly appointed proletarian ministers going to the palace to be sworn in gave rise to much snobbish tittering. Would these horny-handed sons of toil know how to wear court dress? Would they even agree to do so? Would their rough manners let them down? In the event nothing untoward happened, but the day that Labour took office was no less remarkable for that. Among the men who swore the ministerial oath was John Robert Clynes,

who began his working life in a Lancashire cotton mill at the age of ten. He was now chairman of the parliamentary Labour Party. 'I could not help marvelling at the strange turn of Fortune's wheel', he later wrote, 'which had bought Ramsay MacDonald the starving clerk, J H Thomas the engine driver, Arthur Henderson the foundry labourer and Clynes the mill-hand to this pinnacle beside the man whose forebears had been kings for so many splendid generations.' George V was thinking along similar lines: 'Today 23 years ago dear Grandmama died. I wonder what she would have thought of a Labour Government!' Grandmama – that is, Queen Victoria – would probably have thought that the political landscape had been turned upside down. It had certainly been changed for ever.

With less than 200 MPs out of nearly 700, the first Labour government faced an impossible task. Nevertheless, it forced through some commendable measures to help the poorest citizens, the ones who had been hit hardest by the slump. Unemployment benefit, for example, was raised from 15 shillings to 18 shillings a week. If a man had a dependent wife, then he received 7 shillings on top, and he

SOUP AND SOCIALISM
The shortlived Labour government did what it could for the poor and unemployed. At the most basic level, this meant providing hot meals at 'poor relief' soup kitchens. Some of those out of work had unemployment insurance, but a government committee appointed by the incoming Conservative administration found that public opinion was 'predominantly unfavourable' to any form of dole because it was thought to encourage idleness. The committee investigated the widespread assumption that the unemployed routinely abused the insurance system, but found no evidence of fraud at all.

QUAY WORKERS

London dockers getting back to work at the end of a strike in 1924. Dockworkers had a reputation for militancy. In 1920 they had provoked a political crisis by refusing to handle arms shipments bound for Poland, then at war with the new Soviet state. In 1922 the dockers' union was absorbed into the Transport and General Workers' Union, but the highly skilled stevedores elected to retain their own union – the National Amalgamated Stevedores' and Dockers' Union. The TGWU men became known as 'whites', from the colour of their union cards, while the stevedores were 'blues'. Rivalry between the two made it harder for dockers to present a united front to employers when industrial conflicts arose.

was entitled to claim 2 shillings a week for each child. So an unemployed man, married with three children, received benefit amounting to 31 shillings a week in the summer of 1924. It was still less than half of what was needed to live on – a government statistician had calculated that a working docker with a wife and three children required a minimum income of £3 13s 6d a week. But previously there had been nothing at all for a wife or children, so the unemployed under Labour were already better off than they had been under either the Liberals or the Tories.

Making an impact in housing

The Labour government's other great undertaking for the benefit of the poor working classes was the 1924 Housing Act, which empowered local authorities to build houses for low-paid citizens – something that no private speculators were doing at the time. 'Are we to remain without houses merely because people with money to invest refuse to invest that money directly in working-class houses?' asked John Wheatley, the main sponsor of the Act, a fiery Glaswegian whom MacDonald had appointed Minister of Health. The answer to his question was a resounding no: a Labour government had a responsibility to house the ordinary people who were the engine of the nation's prosperity, or at least of its recovery.

The health and well-being of the people who would live in the new houses was paramount. Wheatley houses were built twelve to an acre on the outskirts of big towns. This relatively low density allowed light and air to surround every home and gave each occupier a patch of garden in which to grow vegetables. It was also written into the Bill that all the houses must have an indoor bathroom (rather than provision for a copper in the scullery). Altogether more than half a million municipal homes were eventually constructed under the auspices of Wheatley's Act, and building homes for ordinary people became one of the primary functions of local councils. In retrospect, this was the main legacy of that first Labour government – a solid, unquestionably sound, bricks-and-mortar achievement.

The Tories return to power

The successes of MacDonald's first administration are all the more remarkable when one considers that it lasted less than a year. In 1925 the baton passed back to the Conservatives under Stanley Baldwin. With Churchill as Chancellor, one of the first acts of the administration was to return the pound to the gold standard, which had been suspended on the outbreak of war in 1914. Reinstatement was intended to restore British prestige and return the economy to its 'normal' pre-war level, but the pound had fallen in real terms, so it merely made British exports artificially expensive in foreign markets. The economy suffered badly as a result.

An even more dangerous economic crisis was looming in the mining industry, where colliery owners had seen their profits fall, and wanted to cut miners' wages.

The miners refused to countenance this, claiming that they were already worse off than they had been in 1914. In April 1926, the owners posted notices saying that employees would be locked out – sacked, in other words – unless they agreed to a much lower wage and a longer working day. It was a deliberate move designed to provoke a showdown and the miners took up the challenge. They turned to the union movement to support them, arguing that if the miners were forced to take pay cuts, then other workers would also be forced down the same route. The TUC agreed and declared a general strike for the first week of May.

THE GENERAL STRIKE OF 1926

Once again, revolution seemed to be in the air. While the unions finalised their plans to paralyse the country, the government made preparations to foil them. Hyde Park in London was turned into a vast depot for food and other essential supplies: some 3000 lorries were parked up there, with military guards posted on the gates, and loyal Post Office workers toiled through the night stringing telephone wires between the blossoming trees. On the eve of the strike, *The Times* wrote portentously that 'unless counsels of reason prevail, we are within a few hours of the gravest domestic menace which has hung over this nation since the

THE STRIKERS

Though the striking workers saw themselves as active participants in a fundamental struggle, for many there was little they could actually do to fill the days. These Scottish miners from Prestonpans colliery in East Lothian (above) could find nothing better to do than sit and play cards, while the political drama played itself out elsewhere. In Plymouth, this orderly column of men (left) are marching not to the barricades, but to a church pew. Dressed in their Sunday best, they are about to attend a special service for strikers at St Andrew's church. Not all clergy were so sympathetic. That same Sunday, 9 May, the Roman Catholic Archbishop of Westminster declared that the strike was 'a sin against God'. Information about what was actually going on was hard to come by, and so was consumed avidly by strikers when it appeared (right). Local branches of the TUC and other left-wing organisations produced newsheets with names such as *The Worker*, but there were precious few means of getting them distributed to supporters. Strikers in the provinces relied on an almost medieval system of TUC 'couriers', who travelled from city to city spreading news by word of mouth and encouraging men to stand firm.

fall of the Stuarts'. And as in the days that led up to and then during the English Civil War, everyone took sides. It was almost impossible to be neutral: everyone was either for the strike or adamantly against it.

The middle classes were almost uniformly against. When the government called for people to take the strikers' places, the white-collared office workers and small businessmen were the first to volunteer to 'do their bit' – as if driving a tram, manning a signal box, or lugging sides of beef were a patriotic duty on a par with fighting the Germans in the war. The ranks of the pro-government men were swelled by students from Oxford and Cambridge, who viewed the strike was an attack on ancient British liberties and responded enthusiastically to the government's call. On the morning of 3 May, great crowds of them could be seen in the quad of the Foreign Office, smoking and laughing and waiting to be given a job to do: most of them were enrolled as special constables.

ARMED GUARDS
Armoured cars – of a type cruelly familiar to the people of Ireland – were used to protect convoys of food during the General Strike (above). In London military muscle was on display throughout the crisis. A pair of destroyers was moored in the Pool of London, where warehouses were full of supplies, and a battalion was stationed close to the docks in Victoria Park – they shared the space with crowds attending pro-strike rallies. As far as the strikers were concerned, armoured cars were deployed for propaganda purposes, as the TUC had already pledged not to interfere with the distribution of food or medical supplies.

READY FOR A FIGHT

Students from Oxford University (top right) pose with their standard-issue tin hats, armbands and wooden truncheons after being enrolled as special constables. On 5 May, at the height of the strike, the government announced that it intended to recruit 50,000 specials in London, and to mobilise 200,000 second-reserve policemen throughout the country. Some received training in combat techniques. By this time, the government had nearly half a million volunteers at its disposal. Most were involved in more peaceable anti-strike work, such as distributing the petrol stockpiled in Hyde Park (right).

DISPLAYING THEIR COLOURS
Not all working-class people were in favour of the strike. These fishermen's wives from Cullercoats, just north of Tynemouth, are demonstrating against it dressed in their traditional shawls. Most of the other workers in the industrial Northeast – the miners above all – were solidly behind the strike action. Some strike supporters resorted to sabotage. On Monday 10 May the Flying Scotsman, which was being driven by volunteers, was derailed close to Newcastle after a section of track had been deliberately removed. Fortunately for all concerned, of the 500 passengers on board, only one person was hurt.

The strike began in earnest that same night when the 'first-line workers' downed tools, among them railwaymen, printers, builders, steelworkers, stokers and labourers in power stations. The decision to bring the printers out was the first tactical error by the unions, as this made it hard to get their views across while the strike was on. The government, meanwhile, produced a newssheet called *The British Gazette*, the combative tone of which was entirely due to the character of its editor, Winston Churchill. On 7 May, the *Gazette* reported the view of Liberal MP Sir John Simon that the strike was 'an utterly illegal proceeding' since it was aimed at the government and not at the employers.

Churchill tried to extend the reach of his propaganda by commandeering the airwaves, but was stoutly resisted by the BBC general manager John Reith ('that wuthering height', as Churchill later called him), who valiantly defended the Corporation's editorial independence. *The Times* managed to publish an edition on 5 May – a single stylographed page with two columns of typewritten news. It cost tuppence, and was snapped up wherever it went on sale.

OVER A HOT STOVE
Ladies Gisborough, Malcolm and Mountbatten in the field kitchens in Hyde Park. Lady Mountbatten (third from left) looks rather overdressed for the job. A few years later, in the hungry 1930s, aristocratic ladies would be making charitable visits to soup kitchens, but for now they showed their solidarity with the middle and upper classes by doling out lunch to government volunteers. Hyde Park was the centre of the government operation to distribute supplies in London during the strike. It was converted into a kind of army base, with guards on the gates, prefabricated barrack rooms and a motor pool. For the well-to-do ladies helping out, Hyde Park was also conveniently close to home.

The shortage of news inevitably led to some wild speculation and rumours. In the first days of the strike, a story spread that a policeman had been killed when strikers overturned an omnibus. No such thing had happened. In fact, there was very little violent conflict during the strike, despite the fierce pickets and armoured cars on the streets. If this was a revolution, it was a rather polite, very British kind of revolution – a fact noted with satisfaction by George V, who wrote in his diary that '… our dear old country can be well proud of itself. It shows what wonderful people we are.' Indeed, the King was more even-handed in his attitude to the strikers than many among the upper and middle classes, saying: 'Try living on their wages before you judge them.'

Such violence as did occur was mostly directed against property. Shops were attacked and looted in Glasgow – tellingly, the most frequently stolen items were men's boots. In London, a printer was arrested for manhandling the driver of a van distributing *The British Gazette*, and then trying to slash the van's tyres. In Castleford a schoolmistress named Isabel Brown was charged with sedition after

making a speech in praise of communism. In court she gave her address as 'Moscow, Soviet Russia'. The unlikely poster boy of the government side was Lord Raglan, who was applauded for presenting himself as a humble volunteer at a railway depot and driving a train from Pontypool Road to Monmouth.

On 11 May, the unions brought out the 'second-line workers': engineers, shipbuilders, woodworkers, textile workers, postmen and those in the distributive trades. Three million workers were now on strike, but the action had already failed in its main aims. The country was still functioning, the strikers had not managed to win the sympathy of the population at large – and the government had not budged an inch on the miners. Two days later, TUC leaders offered to call off the strike as a prelude to further negotiations, then, despite not receiving any government assurances or guarantees, they called off the strike anyway. The miners held out on their own for seven months until privation and hunger drove them back to the pits to cut coal for longer hours and much reduced wages.

STANDING ROOM ONLY
In the absence of the usual buses, these office workers (above) seem to be enjoying the experience of commuting in a steam-powered lorry. The chuffing lorry looks a slightly more prestigious place to be than in the cattle-cart it is towing behind. These three self-satisfied volunteers (right), standing at the front of a steam engine at Waterloo Station, seem quite content to swap their usual work for driving a train. The 'BBB' daubed on the engine's nose refers to their surnames – Bellairs, Barton and Bruce.

THE DECADE'S END

The final years of the decade were altogether more sombre than the first. Frenzied stock market activity in America fuelled an economic boom through the 1920s that came to a catastrophic end in October 1929. Share prices collapsed, banks failed and the US economy imploded. One by one, the trading nations of the world were sucked into the vortex of economic depression. But even before the cataclysm impacted in Britain, something had changed in the zeitgeist. The long, heady party had petered out and a kind of nationwide hangover had set in. Politically, there was a retreat from confrontation and a general shuffling towards the centre ground. The Labour Party, chastened by the failed militancy of its left-wingers, settled down to the task of making itself an electable alternative to the Tories.

In the wake of the General Strike, the ruling Conservatives realised that a little social conscience was in order. The major achievements of Stanley Baldwin's second term were the Pensions Act of 1928, put forward by Neville Chamberlain, and the Local Government Act of 1929 which made local authorities responsible for the destitute, putting an end to the archaic and hated Poor Laws.

A third accomplishment of Baldwin's second spell in office was the lowering of the voting age for women from 30 to 21, finally giving women equal franchise status with men. Emmeline Pankhurst, the field marshall of female suffrage, lived just long enough to see the new Bill pass into law. When she died, in June 1928, her obituary in *The Times* was generous and respectful: 'Whatever views may be held as to the righteousness of the cause to which she gave her life, there can be no doubt about the remarkable strength and nobility of her character …'.

In 1926 Germany was admitted to the League of Nations and the Great War seemed done with at last. The sense of closure gave rise to new assessments of the conflict. Wilfred Owen's pain-filled poetry became more widely known and his anguished indictment of the 'old lie' – that it is 'sweet and proper to die for one's country' – slowly became the orthodox view. Richard Aldington's anti-war novel *Death of a Hero*, published in 1929, expressed all the bitterness and anger of a war-scarred generation. That same year the English translation of *All Quiet on the Western Front* appeared. The tone of Erich Maria Remarque's account of a German platoon's experience at the front was gentler than Aldington's book, but his message was no less forceful for that.

Looking to the future

By the end of the decade there was an entire generation of adults who had not taken part in the war. If there was a gulf in British society, it was not so much between rich and poor, or north and south, as between those who had suffered the blood and mire of Flanders, and those who had not. For better or worse, the uncertain future belonged to those who had not – a point made rather more lyrically by Winston Churchill in *The World Crisis*, his account of events during the years from 1911 to 1928. 'Merciful oblivion draws its veil', he wrote. 'The crippled limp away; the mourners fall back into the sad twilight of memory.'

AUF WIEDESEHEN, PET
Late in 1929 the last of the British troops left the occupied German Rhineland, and the last visible vestige of the Great War departed with them. The men in this photograph are a new generation of Tommy: both they and the friendly German girls seeing them off are too young to have taken part in the war that, before long, would become known as the First World War. For now, reconciliation was in the air and to many it seemed hopeful that Britain and Germany would henceforth be friends to each other. But just three years later a new leader – Adolf Hitler – came to power in Germany, and the old international enmities stirred again. Lasting peace would only be found after a new and even more terrible war.

'New youth is here to claim its rights, and the perennial stream flows forward, as if the tale were all a dream.'

Winston Churchill in *The World Crisis*, a decade after the Great War

1930s

1930s
FROM HIGH
TO LOW

The decade would be remembered for the Great Depression, sparked by the Wall Street Crash of November 1929, but it opened in hope and glory. This was the great age of the air adventurer and the public imagination was transfixed above all by the 'aviatrix', the plucky girl flyer piloting her flimsy biplane alone across oceans and deserts. Britain had her very own air adventuress: Amy Johnson from Kingston upon Hull. Slight, slender and beautiful, she was the brave and battling heroine who kept spirits up as the Depression began to bite deep.

SHIPBUILDING NATION   The rudder of the SS *Arctees* launched in 1934 from the yard of the Furness Shipbuilding Company, Stockton-on-Tees. Already in decline in the 1920s, shipbuilding would be one of the industries hit hardest by the Depression.

ADVENTURES IN THE AIR

On 5 May, 1930, Amy Johnson took off from Croydon, then London's major airport, for the 11,000-mile flight to Australia. She was 27 years old and alone at the controls of a second-hand de Havilland Gypsy Moth biplane that her father had helped her to buy. The plane was named 'Jason' after the trademark of her father's fisheries company in Hull. Nineteen and a half days later, Johnson landed at Darwin in northern Australia. In recognition of the achievement, she was awarded a CBE at home, while the Australians honoured her by giving her their No 1 civil pilot's licence. Her aircraft was preserved at the Science Museum in Kensington. The public loved her. They sang: 'Amy, wonderful Amy / How can you blame me / For loving you?'

The pilots of heavier-than-air machines were the heroes and heroines of the day, but it was thought that the future of commercial passenger flight lay in huge airships, rather than frail and tiny aeroplanes like Amy's. The huge, gas-filled

'AMY, WONDERFUL AMY'
The public adored Amy Johnson, and it is easy to see why. She was courageous, down-to-earth and not afraid to get her hands dirty – she was the world's first fully qualified female aircraft mechanic. She poses happily here in her oil-stained overalls, while working on the engine of her de Havilland Gypsy Moth, a single-engine, wood-and-fabric biplane with an open cockpit. The photograph was taken in March 1930. A few weeks later, she was smashing the England to Australia flying record. On her return, an estimated million people lined the route from Croydon to London to welcome her home.

BIG NEWS

Crowds gathered in Fleet Street to welcome Amy Johnson after a record solo flight in December 1932. This time it was from London to South Africa. The Daily Express building was – and still is – a dramatic Art Deco statement, with polished black façade. It had all the flash and panache of its proprietor, the ebullient and crusading Canadian press baron, Lord Beaverbrook. He had turned the *Express* into the most widely read newspaper in the world, locked in unending combat with Lord Rothermere's *Daily Mail*. The two media moguls cooperated briefly to attack free trade and to found the United Empire Party, but normal service was soon resumed as they resorted to their usual state of circulation warfare.

bodies were not fast, but they carried passenger compartments beneath them that were spacious and lavish enough to have grand pianos and dining areas, and to carry passengers in style. The British Empire covered a quarter of the land surface of the planet, and 'Imperial air routes' were planned to stitch it together. A few months after Amy's successful solo venture, an airship proving flight was planned.

The R101 airship disaster

The giant R101 set out from Cardington, Bedfordshire, at 7pm on Saturday 4 October, 1930. The airship was already famous. It had cruised over London – the press described it as 'large as the *Mauritania*', the famous ocean liner – and its sister ship the R100 had successfully flown to Canada. The destination this time was India, with men of the Air Ministry on board, including the air minister, Lord Thompson. A few hours after taking off the airship hit a violent rainstorm near Beauvais, 40 miles from Paris. Low cloud prevented the captain, Flight Lieutenant Irwin, from flying at altitude. The mass of rainwater on top of the gigantic flight envelope forced the airship lower, then gusting winds appear to have damaged the nose, pushing the ship into a dive. Irwin ordered all engines to slow, trying for a safe emergency landing. At 2am, the R101 hit the ground. Although the impact was gentle, the hydrogen gas bags exploded and flames

DOOMED GIANT

The R101 in its hangar at Cardington in Bedfordshire in 1930. Airships were thought well-proven by now. The Admiralty had built two hydrogen-powered airships on the lines of the German Zeppelins after the war. The R34 crossed the Atlantic to Long Island safely in 1919. The first man to arrive in America by air from Britain was a Major Pritchard, who leaped from the airship by parachute to give instructions to the ground-crew. A stowaway was found in the gas bags. The trip took 108 hours, but it was still thought that airships were the future of commercial flying. The R100 and R101 were luxury craft. Here (right) waiters serve members of a Dominions Conference at smartly laid tables in the dining room of R101. The R100 made a successful flight to Canada in 1930 and it was hoped that the R101, which had some structural alterations made to her, would prove even more triumphant on her test flight to India.

enveloped the passenger gondola below the airship. Forty-eight passengers and crew, including Lord Thompson, were burned to death. Only eight men, all of them crew, survived. Among them was the wireless operator, who telephoned the news to the Air Ministry from Beauvais. The Sunday newspapers in Britain printed special editions during the day. The French declared a day of national mourning.

Two days later there was a bizarre twist to the story. The director of the National Laboratory for Psychical Research, founded in 1925, was investigating the powers of a medium called Mrs Garrett. During the session, she began relaying messages from Flight Lieutenant Irwin who had died in the crash. He was said to have complained through her that the engine capacity had not been increased when the airship was enlarged, so the ship was underpowered. He also said the gas-bags had been leaking, and there had not been enough trials. These points were later confirmed by the official enquiry, which found that the immediate cause of the disaster was gradual loss of gas through holes in the gas-bags.

The destruction of the R101, which had cost the huge sum of £500,000 to build, put paid to the hopes of Britain developing regular intercontinental airship passenger services. The Air Ministry stopped building the craft, the R100 was dismantled and the base at Cardington was closed. It was an omen, not just for travel by airship, but for the high hopes for the Thirties.

IN ECONOMIC MELTDOWN

It was clear that the British economy was in crisis. Deep, across-the-board cuts in public spending were looming closer. The first casualty was the Labour government of Ramsay MacDonald. When it had come to power, in June 1929, the number of registered unemployed stood at 1,163,000, a little under 10 per cent of the workforce. By June 1930, as the effects of the Wall Street Crash rippled out across the world, the number had risen to almost 2 million. At the end of 1930 it hit 2.5 million. The position of the working man was now more perilous than at any stage since the end of the Napoleonic wars.

It did not help that MacDonald was trying to run a minority government. Labour had won more seats than the Conservatives in the 1929 election – 287 to the Tories' 260 – but they had polled fewer votes and did not have an overall majority: the balance of power was held by 59 Liberal MPs. In their campaign Labour had made an 'unqualified pledge' to deal with unemployment. As the jobless numbers spiralled out of control, this became a huge embarrassment for MacDonald and his Chancellor, Philip Snowden, who had no solution to the abyss facing the country. Part of the problem lay with the Prime Minister himself. The charismatic MacDonald had risen from lowly beginnings to now be heading his second Labour administration, but the Socialist beliefs that had driven him had dissipated. A former admirer said of him that 'he does not believe in the creed we have always preached'. He was touchy, hated criticism and had little grasp of economics. 'Unemployment is baffling us. The simple fact is that our population is too great for our trade', he wrote in his journal. 'I sit in my room in Downing Street alone and in silence. The cup has been put to my lips – and it is empty.'

Unemployment was equally baffling to the minister in charge of it, Jimmy Thomas, former boss of the railwaymen's union. Thomas made much of being a man of the people – wags said that he dropped his aitches with as much care as a woman applying make-up – and he was frantic at his powerlessness to help.

New political parties
As a sense of drift ate into the Labour Cabinet, the party's brightest young star, Sir Oswald Mosley, left to found his New Party. Meanwhile, another new party had been founded by two press barons. In 1930 Canadian-born Lord Beaverbrook started an 'Empire free trade crusade' and his flagship paper, the *Daily Express*, began to print the small crusader on its front page, which it carries to this day. Beaverbrook wanted a tariff put on all goods coming in, with preference given to goods from the empire. *Express* editorials attacked the principles of free trade as Victorian and outdated. Lord Rothermere, owner of the *Daily Mail*, agreed and the two cooperated in founding the United Empire Party. A quarter of a million readers contributed £100,000 to the party's funds. Predictably, the two moguls fell out, backing rival candidates at a by-election in Paddington in October 1930. The seat was won by Beaverbrook's Empire Crusader, Vice Admiral Taylor. Another Crusader was elected for Islington East, but this was the party's high point.

Shaken to the core
By the early summer of 1931, the government was in crisis. The trade unions were antagonistic. The radical left-wing MPs of the Independent Labour Party, though nominally allies, were in more or less permanent rebellion. The morale of the

STRIKING TO NO AVAIL
In the worst-hit industries – shipbuilding and shipping, iron and steel, coal, textiles, heavy engineering – whole communities were laid waste. At first, many workers believed industrial action might help. Here (top left), striking shipyard workers gather outside the offices of the TGWU in Tooley

Street, London, in May 1930. Earlier that year, the miners above staged an underground 'sit-in' at their colliery in the North over pay and conditions; here, they are seen leaving, their eyes shielded by visors against the unaccustomed daylight.

The worst year for strikes was 1931 with 6.9 million days lost; 1932 was little better,

with 6.4 million. By 1934 industrial action had abated and fewer than 1 million days were lost to strikes that year. Though there was an upsurge in 1937, the great crisis in labour relations had passed.

The suffering in mining communities in the Thirties was acute. In its heyday, coal-mining employed 1.2 million men, but by

1931 two-thirds of men in some pit villages were without work. More than 40 per cent of miners were out of work in 1932 – and the number was much higher in the inland valleys of Wales, in Merthyr, Rhondda and Aberdare. Even by 1935, when the worst of the Depression had lifted in other sectors, a third of miners were still left idle.

Parliamentary Labour Party (PLP) was in tatters. The agreement with the Liberals was beginning to splinter. Dismal by-election results added to the gloom. As if in physical reflection of the shaky political state, the Dogger Bank earthquake – the largest ever in Britain at 6.1 on the Richter scale – shook the country in June 1931.

The public finances were caught in a vicious circle. In 1931 tax yields fell by almost a third from their 1928 level, while the cost of unemployment benefit soared from £12 million to £125 million. Exports halved in value. The £40 million government deficit was expected to double in 1932. The collapse of the Austrian bank Kreditanstalt sparked bank collapses in Germany and hit the City of London, which had made large loans to Germany. Foreign creditors, mainly French, sold sterling. In less than a month the Bank of England was down £60 million in bullion and foreign exchange reserves. Before leaving for America on holiday,

THE COALITION CABINET

A small crowd gathers at the gates of Downing Street on 24 August, 1931, waiting for news at the height of the government crisis (left). The next day, ministers of the new and as yet unelected National Government were photographed in the garden of 10 Downing Street (right). They are, standing left to right: C Lister; Jimmy Thomas, now Dominions Secretary; Rufus Isaacs, Marquis of Reading, briefly Foreign Secretary; Neville Chamberlain, soon to be Conservative Chancellor of the Exchequer; and Sir Samuel Hoare, Viscount Templewood, Conservative Secretary of State for India. Seated, left to right: Philip Snowden, the beleaguered Chancellor; the Conservative Party leader Stanley Baldwin, now Lord President of the Council; Prime Minister Ramsay MacDonald; Herbert Samuel, the Liberal Home Secretary; and Lord Stanley, Parliamentary and Financial Secretary to the Admiralty.

When free trade was dropped, and Imperial Preference brought in by the Ottawa Agreements of February 1932, Snowden and Herbert Samuel both resigned. Neville Chamberlain, the coming man, said that Ottawa was 'the crowning achievement in a year wonderful with endeavour'. Preference for Empire goods was followed by 'most-favoured nation' trade treaties with Argentina and the Scandinavian countries. Marketing boards were set up for milk, potatoes and hops, while British wheat was guaranteed a share of the market. What was perhaps most remarkable was that this huge extension of state control was largely Conservative-inspired.

Montagu Norman, governor of the Bank of England, said that ration books should be printed 'in case the currency collapsed and the country had to revert to barter'. Bankers warned that sterling would fall off the precipice unless confidence was restored by a more balanced budget.

The Chancellor pressed his Cabinet colleagues for cuts. On 31 July, the day Parliament rose for the summer recess, he tried to hustle them into agreement: he released a report, without warning, that predicted a budget deficit of £120 million by the following spring and recommended spending cuts of £96 million, including a 10 per cent cut in the dole. Snowden's aim was to soften up opinion in Britain to accept drastic action, but instead the run on the pound worsened. Ministers were recalled and on 21 August agreed to £56 million in cuts, mainly from public sector salaries, but even this was so far short of the recommended £96 million that it failed to prop up sterling. Two days later, the Labour Cabinet voted 11 to 9 for the cut in unemployment benefit, but the dissenting minority – who included Arthur Henderson, then Foreign Secretary – was too large to ignore. Believing it to be the end of the road for his government, MacDonald came out of the bad-tempered meeting and said: 'I'm going off to the Palace to throw in my hand.'

Forming a national coalition

When MacDonald arrived at the Palace, George V gave him some good advice. He suggested that MacDonald remain as Prime Minister, at the head of a new National Government. The next day, 24 August, 1931, MacDonald was back to tell the King that Stanley Baldwin, the Conservative leader, had agreed to serve under him in a new National Government. It was, Baldwin said, 'for a limited period. There is no question of a permanent coalition.' But in fact that is precisely what happened: Britain would have a national coalition government until 1945. Four Conservatives joined MacDonald's 10-man Cabinet, including Baldwin and Neville Chamberlain, soon to replace Snowden as Chancellor.

For a while it seemed MacDonald's finest hour – 'money was saved, England was saved' – but the bulk of the Labour Party refused to follow its leader and most

Labour MPs passed into opposition. The split in the party was long-lasting and bitter. MacDonald and the few who remained with him – Snowden and Jimmy Thomas, the former railwayman now Dominions Secretary – were reviled as traitors and Tory lackeys and expelled from the party. For good measure, Thomas was also thrown out of the National Union of Railwaymen.

Pay cuts all round

On 9 September, 1931, Snowden announced salary cuts of 10 per cent for all government employees. Savings of £25 million were to be made in unemployment benefit: a single man's dole fell from 17 shillings a week to 15s 3d. Labour MPs attacked their erstwhile colleague as a Scrooge, he called them Bolsheviks. The King volunteered for a cut in the Civil List payment he received from £470,000 to £430,000. The Prince of Wales presented the Exchequer with £10,000 from his £65,000 income from the Duchy of Cornwall. The American philanthropist Edward Harkness gave £2 million to be spent 'for the benefit of Great Britain'.

The Admiralty now announced pay cuts across the board for all ranks in the Navy. For officers, the cuts equated to around 10 per cent, but for many lower ratings – and therefore the lowest paid – the cut was more like 25 per cent. Jolly Jack Tar was understandably upset and sailors on ships at anchor off Invergordon on the Moray Firth, including the powerful battleships *Rodney* and *Nelson*, made a stand. At 6am on 15 September, they refused to put to sea for exercises. There was loose talk of training the ships' 16-inch guns, which could throw a one-ton shell for 20 miles, on Ramsay MacDonald's house at nearby Lossiemouth.

This was by no means a full-blooded mutiny – the men still stood to attention when Marine bands played 'God Save The King'. The only coherent demands were in a 'loyal manifesto' dictated by Len Wincott, a seaman aboard the cruiser *Norfolk*, which beseeched the Admiralty to 'amend the drastic cuts in pay which threaten tragedy and misery amongst the families of the lower deck'. The First Lord of the Admiralty was Austen Chamberlain, elder half-brother of Neville, who realised that the cuts were deeply unfair. He was conciliatory and ordered the ships of the Atlantic Fleet to disperse to their home ports, promising to look into the men's grievances. It worked. Two days after the mutiny had started, it fizzled out. The cut was evened out at 10 per cent across the board, and although it was still disproportionately unfair to lower rankings it was more acceptable.

The only other group to have a pay cut restored – this time in full – were the judges. Sir William Holdsworth, a flamboyantly moustachioed professor of English law at Oxford, argued that it was wrong for judges to suffer because they had to try cases which 'involve enormous amounts of money'. Since a 'wrong decision may inflict on a litigant the unmerited sacrifice of a sum which vastly exceeds the annual savings on all judicial salaries', it was wrong to expose judges to the same cuts as other civil servants. The logic was utterly self-serving – no lawyer argued

NAVAL ACTION
Cadets doing PT on the deck of the Royal Navy battleship HMS *Ramillies*. What began in the Fleet at Invergordon as an angry protest against the Admiralty's proposed pay cut would end with the government being forced to suspend sterling from the gold standard. Having bungled the pay cut, the Admiralty made matters worse by trying to hush up news of the sailors' refusal to put to sea. It trickled out, of course, and was blazoned as a full-scale mutiny by the press at home and abroad. Gold poured out of London once more and sterling tottered. The pound found its new value at around 70 per cent of its old gold-backed value.

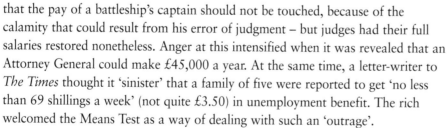

that the pay of a battleship's captain should not be touched, because of the calamity that could result from his error of judgment – but judges had their full salaries restored nonetheless. Anger at this intensified when it was revealed that an Attorney General could make £45,000 a year. At the same time, a letter-writer to *The Times* thought it 'sinister' that a family of five were reported to get 'no less than 69 shillings a week' (not quite £3.50) in unemployment benefit. The rich welcomed the Means Test as a way of dealing with such an 'outrage'.

The Admiralty bungles again

The judges got away with it, but the Admiralty got it wrong again. Despite a promise of no reprisals following the settlement brokered by Chamberlain, 24 ratings were dismissed as ringleaders and punishment gunnery drills were inflicted on others. Worst of all, it tried to hush up the entire incident. But seamen like Fred Copeman, an idealist who later fought with the International Brigades in Spain, were not to be silenced. The press, denied a proper briefing, blew the incident up as a full-scale mutiny, which had unthinkable consequences. The Royal Navy was the symbol of British might, keeping the sea lanes open to the empire. Foreign newspapers splashed the story across front pages: Britain, they claimed, was on the verge of mutiny. Investors took panic again and another £43 million flooded abroad in less than four days. The pound could not withstand such pressure.

THE ELECTION TRAIL
Ramsay MacDonald campaigning for his new National Government among the mining communities of Co Durham. This photograph was taken at Haswell Plough, near Seaham, on 13 October, 1931 – his 65th birthday. The Liberal Party tried to woo women voters (top), while the government clearly intended to win over Labour voters with this poster (above). In the event the coalition National Government won votes right across the political spectrum and returned to Parliament with a huge majority.

Abandoning the gold standard

Gold was the internationally accepted means of exchange, but the strains of the slump had made sterling grossly over-valued – and the markets knew it. The National Government bowed to the inevitable. Britain came off the gold standard on 21 September, 1931. It was a huge shock. According to the writer Alec Waugh, '"Safe as the Rock of Gibraltar" and "Safe as the Bank of England" had been the two pillars that sustained our way of life. Now one of them was gone.'

It was forbidden to take gold out of the country for six months. The 1925 Act which required the sale of gold at a fixed price was suspended. The price could float and find its own daily level. The bank rate was raised from 4½ per cent to 6 per cent. The stock exchange closed for the day to enable brokers and jobbers to adjust. The public were assured that, as one headline put it, there was 'No Need For Alarm', but it was the final evidence for Britain's wealthier classes, if any were needed, that the good life of the Twenties was over.

Sterling fell by about 30 per cent and the effect was felt immediately in hotels and resorts across the South of France, the Tyrol, Switzerland and Italy. They were left half-empty as the newly impoverished British came home. Soon, foreign travel was said to be unpatriotic. Cruises, where sunshine was priced in pounds, soared in popularity. Nerves were calmed in October by Noël Coward's *Cavalcade*, a sentimental celebration of things British – the Boer War, Mafeking, stiff upper lips on the *Titanic* and in the Great War – threaded together by a string of popular songs. The show ends on a high patriotic note as a decadent nightclub blues is drowned out by a soaring 'God Save the King' sung by the whole cast. The royal family attended the second night, and the *Daily Mail* serialised it.

National landslide

Two weeks later, in October 1931, the National Government went to the country. It felt it needed a 'doctor's mandate' from the people to deal with the economic sickness. The election was a disaster for the Labour Party, which was woefully ill-prepared, its policies vague, impractical and over-optimistic: 'Bolshevism run mad', said the 'traitor' Jimmy Thomas. Most of the party's pamphlets and posters had to be shredded because they still bore the name or picture of the 'arch-traitor' Ramsay MacDonald. The ones they did run made great play of the Invergordon incident, carrying a picture of the wartime battle of Jutland. The Royal Navy, it said, had thrashed the German Kaiser then and it had now beaten Montague Norman, the governor of the Bank of England.

The Tory press branded this an insult to the Navy, but it need not have worried. The voters approved, massively, of National candidates, electing 554 of them. All of Baldwin's Conservatives ran on National tickets, and 470 were rewarded with seats. Only 46 Labour MPs and a rump of 16 Liberal rebels were elected. The new Cabinet had 20 members. MacDonald remained Prime Minister, with three other National Labour ministers. Sir John Simon, one of five Liberals, became Foreign Secretary. But the real power – and all the key economic posts apart from the Board of Trade – lay with Stanley Baldwin and ten other Tories.

Yet another financial crisis followed in March 1932 when the Swedish 'match magnate', Ivar Krueger, shot himself through the heart in his Paris apartment. Stock markets round the world tumbled further. Sympathy for him waned when it was found that he owed £50 million and had forged 42 Italian Treasury Bonds, with a face value of £500,000 each, in an attempt to prop up his ailing fortune.

TOUTING FOR GOLD
Gold became much in demand following the suspension of the gold standard – and there was no shortage of men, like these two in London in 1932, willing to tramp the streets carrying sandwich boards advertising those who were keen to buy. There was a growing fear that paper money might not be worth the paper it was written on, now that it no longer had a guaranteed link to the value of gold.

SPRINGS OF HOPE

There was no doubt that the British were less religious than they had been in their parents' generation. In York, for example, Sunday attendance had fallen from 35.5 per cent of people in 1901 to just 17 per cent in 1935. The 'Sabbath' had turned into the 'weekend', a time for gardening, hobbies, sports and rambles more than prayer. Nonconformists, pillars of the Liberals, declined as much as their party in their old heartlands in Wales, Cornwall and the West Midlands.

But even though society had grown more secular, public morals were still subject to old standards. Attitudes remained firmly against divorce, artificial birth control, obscenity, alcohol, homosexuality and the 'Continental Sunday' characterised by the opening of libraries, galleries and museums. No first class cricket or football was played on Sundays. Pub doors remained shut in parts of Wales and Scotland. Parliament was opened by prayers. The crowd at the Cup Final sang the hymn 'Abide With Me'. Prayers were said each day in schools, prisons, law courts, on warships and in the army. Britain was still a consciously Christian country: every child knew the Lord's Prayer and a carol or two.

The Church remained a powerful influence – somewhat to everyone's surprise. A new cathedral for Guildford was designed by Edward Maufe in 1932. Some traditions were being relaxed: existing cathedrals followed Canterbury in opening for visitors between services on Sunday, and women were allowed in without hats. T S Eliot's new play *Murder in the Cathedral* caused a sensation at the Canterbury festival. It portrayed the killing by four knights of Thomas Becket in 1170, after Henry II was heard to mutter that he wished to be rid of 'this turbulent priest'.

The Oxford Mission

Piety was left largely to nonconformists and Scots puritans. People went to Anglican services out of habit, for the singing, local gossip, or as a preliminary to a Sunday session in the pub – 'thirst after righteousness' – as much as for worship. So in 1931, when the Archbishop of York, William Temple, led a week's mission to Oxford, its impact was unexpected.

On the final evening, a packed audience joined Temple to sing 'When I survey the wondrous Cross'. After the first verse, he stopped them to point out that the next verse had 'tremendous words'. They looked at Isaac Watt's words on their hymn sheets: 'Were the whole world of nature mine / That were an offering far too small / Love so amazing, so divine / Demands my soul, my life, my all.' If they believed those words from the bottom of their hearts, Temple instructed, they should sing them as loud as they could. If they didn't mean them, they should stay silent. He went on: 'If you mean them even a little and want to mean them more, sing them very softly.' It was brilliant theatre. As one member of the congregation later recalled, to hear these words whispered by two thousand young men and women was 'an experience never to be erased from my memory till the whole

BELIEF IN FRESH AIR
The fad for 'Healthy Living' in the Thirties went as far as open-air lessons, like this one taking place in St James's Park in London.

A chill and misty February morning looks anything but healthy for the pupils in their neat caps and blazers, huddled under blankets for warmth.

tablet is blotted'. The vicar of the university church believed the Oxford Mission 'stopped the rot' in Christian life and was a decisive moment when 'the tide began to come in', he said, alluding to Matthew Arnold's great Victorian poem on the sea of faith ebbing away. Hope and idealism, it seemed, could still break through.

In 1932 the Oxford Group, which had been founded by an American evangelist in the Twenties, began to get the attention of popular newspapers. The *Daily Express* ran a series of pieces by young men on the revival in religious feeling. They included 'Bunny' Austin, the tennis champion, who said that he thought Jesus was neither meek nor mild, but 'a man magnificently built, tall and strong' – rather like himself. The Group believed in public confession of sins and gained so many followers that the Albert Hall was hired for their confessionals.

New schools of thought

Experiments were made in 'free' schools – free of discipline, not fees. The most famous was A S Neill's Summerfields. It specialised in problem children (observers claimed they were usually the offspring of problem parents) who broke windows, wrote swear words on the walls, played truant and stole. Neill said that he made Summerfields for the children, rather than the other way round. His proud boast was that he had discovered that children are born sincere, and remain so if they

GREAT SOUL
In 1931 Mahatma Gandhi, the charismatic leader of the Indian independence movement, visited London to discuss a new federal constitution with the British government. He had recently been released from a brief prison sentence in India, imposed for defying the unpopular salt monopoly of the British Raj. Although his visit was not a political success, he was greeted with much goodwill by the British public, as this photograph with textile workers in Darwen, Lancashire, shows (above). This was generous of them, for a central part of Gandhi's protest against British rule was that India should spin its own cotton into thread to be woven into cloth, rather than importing cloth made in the mechanised Lancashire mills. The home-spun dhoti he wore was a symbol of this protest, as much as of his humility and simplicity.

are not warped by conventional education. 'Some turned out sincerely good, a few stayed sincerely bad', Robert Graves wrote. 'Everything got broken.'

Another no-discipline school was run by Bertrand Russell and his wife, Dora. The Russells believed that the development of 'personality' through free expression was more important than book-learning, which could be picked up later. The problem with this, Graves noted, arose when children went home for the holidays and expressed themselves as they had at school, by swearing or smashing something. They were then 'repressed' by irritated neighbours and relatives.

The urge for peace

Peace was in the air in the 1930s, with peace conferences held in Montreux, Lausanne, Genoa and other pleasant towns by lake or sea. Each was briefly swamped by delegates, interpreters and journalists, ending with an over-optimistic final communiqué, then the show moved on. The first World Disarmament Conference, held under the League of Nations banner in Geneva in 1932, turned into farce. The Soviet Union proposed complete disarmament, but it knew that the Western capitalist nations would not agree. A proposal to ban bombing from the air was vetoed by Sir John Simon, the British Foreign Secretary: India was restless as the 'civil disobedience' campaign led by Mahatma Gandhi gathered pace and the cheapest, most effective way to deal with turbulent tribesmen on India's Northwest Frontier was to send RAF biplanes to bomb them. Another proposal, to limit tanks to 8 tons, was also rejected by the British, who were testing 16-ton tanks, and by the French, who were experimenting with a 60-ton monster.

Students at the Oxford Union carried a motion in 1933 to refuse to fight for King and Country if called upon to do so. A League of Nations 'peace monarch' was proposed, to reign from Geneva. Peace campaigners picked names at random from German telephone directories, and sent them postcards saying that the writer was resolved to practice non-resistance. Dr Maude Royden tried to raise a peace army, whose volunteers would march to the front line in a war and occupy no man's land between the two belligerents, obliging them to call off the war or shoot innocent civilians. It was perhaps as well that this was not put to the test.

'It was difficult to find a scientist who did not believe that the scientific-technological-industrial revolution, accelerating under his eyes, was not doing incomparably more good than harm.'

C P Snow, physicist and novelist, on the confidence of scientists in the Thirties

Technological strides

It was as well, too, perhaps, that the peace activists were not aware of the progress being made in nuclear fission and other areas, as British scientists and engineers enjoyed something of a golden era. The team of physicists at the Cavendish Laboratory in Cambridge – James Chadwick, John Cockroft, P M S Blackett and E T S Walton – were leading the world with their research. In 1932 Cockroft and Walton were the first to 'split the atom', causing a nuclear reaction by using artificially accelerated particles. Chadwick discovered the neuron in 1934, confirming that Lord Rutherford had been correct in postulating its existence back in 1920.

continued on page 371

A NEW AGE OF TECHNOLOGY

The Thirties saw a massive spread of services that we take for granted today. All over the country the infrastructure was being built to ensure that people everywhere could have access to the telephone, to the new wireless programmes broadcast by the BBC and to the benefits of electric power. The developments in radio led to radar, which would prove invaluable when war broke out at the end of the decade.

NEW COMMUNICATIONS Telephone engineers fix telegraph wires to insulators near Staines in Middlesex in 1933 (left). The engineers were employed by the Post Office, since telephone services had evolved from the telegram service: the poles they are working on were still called telegraph poles. Most telephones were now on automatic exchanges and the old upright models, where the user had to juggle with the microphone and a separate earpiece, were being replaced by sleek all-in-one handsets. The lady in the telephone box below – as unmistakably British as red pillar boxes and double-decker buses – is holding one of the new devices. The Post Office was a big employer, and the rise in the number of telephonists in business and the civil service created many new jobs.

The men building a new wireless station near Baldock in Hertfordshire in 1930 (below right) were part of a huge expansion that would enable most people across the country to pick up BBC broadcasts. The impact went far beyond news and entertainment. By the end of the Thirties, around 11,000 elementary and secondary schools in mainland Britain had radio sets and tuned in to the BBC's excellent educational programmes.

"This is not the age of pamphleteers. It is the age of the engineer. The spark-plug is mightier than the sword."

Lancelot Hogben, professor and author

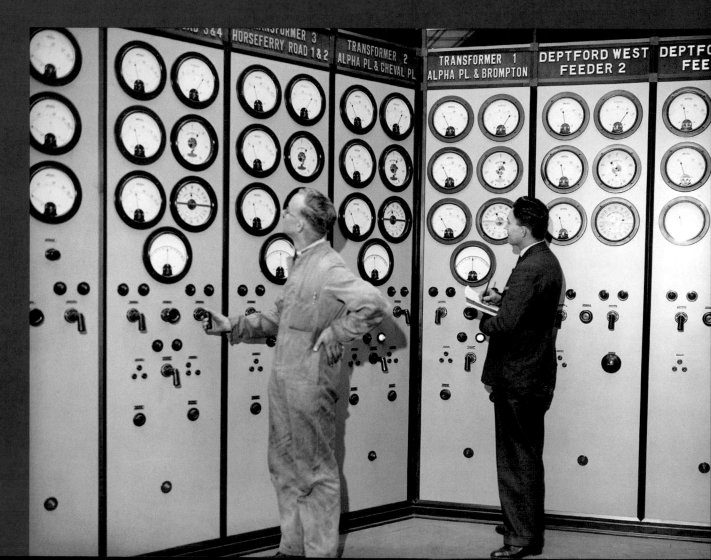

ELECTRIFYING THE NATION
Electricity was the key source of energy in the Thirties, and constructing the supply system was a massive project. Here (far left), a 51-ton stator – the stationary component of a generator – built in Birmingham is delivered for installation at a power station in Wembley in 1933. Battersea power station was built on the river right in the heart of London: these technicians (bottom left) are checking dials monitoring transformers and feeders in late 1932. The two lofty workmen (centre left) were at work on the insulators of the Central Electricity Board towers at Dagenham. By 1933, the National Grid of high-voltage transmission lines was almost complete, and Britain had one of the world's best electricity supply systems. Electricity had the effect of shifting industry from the North and Wales to the Midlands and Southeast. By 1938 the electricity industry was employing 325,000 – double the figure for 1924.

The number of electricity consumers shot up from just 730,000 in 1920 to 9 million by 1939. New customers were being added at the rate of 750,000 a year, and two in three houses were wired up. The first wave of electrical appliances in homes were vacuum cleaners, refrigerators, cookers and radios, but electricity was reaching into every part of life. It powered broadcasting, the cinema, trains, trams and trolley buses. It was used in the new dangerous-looking machines for permanent hair waves: this intrepid woman (near left), seen in 1934, seems on the point of being electrocuted rather than coiffured. The team of workers below are constructing an electrical clock at Paddington Station in 1935.

A GALLERY OF PRIZE-WINNERS

British scientists were at the very forefront of new research and development in the 1930s and reaped a host of Nobel prizes in physics, chemistry, and physiology and medicine. The three in the top row are among the immortals. Ernest Rutherford (near left, in 1932), born one of 12 children of a wheelwright in New Zealand, grew up to be one of the greatest pioneers of sub-atomic physics. Scholarships got him to the Cavendish Laboratory at Cambridge, where he discovered three types of uranium radiation. While at Manchester, he won the Nobel prize for chemistry and developed the concept of the 'Rutherford-Bohr atom' of nuclear physics. Becoming Cavendish professor at Cambridge, he predicted the existence of the neutron. Rutherford's colleagues at Cambridge included the Irish physicist Ernest Walton (far left) and John Cockroft (centre), who disintegrated lithium by proton bombardment in 1932. They were jointly awarded the Nobel prize for physics in 1951. Cockroft became the first director of Britain's Atomic Energy Establishment at Harwell in 1946. Other members of the Cavendish team included Patrick Blackett (middle row, far left), who developed a device for studying cosmic radiation, winning a Nobel prize in 1948, and James Chadwick (middle row, centre), who won the Nobel prize for physics in 1935 for discovering the neutron.

Eminent scientists working in other fields included Walter Haworth (middle row, near left), professor of organic chemistry at Birmingham. In 1937 he shared the Nobel prize for chemistry for his work in determining the properties of Vitamin C. The physiologist Henry Hallett Dale (bottom row, far left) worked on the chemical transmission of nerve impulses, winning the 1936 Nobel prize for physiology and medicine with the Austrian Otto Loewi. Dale also discovered acetylcholine. The physiologists Edgar Adrian (bottom row, centre) and Charles Sherrington (near left) shared the Nobel prize for physiology and medicine in 1932 for their work on the function of neurons. Adrian did important research on electrical impulses in the nervous system. He was a pioneer in the study of epilepsy and brain lesions. Sherrington researched reflex action.

Chadwick also built Britain's first cyclotron in Liverpool in 1935, the same year that he was awarded the Nobel prize for physics.

Cathode ray tubes and electronic cameras were pioneered in Britain by Isaac Shoenberg, director of research at EMI from 1931. EMI and Marconi, another British company, provided the equipment for the world's first regular television service, launched by the BBC from Alexandra Palace in 1936. An offshoot was Radar, the radio location of aircraft. The government gave £10,000 for research into the radar techniques, which proved a bargain in the hands of the brilliant Scottish physicist Robert Watson-Watt. The first radar masts for detecting enemy aircraft were being built on the Kent and Essex coasts in 1936, the year that a Spitfire first flew. Four years later, the combination of fine fighter aircraft and radar to guide them to the squadrons of approaching enemy bombers was to save the nation.

The BBC was the main force in television and radio research. But most developments came from the private sector and the R&D efforts of electronics companies like EMI and Marconi, aircraft builders, engineering firms and chemical giants. Despite the economic problems, investment in research tripled between 1930 and 1938, providing a big pool of scientists and engineers. It was to prove essential to the future war effort.

Scientists – or 'boffins' as they were popularly known – were much admired by the public, who soaked up books on astronomy, natural history and geology. Sir James Jeans, an expert in quantum theory and stellar evolution, drew a mass readership for books such as *The Universe* and *The New Background of Science* in 1933. *Mathematics for the Million* and *Science for the Citizen* were bestsellers in 1936 and 1938 for Lancelot Hogben, a professor of zoology.

PRESS WARS

It was a wonderful time to be a reader of popular newspapers. Circulation battles reached such intensity it was said that a whole Welsh family could be clothed from head to foot for the price of eight weeks' reading of the *Daily Express*, which showered Wales with free gifts. The left-wing *Daily Herald* began it by offering readers a set of Dickens novels in 16 volumes for 11 shillings, which it said was 'worth four guineas'. The paper's owner, Lord Southwood, claimed that a profit could be made on 11 shillings. The *Daily Express, Daily Mail* and *News Chronicle* hit back, offering their readers Dickens sets for 10 shillings, selling more than 300,000 sets between them and losing £36,000 in the process. Canvassers were sent round the country lavishing cameras, tea-sets, cutlery, coats, shirts and trousers on those who signed up as registered readers. After giving away thousands of pairs of silk stockings, the *Daily Express* returned to books, offering 12 volumes of classic novels for 10 shillings. The magazine *John Bull* retaliated with 12 volumes of classic novels for 8s 9d. The *Express* dropped its price to 7s 6d, and sold 115,000 sets for a loss of £12,000. The *Herald* turned to 'four guinea' encyclopaedias at 11 shillings – and was undercut by the *Express*.

It cost a proprietor real money to wage war. The *Daily Herald* (years later to be reborn as *The Sun*) spent £1,325,000 in boosting its circulation from 400,000 to 1,750,000, a cost of about £1 per reader. Beaverbrook spent his money to

greater effect bringing in 300,000 new readers for an outlay of £123,000, or 8s 7d a reader. When the press wars finally ended, the *Express* had a circulation of more than 2 million – the largest for a daily paper anywhere in the world.

Charles Dickens reappeared in a final *Mail* versus *Express* skirmish. The great Victorian novelist had left behind him a Life of Christ, written for his children, but specified that it was not to be published until they had all gone. The death of Sir Henry Dickens, last of the children, released it and the *Daily Mail* paid £40,000 – about £1 a word – for exclusive rights. The *Express* waited for the first promotion posters to go up, then took the gloss off the *Mail*'s scoop with an article revealing that late in life Dickens had an affair with the actress Ellen Ternan.

'The Conciliator'

The most influential journalist of the day was Geoffrey Dawson, editor of *The Times*. Dawson was ferociously bright, a fellow of All Souls College, Oxford, and a former civil servant in South Africa who mingled easily with the Establishment. It was his second stint in charge at *The Times*. He had been editor under Lord Northcliffe from 1912 to 1919, but resigned over the way the proprietor used the paper to promote his own political interests. Dawson returned in 1923 after Northcliffe died and ownership passed to fellow Old Etonian, John Jacob Astor.

DAILY BREAD
Workmen dismantle the famous clock as part of the remodelling of the *Daily Telegraph* building in Fleet Street (left). The British press was a phenomenon. No other country got near its massive circulation figures. The two big quality dailies, *The Times* and the *Telegraph*, sold almost a million copies a day between them. The *News of the World* reached a Sunday circulation of 3.8 million in 1939 – and its great rival, *The People*, was snapping at its heels. Circulation wars took many forms – offers for cheap editions of Dickens and Shakespeare, cash prizes, free pairs of socks and stockings. Here (below), in keeping with the 'Hungry Thirties', the *Daily Express* is subsidising loaves of bread.

Ironically, Dawson now began using *The Times* to further his own ideas, much as Northcliffe had once done. He was close to both Baldwin and Chamberlain and, after Hitler came to power in 1933, he actively endorsed their policies of appeasement. He was an old friend and dining companion of Edward Wood, who as Lord Halifax became a pro-appeasement Foreign Secretary, and he was also part of the so-called 'Cliveden set', which met at the Astor's country house, Cliveden in Buckinghamshire, and favoured friendly relations with Nazi Germany. Finally, Dawson was a member of the Anglo-German Fellowship. With all of these connections on the part of its editor, small wonder that *The Times* made little reference to German anti-semitism. 'The Thunderer', as the paper had once been called for its robust views, had become 'The Conciliator'.

Dawson can take the credit for one long-lasting innovation: in January 1930 *The Times* ran its first crossword puzzle. Within a few weeks, its editorial boasted that the best brains in the country – 'ministers of the crown, provosts of colleges, King's Counsels and the rest' – were finding the crossword 'just the thing to fill up odd moments'. One such was M R James, provost of Eton and author of bestselling collections of ghost stories, who boiled his morning eggs for the time it took him to complete the crossword and, the paper said, he 'hates a hard-boiled egg'. On 1 March, 1930, the paper published an all-Latin puzzle, confident that the men who ran Britain were comfortable with the classics. Readers who knew the answer to 'Horace calls Tarentum this' (Lacedaemonium) might, like Dawson, be a trifle self-satisfied and fixed in their ways. But they were most unlikely to abandon the nation's traditional values for the frenzy and mass murder that was infecting the elites of Soviet Russia and Germany.

Daily, weekly and monthly variety

The British were the most voracious newspaper readers on the planet. Provincial newspapers were strong – 'God the Father, God the Son and God the *Yorkshire Post*', as they said in 'God's own county' – but the nationals were a phenomenon, selling some 10.5 million copies a day. Most of that went to the popular papers, with eye-catching photographs and strip cartoons, but *The Times* and *Daily Telegraph* sold almost a million between them – the lion's share to the *Telegraph* – and minorities were also catered for. The communist *Daily Worker* was founded in 1930. The *Daily Herald* was backed by the TUC. The *News Chronicle*, the *Manchester Guardian* and the *New Statesman* magazine were generally sympathetic to the Left.

Picture Post, a topical news magazine of photographic essays, was launched in 1938. Within a year it had a circulation of 2 million. The most successful women's magazine, meanwhile, was *Women's Own*, which progressed so well from its launch in 1932 that it was joined five years later by *Woman*, a rival with a mix of romantic short stories, recipes, fashion, cosmetics and hints on running a home.

Almost all the papers printed horoscopes – only the *Daily Herald*, *Sunday Times* and *Observer* felt it to be beneath their dignity. The best-known astrologer was R H Naylor of the *Sunday Express*, who also wrote for a bestselling sixpenny monthly, *Prediction*, which covered the ground from palmistry to hypnotism. *Old Moore's* had been the most famous almanac since correctly predicting a snowfall on Derby Day in Victorian times. But the title had never been copyrighted and the troubled times gave such a boost to the prediction industry that nine *Old Moore's* – each with different predictions – were published every Christmas.

WEEKLY ESCAPE
Comics were read avidly by children from all backgrounds, allowing them to escape to a world of heroes and daring-do, like this boy glued to his comic stretched out on the window-ledge of his terraced home. 'What child', asked George Orwell, 'bound all day by an elementary school classroom or the walls of a factory does not long to be cruising, skating, riding or giving a garden party in an Emir's palace?' In 1939 Orwell wrote a famous essay on 'Boys' Weeklies', in which he observed that they had two basic beliefs: that 'nothing ever changes, and foreigners are funny'. The French were always Froggies and had pointed beards, the Italians were Dagoes and played barrel-organs, the Chinese had saucer-shaped hats and pigtails.

Children's comics were another fantastic growth area. The old much-loved staples, *Gem* and *Magnet*, usually carried a single story, written by the same person. It is not surprising, then, that a raft of new comics – *Wizard, Rover, Skipper, Hotspur, Champion, Modern Boy* – now appeared for boys. Dedicated comics for girls included *Crystal*, which featured The Fourth Formers at St Chads School, and *Silver Star* offering romantic serials such as 'Love's Sinner' for older readers.

Each issue had seven or eight different serials, so they gave their readers much greater variety. School stories aside, the favourite subjects of the new boys comics were the Wild West, the Frozen North, the Foreign Legion, the Great War (Air Force or Secret Service, never the trenches), Tarzan-type jungle stories, football, Robin Hood, Cavaliers and Roundheads, and scientific invention. Orwell found that 'Death-rays, Martians, invisible men, robots, helicopters and interplanetary rockets figure largely', and he credited H G Wells with being the father of this 'scientifiction': his classic, *The Time Machine*, had been popular since 1895. Wells was still writing, but *The Shape of Things to Come*, published in 1933, was not a piece of futuristic sci-fi but a warning against the evils of Fascism.

Vicar unfrocked

The most read-about churchman of the Thirties, to the chagrin of the Anglican Church, was the rector of the little village of Stiffkey in Norfolk. At Norwich Cathedral on 21 October, 1932 – Trafalgar Day, as it happened, which celebrated Horatio Nelson, a man born in a vicarage not far from Stiffkey – the bishop of Norwich, with the dean and canons, proceeded in solemn state to the Beauchamp chapel. They had come to pass judgment on Rev Harold Davidson, who scurried in after them, a little late, clutching a silk top hat and accompanied by his sister.

Davidson had arrived in Stiffkey aged 31 in 1906. He held services every Sunday, then on Monday left his wife and five children in the rectory and caught the train from Wells-next-the-Sea to London. There he spent the rest of the week badgering young girls with faintly lewd suggestions. Some were prostitutes, others were waitresses in ABC tea shops and Lyons Corner Houses. Some were amused by the old man. Some were not. The bishop defrocked him for conduct unbecoming and Davidson left the cathedral, shouting angrily, as a layman.

Now penniless and abandoned, Davidson took to amusing the public to keep body and soul together. One of his stunts, threatening to starve himself to death in a barrel on Blackpool sands, got him arrested on a charge of attempted suicide. He was acquitted and won £382 in an action for damages against Blackpool Corporation. His notoriety grew – he pulled in large crowds with a dead whale at a Bank Holiday fair on Hampstead Heath. A circus hired him to appear with lions in a cage. This, alas, was his undoing. He and the lions were a sideshow at Skegness in July 1937 when a lion began to maul him. The trainer, aptly enough a 16-year-old girl, Irene Violet Sumner, made valiant efforts to rescue him. In vain.

Monster of the deep

The great diversionary story of the decade was the Loch Ness Monster. In 1933 an AA patrolman claimed to have seen a serpent-like shape in the waters of the loch. Other claims rolled in, from residents and tourists alike. A big game hunter went to investigate and found a strange spoor in the shingle. The Natural History Museum said that the spoor resembled that of a hippopotamus. The scientist Sir Arthur Keith said that the monster might be a reptile with legs, but he suspected an illusion and that a psychologist would be more useful than a zoologist.

'Nessie', as the monster was affectionately called, did marvels for the Scottish tourist trade. Theories abounded. A local ghillie said it was an old blind salmon. A visitor said they had seen it crossing a road with a sheep in its mouth. An old woman disappeared – when her body was found on the moors, it was said that she had been carried there by the monster. The Royal Scottish Museum thought it might be a large tuna or shark that had come in from the sea. A popular theory was that it was a whale that had entered the loch when it was small, and was now too big to get back to sea. A popular film, *The Secret of the Loch*, showed only the odd glimpse of underwater shapes, but enough people saw it for the profits to endow a bed for divers at Greenwich Hospital.

News of Nessie spread. A Japanese paper described the monster wandering the heaths where Macbeth had met the three weird sisters. The *Berliner Illustrierte* said the monster had been caught and was on exhibition in Edinburgh. It ran pictures of it taken by the 'famous Scottish zoologist, Professor MacKeenkool'. The issue was dated 1 April, showing that some Germans, at least, still had a sense of humour. As the decade continued, such laughs would be at a premium.

MISGUIDED VICAR
The Rector of Stiffkey, Harold Davidson, with his daughter Patricia after a court hearing at Church House, Westminster, on 30 March, 1932. The case followed scandalous allegations that his work with prostitutes in London was not the sort of behaviour expected of a man of the cloth. His case gave the newspapers much to moralise about. He was defrocked later that year and eventually came to a much stickier end, attacked by a lion in Skegness.

BIRTH OF A LEGEND

This well-known picture of Nessie, the Loch Ness Monster, was first published on 19 April, 1934, following widespread reporting of a sighting the previous year. It was one of two images known as the 'surgeon's photographs', supposedly taken by Colonel Robert Kenneth Wilson. It was later revealed to have been a hoax by Christian Spurling, who claimed on his deathbed that he had helped big-game hunter Marmaduke Wetherell to stage the picture, also aided by Wetherell's son, Ian. But by then the story of Nessie had taken on a life of its own.

The group of monks below, angling on Loch Ness, are from the nearby Fort Augustus Abbey, where most of the resident order claimed to have seen the monster. The Father Superior said that he had been aware of it for some years. It was said that references to a monster being present in the loch went back all the way to St Columba in AD 565, when the saint was reputed to have prevented the monster from eating a Pict.

1930s

UNEQUAL FORTUNES

From 1931 to 1935 the number of people officially classed as unemployed in Britain never dropped below 2 million. In the bleak winter of 1932–3, the total climbed to almost 3 million. In other words, a quarter of the working population was out of work. One in four passed their days in enforced idleness, on a street corner, in a library reading room. These official statistics excluded farm labourers, the self-employed, married women and others, which meant that the true unemployment figure was even higher.

A PLEA FOR WORK A man makes his own protest against unemployment with a home-made sandwich board in 1935.

THREE ENGLANDS

Seasonal unemployment could swell the ranks of the jobless. Farms required more hands at harvest than at other times of the year. Building labourers were laid off in the winter, as were waiters and fairground staff in summer resorts such as Blackpool and Brighton. Even in the otherwise healthy car industry, winter was a slack time, for cars sold best in spring and summer.

Since the 1930s slump was global, the effects of it were, too. Countries such as Argentina, Canada, South Africa and Australia had all lost customers for their food and wool, and as a consequence had less capital with which to buy manufactured goods from Britain. By 1929 British exports had crept back up to just over three-quarters of their pre-war level, but two years later, in 1931, they had plummeted back to just half the level they had been in 1913.

Two towns
As Dickens wrote in *A Tale of Two Cities*, his novel set in London and Paris at the time of the French Revolution, 'It was the best of times. It was the worst of times.' His words could equally have applied to the state of Britain in the 1930s. Choose two cities or towns. Let Dagenham in Essex be one, the prosperous one. London County Council was building its largest new housing estate there. It had 18,000 houses in 1930. The Londoners who were rehoused there found gardens, bathrooms, kitchens and electric light waiting for them in homes that were palaces compared to the slums they had left behind in the East End. Ford built a brand new factory nearby on a green field site. The whole place purred with prosperity. Ford was doubling its workforce every three years.

Now consider Jarrow, on the south side of the Tyne in what was then County Durham (now Tyne and Wear). Jarrow had industrial pedigree when Dagenham was still green fields. Palmer's shipyard pioneered rolled armour plate there in 1856. It built hundreds of proud warships, colliers and cargo vessels. Palmers was the town's lifeblood, employing three men in four. In 1930 the yard was reeling. By 1933 it was finished. The only great ship that came to Jarrow was the *Olympic*, sister ship of the *Titanic*, and she came to be broken up for scrap. Ellen Wilkinson, Jarrow's Labour MP, wrote a famous book called *The Town That Was Murdered*. Where Dagenham teemed with new life, Jarrow was dying.

A traveller's view
When the writer J B Priestley journeyed across England in 1933, he found 'three Englands'. The first was Old England, the country of cathedrals, manors and inns, parsons and squires, the place that appeared on chocolate boxes and Christmas

COUNTRY MEETS TOWN
In a photograph from 1934 that seems to epitomise two of Priestley's 'three Englands', harvesters gather their crops almost under the shadow of the great Cunard White Star liner *Queen Mary*, then being built over the water at John Brown's shipyard on Clydebank. Britain's agriculture and shipbuilding were hard-pressed by the economic conditions of the 1930s, leaving many workers unemployed. Both would be rescued only by the coming of war, which created unprecedented demand for ships and homegrown produce.

cards. It was as alien to the real England, Priestley said, as a horse and trap was to the motor-racing circuit at Brooklands. Another traveller, H V Morton, wrote of the 'economic and social cancer' behind the beauty of the countryside. Everywhere, he said, the story was the same: cornland going back to grass, estates breaking up when the owners died, farmers crippled by mortgages, even keeping cattle was a folly when 'the Roast Beef of Old England comes so cheaply from the Argentine'.

The price of corn fell to 20s 9d a quarter – less than £1 and the lowest it had been since the Civil War nearly 300 years before. In East Anglia, farmers were losing at least £5 on every acre of wheat, 5 shillings on every sheep. Land was worth a quarter of what it had been before the Depression. Fields were abandoned to brambles and weeds. Farmers demonstrated with banners that read: 'Wanted in 1914. Abandoned in 1930.' Such protests had no effect. The cities wanted cheap food and that meant Canadian wheat and frozen New Zealand lamb.

Crumbling country estates

In some great houses on once profitable estates, the families retreated from wing to wing, the roofs and casements rotting behind them. A third of the great houses of Shropshire disappeared in the decade. The owners of sporting estates were hard hit by the cumulative effects of the Wall Street Crash. The American sportsmen who had paid top dollar to shoot in Britain had disappeared. By 1932, the makers of sporting guns faced ruin. Arable farming was the hardest hit. More than 3 million acres passed out of cultivation between the wars. Market gardening fared better, expanding with demand from canners for fruit and vegetables.

In this climate weekenders began to snap up country cottages as people left the land. Farm workers in East Anglia earned as little as 30 shillings a week and their diet hardly differed from that of the poor in industrial cities. A supper of white bread and margarine, tinned sardines and tea was the main meal, with bread and cheese and pickles at midday.

Industrial England

The second England identified by Priestley on his journey was 19th century England. This was the industrial nation of coal, steel, cotton, wool and railways. It took up much of the Midlands and the North, but could also be found elsewhere, with row upon row of back-to-back houses, square-faced chapels, mill chimneys, slag heaps and tips, pubs, railway yards, slums and fried fish shops. For the better-off there were detached villas with monkey-puzzle trees, grill rooms, good-class drapers, and Unionist and Liberal clubs. But once they had made a tidy fortune, the tough and enterprising slipped out of this 'mucky England of their making' and settled instead amid the charms of Old England, where their children, 'well schooled, groomed and finished', were soon little different from the old land-owning families.

In Leeds, there were 33,000 back-to-back houses, built 70 to 80 to the acre, with small and squalid rooms. Industry had turned the once green and pleasant land into a 'wilderness of dirty bricks', with blackened fields and poisoned rivers. Priestley found this state of affairs in Wolverhampton, St Helens, Bolton, Gateshead, Jarrow and Shotton. It was as if the country had 'devoted a hundred years of its life to keeping gigantic sooty pigs'. He thought that Hebburn on Tyneside looked as much like an ordinary town as 'a dustbin looks like a drawing-room'. Its shipyards were silent and rotting, its skilled men hanging about the streets as if 'waiting for Doomsday'. Each day, men who had built fine ships went out in a down-at-heel old ship's boat to catch a few fish to give to the families of the unemployed. The town's spirit was not yet broken – it had an orchestra, a ladies' and a children's choir, gym classes, a camping and rambling club – but Priestley felt its self-respect was draining away. This was a working town and it had no work.

> The less lucky in industrial England 'were very unlucky indeed ... [with] monstrously long hours of work, miserable wages, and surroundings in which they lived like black beetles at the back of a disused kitchen stove.'
>
> J B Priestley in *English Journey*, published in 1934

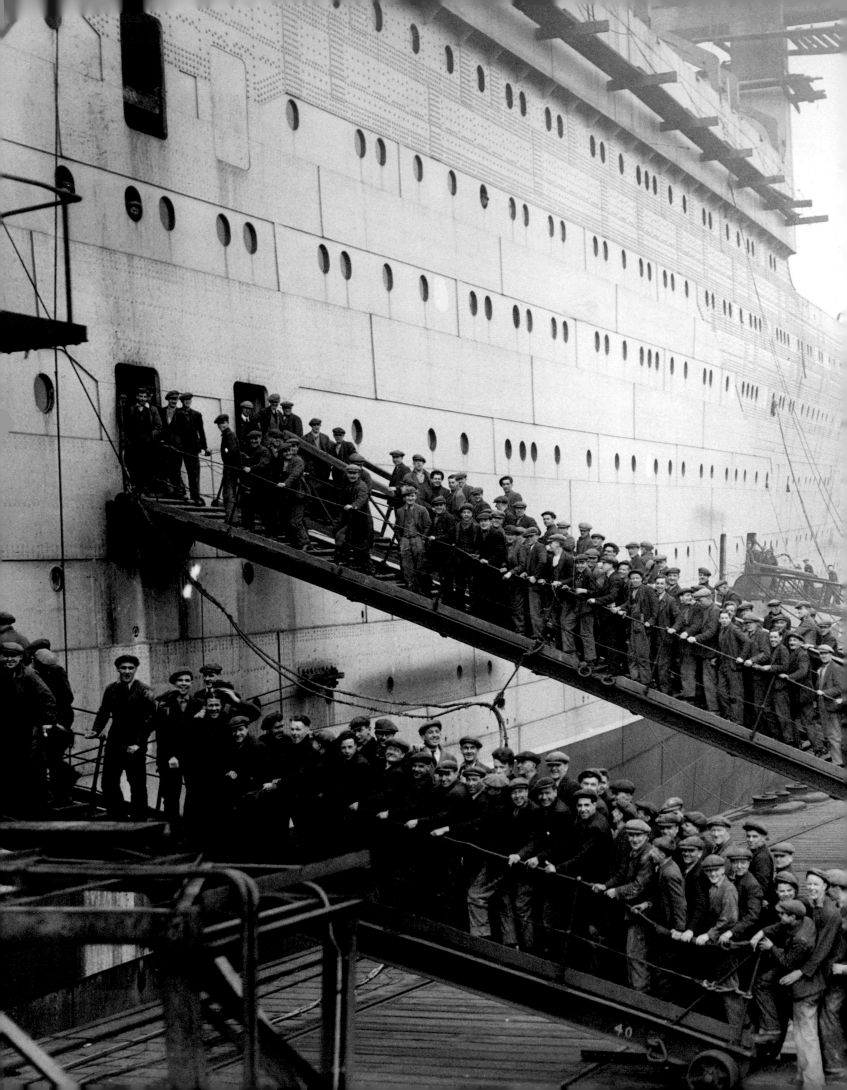

BUILDING OCEAN LINERS

Some of the hundreds of men employed to build the *Queen Mary* return to complete their shift after the dinner break. At this stage – March 1935 – the ship was still known in John Brown's shipyard as 'Liner 534'. A huge range of skills was needed to build a great ocean liner, the biggest, most sophisticated, luxurious and arguably most beautiful mode of transport ever created. She needed joiners, precision engineers, plumbers, welders, glaziers, electricians, boilermakers and above all riveters. Every piece of the ship's hull was held together by rivets, literally millions of which would be hammered home in the construction of a liner. The smiling rivet boy below is Patrick Breslin. He worked on the *Queen Elizabeth*, which was commissioned from John Brown's yard in 1936, the year the *Queen Mary* made her maiden voyage.

HAMMER AND CHAIN
Work in industry could be dreary and monotonous almost beyond endurance. This 'chain gang' of men are manufacturing giant chains and testing the links with hammers in the steel foundry of the Pontypridd Chain Works. By the time this photograph was taken, in March 1937, the worst of the slump was over, but men like these in Welsh industry were still relieved and happy to be in work.

The 'third England'

Priestley thought the true birthplace of what he identified as the third England was America. It was a brand new place of arterial roads and by-passes, petrol stations, giant cinemas and dance halls, cocktail bars, Woolworths, 'factory girls looking like actresses', greyhound tracks and swimming pools. Coming into London from the north he passed miles of semi-detached houses, all with garages and wireless sets, where people read magazines about film stars, and possessed things like tennis rackets that were quite unknown in the terraces of industrial England.

People needed money to live in this new materialistic world, but not that much. Its clean factories – all glass, white tiles and chromium plate, a far cry from the grimy brick-built mills of the North – mass produced cheap luxuries and new electrical goods such as vacuum cleaners, electric toasters and gramophones. It was, Priestley thought, a democratic place: '... in this England, for the first time in history, Jack and Jill are nearly as good as their master and mistress.' It was cleaner, tidier and healthier than industrial Britain, but Priestley, who hailed from Bradford, could not help thinking it had fewer 'solid lumps of character'.

Regional differences

The figures backed Priestley up. The situation was worst in heavy industry and the mines; pottery workers and seamen were also hit hard. The old Victorian backbone of the country was almost broken, and shipbuilding had fared worst of all. By 1932 almost 60 per cent of shipyard workers were without a job. The great Cammell Laird yard in Birkenhead had just a single dredger on its order book. Iron and steel and the mines were in dire straits, too, with 48.5 per cent and 41.2 per cent of workers unemployed. Cotton was slightly better, at 31 per cent. The average unemployment across all industries was 22.9 per cent, but since this figure included the grim totals for the old industries, the real contrast was much greater. Some towns, like St Albans and Oxford, barely felt the slump at all.

The pain was regional, sometimes microscopically so. In South Wales, for example, three-quarters of the men in Brynmawr and Dowlais and two thirds of men in Merthyr had no work in 1934. In contrast, towns a few miles away on the coast were little affected. The anthracite and tinplate areas in the coalfields of west

Wales and the Neath and Swansea valleys, also suffered less than the east. Between them, the Merthyr, Rhondda and Aberdare valleys had half the unemployed of South Wales. In an attempt to address the situation, in 1934 the government created 'special areas' for state aid. These embraced South Wales, Tyneside, West Cumberland and industrial Scotland. Northern Ireland was badly hit, too, its shipyards and linen mills idle, but it lay beyond the scope of Westminster legislation. Together, these areas had two-thirds of all Britain's unemployed.

It was difficult for the depressed areas to recover. Unemployment was not only much higher there, but it lasted far longer. The new industries, powered by electricity, located themselves close to the big consumer markets of the Southeast and the Midlands, with the result that only a small fraction of the jobless in the Southeast were out of work for more than a year, compared to more than a third in Wales. The jobless rate in London and the Southeast never went much above 6 per cent and the Midlands, too, were relatively unscathed. Wales and Northern Ireland were four times worse off. It was only occasionally that a run-down region found itself well-placed for a growth industry. ICI brought chemical plants and much needed employment to Teesside near the decaying Durham pit villages and the silent shipyards of the Wear.

BEANS MEANS … WORK
Women canning green beans on a production line at Wisbech in Cambridgeshire in 1934. The Thirties saw a big increase in the amount of produce grown and canned in Britain. The work was still labour intensive, but production line techniques were honed throughout the decade. The increase in productivity would be a vital factor in the coming war.

BLEAK BRITAIN

Idleness made the mills and industrial towns appear darker and more satanic than ever. For mile upon mile, the landscape was slag-heaps, scrap metal, rotting wharves, weed-infested shunting yards and gaunt men sifting through coal tips or fishing by the banks of a scum-cold canal. The writer George Orwell felt that it was a 'kind of duty' for the better-off to see and smell the labyrinthine slums.

Orwell caught an essence of the depression from a train window. At the back of one slum terraced house, he saw a young woman kneeling on stones, trying to unblock a drainpipe with a stick. He saw her clearly, 'her sacking apron, her clumsy clogs, her arms reddened by the cold'. Her face was round and pale, the exhausted face of the slum girl worn out by need and toil, with the most desolate expression he had ever seen. What he saw was not the ignorant suffering of an animal. 'She knew well enough what was happening to her', he wrote, 'understood as well as I did how dreadful a destiny it was to be kneeling there in the bitter cold, on the slimy stones of a slum backyard, poking a stick up a foul drainpipe.'

Voluntary help

Charities and volunteers were a tremendous force in offsetting poverty. The Rotary clubs, the Inner Wheel, the Women's Institute had thousands of members doing their bit to help. Volunteers manned soup kitchens, packed Christmas parcels for needy families, or helped to pay for recreation halls and allotments. Towns Women's Guilds helped the blind, orphans, unmarried mothers, prisoners, aged governesses, shipwrecked sailors and many more. Family planning clinics and a quarter of maternity and child welfare centres were kept going by voluntary effort. There were 1,013 voluntary hospitals in 1935, providing a third of the country's hospital beds, kept afloat by flag days, appeals, bazaars and donations.

Individual benefactors were important. The Carnegie UK Trust, founded in 1913 by the Scots-born American industrialist, continued to fund all manner of social projects from public libraries to village halls and music festivals. An Indian steel magnate set up the Ratan Tata foundation for social work. Edward Harkness, an American whose family had made a fortune in Standard Oil, was another man of great generosity. He provided £2 million in 1930 for the Pilgrim Trust and to endow scholarships, 'prompted by his admiration for what Great Britain had done in the 1914–18 war, and by his ties of affection for the land from which he drew his descent'. The most spectacular philanthropist of all was a home-grown tycoon. Lord Nuffield had started work as William Morris in a bicycle shop at 16. By 1940 he had given more than £10 million to charity. His money came from his car manufacturing plants, the biggest at Cowley in Oxford. He gave £4 million to the university, £2 million to medical research, and £1 million to found a new post-graduate college of social sciences.

SCRAP FOR SALE
Potential customers rout about in a scrapyard in Leeds in 1935, on the lookout for cheap spare parts. There was plenty of demand. The car industry was one of the great successes of the decade. By 1939, Britain had 2 million privately owned cars, a 20-fold increase since 1919. The cost of a small car like an Austin Seven was just half what it had been in the Twenties.

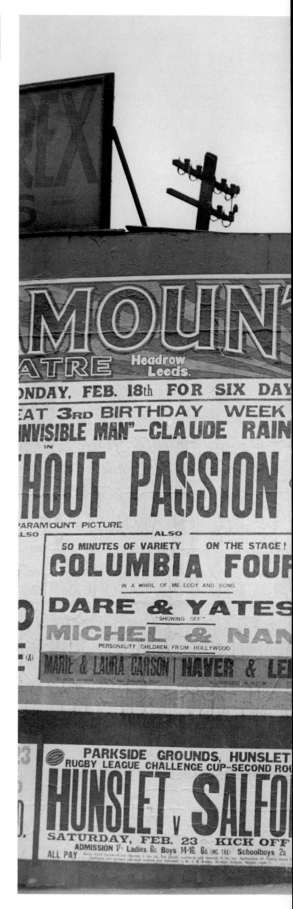

Orwell's insight

The poor lived on white bread and margarine, cans of corned beef or sardines, potatoes and sugared tea. They had no fresh fruit, no nourishing wholemeal bread. The result, Orwell said, was the 'physical degeneracy' on view in the industrial towns. The people of Sheffield, for example, were physically so small they seemed to be 'a population of troglodytes'. Few had their own teeth: anyone over 30 who did was considered abnormal. In Wigan, Orwell stayed in a house with five people, where the youngest, a boy of 15, was the only one with a single tooth of his own. 'Teeth is just misery', a woman said. It was best to 'get shut of them'.

Orwell described a house in the Scholes quarter of Wigan that cost 9s 6d a week to rent. It was a two up, two down, with a coal hole. The walls were falling to pieces, water came through the roof, the floor was lopsided and the windows did not open. In another, smaller house – a one up, two down – with a leaking roof he found a family of ten, eight of them children: the corporation recognised they were overcrowded, but could not find a more suitable house for them. None of these houses had baths or lavatories. These were streets of back-to-backs, with two houses built as one, so that each side had a front door. The front houses faced onto the street, the back houses onto a yard with the lavatories and dustbins.

UNEMPLOYED IN THE THIRTIES
A man looks out over an industrial landscape as blighted and forlorn as the lives of the unemployed (right). The wreckage left behind by the decay of old industries, the heaps of cinders, the crumbling bricks and broken windows of abandoned factories, was like the detritus of a great war. The unemployed flocked to libraries (above), to scan the jobs columns in the papers, but also simply to pass the time by reading. More books were issued by public libraries in the Thirties than ever before. About 100 million book loans were made in 1930 and nine years later the figure had climbed to 247 million. As well as public libraries, there were 'twopenny libraries' in stores like Boots. Book Clubs were founded throughout the decade, catering for the politically left, right and centre. And Allen Lane published the first sixpenny Penguin paperback in 1935.

'Unemployment is not an active state. Its keynote is boredom – a continuous sense of boredom.'

from a report on unemployment published in the 1930s

LIFE ON THE DOLE

The average unemployed family had an income of about 30 shillings a week. A change in diet accompanied the loss of a job: meat, eggs, fresh vegetables, butter and milk usually disappeared, to be replaced by margarine, condensed milk, bread and potatoes. George Orwell was shown the weekly budget of an unemployed miner and his wife. They had two children, one aged two years, the other 10 months. Here is how they spent their 32 shillings a week dole money:

Rent	9s ½d
Clothing Club	3s
Coal	2s
Gas	1s 3d
Milk	0s 10½d
Union fees	0s 3d
Insurance	0s 2d
Meat	2s 6d
Flour	3s 4d
Yeast	0s 4d
Potatoes	1s
Dripping	0s 10d
Margarine	0s 10d
Bacon	1s 2d
Sugar	1s 9d
Tea	1s
Jam	0s 7½d
Peas, cabbage	0s 6d
Carrots, onions	0s 4d
Quaker oats	0s 4½d
Soap, powders	0s 10d
TOTAL	£1 12s 0d

In addition, the family got three packets of dried milk a week for the baby from the Infants' Welfare Clinic. Orwell noted that the list left out many items: pepper, salt, vinegar, matches, razor blades, wear and tear on furniture and bedding, and so on. It included no 'luxuries', like beer or tobacco. If the man of the house smoked or drank, there would have to be a reduction in some of the staples in the list. Clothing Clubs, into which this family was paying 3 shillings a week, were run by big drapers in all the industrial towns. It was only through them that the unemployed were able to buy new clothes.

Those living on the front might have a walk of 50 yards or more to the lavatory. In mining districts, subsidence from underground workings sometimes canted whole streets at an angle – jammed windows were commonplace.

Legend had it that the worst landlord was 'a fat wicked man, preferably a bishop', who lived high on the hog off his extortionate rents. The reality, Orwell found, was that it was the poor landlord – perhaps a widow who had invested all her money in three back-to-backs, inhabiting one of them and living off the rents of the others. She would never have the money for repairs. So roofs leaked, bugs thrived and as the houses became more decrepit they became more and more crowded, with the desperately poor spreading the rent among them.

Wigan – for all George Orwell and the music-hall jokes about 'Wigan Pier' – was by no means the worst. H V Morton was rather charmed by it. He liked its Italian gardens and the lake in its park, and the way the corporation insisted that buildings on the main streets were in Tudor style. He thought it was 'a spa' compared to Wednesbury and the Staffordshire pottery towns.

The hated Means Test

The drop in income for families when a job was lost was brutal. In Stockton-on-Tees, for example, families with a wage earner averaged £2 11s 6d a week, compared to families on the dole who had just £1. A study for the Ministry of Labour in 1937 reflected this, showing falls in income of between 45 and 65 per cent. During the row over the Means Test, dieticians worked out the minimum sum that a human being needed to stay alive. They estimated it at 5s 9d a week.

The dole, as unemployment benefit was generally known, was only paid as a right for 26 weeks. After that, claimants were subject to the despised Means Test

THE HARDEST LIFE OF ALL

Miners suffered worst from unemployment, particularly in Wales, where these miners were photographed outside their cottages in Ebbw Vale on a bleak December day in 1934. That year, half the miners in the Methyr valley and 45 per cent in the Rhondda were out of work. The life they yearned to return to was brutal, but at least their families were better off than when there was no work. In 1930 these two miners (top right) stripped down to their underwear to cope with the intense heat underground at Tilmanstone Colliery in the Kent coalfield. The photograph was made possible by the recently developed 'Sashalite', a safe flash light which replaced earlier dangerous flash illumination in photography. Boys could start down the pit as young as 14 years. These pit boys (bottom right) are learning how to handle and harness a pit pony at Manvers Main Colliery at Mexborough in 1935. Training was vital, for the mines were death-traps. Over the five years to the end of 1931, more than 5,000 men and boys died in the mining industry, while 800,000 were injured.

conducted by the local Public Assistance Committee (PAC), which had replaced the Poor Law Guardians. The maximum payment for a man was 15s 3d a week, but this was only paid if the PAC was satisfied that the claimant had no other income – no savings, no relatives helping out and no part-time work. The process was humiliating for respectable, hard-working men, many of them skilled, who felt themselves treated no better than vagrants under the old Poor Law. The 'relieving officers' who assessed a man's means visited his home, nosed into his life, looked at his furniture – and sometimes suggested he sell some of it. Dole money was cut if he had savings, or money coming in from sons and daughters, or if a pensioner lived in the household. It was an offence to keep any resources concealed.

Many were found ineligible for benefit, while for many others it was reduced. In Lancashire, for example, it was claimed that only 16 per cent were awarded full benefits, and that a third were debarred outright. Over the country as a whole, half of applicants got less than the maximum. There were cases where children and grandparents had to leave the family home because their earnings and pensions would have led to the head of the family having his dole money stopped. The savings for the government in the first year were £24 million, but the cost in humiliation and family hardship was high. An unemployed Birmingham man killed himself after his benefit was cut to 10s 9d a week, with the threat of it being cut altogether. The coroner declared it 'very distressing' and found that the Means Test had been the final straw in rendering him 'temporarily insane'.

Men cycled miles to look for work, or hung around factory gates, hoping for a few hours of casual work. In the mining districts, they went coal-picking, sifting through the slag heaps for scraps of coal. In Wigan, George Orwell saw men with

sacks and baskets scrabbling on slag-heaps that gave off sulphurous smoke from fires smouldering beneath the surface. He watched as some 200 ragged men, each with a sack and a coal-hammer, waited for a train carrying fresh slag from the mines. With the train doing almost 20mph, they hurled themselves aboard. It was dangerous: one man had lost both legs under a train a few weeks before Orwell's visit. At the slag-heap they shovelled the dirt out, while wives and children below picked out lumps of coal, the size of eggs or smaller. Then they trudged the two miles back to Wigan, with perhaps ninepence worth of coal in their sacks. And though it was waste coal, it was still theft to take it. Now and again, a colliery company prosecuted a man for coal-picking. The local magistrates would fine him 10 shillings, and his fellow coal-pickers would raise the money among themselves.

Protesting against the Means Test

The struggle to survive bred fatalism, depression and apathy, but little violence and no revolution. The National Unemployed Workers Movement (NUWM) was the most militant. It was closely allied to the Communist Party and official Labour leaders distrusted it, the more so after NUWM marchers clashed with police in Bristol in 1931 on their way to lobby the TUC conference. NUWM membership peaked at a claimed 100,000, and there were further clashes with police in Belfast, Birkenhead, Manchester and London in autumn 1932 as it campaigned against the Means Test. The fighting went on for three days in Birkenhead, with bottles and park railings used as missiles. Police charged at a demonstration in Parliament Square in Westminster.

NORTHERN MILL TOWN
A view of Colne in Lancashire shows the price Britain had paid for being the first workshop of the world. On this summer day in 1930 it was at least possible to look out across the town, which was more often obscured by smoke drifting from the factory chimneys. There was a meanness – to the barrack-like factories, the tiny terraced cottages, the filthy rivers and streams – that smacked of the elevation of profit above principle. D H Lawrence complained in 1930 that the industrialists in the 'palmy Victorian days' had condemned their workers to 'ugliness, ugliness, ugliness: meanness and formless and ugly surroundings ... great hollow squares of dwellings ... little four-room houses with the "front" looking outward into a grim, blank street ...'

A million people were said to have signed a petition demanding the scrapping of the Means Test. It was carried by 2,500 marchers to London, who were greeted by crowds of workers in Hyde Park. The police charged with batons and a hundred people were injured in violent scuffles. Most newspapers used the presence of the NUWM to brand the marchers as Reds, claiming they had used the 'Bolshie' (Bolshevik) tactic of baiting the police. The petition was never delivered to Parliament. According to one story, probably apocryphal, it was left in a London Underground cloakroom for safekeeping and the cloakroom lost it. Unsympathetic cynics observed that this avoided a re-run of the Chartist petition of 1848, where two-thirds of the signatures were found to be forgeries.

In 1935 the creation of the unpopular Unemployment Assistance Board, which superseded PAC in dealing with the long-term unemployed, sparked a fresh burst of trouble in Wales and Sheffield. The NUWM's influence, though, was now waning. The most common attitude among miners in Durham, a report found to some surprise, was the determination to 'make the best of things'. There was little sense of grievance. Only a tiny proportion of the young unemployed in South Wales were politically motivated. It was wrong, another study said, to assume that their want and discontent were expressed in revolutionary attitudes.

The Jarrow March

The 'Jarrow crusade' was one of the few hunger marches not run by the NUWM. It was deliberately non-political, and its appeal to the public was all the more powerful for it. It was also one of the smallest marches. Just 200 Jarrow men

SOUTHERN STREETS
The narrow streets around Whitechapel High Street in London's East End had seen waves of Jewish immigrants. By 1938 a few Indians had arrived as well, like these smartly dressed young men. Although new houses were being built on greenfield sites out of London, slum clearance in cities was slow. Across the country, more than half a million dwellings were waiting to be demolished under the slum clearance acts, and another 350,000 'marginal dwellings' were slums in all but name.

walked to London with a petition. Local Conservative as well as Labour officials helped to organise it, and it was made clear that their crusade had nothing to do with a much larger march organised by the NUWM at the same time. Newspapers and news-reels felt it safe to give sympathetic coverage to such a non-Red march. The marchers were greeted with great goodwill in towns and villages along the way and in London at the end, but although it has become the lasting symbol of the Depression in Britain, it achieved very little for Jarrow at the time.

It is a small but important detail that Ellen Wilkinson, Jarrow's Labour MP who was instrumental in organising the march, was an ex-communist. She had been a founder member of the Communist Party in Britain in 1920, but after four years, disillusioned by its totalitarian ways, she turned her back on it to re-enter the democratic mainstream of British politics. She would become the country's first woman education minister, in Attlee's post-war Labour government.

Consensus and coalition

Europe was falling prey to two giants of evil, Stalin and Hitler, and to the new creeds of communism and fascism. Britain was a different world. The few native communists and fascists were noisy, but they were never more than fringe. Not a single fascist was elected to Westminster in a decade when they were triumphant in Italy, Germany and ultimately in Spain. Communist MPs could be counted on the fingers of one hand. In Britain, consensus and coalition were the order of the day.

So was social flexibility, although this should not be exaggerated. The top 1 per cent of the population was not as spectacularly rich as before the Great War, when it owned 69 per cent of the nation's wealth. By 1936 the figure was down to 55 per cent, but most of the drop had not gone to the poor. Far from it. The drop for the wealthiest had been absorbed by the rest of the top 5 per cent, who in 1937 had 79 per cent of all wealth. The great majority of people in Britain had very little personal property at all. Some 8 million families – three-quarters of the population – would have realised less than £100 by selling all they owned.

In Victorian days, industry had been the wealth-creator. In the 1930s, four in every five millionaires had made their money in commerce and finance. They were bankers, stockbrokers, insurers, shipowners, retailers, merchants. A third lived in London: the provinces no longer had as much clout. The public school strangle-hold was firmer than ever. The great majority of Conservative MPs – and in the Thirties most MPs were Conservatives – came from public schools, as did 190 of the 271 top civil servants. Public schools produced more than three quarters of bishops, deans, high court judges and directors of the major banks. Nine in ten directors of the big railway companies were former public schoolboys, as were four in five senior managers in the steel industry. A study in 1931 showed that 524 of the 691 holders of 'high office' in church, state and industry were public schoolboys, with over a third coming from just five schools: Eton, Harrow, Winchester, Rugby and Marlborough. The ratio had scarcely budged by 1939.

And yet Ramsay MacDonald's upbringing in poverty in Scotland did not prevent him becoming the most powerful man in the land. Philip Snowden, his chancellor, was born in a two-roomed hovel near Keighley in West Yorkshire, a weaver's son who became a viscount. The Liberal Rufus Isaacs was one of nine children of a Jewish fruit merchant from Spitalfields in London. Neither his class nor his religion prevented him from becoming the Marquis of Reading, ambassador to Washington and viceroy of India.

THE HUNGER MARCHES

The Jarrow Hunger March is the unemployed crusade that has gone down in the collective memory, but in fact hunger protests took place throughout the 1930s as people marched on London from areas of high unemployment to ask, not for charity, but for the right to work to earn a living. None of the marches achieved their aim, but they did raise awareness of the problems faced by the working class in some parts of the country.

ACTIVE PROTEST

After its victory in the 1931 election, the new National Government immediately introduced the Means Test. This cut unemployment benefit payments for anyone who had some savings to fall back on, or with relatives who could help them. The result was that most people did not get the full unemployment benefit. There was fierce anger against the test and those who administered it, but above all against Ramsay MacDonald and the old Labour leaders who were accused of class betrayal. A National Hunger March on London was organised in 1932. A million people signed the petition, carried by the 2,500 marchers, demanding the abolition of the Means Test. These men (below) marched down from Yorkshire; the photograph was taken at King's Cross station as they returned home that November. The dole was just enough to keep body and soul together, and no more. Labourers in the country could eke it out by keeping rabbits and growing vegetables, but in industrial areas there was little that men could do other than scour coal tips for fuel. And the real hardship began when the dole ran out after the 26 weeks for which it was payable.

'The men do not want charities. They want jobs.'

Ellen Wilkinson, MP for Jarrow, from *The Town That Was Murdered*,
an account of the Jarrow March published in 1939

THE JARROW MARCH

On the long trek down from Tyneside, the Jarrow marchers were fed and offered shelter by well-wishers along the way (bottom left). The photograph above was taken as they passed through the village of Lavendon, near Bedford, some of the men playing mouth organs to keep up their spirits in the rain. On reaching London on 31 October, 1936, they were led through Hyde Park by their MP, Ellen Wilkinson (top left). The marchers carried a petition begging the government to act over unemployment, which had reached a staggering 75 per cent in Jarrow after the big shipyard, Palmers, laid the men off. The marchers gained much sympathy from the public and the press, for they conducted themselves with dignity and no hint of 'Bolshiness' (behaving like Bolsheviks) to frighten off the popular newspapers. But the shipyard stayed idle, apart from a little shipbreaking – sad work for men who had proudly built ships, not broken them up.

A VERY BRITISH FASCIST

It is ironic that the great extremist of the time, far from being radicalised in a slum, was a 6th baronet. Sir Oswald Mosley, Blackshirt leader and fan of Mussolini and Hitler, was born in 1896 to a wealthy family of country squires with an estate at Rolleston that employed 30 gardeners. The men in the family were traditionally boxers. They staged bouts in the ballroom, like Regency rakes. Following the tradition, Mosley was an accomplished boxer as well as a swordsman. During the Great War he had served in the trenches and in the Royal Flying Corps.

Mosley was first elected to Parliament in 1918, aged just 21, as Conservative MP for Harrow. Unhappy with the government's position on Ireland, he crossed the floor of the House to become an Independent. By 1924 he had joined the Labour Party. Elected Labour MP for Smethwick in 1926, he was hailed as the Party's golden boy, its most brilliant young member. Almost everyone, according to social reformer Beatrice Webb, thought of him as a future leader. Labour was a party of plebeians and plain men, she explained, and hitherto MacDonald had no competitor in 'personal charm and good looks … and the gift of oratory. But Mosley has all three, with the élan of youth, wealth and social position added to them.' He was a brilliant speaker and debater, he worked hard and he had ideas. But there was always a streak of impatience, instability and violence about him.

In 1930 Mosley was junior minister for unemployment under Jimmy Thomas, whom he despised. He wanted action and proposed a radical programme of public works to be financed by government loans. When MacDonald turned it down, Mosley resigned from the government and the Labour Party. In a fierce speech to the Commons on 29 May, he warned that if nothing was done Britain would sink to the level of Spain, a dreadful fate for a country that within everyone's lifetime had 'put forth efforts of energy and vigour unequalled in history'.

The New Party

Mosley's next move was to form his own political party – the New Party. At first its future seemed bright. Osbert and Sacheverell Sitwell joined, along with the young photographer Cecil Beaton, the left-wing Oliver Baldwin, Stanley's rebel son, and the equally leftist ex-Labour MP and Old Etonian, John Strachey. Literary figures who joined the New Party included Christopher Isherwood, whose Berlin stories inspired the musical *Cabaret*, and the diarist and diplomat Harold Nicolson. These were interesting men, but Mosley did not keep them for long. In April 1931, the New Party candidate Allen Young took 16 per cent of the vote in a by-election. By summer, Young and Strachey had left. Of 24 candidates fielded by the New Party in the general election of October 1931, only two managed to save their deposits. By April 1932 Mosley had formally disbanded the party.

He was, his friends thought, wildly impulsive and arrogant. They suspected that he would now 'play the He-man'. Beatrice Webb wrote that 'The British electorate would not stand a Hitler … Mosley has bad health, a slight intelligence and an unstable character. He lacks genuine fanaticism. Deep down in his heart he is a cynic. He will be beaten and retire.' She would turn out to be right. But for now, Mosley displayed a taste for street-fighting that echoed the fascists on the

FASCIST OFFENSIVE
Sir Oswald Mosley in full cry at a meeting in 1934 (near right), as membership of his British Union of Fascists (BUF) was beginning to build. His veneer of sophistication and stage presence made him seem more significant than he was. He had glamour and was a powerful orator, but he was too obviously a pale pastiche of Mussolini and Hitler – Malcolm Muggeridge called him 'the Lilliputian Führer'. Moseley's black-shirted admirers – seen here (far right) giving him the classic Nazi salute on 4 October, 1936, shortly before provoking the Battle of Cable Street – were almost comically theatrical, compared to the truly menacing Blackshirts and Brownshirts in Italy and Germany. Some of his women fans were photographed in their blackshirts, berets and A-line skirts while on parade in Liverpool in 1935 (bottom right). They have a slightly bashful air, as well they might. Mosley tried to exploit the political tensions thrown up by the slump, but the British Union of Fascists never came remotely close to power. It was all bark and no bite, and failed to attract the vast majority of the British public. Not a single BUF member entered Parliament.

Continent. He used the communists, who broke up his meetings, as an excuse for veering to the extreme right. Mosley said this 'forces us to be fascist', Nicolson noted in his diary. Uniforms were discussed. 'I suggest grey flannel trousers and shirts', said Nicolson. His notion of making them look like schoolboys did not go down well and he, too, was soon gone, to become a National Liberal MP.

Mosley visited Rome in January 1932 and met Mussolini. He was impressed. When he launched his new British Union of Fascists (the BUF) in October 1932, he issued members with sinister – but vaguely ludicrous – black shirts. Shirts were big with demagogues: Mussolini's followers were blackshirts, Hitler's were brownshirts. A little later, in Argentina, Peron's devotees were the Shirtless Ones.

Setting out his stall

Mosley's 'Mein Kampf' was *The Greater Britain*, a book he wrote in the summer of 1932. He argued that Britain was in crisis. If no action was taken, she would sink from imperial grandeur to decadent weakness, as Spain had done. The innate intelligence of the Anglo-Saxon race gave hope for the future. To exploit that superiority, Mosley would rule a well-disciplined state with a small cabinet. Parliament would survive, but with limited powers. Much of its work would pass

THE BATTLE OF CABLE STREET
Anti-fascist protesters put up barricades in Cable Street on 4 October, 1936, to prevent Mosley and his followers from marching through the East End of London (left). They clashed with police (above) and with Mosley's men in what was called the Battle of Cable Street. Most people, though, were utterly unmoved by extremists on Left or Right. They found the clenched fist salutes of the Reds as distasteful as the outstretched arms of the fascists. Moderation prevailed.

to 24 corporations, each representing a particular industry. Capitalism would remain, but under tight state direction. The aim was self-sufficiency in an imperial trading bloc. Cheap foreign imports would be banned, with British industry able to pay high wages and hire the unemployed. The powers and freedoms of trade unions would be curtailed. Women were to be encouraged to stay at home rather than compete with men for jobs.

All this was radical, but Mosley sought to soothe the public with his respect for tradition – the monarchy, Church and Empire – and for a time the BUF did not fare badly. By February 1934 its membership stood at 17,000 and this trebled to around 50,000 after Lord Rothermere's *Daily Mail* began to champion the BUF. It did not last. In June 1934, at a rally at London's Olympia, Blackshirt stewards brutally beat up some hecklers. The same month, Hitler's ruthless murders of his Nazi critics in the 'Night of the Long Knives' highlighted the dark side of fascism. Rothermere was no fascist, he was a reactionary Tory. He withdrew his support in July 1934 and within a year or so membership had all but evaporated, down to around 5,000.

The BUF staggered on thanks to Mussolini, who between 1933 and 1936 sent it some £60,000. The party campaigned in 1935 against British support for League of Nations sanctions on Italy over Mussolini's invasion of Abyssinia, but it cannot be said that Il Duce got much for his money. Mosley, remembering the humiliation of his New Party at the polls in 1931, put up no candidates at all for the 1935 election. Instead, he produced the rather lame slogan, 'Fascism Next Time'.

Anti-Semitism backfires

One of the New Party candidates in that disastrous election of 1931 had been a Jew – Kid Lewis, a welterweight boxing champion, who lost his deposit standing for his home constituency in Whitechapel. But gradually Mosley came to adopt an anti-Semitic stance that had more in common with German Nazis than Italian fascists. In May 1934 Jews were barred from the BUF. This struck a chord with some in London's East End, which by now had a large and not as yet fully assimilated number of Jewish immigrants – a third of all Jews in Britain lived in the East End. BUF members attacked Jews and their property amid considerable violence, most notoriously in the Battle of Cable Street on 4 October, 1936, when a march of 1,900 Fascists was blocked by tens of thousands of protesters. In the municipal elections of 1937, the BUF came second in a number of East End seats, but it was not close to winning in any of them.

The violence in London made people elsewhere more, not less, sympathetic to the Jews. The BUF obsession with 'the Jewish problem' alienated the vast majority of Britons, for whom the problem was non-existent. The troubles in the East End led the government to pass the Public Order Act in 1936. This banned political uniforms and gave the police powers to ban or re-route any provocative march they deemed might cause trouble. Young men who had welcomed the chance to march in BUF uniform and have a rumble with protesters found this amusement withdrawn. The party became smaller – and more middle-class – by the month.

BATTING FOR THE OTHER SIDE
Soviet agents were more successful in recruiting from young and privileged students at Cambridge University than they were among workers, whose innate patriotism made them suspicious of flirting with Moscow. Anthony Blunt (right, on the left) was the son of the chaplain to the British embassy in Paris. He was first an undergraduate, then from 1932 a fellow of Trinity College, Cambridge. He met his fellow traitors – Guy Burgess, Kim Philby and (below) Donald Maclean – while at Trinity. Blunt supplied the names of other likely recruits to his Soviet spymasters. After the war, he helped Burgess and Maclean to defect to the Soviet Union just before their treachery was revealed. Donald Maclean was the son of a Liberal Cabinet minister, whose betrayal of national secrets began when he joined the Foreign Office in 1935, and continued until he fled and defected to Moscow in 1951.

THE COMMUNIST CONNECTION

For all the talk of 'Red Clydeside' and the 'little Moscows' in South Wales, the communists fared little better in Britain than the fascists. Party membership was around 7,000 for most of the Thirties, reaching a brief peak of 18,000 late in the decade. They were, though, very active. The propaganda in the party paper, the *Daily Worker*, embraced the arts and book pages, where films, theatre and writing were all seen in Marxist terms. It tried to appeal to the working man, with sports pages covering football and boxing, as well as the decidedly non-Marxist 'Sport of Kings' – horse-racing. The party churned out pamphlets by the hundred thousand, which were sold on street corners by eager volunteers.

Communist Party membership represented only those who were willing to devote themselves to the cause. The number of general sympathisers, or 'fellow travellers', was higher and might have been greater still had the British Communist Party not been so slavishly under Soviet control. It raised so little money on its own behalf it became dependent on handouts from Moscow. This involved it in tortuous efforts to reflect Stalin's will, which in turn alienated patriotic British workers who were suspicious of foreigners.

Communist candidates were trounced in the 1931 general election, most of them losing their deposits. Later, they gained some useful publicity from the clashes with Mosley's Blackshirts. Moscow also moderated its hostility to Western governments as the increasing power of the Nazis in Germany forced it to seek allies in the West. The party only put forward two candidates at the 1935 election. One of them, William Gallacher, was elected for West Fife. This 'popular front' period, when the party relaxed some of its scorn for others on the left, saw it gain members but it never had any real hold on the working class.

Middle-class sympathisers

Intellectuals were altogether more susceptible. It was now that the Communist Party recruited three undergraduates at Trinity College, Cambridge: Guy Burgess, Donald Maclean and Anthony Blunt, later infamous as traitors. Burgess was the grandson of an admiral and an Etonian. He was a Gladstone Memorial Scholar at Trinity. Maclean's father was the president of the Board of Education when he went up to Cambridge in 1931. The other man in this little nest of spies was Kim Philby, who had gone up to Trinity in 1929. His father was St John Philby, an Arabist and adventurer, who was political adviser to Ibn Saud in Saudi Arabia.

The gullibility of apologists like the playwright George Bernard Shaw was astonishing. 'GBS' visited the Soviet Union in 1932, at the height of his fame. He was driven through Moscow and to selected parts of the countryside when farms were being turned into collectives by the state. 'Tales of a half-starved population dwelling under the lash of a ruthless tyrant' were nonsense, he later wrote in *The Times*. There were 'crowds of brightly dressed well-fed happy-looking workers'. Also, he added, 'in the USSR, unlike Britain, there is freedom of religion'.

Even as Shaw was writing such words, millions of Ukrainians were starving to death in a deliberate terror-famine. Tens of thousands were shot, and millions taken to labour camps in Siberia, where they died of cold, overwork and starvation. Yet even today the mass murders in villages and work camps in the Soviet Union during the Thirties remain less notorious than the wartime Nazi concentration camps. Many on the left turned a blind eye. But the outlines were

OVERALL PROTEST
The League Against Imperialism sets out its position in Trafalgar Square in August 1931. Little support was forthcoming. Britain was still the greatest imperial power in the world. The majority of Britons may not have been as proud of the Empire as they had been in the heyday of Victorian jingoism, but few were ashamed of it, either, and they had little time for the siren songs of crypto-communists like these. In reality, 'anti-imperialist' often meant 'Stalinist', and as such 'anti-imperialists' were inflicting inhumanities in Soviet Russia on a cold-blooded scale undreamt of in British colonies.

known. Independent-minded journalists like Malcolm Muggeridge exposed them in reports from Russia – and were expelled. Intellectuals who witnessed Communist Party tactics in the Spanish Civil War, like George Orwell and Arthur Koestler, became aware at first hand of the evils of Moscow-style communism. At show trials in Moscow, Henry Thornton and three other manifestly innocent British engineers working on a project in Russia for Metropolitan Vickers were accused of 'deliberately wrecking' the Soviet economy. Worse than this black comedy were the trials in which Party leaders pleaded guilty to working for British and French intelligence, and were then shot.

As the decade progressed, the British and French were becoming outnumbered in Europe by those living under dictatorships. It is only with hindsight that they can be criticised for not regarding the Nazis as the greater menace. In the pre-war period, far more died from bestial treatment by Stalin than as yet from Hitler.

THE GAME GOES ON

As ever, sport helped to keep minds off the evil doings across the water. The 1930s were a golden era for cricket. The London County Council had 350 pitches, and a thousand clubs applying to use them. The game was even more popular in the North. The Roses matches between Lancashire and Yorkshire had a national following. Jack Hobbs, who was the first cricketer to be knighted, opened the batting for England in his last Test match in 1930, but he went on playing for Surrey until 1935, when he was well into his 50s. By then, he had scored 61,237 runs in first-class matches, a record that still stands. Hobbs and Herbert Sutcliffe were an unrivalled pair of openers, and all-rounder Wally Hammond was at his peak, scoring 3,000 runs in Tests against Australia. Hedley Verity set a first-class record in 1932 by taking all 10 wickets for 10 runs against Nottinghamshire.

BBC broadcasts of Test matches attracted huge audiences. 'Live' coverage from far-flung matches was enabled by telegrams sent from the ground detailing each ball bowled, which the 'commentator' used to describe the game. Celebrities and intellectuals had yet to pose as football fans. Cricket was the game.

The sensational cricket story of the decade was the MCC's 'Bodyline' tour of Australia in 1932–3. The MCC won the Ashes, but the Australians claimed that this was only because of dangerous bowling by Nottinghamshire fast bowler Harold Larwood. The English captain, D R Jardine, defended what he called 'leg-theory' bowling, insisting that it was fair. It was certainly effective: even the great Australian batsman Donald Bradman struggled to cope. Larwood was a slender, almost slight figure, but he bowled with extraordinary power and pace. The Australians called his bowling 'preventable brutality' and threatened to call off the Ashes tours. Larwood was not selected when the Australians next toured England. He felt betrayed by the cricket establishment – with good reason.

Larwood was thus not part of the record-breaking team of 1938. In the Fifth Test against Australia at the Oval, in August 1938, England scored 903 runs for seven wickets declared. The margin of the win – an innings and 579 runs – remains another Test record. A 22-year-old Yorskshireman, Len Hutton, stayed at

A GREAT BRITISH BATSMAN
Jack Hobbs (below) played his first game for Surrey in 1905. He was still going strong in the 1930s: 98 of his 197 first-class centuries – the highest total in the history of cricket – were made after he turned 40.

BODYLINE CONTROVERSY

The great cricket story of the decade was England's victorious tour of Australia in 1932–3. The fast bowler Harold Larwood (left) was a phenomenon. He was only average height and build, but his pace, strength and near-perfect rhythm enabled him to bowl at over 90mph. Encouraged by the England team captain, D R Jardine, Larwood pitched the ball on the leg side, so that it rose sharply at the Australian batsmen. At the time batsmen were protected only by leg pads, with no helmet or body padding. As the struggling batsmen fended the ball off, a ring of English slips and other fielders gobbled up the catches. Jardine defended it as 'leg-theory' bowling. The Australians – outraged by the bruises Larwood inflicted and his large haul of wickets – called it 'bodyline' and 'brutality'. England won the Ashes and Jardine wrote a best-selling book about the tour (below), but the Australians complained so bitterly the government felt obliged to intervene. Jimmy Thomas, the Dominions Secretary, summoned MCC members to Downing Street. Cricket, he said, was the main sentimental link between Australia and the Mother Country and he urged them not to strain Anglo-Australian relations any further. As a result Larwood, a bowler whose brilliance had tamed even the great Donald Bradman, never played Test cricket again.

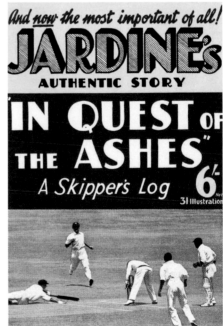

the crease for 13 hours to score his 364 runs. Don Bradman, Australia's captain, was the first to shake Hutton's hand when he broke the old record of 334 held by Bradman himself. Hutton ran six miles between the wickets, before eventually being caught. His score stood as a record until 1958 when Garfield Sobers hit 365 not out against Pakistan in Jamaica. Despite the spread of cricket around the empire, the game in England was still divided into 'Gentlemen' and 'Players', or amateurs and professionals. Separate dressing rooms were common. County sides were captained by amateurs and so was the MCC. Wally Hammond reverted to amateur status in 1938 to be able to captain Gloucestershire and England.

Sweepstakes and football pools

The arrival of two new forms of gambling gave the very poorest dreams of riches to keep them going. The Irish Sweepstake was started in Dublin in 1930 and soon became hugely popular with the British public. Public lotteries were forbidden in

GAME, SET AND MATCH
Fred Perry leaps the net after winning the men's singles final at Wimbledon in 1935. Perry, the son of a Labour MP, came into the game late. He was the world table tennis champion in 1929 and only took up tennis when he was 19. Between 1933 and 1936, when he turned professional, he won every major amateur title, including the US singles three times and the Australian and French championships. He was Wimbledon champion three times and the last British man to lift the trophy.

Britain (though clubs were allowed to run sweepstakes for members), but the Post Office could not stop people buying tickets in Dublin without censoring the mail. Over the decade, the Sweepstake took in more than £60 million, of which £14 million went to Irish hospitals and £2 million to the Irish government in taxes. Politicians in Britain were urged to copy it, but were nervous of antagonising Nonconformist voters implacably opposed to all forms of gambling.

Meanwhile, the football pools rocketed to popularity in Britain and by the late Thirties had overtaken the Sweepstake. The pools were based on guessing the football results, with each entry costing as little as a penny. Profits and overheads were deducted from the total wagered, and the remainder was distributed among the winners. A vast army of agents covered the country from town to village, distributing coupons and collecting takings. Most entries, though, came through the post. The volume was so huge that extra postmen were employed on Mondays and Tuesdays, when the new coupons were delivered.

The pools were heavily advertised in the popular papers and also promoted on Radio Luxembourg and Radio Normandie, two commercial radio stations broadcasting from abroad. The growth was startling: 10 million people were soon doing the pools, hoping that their 2s 6d stake would win them a £22,000 fortune. During the 1934–5 season, at least £20 million was spent on the pools. A year later, that had doubled, and politicians and churchmen were fretting over the money wasted, in small but regular amounts, by families that could ill afford it.

THE GREAT OUTDOORS

There was huge enthusiasm for outdoor pursuits in the Thirties. The Lake District was popular with hikers: these two young women (below) are admiring the view from the famous Wishing Gate at Grasmere in 1935. One organisation at the heart of making the outdoors more accessible was the Youth Hostel Association (YHA), founded in 1930. The movement was a stunning success. The YHA opened its first permanent hostel at the City Mill in Winchester in 1931 and by 1939 it had 297 hostels and 83,418 members in England and Wales. Separate associations in Scotland, Ulster and Eire brought the total number of hostels in the British Isles to 397, with 106,000 members clocking up more than half a million nights in them. Ramblers clubs sprang up across the country and a National Council of Ramblers was set up in 1935. Much of Britain was out of bounds, with bailiffs and gamekeepers keeping a close lookout for trespassers. Ramblers now lobbied for greater access and persuaded the Ordnance Survey to mark footpaths on maps to show where walkers had rights of way.

A change of leader

It was a sign of Britain's underlying stability that there were just three prime ministers over this turbulent decade – the nation's closest allies, the French, could get through that many in a fortnight. Furthermore, the changeovers were smooth and crisis-free. In June 1935 Ramsay MacDonald retired and Stanley Baldwin returned to Number 10. Nothing stuck to 'honest Stan'. He liked to be thought of as a country worthy, torn from reading Wordsworth to do his duty for the nation. He was very much a part of Old England. He was Rudyard Kipling's first cousin, and his aunt was married to the pre-Raphaelite painter Edward Burne-Jones. He was a patriotic and generous man. In 1919 he had spent £120,000, a fifth of his fortune, on War Bonds and presented them to the government. The letter he wrote to *The Times*, suggesting that the 'wealthy classes' should follow suit, was signed 'FST' – he was then Financial Secretary to the Treasury. No one realised it was Baldwin, as he intended, and only one person is believed to have followed his example. He called a general election in November 1935 and the National Government was returned with a large, if slightly reduced, majority.

Signs of recovery

As the decade went on, the recovery was based on cars, bicycles, electrical goods and, from the mid-1930s, rearmament centred on the aircraft industry in Coventry and Bristol. People moved where the work was. The booming industrial estates at Slough, for example, sucked in labour from the Welsh valleys. The Midlands car, van and lorry plants attracted families from the North and Scotland. Electricity

WHITE-COAT WORKERS

Women making radios in a clean modern plant in 1938. Conditions in the booming electricity-powered industries were better by far than anything that had gone before. The workers here all have the benefit of individual electric lighting to help them see what they are doing. Radio had moved rapidly since the first post-war crystal sets requiring complicated aerials and headphones. Valve sets with integrated loudspeakers came in. Many were powered by an accumulator – something like a car battery – that needed recharging from time to time, but by the Thirties there were also mains electricity radio sets. Reception was vastly improved, so that sound quality was excellent in all but the worst atmospheric conditions. Prices tumbled, too. Currys were selling two- and three-valve sets on hire purchase for one or two shillings a week. The number of radio licences, which stood at just 36,000 in 1922, had passed the 2 million mark four years later and reached 8 million in 1939.

was the key. The National Grid was all but complete by 1933, with new power stations connected by a grid of high voltage power lines. Electricity output quadrupled in the 15 years leading up to the war, and the numbers employed in the electricity industry reached 325,000. The one house in three that was wired for electricity in 1930 had become two houses in three by 1939. The impact on industry was perhaps even more dramatic. Factories powered by electricity were utterly different to the blackened buildings of old plants powered by coal, with their belching chimneys and sirens sounding each shift. The fine new factories along the Great West Road into London had scarcely a chimney between them. They made the new products of the new industries: potato crisps, scent, toothpaste, fire extinguishers, bathing costumes.

The Hoover plant at Perivale was a symbol of this modernity, built in stunning Art Deco style. It was light and elegant, constructed of steel, glass and concrete, and set amid lawns and flowerbeds. The arterial road beside it carried the trucks and vans that supplied the factory with parts and then distributed its brand-new vacuum cleaners to the thriving markets of the Southeast. No railways, no coal, no noise, no smoke. Hoover boomed. In the very worst years of the Depression, between 1930 and 1935, sales of vacuum cleaners increased twelve-fold, up from 37,550 to 409,345. Other electrical appliances – refrigerators, cookers, heaters, radio sets, reading lamps – also brought work and good wages to those that made them and an improved quality of life for the families who could afford them.

Cars became another major new industrial employer. In 1924 Britain had produced 146,000 motor vehicles. By 1937 the half-million-a-year mark had been passed. The number had risen every year – even in the worst of the slump from 1929 to 1933. Cars brought vibrancy and good wage packets to Dagenham and also to the Midlands at Coventry, Birmingham, Luton and Oxford.

Advances in plastics and artificial fibres gave fresh impetus to chemicals. 'Rayon' and other yarn was used in clothing. Plastic, often as 'Bakelite', became a standard material for radio sets. ICI, the giant chemicals combine put together in 1926, did well across a wide range: fibres, synthetic dyes, pharmaceuticals, fertilisers. The industry was employing 100,000 by the time the war broke out.

Population and productivity

Changing demographics helped. A falling birth rate meant that the 15 to 64 age group was growing faster than the population as a whole. In mid-Victorian days, that group accounted for less than 60 per cent of total population. By 1937 it was within a whisker of 70 per cent. These were people at the peak of their producing and consuming powers, boosting both national output and consumption.

Technology gave another boost. Mass production revolutionised productivity in everything from cars to radio sets. Electricity not only spawned new industries, it transformed old ones. Electric coal cutters in the pits and power tools in engineering led to big rises in output. Credit instalment plans – better known as hire purchase, or the 'never never' – were another factor, making it easier for consumers to spend. J Gibson Garvie, the boss of United Dominions Trust, a major credit supplier, hoped that 'the principle of instalment-buying will eventually prove the spearhead of an advance to a fuller civilisation'. It was already producing an indebted one with 'repo' – repossession from families that could not keep up payments – increasingly common. Ellen Wilkinson, Labour MP for Jarrow, got a private member's bill through Parliament that meant defaulters were at least partially reimbursed for what they had paid out.

The thousand-odd chain stores built between the wars shrugged off the Depression. Marks & Spencers opened 129 brand-new stores between 1931 and 1935, and enlarged 60 more. Turnover, impressive at £2.5 million in 1929, grew tenfold over the next ten years. Most medium-sized towns now boasted a Marks and Sparks, a Sainsburys or Lipton's, and a Woolworths. Between them they made a big range of food, clothes and household goods readily available. It was the beginning of the threat to small grocers and traditional corner shops.

CARS FOR THE MASSES
Workers on an assembly line at the Morris car plant at Cowley in Oxford rub down the bodywork after its first coat of paint. Perhaps surprisingly, the Thirties were boom times for car factories. In 1919 there had been around 100,000 cars on the roads. Twenty years later, that had ballooned to 2 million. No longer was a private car an unimaginable luxury. The cost of an Austin Seven had fallen to £120 by the early Thirties, and small Morrises sold for between £100 and £200. Traffic lights, roundabouts and 'Belisha beacons' at pedestrian crossings were all introduced to help control the ever-increasing number of cars on the roads. Even so, road safety was an issue: the death toll was far higher than it is today, reaching 7,300 in 1934.

1930s
UNCERTAIN TIMES

On 20 January, 1936, George V held his last Privy Council meeting in his bedroom at Sandringham. He could barely sign his name, and he soon lapsed into a coma. Rudyard Kipling had died shortly before. 'The King has sent his trumpeter ahead', they said. Lord Dawson, his doctor, issued a bulletin that read: 'The King's life is moving peacefully towards its close.' He would not last the night. George had come to the throne in 1910 amid a constitutional crisis. He not only steadied the ship with dignity and compassion, but also steered the monarchy through the storms of the Great War. His death would provoke an even bigger crisis for the royal family as his eldest son, Edward VIII, proved unsuitable to succeed him.

RADIO KING George V preparing to deliver his Christmas message from Sandringham in 1933 (left). His first Christmas message had been broadcast the previous year, with a script written by Rudyard Kipling, starting a royal tradition that continues to this day.

THE ABDICATION CRISIS

Famously, George's last words were reported to be 'bugger Bognor', as in the seaside resort of Bognor Regis, but this is probably apocryphal. The new King's first action was a deliberate break with the past. 'I'll fix those bloody clocks', said Edward, referring to the clocks at Sandringham that his father and grandfather had kept on 'Sandringham time', half an hour ahead of the rest of the country. All the clocks in the house were now changed to GMT.

George V was dearly loved and deeply mourned. Almost a million people queued to file past the bier and pay their last respects. His eldest son and new monarch Edward VIII was also popular. Known as David in the family while he was Prince of Wales, he was slender and blond, an 'adored Apollo'. He wore his uniforms well, was a good horseman and polo player, yet there was a fragility to his slight frame and a melancholy in his eyes and mouth hinting that, though he sought pleasure, he did not find it. He was the symbol of Young England, seen with jobless miners in South Wales and dancing the Charleston in Mayfair.

The Prince was always at odds with his father, and his natural charm and grace were in stark contrast with two of his brothers – the awkward, stammering Duke of York, and the plodding, witless Duke of Gloucester. So too, though, was Edward's selfishness. He was obsessed with fashion, with 'smart nightspots, louche weekends, horseplay, jazz and jigsaw puzzles'. He had sympathy with the poor, but he spent his time pleasure-seeking with rich socialites.

Indiscretion and informality

Edward had enjoyed a love affair with Freda Dudley Ward, a married woman described as 'discreet, pretty … and pleasure-loving'. They had met during an air raid in 1918. By the Thirties the affair had turned to friendship, but in May 1934 when Mrs Dudley Ward rang St James's, as she often did, the telephonist was

A MUCH-LOVED KING
Although a dyed-in-the-wool conservative – his great passion was stamp collecting and he persisted with his beard long after they had fallen out of fashion – George V was broad-minded on many social issues and not afraid to embrace change. The nation celebrated his Silver Jubilee in 1935. His death at Sandringham in January 1936 touched the world. Thousands of schoolchildren sent messages of sympathy to his widow, Queen Mary. These boys at the Hugh Myddleton school in Clerkenwell, London (left), are observing two minutes silence as a mark of respect. The public were particularly touched by news from Tibet that the monasteries had spent a day in prayer for the King. According to the writer Robert Graves, the common refrain was that 'He was a good man and we shall miss him'.

THE PEOPLE'S PRINCE
A great throng of schoolchildren cheer the Prince of Wales during his visit to Ponciau Banks recreation ground, lighting up a dreary day in North Wales in May 1934. The prince was hugely and deservedly popular with the British public. For all his natty dressing and night-clubbing, his visits to depressed mining and factory towns showed real interest and sympathy for the working class.

embarrassed: 'I have orders not to put you through', she said. Edward had met someone else – a 37-year-old divorcée, who was still there when he became King.

Edward's short reign was to be described as a 'blaze of indiscretion'. The cause of the fire was an American woman, Mrs Wallis Simpson. She had been born Bessie Wallis Warfield in Baltimore, but was always known as Wallis. After an unhappy first marriage, she had moved to Europe and married Ernest Simpson, but the marriage failed. (Ironically, it had been in the house of Ernest Simpson's sister that the Prince of Wales first met Mrs Dudley Ward.) Wallis had now, as Stanley Baldwin put it, 'stolen the fairy prince'. She was chic rather than feminine. Part of her attraction to Edward was that she showed him no deference, as her home-grown rivals did. She was quite willing to bully him, getting him to paint her toenails or fetch her cigarettes – and he adored her. He neglected his duties to see her, and even showed her confidential government papers. His private secretary was appalled at her influence: 'before her the affairs of state sank into insignificance ... every decision, big or small, was subordinated to her will'.

CELEBRITY COUPLE
Edward VIII, still uncrowned, on holiday with Wallis Simpson in the summer of 1936. All the world seemed to know that Edward was in love with Mrs Simpson – except the British public. The American and Continental papers were full of the couple's affair. In those more deferential days, the British press breathed not a word of it. Many in London society, though, were aware of the situation and knew that a constitutional crisis would follow if he insisted on marrying the twice-divorced American.

A bitter dispute was at the bottom of this and other rows. The Prince of Wales and his father more or less detested one another. Court life was dull, but it was respectable. David had sown his wild oats. Now he was expected to set aside his own pleasures, as Prince Hal had put away Falstaff when he became Henry V. But Edward showed no sign of doing so. He hired a yacht, the *Nahlin*, for a reputed £250,000 and spent the summer of 1936 cruising round the eastern Mediterranean with Mrs Simpson and friends. 'Vive l'amour!', the Yugoslav papers cheered as the *Nahlin* sailed down their coast.

There was homegrown gossip, too. On one occasion the King had his brother, the Duke of York, deputise for him at the opening of an Aberdeen hospital, while he went to a nearby railway station to meet Mrs Simpson. The staff at Balmoral were flummoxed at the way formality crumbled: curtsies were 'scarcely required'. No word of such doings appeared in the British press, though *The Times* dropped hints that a sovereign 'should be invested with a certain detachment and dignity … which are not so easily put on as a change of clothes'. The affair might be common knowledge among journalists and in London society, but it was also etiquette that, since the royals could not comment, it was unfair to mention their foibles. The last time this rule had been broken, Robert Graves wrote, had been by a sporting newspaper in the 1880s when Edward VII, had been Prince of Wales. There was 'nothing whatever between the Prince of Wales and Lillie Langtry', the newspaper announced, adding a week later: 'Not even a sheet.'

The American press, understandably, was full of the couple. Never, it was said, had there been such a human-interest story since Antony and Cleopatra. The *News Chronicle* ran a front page story that Mrs Simpson was going to Ipswich to get a divorce and the judge at the hearing was startled to find his court full of American reporters. It was the bishop of Bradford, Dr Blunt, who inadvertently triggered the story breaking to the British public. Dr Blunt planned to use a diocesan conference to urge the King to take the Christian aspect of his coronation seriously. The bishop hoped that Edward realised that he needed divine grace, but wished 'he gave more positive signs of his awareness'. On 30 November, following his usual practice, Dr Blunt sent a copy of his speech to the *Yorkshire Post*. The next day, the *Post* printed his comments and the dam burst in the press. Rumours flew. Mrs Simpson was to be made Duchess of Lancaster, it was said, before marrying the King.

Taking sides

Baldwin discussed the matter in Cabinet and sounded out the dominion governments, for the monarch was the formal political link between Britain and the empire. They found a twice-married woman, who was also a commoner and a foreigner, too much to stomach. 'Most ordinary people were for the King', said Graves. 'Most important people were against him.' Churchill and Beaverbrook were the core of the 'king's party', though it was said that they supported him as much to get rid of Stanley Baldwin as from personal loyalty. Mosley was for him. Edward himself flirted with a morganatic marriage: he would marry Mrs Simpson without making her queen and any children would drop any claim to the throne. Baldwin would not have it. The king's wife must be queen, and her issue heirs to the throne. 'God save the King', loyalists shouted, 'from Mr Baldwin.'

The country was in the hands of Old Men and to them Edward seemed to be contemptuous of the values of their generation. Prime Minister Baldwin was almost 70, deeply conservative and a champion of morality in public life. The archbishop of Canterbury was 71-year-old Cosmo Lang, a Scot and former dean of divinity at Oxford, who did not mince his words. He said it was strange that the King 'should have sought his happiness in a manner inconsistent with the Christian principles of marriage … within a circle whose standards and ways of life are alien to all the best instincts and traditions of his people'. Palace officials were also hostile – Edward had replaced some of them. The King rarely went to church, they whispered, he disliked protocol and showed it publicly.

Mrs Simpson removed herself to France. The A-word, 'Abdication', was mentioned in the *Daily Mail*. Communists and Fascists found common cause for once. 'There is no crisis in all this business for the working class', said Red leader Harry Pollitt. 'Let the king marry whom he likes.' Mosley placed his Blackshirts behind the King because, it was said, the King was a Nazi sympathiser.

On 10 December it was all over. Baldwin read out the King's statement of abdication in the Commons. The following day Edward gave a farewell address to the nation on the BBC, then he slipped across the Channel, on a dark warship, as the Duke of Windsor. On 12 December Edward's brother, the Duke of York, as proclaimed George VI. It was an excuse for some misquoted Shakespeare: 'Now is the winter of our discontent made glorious summer by this son of York.'

THE NEW ROYAL FAMILY
After dining with his brother, who had just abdicated, the new King George VI returns to his home in Piccadilly in December 1936 (above left). The contrast between the two brothers could not have been greater. Where Edward was outgoing and flamboyant, George was shy, with a stammer that he strove to overcome in public speaking. Where Edward lived the high life and had affairs with married women, George married young and had a happy family life. This photograph of his wife Elizabeth, then Duchess of York, and daughters Elizabeth and Margaret Rose was taken in March 1935, before the abdication crisis arose. George neither wanted nor expected to become King, but he accepted the challenge as his duty.

THE BBC – A NEW INSTITUTION

It was fitting that the King bade his farewell on radio, for this was the medium of the age. The new valve sets with built-in speakers, either powered from the 'mains' or 'wireless' powered by an accumulator, all but did away with the old crystal sets with headphones. The best were sleekly designed in Bakelite, the new plastic, and were the work of famous designers like Serge Chermayeff and Misha Black.

The BBC had a monopoly of home broadcasting with the only competition coming from Radio Luxembourg and Normandie, commercial stations in Europe which made their money from advertisements. Their ads for hot drinks – Ovaltineys, the Horlicks Tea Hour – were known to all. The BBC was funded by the radio licence of 10 shillings a year. With more than 8 million issued by 1939, this was enough to fund the organisation in style. In 1932 it moved its headquarters to Broadcasting House in Portland Place, a fine art deco building.

The BBC's output was largely highbrow at first, with classical music and serious drama. The BBC Symphony Orchestra started in 1930 under Adrian Boult and became the main orchestra for the annual 'proms', later broadcast from the Albert Hall, with talks by heavyweight musicians like the conductor Malcolm Sargent. There was also a popular music series called 'This Symphony Business', in which a self-confessed philistine allowed himself to be charmed by serious

NEWS FROM THE RING
Still black with coal from working in a South Wales pit, Richard Farr, the brother of heavyweight boxer Tommy Farr, listens anxiously to the radio with his family for news of Farr's world title fight against Joe Louis in 1937. Louis, known as the 'Brown Bomber', was unbeaten world champion for a record 12 years, inflicting 25 defeats on his opponents – including Tommy Farr. Through radio, sports fans were able to listen at home to live coverage of their favourite sport. At first, because of pressure from evening papers, the BBC did not broadcast results. But the rule was relaxed, and by 1939 most important sporting events were being covered.

music. It supported British composers such as Constant Lambert and William Walton, and the last works of Frederick Delius. The BBC Theatre Orchestra first broadcast in July 1931, followed before Christmas by the BBC Chamber Orchestra.

Changing audience habits

By the late 1930s more varied light entertainment with dance bands, popular singers, comedians and sport was in the ascendant. The regional studios unearthed talent from across the country. Kathleen Ferrier made her debut in Newcastle in 1939. Wilfred Pickles auditioned in Manchester. They soon moved to 'the Smoke', as smog-ridden London was known. 'All the good men go to London', Pickles noted. 'I wonder why?'

Serial plays were broadcast on Sundays – *The Count of Monte Cristo* and *Les Misérables* were two of the most popular – and gained such large audiences that clergymen complained: not only were congregations diminished, but they themselves missed out on episodes. Cinema and theatre proprietors were most annoyed by *Bandwagon* at 8.15pm on Wednesdays, as their midweek takings dropped by as much as a third. Women's Institute meetings and evening classes were rearranged to Tuesdays or Thursdays. It was the annual Royal Command Variety performance that was the real bugbear for show business. It was so popular on the BBC that cinemas, music-halls and theatres ran to near-empty houses. The BBC at first agreed to pay a large sum to charity for the broadcasting rights. This was good for charity, but it did not tempt the audience away from their radio sets. Complaints multiplied, and in 1938 the BBC was forced to abandon the broadcasts altogether.

Sometimes radio saved a show. Once a fortnight the BBC ran 30-minute extracts from plays and musicals and it was often on the strength of this that people went to see a show in a London or provincial theatre. *Me and My Girl* was a classic example. Its Christmas run at the Chelsea Palace in 1937 was almost over when the BBC broadcast an excerpt, including 'The Lambeth Walk' sung by Lupino Lane. It gave the show a new lease of life.

As far as the British public was concerned, the BBC could do little wrong, but it was too successful by half for the popular press. At first, the BBC was careful not to broadcast the results of big horse races like the Derby for fear of hitting evening newspaper sales. Listeners heard the pounding of hooves and roar of the crowds, but the results were kept quiet until the 6pm watershed when the evening papers would no longer be harmed. This rule was gradually relaxed for sporting events, but no news was broadcast between midnight and 6.00pm, due

ENJOYING THE LAMBETH WALK
Actor and director Lupino Lane fronts the chorus line in *Me and My Girl*, alongside musical comedy star Teddie St Denis, at the Victoria Palace, London. The show had been about to close after just a short run at the Chelsea Palace at Christmas 1937, when the BBC broadcast Lane singing 'The Lambeth Walk'. He played a cockney who inherited an earldom and delighted guests at a smart dinner party with an old London song: 'Any time you're Lambeth way / Any evening, any day / You'll find us all / Doin' the Lambeth Walk.' The song became a huge hit and a dance was invented to go with it, which took off after the Duke and Duchess of Kent were said to have danced it. The dance spread to America, reversing the usual westward flow of music, and soon even the Czechs were forgetting their political troubles with its infectious gaiety.

to pressure from the press barons to preserve a news monopoly for their papers. The only exceptions were events of national concern, such as the crash of the R101, the death of George V and the political crisis of 1938.

Spreading its wings

The BBC helped to stitch the far-flung dominions and colonies together. The Empire Service (later the World Service) started in 1932. The first foreign language broadcasts were made in Arabic in 1938. European services began on the eve of the war in German, French, Italian, Spanish and Portuguese as well as English. They would later prove critical in counteracting German – and Soviet – propaganda. Alistair Cooke began presenting *The American Half-Hour* in April 1935, a forerunner of his record-breaking *Letter from America*. Another area where the BBC shone was in its schools broadcasts: by the end of the decade, 11,000 schools were listening in to its teaching programmes.

The great sporting events became enshrined in radio programming: the Oxford–Cambridge boat race, the FA Cup Final, the Grand National, tennis at

Wimbledon and cricket Test matches. Remembrance Day drew huge audiences, as did the King's Christmas Day message, inaugurated by George V in 1932. Radio helped to give Britain the strong sense of identity that foreigners remarked on. It was natural that Edward VIII's abdication message was carried by radio, so that the whole country could hear it. And Prime Minister Neville Chamberlain used it to announce the declaration of war with Germany on 3 September, 1939.

The start of TV

The world's first regular television service began from BBC studios at Alexander Palace in north London on 2 November, 1936. Sir John Reith, the BBC's founding father, refused to be televised as part of the ceremony. Television, he said, was an 'awful snare'. Only those within 35 miles could pick up the signal. For its first outside broadcast, on 12 May, 1937, the fledgling service televised George VI's coronation procession – around 10,000 were able to watch it. Then it was the tennis at Wimbledon in June. It could only cover the finish of the 1938 Boat Race, but it kept viewers up to speed with model boats on a mock-up of the course. A few weeks later it was at Wembley for its first FA Cup Final. Richard Dimbleby was at Heston airport on 30 September, 1938, for BBC radio and television to report on Chamberlain's return from Munich. Television also gave advance warning of the Second World War to the 20,000 homes who by then had TV sets:

FOOTBALL ON TV
Arsenal players crowd round the camera after playing in the first football match to be filmed for television anywhere in the world, on 16 September, 1937. The game was of no importance – Arsenal first team were playing their own reserves – but the occasion was a milestone in television history. TV sets were still rare and expensive. Only a few thousand viewers watched the historic grainy pictures, but they gave an unforgettable glimpse into popular broadcasting in the future.

on 1 September, 1939, in the middle of a Mickey Mouse cartoon, screens suddenly blacked out. It was feared that German bombers might home in on the signal, so the service was suspended for the duration of the war. When it restarted on 7 June, 1946, the very first programme shown was the interrupted Mickey Mouse.

The television service had only three announcers in the decade. Leslie Mitchell was the first in 1936 – he was also the first on ITV, in September 1955 – then Elizabeth Cowell, a tall and imposing lady, and Jasmine Bligh, the strikingly beautiful niece of the Earl of Darnley and a descendant of Captain Bligh of the *Bounty*. The ladies wore evening dress after 6pm. They had to learn their lines – no autocues in those days – and theatrical training helped. Jasmine Bligh re-opened the service after the war: 'Good afternoon, everybody', she said. 'How are you? Do you remember me?' Despite its small budget, the service had style in plenty.

FIRSTS IN THE AIR AND AT SEA

In hindsight, more important than the abdication was a little noticed event at Eastleigh aerodrome, now Southampton airport, in March 1936. A new fighter plane, the Supermarine Spitfire, had its first test flight. It handled so perfectly that the test pilot, Captain 'Mutt' Summers, told the engineers on landing: 'Don't touch anything'. The Spitfire was the final masterpiece of the designer R J Mitchell. He was dead within a year, but his creation has a touch of immortality about it.

The public first saw the Spitfire at the Hendon Air Display in July 1936, and were entranced by the grace of its elliptical wings and the growl of its Rolls-Royce Merlin engine. It was more complicated to build than the Hawker Hurricane, whose maiden flight preceded it by four months, and more Hurricanes than Spitfires would fight in the Battle of Britain, but it was the Spitfire that captured the heart and mind. The first RAF order was for 310 aircraft, at a cost of £6,033 each, and the first one rolled off the assembly line in May 1938. When production ended ten years later, 20,351 Spitfires had been built. One had flown at 606mph, within a whisker of 1,000km/h; another had reached an altitude of 51,550 feet.

> 'If you handled it properly it would never get away from you. There are many pilots alive today who owe their survival to this remarkable quality in the Spitfire.'
>
> Jeffrey Quill, Supermarine Spitfire test pilot

Mitchell's brief had been to create a fast monoplane fighter that exploited the power of the Merlin engine to the full, while retaining the manoeuvrability of the RAF's existing biplanes. He succeeded triumphantly, producing a very forgiving aircraft. One Spitfire lost its propeller in a high speed dive, yet the pilot was able to glide 20 miles to his home airfield. The Elizabethans used the term 'Spitfire' to describe a fiery temperament. It was suggested by a director of Vickers-Armstrong, Supermarine's parent company, who called his young daughter 'a little spitfire'. Mitchell thought it was 'just the bloody stupid sort of name they would choose'.

Luxury liners

Another great maiden event took place in Southampton at the end of May 1936. The transatlantic liner *Queen Mary* sailed on her first voyage for New York. As with the Spitfire, built in response to the German fighter plane, the Messerschmitt 109, the *Queen Mary* was in part a response to the German ocean liners *Bremen*

continued on page 426

MAJESTIC LINER
The *Queen Mary*, almost completed, is admired by a crowd at Clydebank in March 1936 (below). The new Cunard ship was a symbol that the worst of the Depression was over, and that trade had begun to pick up. The rivalry between the great French, German and British transatlantic liners was intense. Their passage times to and from New York were published in the papers and much national pride was tied up in them. The crossing on the *Queen Mary* was truly luxurious for those who could afford it. These passengers (left) are dining in the splendid cabin class restaurant during the liner's maiden voyage from Southampton to New York. The radiating light on the map pinpoints the ship's position.

THE PURSUIT OF SPEED

A love of speed and world speed records marked the Thirties. The 'Triple Crown' embraced the land, air and water speed records – and Britain held them all.

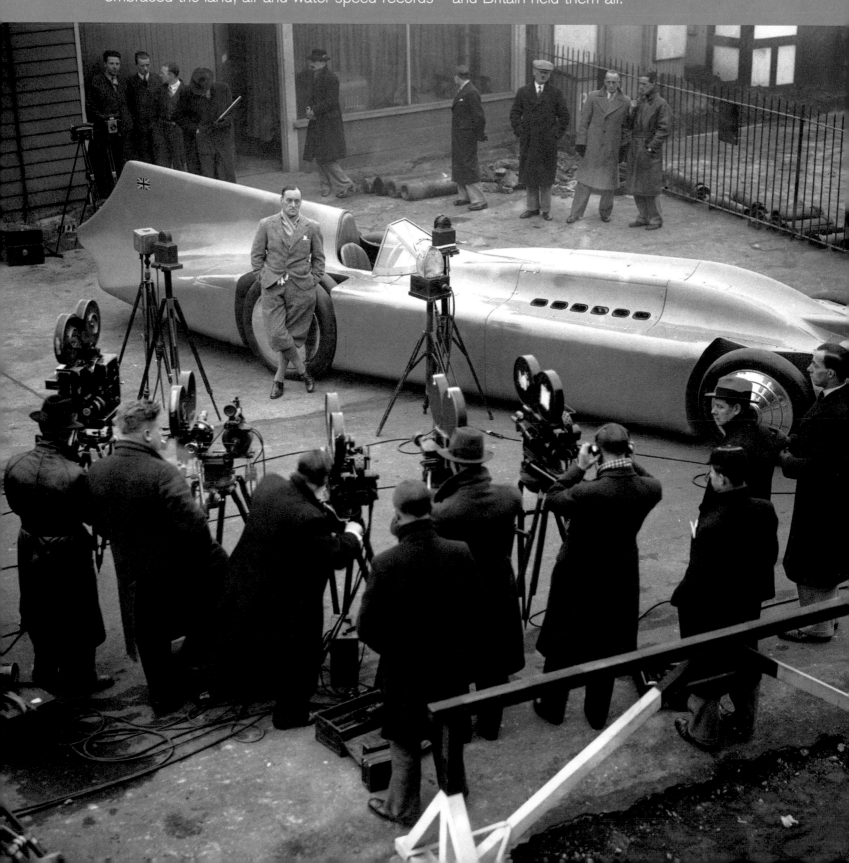

RECORD-HOLDERS

Malcolm Campbell poses with his improved *Bluebird* in January 1935 (left, below). The car had 2,450 horsepower and Campbell would soon use all of that to become the first man to break the 300mph barrier on land, hitting just over 301mph at Bonneville Salt Flats in Utah in 1935. For his early land speed attempts, he drove on the Pendine Sands in Carmarthenshire, but on one occasion his car almost sank in quicksand and he transferred to salt flats in America. He reached his fastest speed on water, 141mph, in 1939. He passed on his passion for speed to his son, Donald, seen here (right) at the wheel of *Bluebird*.

Sir Henry Segrave (below) held the land speed record before Campbell. He is seen here travelling at more than 100mph on the Brooklands circuit in 1930. In June that year he was killed in his boat *Miss England* while breaking the water speed record on Windermere. 'Did we do it?' he asked his rescuers. They nodded, and he died. The following year, George Stainforth broke the world airspeed record, flying at 407.5mph in a Supermarine S.6B seaplane, ancestor of the Spitfire, at Lee-on-Solent.

and *Europa*. The hull was laid down by
John Brown's yard on Clydebank in
December 1930. Work stopped after a year
when Cunard, her owners, were hit by the
Depression. The government agreed to loan
them enough to complete her and her sister
ship, the *Queen Elizabeth*, on condition that
they merged with the rival White Star Line.
Queen Mary was launched in September
1934, shooting down the slipway faster than
expected and almost grounding on the
opposite bank. By the time she was fitted
out, she had cost £3.5 million – enough to
buy 580 Spitfires. It was said that Cunard
wanted to call her *Victoria*, but when they
asked George V for permission to name her
after Britain's 'greatest queen' he replied
that his wife would be most pleased. She
journeyed to Clydebank to launch her.

The *Queen Mary*'s gross tonnage was
80,744. This would have made her the world's largest liner, but the French had
increased the tonnage of her rival, the *Normandie*, from 79,000 tons to 83,000
by enclosing a passenger area on a boat deck. The *Queen Mary* had her revenge,
though. Her captain, Sir Edgar Britten, had to slow her on the last day of her
maiden Atlantic crossing when she ran into thick fog, but it was not long before
she took the Blue Riband from *Normandie* with an average speed of 30.14 knots
westbound and 30.63 knots eastbound. Fitted with new propellers, the *Normandie*
reclaimed the prestigious record in 1937, but the *Queen Mary* won it back in
1938 with a record that stood until 1952.

STEAM POWER
Another speed record came to Britain in
1938. On 3 July train Driver Duddington,
seen here (above) with his fireman, steered
steam locomotive *Mallard* – the Gresley A4
Pacific no. 4468, as every train spotter
knew – to 126mph. It was the fastest speed
achieved by steam power anywhere in the
world. The streamlined locomotive was
almost brand new and belonged to the
LNER, the London & North Eastern Railway.
It achieved its record speed on the
downslope from Stoke Summit to
Peterborough on a London-to-Newcastle
run. Although it maintained 126mph for just
185 feet, the Doncaster-built Mallard did
manage to keep up an average speed of
over 120mph for five miles on this stretch,
all the time hauling a seven-coach train.
Mallard remained in service until 1963,
clocking up 1,426,260 miles. No steam train
has ever beaten its proud speed record.

STEADYING THE SHIP OF STATE

George VI worried lest the abdication should cause the fabric of the monarchy to
'crumble under the shock and strain of it all'. It was more robust than he thought.
A Republican motion in the Commons was supported by just five MPs. The date
of the coronation was still that fixed for Edward VIII – 12 May, 1937. References
to Edward were taboo, though some banners in the East End defiantly read
'God Bless our King and Queen AND the Duke of Windsor'. The event was a
huge celebration, a last hurrah, it seemed, as dark deeds spread on the Continent.
Most of the crowned heads of Europe or their heirs apparent attended, though
not the King of Italy, whose new title of Emperor of Abyssinia the British did not
recognise. With unintended irony, Spain, in the throes of its civil war, sent a

Republican minister. After the ceremony, a crowd of Cup Final proportions – 100,000 or so – gathered outside Buckingham Palace. The Royal Family appeared four times. In the evening, the King made a broadcast committing himself to serve the nation, his speech having only a trace of his stammer and shyness.

No disloyal demonstrations were recorded that day anywhere, although in Dublin the IRA blew up a statue of George II. The village tradition of celebrating coronations with gusto continued. Peels were rung on the church bells in the morning and after the service the strong Coronation ale brewed by many local breweries was drunk. Children danced round maypoles plaiting red, white and blue ribbons to the tune of 'Come, Lassies and Lads'. The afternoon was given up to village sports, tug of wars, tip and run cricket, and band races, where contestants had to play an instrument as they ran. A feast was held, followed by fireworks in the evening, torchlight processions and a bonfire.

On 19 May the new King and Queen drove to the Guildhall for lunch with the Lord Mayor. A grand review of the Fleet was held at Spithead later in the month. Eighteen other navies sent warships. The King sailed round the lines of ships in the royal yacht, and boarded the flagship to order rum to be broken out: 'Splice the mainbrace!' The BBC had commissioned a former naval officer, Thomas Woodrooffe, for live commentary on the illumination of the fleet that night. Unfortunately, he enjoyed the ship's hospitality a little too much and was rather 'tired and emotional' by the time he was called on to broadcast at 10.45pm. 'The whole fleet is lit up', he rambled. 'I mean lit up with fairy lamps. It's fantastic … it's fairyland … When I say lit up, I mean outlined with tiny

HISTORIC OCCASION
The balcony of Buckingham Palace after George VI's coronation at Westminster Abbey. Queen Mary, widow of George V, is in the centre, flanked by the new King and Queen, with the young princesses, Elizabeth and Margaret, also wearing little crowns. A smiling Princess Elizabeth seems to take the event calmly and confidently in her stride. The abdication of her uncle meant that she was now heir to the throne. The BBC covered the coronation procession on TV, the first live outside broadcast in the world. The ceremony took place on 12 May, 1937, the same day that had been fixed for Edward VIII, who was now to spend his life abroad as the Duke of Windsor. A thousand special trains carried people to London from across the country for the celebrations. The decorations in Selfridges store on Oxford Street were so magnificent that an Indian rajah bought them to take home with him to embellish his palace.

lights ...' Then the illuminations were switched off. 'It's gone! It's gone! There's no fleet. It's disappeared ...', cried Woodrooffe. 'There's nothing between us and heaven. There's nothing at all.' The BBC engineer mercifully faded him out.

The new Royal Family proved to be very popular. A favourite newsreel showed them at the Duke of York's Camp for Boys, where the King joined them in singing 'Under the Spreading Chestnut Tree'. He looked relaxed in an open-necked shirt, the Queen was hatless, and the two princesses – adored by all – were simply dressed in blouses and skirts. The lack of pomposity was beguiling.

As to the Duke of Windsor, he married Mrs Simpson in a quiet wedding at Candé in the Loire on 3 June, 1937. Some at home remained attached to him, and bitter with Baldwin and the Church, but *The Times*, Church House and other high places of the establishment continued, Malcolm Muggeridge noted, to treat the Duke with 'that frigid, calculated hatred which the English upper classes reserve for those they have unremuneratively adulated'. The Duke and Duchess of Windsor visited Germany, ostensibly to study its social services, and met Hitler in person. The meeting was ill-advised, adding fuel to accusations of pro-Nazi sympathies. The Duke was persuaded to give up public life and live quietly.

George VI turned out a fine king. There are few grounds for thinking that the Duke of Windsor would have done better, but his behaviour over the abdication was faultless. He made no attempt to divide the country by playing on the great reservoir of public goodwill he had built up. But it was a sad end to a gilded youth. He had hoped to be 'Edward the Innovator', but could credit himself with only two changes: inaugurating the King's Flight of aircraft, and allowing the Yeomen of the Guards to shave off their beards. He was best known, perhaps, for the distinctive 'Prince of Wales' checks and the 'Windsor knot' in ties, and the relaxed style that he brought in proved lasting.

Baldwin bows out

The Coronation was Baldwin's swansong. As Prime Minister he came through several crises – the Depression, national strikes, the abdication, the outbreak of the Spanish Civil War – but he ignored warnings of the growing menace of the Nazis and German rearmament, and kept Winston Churchill in the wilderness. As the news from Europe darkened, Baldwin was not the only one who thought it was time for him to go. He saw George VI crowned, having brought him to the throne, and wisely decided to retire. He became an earl, and retired to Worcestershire.

His successor was Neville Chamberlain, son of Joseph, the fiery Victorian premier. Neville had been a sisal planter in the West Indies before coming back to become Lord Mayor of Birmingham. He was brisk, businesslike and unremarkable, with bushy eyebrows and a drooping, old-fashioned moustache. His Cabinet had two former foreign secretaries, Sir John Simon, who replaced Chamberlain as Chancellor, and Sir Samuel Hoare, who had mishandled diplomacy over Mussolini's invasion of Abyssinia (now Ethiopia) and was rewarded for his blunders with the Home Office. The new War Minister, a critical post in troubled times, was Leslie Hore-Belisha. He had been an effective transport minister, and now did his best to modernise the army in the face of generals who were fonder of the horse than the tank. The manual *Cavalry Training* devoted 23 pages to exercises with the sword and lance. Armoured cars were dealt with in a single aside: 'The principles of field operations in Cavalry Training (Horsed) are in general applicable to armoured car regiments.' It was not a good omen.

WELSH WORDS
Browsers at the annual Welsh Book festival in 1936 (right). Wales retained a strong sense of its own identity. Welsh was still widely spoken and read, and Eisteddfods and other Welsh festivals were well supported. But there was little demand for self-government, despite South Wales being hit harder by the Depression than almost any other region of Britain. The introduction of bilingual teaching and disestablishment of the Church of Wales removed two of the major grievances. Welsh nationalists were bookish folk, professors or students who wanted to revive Bardic culture, rather than agitators. Some Welsh lecturers did try to set fire to an RAF depot in protest at the desecration of local beauty spots, but there was nothing to compare to the violence of the IRA.

A FONDNESS FOR LITERATURE

The British read as never before. Book sales rose almost fourfold in the Thirties, reaching 26 million in 1939, when public libraries reported almost 250 million book borrowings. Mobile libraries reached out to remote villages, and there were also 'tuppenny libraries' attached to tobacconists, sub-post offices and chain stores like Boots. Allen Lane began publishing Penguin paperbacks in 1935. The first two were Ernest Hemingway's *A Farewell to Arms* and *Ariel*, André Maurois' biography of Shelley. They cost 6d a copy, the same as a packet of cigarettes.

Penguins were followed by the more educational Pelicans. Penguin Specials were published on the important questions of the day. Book Clubs flourished, most famously the Left Book Club, founded by the publisher Victor Gollancz in May 1936, soon to have 60,000 members. The dandyism of the Twenties gave way to social concern. The 'new poets' – W H Auden, Stephen Spender, Cecil Day Lewis – 'got in touch with reality' with verses on electricity pylons, and were on the left. George Orwell, an unequalled essayist, lived down his Eton schooldays by writing and literally being *Down and Out in London and Paris*, and getting to grips first-hand with slums in *The Road to Wigan Pier*.

Murder mysteries and detective stories reached their height. Some best-selling authors were American, like Ellery Queen, but the natives were not outclassed. Dorothy L Sayers wrote with panache and style, creating Lord Peter Wimsey as her hero and perfecting the English village setting in her bell-ringing tale, *The Nine Tailors*, in 1934. Agatha Christie's Miss Marple, was equally at home in St Mary Mead. She first appeared in 1930 in *Murder at the Vicarage*. Christie gave more exotic locations to Belgian detective Hercule Poirot, her other great creation, with *Murder on the Orient Express* in 1934 and *Death on the Nile* two years later.

It seemed surprising that two Englishwomen of such impeccable background should have been so at home with crime and murder, but they were racier than their readers knew. Agatha Christie had divorced her first husband, a rarity at the time. Her second husband was the archaeologist Sir Max Mallowan. Dorothy Sayers was a blue-stocking with a first in modern languages from Oxford, but she also had an illegitimate son and, almost as shocking, had worked in advertising. Both women were religious. Sayers was a great Christian apologist, writing the BBC series *The Man Born to be King*, and translating Dante's *Inferno*.

In literature, D H Lawrence died in 1930. P G Wodehouse's immortal characters – Lord Emsworth, Gussie Fink-Nottle, Bertie Wooster and Jeeves – were still going strong. The classic *Right Ho Jeeves* appeared in 1934. Wodehouse described his work as 'a sort of musical comedy without music and ignoring real life altogether'. Frank Richards entertained children with tales of Billy Bunter of Greyfriars School. Arthur Ransome's classic *Swallows and Amazons*, telling of children's adventures in boats in the Lake District, was followed by a string of others. Ransome had been a correspondent for the *Guardian* in revolutionary Russia and married Trotsky's secretary. The influential Sitwells spun fashions in music, pictures and interior design: Osbert was a novelist, Sacheverell a romantic poet and expert on baroque art, Edith a talented poet who turned to prose.

Painters and sculptors

The most original artist of the day was the eccentric Stanley Spencer, who grew up in Cookham, a sleepy village by the Thames. Drawing on his experiences as a medical orderly in the Great War, he painted the haunting images of army life in the Sandham memorial, a powerful tribute to the fallen. L S Lowry was painting his distinctive pictures of Lancashire industrial towns, in greys and blacks and brilliant whites, with stick figures beneath the smoking chimneys.

Jacob Epstein caused a stir in 1931 with 'Genesis', a large marble sculpture of a pregnant woman. It was, the *Sunday Express* declared, 'so gross, obscene and horrible that no newspaper has ever published a full picture of it.' The publicity did the exhibition the power of good, persuading thousands to pay their shilling for entry, though it was noted that many averted their eyes in front of the statue. The young Henry Moore and Barbara Hepworth were just starting their careers.

ART DECO HOME FOR PENGUINS
Art Deco was the iconic architectural style of the age and one popular example was the much-visited concrete Penguin Pool at London Zoo (right). It was designed by Berthold Lubetkin who had left Soviet Russia for Paris, where he was influenced by the great Le Corbusier, before coming to London to set up his own architectural design company, Tecton. After his famous work at the Zoo in 1933, he designed a block of high-rise flats, Highpoint I in Hampstead, that was praised for giving a sense of real quality to high-rise housing. His Finsbury Health Centre was another landmark building.

CREATIVE SOULS

The ballerina Margot Fonteyn, photographed in 1937 (left). She spent her whole career with the Royal Ballet, creating many roles with Ninette de Valois and Frederick Ashton as choreographers. The sculptress Barbara Hepworth is seen here with her 'Mother and Child' (bottom left). She and her husband, the painter Ben Nicholson, were members of 'Unit One', a group of abstractionists who set themselves up against the 'unconscious school' of Expressionism. Stanley Spencer (below) was never part of any movement, a reason perhaps why he was so underrated, an eccentric who tackled unfashionable religious subjects with powerful originality.

The British had a particular genius for detective stories. Agatha Christie (top right) created two immortals in Hercule Poirot and Miss Marple. She also wrote plays, like *The Mousetrap*, and her novels begged to be filmed. The portly and good-humoured G K Chesterton (far right, below) created another memorable character in the detective-priest Father Brown. He was also a fine biographer and poet. H G Wells (far right, top) published *The Shape of Things To Come* in 1933, urging people to confront fascism before it was too late. Daphne du Maurier (right, below) was the beautiful daughter of the actor-manager Gerald du Maurier. She was a brilliant romantic novelist, with a splendid sense of plot and character. Several of her bestsellers, including *Jamaica Inn* (1936) and *Rebecca* (1938), were made into successful films.

1930s
THE SHADOW
DESCENDS

A ghastliness was loose in Europe, the writer Aldous Huxley said, 'an invisible vermin of hate, crawling about looking for blood to suck'. Hitler's lust for power and violence had been clear from the Night of the Long Knives in June 1934, when the SS – Hitler's personal bodyguard under the command of Heinrich Himmler and Reinhard Heydrich – had murdered hundreds of influential Nazis, including his rival Ernst Rohm. Now, in defiance of the Versailles Treaty, Germany was openly rearming. In March 1936 Hitler sent troops into the demilitarised Rhineland zone. Then, in October, he established the Rome-Berlin 'Axis' with Mussolini's Italy, creating a fascist bloc in the heart of Europe.

TEST DRILL During the last days of peace in 1939, office workers practise evacuating to their air raid shelters. The government feared that real air raids, when they came, would create mass panic.

THE LOOMING WAR

The Japanese war in China began in July 1937. The invaders were in Peking (Beijing) by August. The British ambassador to China was wounded in his car, but the incident was hushed over. By September the Japanese were in Shangai. In December they stormed Nanking (Nanjing), the Chinese capital, in scenes of horrific mass rape and murder. They pushed on 500 miles up the Yangtse Kiang river past Hankow in 1938, and also occupied Canton in the South. China was too distant to cause much of a stir in Britain, but it should have set loud alarm bells ringing. Hong Kong and Malaya were uncomfortably close to the newly aggressive Japanese, while Burma and even India were not that far away.

The government response, as it was to Germany's actions, was appeasement, a policy that the minister Oliver Stanley said was 'peace with as little dishonour as possible'. It was a popular policy, for all the warnings that 'mere cooings' would not placate the 'monster of German militarism'. For many, Hitler seemed a lesser menace than Stalin. Only the perceptive realised the scale of the mass killings in Soviet Russia, but Stalin's show trials of 'Trotskyites' were another matter. There was revulsion when Marshal Tukhachevsky and seven other generals were shot. The marshal had been at George V's Jubilee in 1935 and was much admired.

By contrast, Hitler appeared relatively sane. To rearm and send troops into the Rhineland were widely seen as understandable and the Germans' own business. George Orwell felt that Middle England – the 'huge untouchable block of the middle class and the better off working class' – was patriotic to the core. If the country was in acute danger, they would rally to its defence. Otherwise, though, they did not feel that anything that happened abroad was any of their business.

The German terror-bombing of the town of Guernica caused outcries and there was popular support for the Republican side in the Spanish Civil War. Captain 'Potato' Jones was hailed a hero when he ran his steamer past the fascist blockade to sail a cargo of potatoes into Bilbao for the starving citizens. But the only decisive action taken by the government followed the sinking of merchant ships bound for Republican ports by 'unknown' submarines, as this was thought a slight to British naval prestige. Anthony Eden, the Foreign Secretary, called a meeting at Nyon in Switzerland. An agreement was made with the French and Italians to patrol the Spanish coasts to protect shipping and the sinkings stopped.

The far-sighted and the men in power

A few saw the future and were afraid. The diplomat Robert Vansittart warned that Britain was incapable of checking Japan 'if she really means business'. He said that 'by ourselves' – meaning without the Americans – 'we must eventually swallow any and every humiliation in the Far East'. Vansittart also feared a catastrophe if Britain remained weak in the face of the German menace. He had personally met Hitler and his henchmen, and unlike Neville Chamberlain had no illusions. In January 1938 Chamberlain removed Vansittart from his post as permanent undersecretary at the Foreign Office and left him in a backwater.

From the backbenches, Churchill was indefatigable in his warnings of Nazi danger and demands for rearmament. Most people thought him brilliant but

VOICE IN THE WILDERNESS
Winston Churchill laying tiles on the roof of a cottage on his estate at Chartwell in Kent in February 1939. He was a bricklayer, too, with an honorary Union card to back his claim, building walls to burn off the energy that he was prevented from putting to the public good by his banishment to the back benches. Churchill would much rather have been fixing the country's defences and armed forces. From as early as 1934, he warned time and again that 'Germany already has a powerful, well-equipped army, with an immense reserve of armed, trained men ... two years from now the German air force will be nearly 50 per cent stronger than our own, and in 1937 nearly double ...' Little or no notice was taken. Memories of the Great War left little appetite among the general public for talk of more war, and the politicians in charge reflected that mood. He railed against Baldwin and then against Chamberlain, Baldwin's successor as Prime Minister, but they were the men in power. At the time Churchill was regarded by many as a warmonger, not as the all-too-accurate prophet that he turned out to be.

'… the trouble is, we are so damned weak. It is Baldwin who has reduced us to this shameful condition …'

Winston Churchill, speaking in 1936 on Britain's failure to respond to the growing strength of Germany's armed forces

unsound. He was remembered for the Dardanelles disaster in the war, for changing parties twice, for championing Edward over the abdication (although he later changed his mind). Lloyd George agreed that Winston had a powerful brain, but added that it was prevented from running true by a 'tragic flaw in the metal'. Baldwin said that the good fairies at Winston's birth had given him daring, imagination, energy and courage, then the bad fairy had spoiled it by denying him wisdom. Asquith had said of him that he had 'genius without judgment'. The Tory R A Butler, who was at the Foreign Office before the war, described him as the 'greatest adventurer of modern political history' – and a 'half-breed American'. Churchill ran Chartwell, his home in Kent, like a miniature of Blenheim Palace, his birthplace. He created lakes and waterfalls, he painted, he ate and drank lustily and he rattled out the articles for newspapers which helped him to stay solvent.

Neville Chamberlain was in utter contrast. With his reedy voice, self-satisfied smile and moral prissiness, he was said to be 'every inch the political haberdasher'.

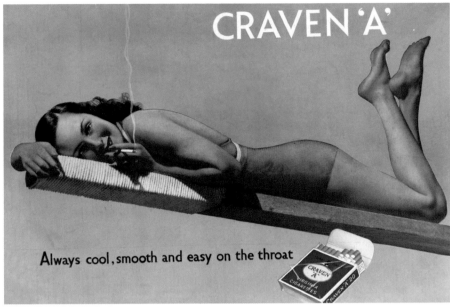

CRAVEN 'A'

Always cool, smooth and easy on the throat

DRINKING AND SMOKING

Pints being pulled in a typical Thirties pub. A remarkable fall in drunkenness had been accompanied by a fall in crime. The British had long been hard drinkers. Drink-related offences, though, fell from 52 per 10,000 inhabitants in the decade before the Great War to just 12 in the Thirties. Beer production fell over the same period from 34 million barrels a year to just 13 million. Seebohm Rowntree, the chocolate manufacturer and philanthropist, noted the new soberness in York. 'One may pass through working-class streets every evening for weeks', he said, 'and not see a drunken person.' The Mass Observation project looked at drinking habits in Bolton. Only a third of adults made a regular weekly visit to a pub. Even on a typical Saturday evening, pub-goers accounted for only one in seven of all adults. A growing number of people smoked, though. Back in 1914, the British were smoking just over 2lb (1kg) of tobacco a head per year. They had doubled that to 4lb by 1938. Spending on tobacco soared from £42 million in 1914 to £294 million in 1939. Some of that rise was due to higher taxes, but advertisements like this one for Craven 'A' (above), as well as images of leading actors lighting cigarettes in countless films, boosted cigarette sales, especially to women.

He wore an old-fashioned wing collar and was seldom seen without his umbrella. His views were stilted and narrow. The Americans were 'a nation of cads', the Russians were 'semi-Asiatic', the French couldn't keep 'a secret for more than half an hour, nor a government for more than 9 months'. Neville had none of his father's eloquence and drive – Joseph Chamberlain had been the powerful colonial minister at the turn of the century – and his close colleagues were no better. At the Treasury, the lawyer Sir John Simon was known as a 'snake in snake's clothing', a man who had sat on the fence for so long, Lloyd George remarked, that some of it had entered his soul. Sir Samuel Hoare had been an advocate of appeasement at the Foreign Office, though he was strongly in favour of penal reform when he moved to the Home Office and was an early and persuasive opponent of capital punishment. Sir Thomas Inskip, the minister responsible for the coordination of Britain's defences, had 'little ability, less power and no perceptiveness'.

To make matters worse, none of Chamberlain's underlings stood up to him and this played to his vanity. One of his officials said that he set himself up on a pedestal, there to be 'adored, with suitable humility, by unquestioning admirers'. He was needled by the least criticism or mockery. He harassed his ministers.

Anthony Eden believed that 'au fond', in his heart of hearts, Chamberlain had 'a certain sympathy for dictators, whose efficiency appealed to him'.

Chamberlain was a bad judge of character, naïve in trusting that Hitler was a man of his word. His desire to have 'no more Passchendaeles', no more Great War-style massacres, was laudable. But what if Hitler wanted them? He thought that peace could be maintained by righting the wrongs of the Versailles Treaty and failed to see that Hitler was half-gangster, half-warlord, utterly bound up in himself. Neither did Chamberlain woo potential allies. He kept the French at a distance and made no serious attempt to shift the Americans from isolationism. He was astonished when his Foreign Secretary, Anthony Eden, resigned.

Eden was young, handsome, impeccably dressed, the son of a baronet, with a fine war record from the Great War. It was less clear at the time that he was also highly strung and subject to mood swings. The Nazis disliked Eden on sight – a 'notorious firebrand' – and he had as little time for them. At first, though, he had agreed with Chamberlain on appeasement. He was, Richard Crossman said, that 'peculiarly British type, the idealist without conviction'. On 20 February, 1938, he resigned, not because he was viscerally against appeasement, but because he thought Chamberlain was too accommodating to Mussolini.

Edward Wood, the third Viscount Halifax, replaced Eden. He was lofty in both height and demeanour, a sincere high churchman, and undoubtedly brave. He had been born without a left hand, but this did not stop him from hunting every Saturday that he could. Hindu terrorists had bombed his train while he was viceroy of India. He went on calmly reading a book of theology, remarking later that he was 'inured to that kind of thing by the Cona coffee machine always blowing up'. Halifax was conciliatory in India and he brought that attitude to Europe. But he had not come across anything like the Nazis and found it difficult to see them as they really were. 'An earnest and honest fellow', Beaverbrook said, 'not quite stupid, but inexperienced in worldly affairs.'

TIME FOR A BREAK

It was easier and easier to 'get away from it all'. The British had long been pioneers of mass tourism – Thomas Cook had invented it. Now, in June 1936, the first Butlins Holiday Camp opened at Skegness. It was sited rather unpromisingly on 200 uninviting acres of turnip fields by the grey waters of the North Sea.

Billy Butlin had begun by running stalls at travelling fairs, like his mother before him. He noticed that the growth of charabancs meant that more and more people were looking for their entertainment on the coast. He leased some sand dunes at Skegness, at first to develop an amusement site. Inspiration for the holiday camp came from a miserable holiday he spent on Barry Island, locked out of his B&B all day in the rain – the standard practice for seaside landladies. Butlin designed his camp to amuse and entertain whatever the weather. There was no need to sit on the chilly beach: the sea, he shrewdly realised, was not an essential part of a seaside holiday. Work began in September 1935, and he almost ran out of funds over a bleak winter. His plans were ambitious. He wanted 600

FAMILY HOLIDAY
Campers at Butlins Holiday Camp in Skegness in 1938 make use of a communal hot water tap for brewing tea. Holiday camps were not new. A few companies, trade unions and charities ran them for employees, union members, the poor and convalescents. But Billy Butlin was the first to build a commercial holiday camp offering

all-in holidays. Meals in modern restaurants, sports facilities and entertainment were all included in the price, under the enthusiastic supervision of 'Redcoats'. The camp at Skegness was an instant success, and Butlin soon opened others at Clacton and Filey. Butlin and his camps caught the communal spirit of the British, and brought out their ability to laugh at themselves.

chalets, with electricity, running water and 250 bathrooms, a Viennese dance hall, fortune-tellers' parlour, a theatre and recreation hall. The camp sported a gym, a swimming pool with cascades and a boating lake. He had the grounds landscaped and filled with tennis courts, bowling and putting greens, and cricket pitches.

This was luxury for people who might not have electricity or a bathroom at home, and it was at a price that working people could afford. All-inclusive, with three meals and entertainment thrown in, it cost from 35 shillings a week (£1.75). There were teething problems in plenty, but people loved it. Capacity at Skegness was doubled and redoubled until it could take 10,000 holidaymakers. A second camp followed at Clacton in 1938, and work started on a third at Filey in 1939.

Butlin built up loyalty by issuing special enamel badges to each camper for the duration of their stay. The badge gave readmission to the camp if they went out. Campers kept their badges from earlier holidays, and proudly wore them all on a ribbon like campaign medals. They were well-made, too, by jewellery makers in London, Dublin and Birmingham. Butlin's staff, the smartly turned out Redcoats, were unmistakable and added to the colour and panache of the camps.

There were also holiday camps for the serious-minded. People at 'Left camps' spent hours in earnest political debate. Amateur dramatics were the staple of drama camps. The routine at music camps began with physical jerks at daybreak. Individual practice on an instrument filled the time between breakfast and lunch. Organised games or a walk led to tea and an impromptu concert in the evening.

The physical exercises at the camps reflected a broad 'keep fit' movement. *The Times* urged in November 1936 that a great national effort should be made to 'improve the physique of the nation'. A fund was started in memory of George V to provide playing fields in the big cities. Women flocked to join the League of Health and Beauty, which ran PE classes. 'Fitness' had originally meant 'fit for military service' and there was a martial aspect to the health cult on the Continent. But where Mussolini was photographed jumping over fixed bayonets, exercise for British politicians did not go beyond a little gentle fishing and a round of golf.

THE AGE OF THE CAR

There had been more motorcycles than cars in 1920, but motorcycle numbers peaked in 1930, then fell by a third over the decade as more people could afford a car. The cost of an Austin Seven fell to £118 and the number of car owners passed 2 million. The 'Big Three' car-makers – Ford, Morris and Austin – were building more than half a million cars a year between them by 1937, and 400,000 people were working in the industry. Vauxhall was growing rapidly in Luton with the Light Six and Big Six Bedford trucks, as vans and lorries took a sizeable share of the retail goods and factory supplies that had once been carried by goods trains.

One result of the growth in car traffic was urban ribbon development. The car spurred house-building on arterial roads and along the by-passes built around congested areas. They were soon lined with houses, shops and petrol stations. This

THE FAMILY HOME AND CAR
The Arsenal and England fullback Eddie Hapgood waves goodbye to his family as he sets off for training in 1936. The vast bulk of the 2.5 million new homes put up between the wars, like the Hapgood's, were built by private developers and not by councils or corporations. The houses were good value and usually solidly built. A new 'semi' could be bought for £450, with a deposit of £25 or so, plus a mortgage at 4.5 per cent. Almost all had electricity and a front and back garden. Pebble dash, 'Tudor' beams and leaded windows added a little individuality. 'Ribbon development' and 'bungaloid growth' were much criticised at the time, but Thirties suburbs have worn well.

was most noticeable on the outskirts of the cities, particularly in the Southeast. Extensions to the London Undergound and the electrification of the Southern Railway also led to road after road of new housing in places like Morden. Advertisements on the tube urged people to 'Stake your claim at Edgware'.

Almost 3 million houses were built in the Thirties as pebble-dash suburbs grew around the cities. Even in 1932, one of the worst years of the slump, more than 200,000 new houses went up. Many families who had lived cheek by jowl in crowded rooms now had a house of their own with a garden. It had always been an English dream to have a house and garden, and this meant that cities sprawled outwards. Cheap cars and new private bus services made development along the main roads practical. They also caused monster traffic jams. 'Road houses' were another sign of the love affair with the car. They were strikingly designed inns, part bar, part restaurant, part entertainment complex. Couples drove out to them to eat and drink, dance, play tennis and swim in summer – and stay overnight with few questions asked. The Great West Road into London had road houses every mile or two with big signs inviting people to 'Swim, Dine and Dance'.

These new suburbs had instant chain stores to cater for them: W H Smith, Sainsbury's, Dewhurst butchers, Express Dairies, MacFisheries, Burton's tailors, big banks, a building society. The houses, often half-timbered with elaborate ridge tiles and porches, cost up to £1,000, and were aimed at people on incomes of around £10 a week. The cartoonist Osbert Lancaster described them as 'By-Pass Variegated' and lampooned them mercilessly: '... some quaint gables culled from Art Nouveau ... twisted beams and leaded panes of stockbroker's Tudor ... a white wood Wimbledon Transitional porch making a splendid foil to a red-brick garage vaguely Romanesque in feeling'. He added that they did 'much to reconcile one to the prospect of aerial bombardment'. This was unfair – the houses were comfortable and generally well laid out, with gardens and a sense of space – but the sentiment was echoed by John Betjeman in his celebrated 1937 poem: 'Come friendly bombs and fall on Slough! / It isn't fit for humans now, / There isn't grass to graze a cow ...'

> The developers have ensured that 'the largest possible amount of countryside is ruined for the minimum of expense.'
>
> Osbert Lancaster, *Daily Express* cartoonist

Slum clearance and new estates

New tenements were built in cities under slum clearance projects. They had broad paved courtyards, where children could safely play, and were a vast improvement on the slums they replaced. The man behind the slum clearance schemes – and the 1935 Housing Act, which laid down enforceable housing standards for the first time – was Lord Kennet, who had lost an arm manning a gun turret as a volunteer in Zeebrugge in 1918. He had been a vigorous minister of health in MacDonald's National Government. He believed in gardens and allotments – 'an Englishman's house is his castle, and his spade and hoe must have their castle too' – and in the use of gas and electricity in place of coal, anticipating the clean air acts.

The design of new estates, though, increased the cleavage between classes. 'Zoning' under the Town Planning Act of 1932 meant that land was developed at one, eight or twelve new houses to the acre. The size of plot made a great

BRAVE NEW HOUSING
Conditions for those lucky enough to be rehoused improved sharply in the Thirties. This new flat (left) is part of a development built by the Bethnal Green and East London Housing Association at Brunswick Street, Hackney, in 1936. The wide balconies were set back from those on the floor below to give them sun and flower boxes were incorporated in the design.

HELPING HAND
A policeman helps children across the road in Cardiff. With road deaths well in excess of 7,000 a year, politicians in the Thirties felt something had to be done. In 1934 a new transport minister, Leslie Hore-Belisha, introduced the striped pole topped with an orange globe that still bears his name. Installed at road crossings like this one (below), Belisha beacons made it safer for pedestrians to cross the road.

difference to the value of each house and thus segregated residents by income. The Campaign for the Protection of Rural England was horrified at the urban sprawl swallowing up farmland. In 1933 it began to promote the idea of a 'Green Girdle' round London. Its campaign bore fruit in 1935 in the Restriction of Ribbon Development Act. The 'Girdle' eventually became the Green Belt.

Tackling road safety

In 1934 Oliver Stanley, the minister of transport, said that road deaths had become a 'hideous and growing blot on our national life'. Upwards of 7,000 people a year were being killed, and tens of thousands injured. Some cottages near dangerous crossroads in the country were said to have become 'unofficial dressing stations', so many crashes took place near them, particularly at weekends. In large towns, the frequent fogs made worse by coal fires led to sudden spikes in accidents. Some local councils had already built pedestrian bridges to protect children at vulnerable spots, often over tram lines near schools. Now, Stanley began a sweeping safety campaign. New road signs – Major Road Ahead, One-Way Street, Roundabout – were brought in. White lines were painted on roads to delineate traffic lanes. Cyclists had to fix reflectors to rear mudguards.

Leslie Hore-Belisha, who took over as transport minister later in 1934, went further. A 30mph speed limit was introduced in built-up areas, although there was no limit elsewhere, just a general regulation against 'driving to the public danger'. It became compulsory to dip headlights when cars passed one another. Cars had to

be fitted with windscreen wipers and splinter-proof windscreens. Hore-Belisha also introduced 'silence zones' in cities at night, where drivers were forbidden to use their horns. The active Anti-Noise League also lobbied successfully to get silencers fitted to pneumatic road-drills. 'Courtesy cops' were equipped with loudspeakers in their patrol cars, their voices booming down the road as they pulled people over to advise them how to drive better. Hore-Belisha also made a driving test compulsory and brought in driving examiners to administer it.

As a result of all these measures the annual death rate fell, but only to around 6,500 – in total, about 120,000 people were killed on the roads between the wars, and well over a million were injured. But at least the accident rate stayed flat, despite the ever-growing volume of traffic. A drive out became a ritual on Sunday afternoons or Bank Holidays. Charabancs, or long-distance coaches, were cheaper and more flexible than trains and were soon used by sports fans and day trippers.

One development the British did not adopt was the motorway. Hitler had started building *autobahnen* in Germany when he came to power, providing thousands of construction jobs. In 1937 the Automobile Association was invited by Dr Fritz Todt, the Inspector General of German Roadways and the driving force behind the autobahnen, to send a delegation to Germany. MPs and county surveyors joined AA officials to see the new roads first hand. The AA concluded that British needs were best met by improving existing roads rather than building brand-new high-speed routes across the countryside. Britain had to wait more than 20 years for its first modest motorway. For now, the East Lancs road linking Liverpool to Manchester was the extent of innovation. George V opened the road and the new Mersey road tunnel connecting Liverpool to the Wirral – the longest road tunnel in the world at the time – on 18 July, 1934.

NEWS FROM EUROPE

The big Continental story at the start of 1938 was the baby expected by Princess Juliana of the Netherlands. It was a girl, born on 30 January. In March German troops upstaged Juliana as they stomped unopposed into Austria. This was the 'Anschluss' in which Austria was annexed as a province of the German Reich. Britain did no more than send a protest note. Churchill demanded a grand alliance to stand against it. Prime Minister Chamberlain responded that that was impractical. He also gave the chairman of John Lewis's department store a 'high-powered rocket' for boycotting German goods.

Chamberlain did, though, accelerate rearmament. The recovery was well underway by now. Rearmament, with its demands for armour plate, explosives, ships, chemicals and uniforms, helped to breathe life back into even the most depressed regions of Britain. The output of cars had doubled over five years. Electrical engineering was flourishing and now shipbuilding and steelmaking made a comeback. Shares on the London Stock Exchange doubled. Robert Graves recorded a string of healthy economic signs on the front page of the *Financial News* on 10 March, 1938. 'English Steel pay 20 per cent … Cammell

> '*Horrible! Horrible! I never thought they would do it.*'
> Lord Halifax, Foreign Secretary, on Germany's annexation of Austria

HONOURED GUEST
Neville Chamberlain is met by a guard of honour on arrival at Oberwiesenfeld airport in Munich in September 1938 (above). The Prime Minister was on his way for talks with Adolf Hitler to discuss German threats to invade Czechoslovakia. He was met by Nazi officials in brown uniforms and a senior SS officer, Obergruppenführer Ritter von Epp (on the far left, dressed in black).

Laird (shipbuilding) Income Rises Sharply ... Royal Mail Lines Pay More ... Dunlop Pays 9 per cent ... Stock Exchange More Confident.'

Hitler's next move

Czechoslovakia had been created by the Treaty of Versailles in 1919, an artificial country made up of Bohemia and Slovakia, with 3 million German-speakers caught up in it in the Sudetenland. Hitler vowed that these 'Sudeten Deutsch' belonged to Germany and that he would see them incorporated in the Reich.

Chamberlain flew to meet Hitler at Godesberg, a pretty little town on the Rhine, on 14 September, 1938. Hitler at first proposed partitioning the Czech state, but then demanded that the Sudentenland must be wholly occupied by German troops. It was, he claimed, the 'last territorial demand I have to make in Europe'. On 24 September Britain and France – and the Czechs – rejected the proposal. Chamberlain said that if France declared war on Germany, Britain would support her. On 27 September the Fleet was mustered, along with volunteer pilots and airmen of the Auxiliary Air Force. Europe was on the brink of war. The same day, the Queen launched the liner *Queen Elizabeth* in Glasgow.

The British, French and Italian leaders met Hitler in Munich at the end of September. The Czechs and their Soviet allies were not invited. When Chamberlain was given 'Heil Hitler' salutes, he doffed his bowler hat in response. On his arrival, he mistook Hitler for a footman. He was only prevented from handing him his hat and coat by a desperate whisper from Ribbentrop.

Chamberlain knew what Hitler thought of the British well enough. Hitler, he said, contrasted the struggle he had gone through in getting to power with the British, still living in their own little world, clinging to ineffective shibboleths like 'collective security', 'disarmament' and 'non-aggression pacts'. He was right – but he himself continued to hang onto the shibboleth of appeasement. The British ambassador in Berlin, the 'dapper, snobbish' Sir Neville Henderson, said that the British would have to allow self-determination to the Austrians and Sudeten Germans under 'suitable guarantees', though he should have known by now that guarantees signed by Hitler were so much wastepaper. It was agreed that German troops would occupy the Sudetenland on 1 October, with the frontiers to be settled by a Four Power commission after a plebiscite.

'In spite of the hardness and ruthlessness I thought I saw in his face, I got the impression that here was a man who could be relied upon when he had given his word.'

Prime Minister Neville Chamberlain on Hitler

Short-lived cheers

Before he left Munich to fly back to London, Chamberlain managed to persuade Hitler to sign a short declaration he had typed out. It declared the 'desire of our two peoples never to go to war with one another again'. It was this piece of paper that Chamberlain famously waved to cheering crowds as he arrived at Heston airport. Large crowds cheered him again when he appeared on the floodlit balcony with the King and Queen at Buckingham Palace that evening. They sang 'For he's a jolly good fellow'. Women cried 'Thank you, thank you' in tears of joy. London's West End filled with rejoicing people, bringing traffic to a standstill. Chamberlain was compared to a 'fairy prince' in one paper. The Swedes gave him a trout stream and the French named streets for him. 'We have looked squarely in the face of evil', the *Sunday Pictorial* assured its readers. 'And we have seen it vanish.'

ICONIC MOMENT
After landing at Heston airport on his return from Munich, Chamberlain waves a piece of paper, an agreement signed by Hitler that the Sudetenland was the last of his territorial demands in Europe. In what seemed a triumph for appeasement, Chamberlain announced to a relieved crowd that this meant 'peace in our time'. It did not. The Munich agreement doomed the Czechs and merely postponed the war for eleven months.

LIFE GOES ON

Evil had not vanished, but for the great British public there was little to be done for now. The cinema was an escape from a dangerous world. Britain had about 5,000 cinemas by 1939 and some 20 million tickets were being sold each week. Some of the new 'Super Cinemas' could seat 4,000. The cinema was cheap – six pence a ticket for a show lasting two or three hours, with two films, a newsreel and perhaps a cartoon or 'short'. The cost was no more than a pint of beer, and it was even less at the 'penny pictures' on Saturday morning matinees. Women could go to the pictures on their own, unlike the pub, and courting couples appreciated the darkness. Lavish decor, thick carpets and deeply cushioned seats brought a touch of colour and extravagance to dreary lives.

The seven cinemas in York had a weekly audience in 1936 of 45,000, half the city's population. This was a growth business. By 1939 the city had ten cinemas and audiences were over 50,000 a week. Nevertheless, the coming of the 'talkies' at the start of the decade had been a disaster for thousands of musicians. Big cinemas had employed orchestras to play through each performance, but with sound they went the way of sub-titles.

The British film industry had some protection from Hollywood. By 1935, 20 per cent of films shown had to be British. The influx of refugees from the Continent helped. The Hungarian Korda brothers were behind hit costume dramas such as *The Private Life of Henry VIII* in 1933, *The Scarlet Pimpernel* in 1934 and *The Four Feathers* in 1939. Alfred Hitchcock was the best British director, and though inevitably he went to Hollywood, he also made some fine films at home, including *A Lady Vanishes* and *The Thirty-Nine Steps*. The official film censor, Major Harding de Fonblanque Cox, was aged 81 and suffered from a type of lethargica that made him fall asleep when anything was put in front of him to read. 'Let us show clean films in the old country', he told the *Sunday Express*. 'I shall judge film stories as I would horse flesh or a dog. I shall look for clean lines.'

YOUNG FILM FANS
The enraptured audience at a children's matinee performance. By 1939 there were almost 5,000 cinemas in Britain – Bolton alone, a town of 180,000 people, had 14. A survey in Liverpool in 1937 found that 40 per cent of people went to the cinema at least once a week, and one in four went twice a week or more.

British documentary makers led the world with films sponsored by the Empire Marketing Board and the GPO film unit. Harry Watt's *Night Mail* in 1936 was a classic. A main aim of the British Film Institute, founded in 1933, was to encourage educational films. Fine films on natural history, on subjects like *The Tawny Owl* and *Rock Pools*, were made by Gaumont British Instructional.

Dance halls were the only real rival for a night out at the cinema and the pub. The Hammersmith Palais de Danse, which opened in 1919, was the archetype. By the Thirties, dance halls were nationwide. In 1930, for example, Rochdale, with a population of around 100,000, had half a dozen dance venues open on Saturday nights, with admission charged between one and two shillings. 'Tea dances' in the mid-afternoon were popular with women and the unemployed.

Ballet was also having a good run. Ninette de Valois and Frederick Ashton were pioneers. The Ballet Club of dancer and teacher Marie Rambert, with Ashton as choreographer, evolved into the Ballet Rambert. Robert Helpmann and Margot Fonteyn were the rising stars of classical ballet in 1939. Ralph Vaughan Williams opened a new composing direction with his ballet *Job*, while in opera Glyndebourne was founded in 1934.

Facing the music

Munich changed nothing. Duff Cooper, First Lord of the Admiralty since 1937, realised this and resigned in protest. *The Week* said that Chamberlain had 'turned all four cheeks to Hitler'. Prague was a 'city of sorrow', British correspondents reported, where solemn crowds gathered to shout: 'We want the whole Republic! We want to fight!' And the Germans were not the only ones with designs on Czech territory: the Poles demanded that areas inhabited by Poles be returned to them. Europe was turning cannibal. Italians listening to a speech by Count Ciano, their foreign minister, began screaming for 'Corsica, Nice, Tunisia, Djibouti'.

Hitler made a speech on 30 January, 1939, demanding the return of lost German colonies. These were far distant, in Africa. It was not, Chamberlain told himself and the nation, the 'speech of a man who is preparing to throw Europe into another crisis'. But Hitler was laying the foundations of his 'Thousand Year Reich'. On 15 March, 1939, his troops occupied the rest of Czechoslovakia. He did not stop with Prague. The former German city of Memel, part of Lithuania since Versailles, was surrendered to him after an ultimatum on 22 March. At last, Chamberlain began to fret that his trust in Hitler was misplaced. 'Is this an attempt to dominate the world by force?' he asked. His War Minister Hore-Belisha warned how little there was to stop him. He wanted a British Expeditionary Force of 19 divisions to be prepared to land in France. Only two were ready for service.

The Spanish war was over. Franco had broken the half-starved Catalan army. Tens of thousands fled over the border to France, where they were interned in camps. In March the Republican cabinet fled and Madrid surrendered. The Fascist successes emboldened Mussolini. On 5 April, without warning, the Italians began bombing Albanian towns. Three days later King Zog fled and began his long exile in Britain. Refugees came in growing numbers. In front of Hitler, Malcolm Muggeridge thought, they were like rabbits faced with the harvester. They gathered in the last corner of Western Europe where the scythe had not reached, where Parliament and books were still unburnt, letters of credit were still valid, the restaurants buzzed with chatter uninhibited by the fear of the secret police, where 'butter was still more evident than guns'. By 1939 some 25,000 refugees had

THE SPANISH CIVIL WAR

Members of a British ambulance unit on the Tardiente Front in the Spanish Civil War in September 1936 (above). The Republican cause was already attracting British volunteers, some as front-line soldiers rather than medical staff. Stalin was arming the Republicans, and sending them Soviet artillerymen and other specialists. Mussolini and Hitler were doing the same for Franco's Fascists, even supplying bomber squadrons. The fact that the dictators had taken sides persuaded the British and French governments to remain neutral, to the fury of the Left. When the Basque and Asturias provinces fell to Franco, some 4,000 Basque children like this little girl (left) were given sanctuary near Southampton. The Right denounced such children as 'Red hooligans' likely to 'corrupt our pure English youth', Robert Graves observed, whilst 'the Left defended them with aggressive sentimental pity'.

In all, more than 2,300 volunteers from Britain and Ireland joined the International Brigades to fight on the Republican side in Spain: 500 were killed. In December 1938, with Franco on the verge of victory, the last 305 British volunteers left by train. Clement Attlee, leader of the Labour Party, was among the crowd who welcomed them at Victoria Station. The fight against fascism was about to get a lot bigger.

FLEEING TO SAFETY

On 12 December, 1938, 502 child refugees arrived at Harwich from Vienna (left) and were then taken by special train to Pakefield Holiday Camp at Lowestoft. Four hundred were Jewish, the others were 'non-Aryan' Catholics or Protestants, or the children of anti-Nazis. The occupation of Austria in March 1938, which had caused them to flee, had been the first violent act of Nazi aggression outside Germany itself. It was a portent of what was to come.

THE BALLOON GOES UP

A crowd in Downing Street read newspapers on the German invasion of Poland, while waiting to hear the British declaration of war. Until now, the press had tried to lighten the air of crisis, with stories like the arrival of the first giant panda at London Zoo. Behind the scenes, though, the government had already been making preparations for war. Rearmament was proceeding as fast as possible, air raid precautions were overhauled, and plans were well advanced for the evacuation of children from dangerous areas.

arrived in Britain from Germany and Austria. Britain was traditionally an asylum for the persecuted – Karl Marx and Lenin included – and many brought their jobs with them. Jews from Leipzig brought the fur trade; others set up tailoring and furnishings factories. Sigmund Freud arrived from Vienna in January 1938.

The final straw

Hitler next turned on the Poles to recover the Polish territory that separated East Prussia from eastern Germany. This was called the 'Polish corridor' and it included the port of Danzig. Stalin offered to send Soviet troops to guard against the German threat, but the Poles, who had suffered Russian help before, declined the offer. Under the Germans, they said, they would lose their freedom. The Soviets would take their souls. On 23 August, 1939, to the surprise of all but the dictators themselves, the German Nazis and Soviet Communists signed a non-aggression pact. It had a secret clause: the two would share Poland between them.

In Britain, the violence in the last days of peace came not from the Continent but from the IRA. Eire was now a republic, but the IRA would not accept continued British rule in the north and began a terror campaign on the mainland. On 25 August, 1939, an IRA bomb in Coventry killed 25 people.

German troops invaded Poland from the west on 1 September. The Soviets would attack from the east a little later. On 3 September, Britain and France declared war on Germany. What followed was aptly called the Phoney War. In the last months of the Thirties, the blackout caused more British deaths than any fighting. The cities were dark, and London was almost childless as evacuation got under way. The blackout was blamed for 1,130 casualties, while the navy had 586, the RAF 79, the army none. But all too real a war was waiting in the wings.

ON THE BRINK OF THE WAR

For most of the Thirties, with memories of the Great War still raw in people's minds, Britain's politicians did all they could to avoid involvement in another war. And the public applauded them for doing so. But at the end of the decade, practically everyone accepted that a stand must be made against Hitler and Nazi Germany. When the declaration of war came, people calmly accepted the situation and carried on – after making sure that as many children as possible were evacuated out of harm's way from the cities to the country. There they would be safer from the German bombers that people knew would make the Second World War more terrifying by far for civilians than the First.

SERVE TO SAVE

CHILDREN AT WAR
Children on the beach at Whitley Bay in Northumberland (now Tyne and Wear) fill sandbags to protect local buildings and shelters (left). More than a million children like these young boys (right), with name tags and gas masks, were evacuated from cities in September 1939. In the cities they left behind, posters in the Air Raid Precaution campaign urged people to volunteer to help save lives and property in bombing raids (above). Many evacuees came from the poorest and most overcrowded slums of the big cities. Their condition often shocked the middle-class and country people who housed them. The children had head-lice, impetigo and scabies, and they were often unwashed. Some had no change of clothes – 'house-holders had to keep the children in bed while they washed their clothes', a report found – while others arrived in garments so verminous they had to be burnt. 'Some children arrived sewn into a piece of calico with a coat on top and no other clothes at all.' The social shock waves caused by the evacuees stirred the national conscience.

BE PREPARED

A message painted on a pavement (below) in Chorlton, Manchester, reminds everyone to carry their gas mask. In the event, poison gas was never used during the Second World War. Women wave goodbye to troops (top right), 'somewhere in England', on 21 September, 1939, as the men march off to war. A family try out their new air raid shelter on hearing the air raid warning (bottom right).

The horrors of the bombing and the fighting were to be terrible indeed, but they had not yet come. The Thirties ended in the Phoney War, with aircraft dropping propaganda leaflets, not bombs, and the troops of the British Expeditionary Force in France doing little more than training exercises. Only in the war at sea, against the U-boats, was there real ferocity. All that would change, brutally and utterly, in May 1940.

WHERE IS YOUR GAS MASK

'This is a sad day for all of us …
I trust I may live to see the day when
Hitlerism has been destroyed and a
liberated Europe … re-established.'

Prime Minister Neville Chamberlain, 3 September, 1939

1940-45

1940 TO 1945

YEAR OF DESTINY

As 1940 dawned, Britain was four months into its second war against Germany in barely more than 20 years. But so far there had been so little action it had been dubbed the 'phoney war'. Evacuees began to drift back home and people grumbled about wartime measures that seemed to have no point. By the year's end, however, the whole country would be on a total war footing.

FOND FAREWELL A soldier and his girlfriend prepare to say goodbye at a railway station in London in June 1940.

A BLEAK START TO THE NEW YEAR

The year began in a snowstorm. In villages and towns up and down the country people woke to find themselves cut off from the outside world. In the cities, the snow added to the perils already faced by people trying to get around in blacked-out streets. A Gallup poll in January revealed that around one in five claimed to have sustained an injury from walking into trees in the dark to falling over an unseen kerb or tripping over a pile of sandbags. It is hardly surprising that many people settled for going to bed early. Or they might listen to the wireless, instead of going out.

The BBC had not as yet developed the sure touch that it would find a few months later. Newspapers criticised much of its output as 'puerile', 'funereal' and 'amateurish'. Almost a third of listeners tuned in regularly to Radio Hamburg's English-language programmes, and in particular to the broadcasts of 'Lord Haw Haw', alias William Joyce. A one-time leader of the British Union of Fascists, Joyce had fled to Berlin a week before the outbreak of war. His opening catchphrase – 'Jairmany calling, Jairmany calling' – would become notorious.

'On the ration'

One particular privation that households had to face had nothing to do with the weather. On 8 January, 1940, food rationing began. It was to last well into peacetime – it did not end officially until 1954. The first foods 'on the ration', as the phrase went, were butter, sugar, bacon and ham. Meat was added in March, followed by preserves, syrup, treacle and cheese. Eventually, rationing reached out to include tea, margarine and cooking fats.

On the whole, the system worked well enough. Everyone over the age of six was issued with a buff-coloured ration book of coupons – those for younger children were green – with special books for gypsies, seamen, travellers, servicemen and servicewomen. The books had to be registered with a local shopkeeper and only that particular retailer could exchange the coupons for food. Initially, the coupons had to be cut out and sent to the local Food Office, but later, to save time and paper, shopkeepers simply stamped the book as proof of purchase.

Queues and points

Eggs and milk were 'allocated' rather than rationed, the allocation depending on supply. The milk allowance was progressively cut, although it remained reasonably generous – it settled at three pints per week, with children under five, pregnant women and nursing mothers being entitled to an extra seven pints. Dried eggs

THE MILK RUN
As the temperature plummeted in January 1940, coal supplies ran out, vegetables froze in the ground and roads and pavements turned to sheets of ice.

People went to ingenious extremes to secure supplies. Though this sled-borne consignment of milk and eggs got through the snow, the milk on the doorstep was usually frozen solid.

GOVERNMENT INFORMATION

KEEPING IT QUIET

It was one of the jobs of the government Ministry of Information to alert people to the dangers of unwittingly giving away information to members of a so-called 'Fifth Column', who were believed to be ready and willing to collaborate with the Germans. The notion that a Fifth Column was active turned out to be pretty much illusory. When a patriotic Cardiff householder accused his neighbour of tapping out Morse code signals to the enemy, it was discovered that the cause of the sounds was a leaky cistern.

Cyril Kenneth Bird, better known to posterity as Fougasse, was one of the cartoonists and humorists employed by the Ministry to get the message of caution across to the public. His eight drawings, all featuring the catch line 'Careless Talk Costs Lives', were soon to be seen practically everywhere, as were other, more serious posters warning against loose talk and rumour-spreading.

The government soon found many other reasons to launch poster campaigns. A compiler of one Mass Observation report commented: 'Take a short walk from the office where this report is being written and you will see 48 official posters as you go on hoardings, shelters, buildings, including ones telling you to eat National Wholemeal Bread and not to waste food … [and] ones exhorting the need to save for victory.' For the government, encouraging people to save was of vital importance in the battle to combat inflation. By 1943, the National Savings campaign was spending more on posters than the Ministry of Food.

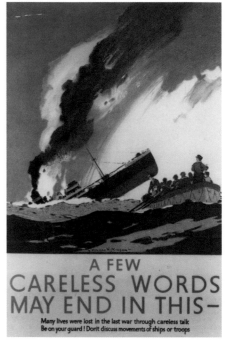

A FEW
CARELESS WORDS
MAY END IN THIS—
Many lives were lost in the last war through careless talk
Be on your guard! Don't discuss movements of ships or troops

BEWARE

Whether alone or in a crowd,
Never write or say aloud,
What you're loading, whence you hail,
Where you're bound for, when you sail.

—ABOVE ALL NEVER GIVE AWAY
THE MOVEMENTS OF H.M. SHIPS

".... strictly between these four walls!"

CARELESS TALK
COSTS LIVES

Don't forget that walls have ears!

CARELESS TALK
COSTS LIVES

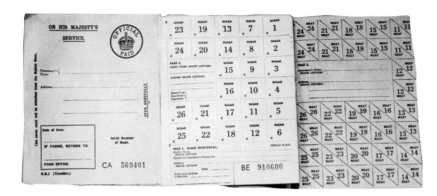

RATIONING
Wartime ration books (above left) were issued to everyone on the introduction of food rationing in January 1940. Initially, few foods were affected, as this well-stocked store, photographed in February 1940, was keen to point out. But as the war progressed, shortages began to bite.

eventually stood in for real ones, the allowance being a tin of dried egg every eight weeks. Fruit and vegetables remained off ration, as did poultry, fish, game, sausages, offal and bread in the shape of the wholemeal 'National Loaf'. But just because something was unrationed did not ensure a plentiful supply. The quest for unrationed foods involved endless queuing – and frequent disappointment.

The queue rapidly became symbolic of wartime hardship. In an attempt to alleviate the burden, a points system was devised by which everyone received around 20 extra points a month to spend anywhere on anything. Of course, there was no guarantee that any specific item would actually be available. Tobacco was treated as a special case. It was never rationed officially, as it was thought this would be bad for morale, but its supply to manufacturers was strictly regulated. This led to periodic cigarette famines and much public grumbling.

A QUEER KIND OF WAR

The actual war news did little to raise anyone's spirits. On 6 January, Leslie Hore-Belisha, the War Minister, was forced to resign – many believed because his reforms had upset the generals. The British Expeditionary Force had set out and was deployed on the Franco-Belgian border, strengthening defences for a German attack that never came. The skies were quiet. The RAF sent bombers over Germany, but rather than carrying bombs, they dropped propaganda leaflets – 18 million of them. Attempts to take the gloves off foundered in the face of government intransigence. When the pugnacious Conservative MP Leo Amery suggested to Sir Kingsley Wood, the Air Minister, that he should set fire to the Black Forest, the horrified Wood replied: 'Are you aware that it is private property? Why, you will be asking me to bomb Essen next!'

Small wonder that the war was nicknamed the 'phoney war' by some, the 'bore war' by others. Neville Chamberlain, the Prime Minister, described it as 'this strangest of wars'. It was certainly a war that Chamberlain appeared reluctant to fight. He had written to his sister the previous November: 'I have a hunch that the war will be over before the spring. It won't be by defeat in the field, but by German realisation that they can't win and it isn't worth their while to go on getting thinner and poorer when they might have instant relief and perhaps not have to give up anything that they really care about.'

'The navy's here'

Things were rather different at sea thanks to the dynamism of the new First Lord of the Admiralty: Winston Churchill, who was called back to office on the outbreak of war. Just before Christmas 1939 the German battleship *Admiral Graf Spee*, pursued by a British squadron, was forced to take shelter in Montevideo harbour in neutral Uruguay. Rather than confront the enemy cruisers off the River Plate's estuary, the *Graf Spee*'s crew, under orders from Berlin, scuttled their own ship. The journalist Mollie Panter-Downes described the action as 'the Royal Navy's Christmas present to the British public'. MP Henry 'Chips' Channon enthused 'already our sailors are being referred to as Nelson's grandsons'.

Then, in February, came the *Altmark* incident. The *Altmark* was a German supply ship and the British government had received information that just before

WINSTON'S NAVY

A crew member from the cruiser HMS *Exeter* gives the thumbs up (left) as he and his colleagues celebrate their victory, in consort with the light cruisers *Ajax* and *Achilles*, over the *Admiral Graf Spee*, a German pocket battleship, in the Battle of the River Plate. It was Britain's first naval success of the war and it gave a boost to the prestige of Winston Churchill, seen above on the bridge of a destroyer. After years in the political wilderness, Churchill had been recalled to office, by a reluctant Neville Chamberlain, as First Lord of the Admiralty. His first speech to the House of Commons following the appointment had been a triumph. Harold Nicolson wrote in his diary: 'In those 20 minutes Churchill brought himself nearer the post of Prime Minister than he has ever been before. In the lobbies, even Chamberlainites were saying "we have now found our leader".'

the Battle of the River Plate she had taken on 299 British prisoners from the *Graf Spee*. She was attempting to return home, steaming cautiously down the Norwegian coast, when she was intercepted by the 4th Destroyer Flotilla under the command of the dashing Captain Philip Vian on board HMS *Cossack*. She had an escort of Norwegian destroyers, having already been searched by the Norwegian navy, who had not found the British prisoners. Under direct orders from Churchill, Vian pursued the *Altmark* into neutral Norwegian waters to rescue the prisoners. When the German ship ran aground a boarding party – some of them armed with cutlasses – stormed onto the *Altmark* with shouts of 'The Navy's Here'. They quickly overcame the crew's resistance and effected a dramatic rescue.

The Norwegian fiasco

Hitler's reaction was characteristically violent, as if someone had trodden hard on an exceptionally painful corn. Grand Admiral Raeder, commander-in-chief of the German navy, had already alerted the Führer to the importance of keeping the shipping route along the Norwegian coast open, so that Swedish iron ore could reach the Reich's hungry armaments industry. Now, German plans for a decisive invasion were hastily advanced. Paradoxically, after months of dithering, the Allies had finally decided to lay mines to block the supply lanes, even though this meant infringing Norway's neutrality. The first were laid on 8 April. The following day, German troops moved virtually unopposed into Denmark and the first wave of an invasion force landed in Norway. The phoney war was over.

EVACUATION

SAFEGUARDING THE CHILDREN

Even before war broke out, Britain was evacuating children from the cities to rural areas less likely to be subject to air attack. The exodus began on 1 September, 1939. As children were marched off with their teachers to railway or bus departure points, many parents wondered if they would see them again. Billeted with strangers, many were homesick at first, but most – like this boy from Shepherds Bush in London (right) – settled into their new country life.

In 1940, with the threat of invasion growing, the evacuation continued from potential invasion areas and cities such as London, Hull and Portsmouth. More evacuees, like these bombed-out children from Southampton (above), joined them after the Blitz began. The final evacuation came in 1944, when more than a million adults and children left the capital in the face of V1 and V2 attacks.

The Norwegians appealed to the Allies for help and British and French troops were sent to their aid, but the campaign was a shambles. The British were woefully ill-equipped for deployment in snow, without snowshoes, skis or even white camouflage jackets. Most of Norway's ports were already in German hands and the Germans had total air supremacy. Nevertheless, a few days before the German landings, Chamberlain assured an audience of prominent Conservatives that Hitler had 'missed the bus' and that no invasion could possibly succeed given the Royal Navy's sea superiority. That particular bubble was soon punctured as it became clear that the Allied attempt to take Trondheim was doomed to fail and the troops were hastily evacuated. At Narvik, where fighting continued, the best that could be said was that it was a stalemate.

On 7 May, Chamberlain rose in the House of Commons to defend his government's conduct of the Norwegian campaign. He was greeted with jeers of 'missed the bus'. Leo Amery denounced him as 'no longer fit to conduct the affairs of the nation', concluding a vitriolic speech by quoting the immortal words of Oliver Cromwell to the Long Parliament – 'In the name of God, go!' David Lloyd George, the veteran Liberal ex-premier, told Chamberlain bluntly that there was 'no better sacrifice the Right Honourable Gentleman could make than to sacrifice the seals of office'. Chamberlain made an appeal to his 'friends in the House' to support him, but his resignation was now inevitable.

> ## 'The trouble with Neville Chamberlain is that he looks at foreign affairs through the wrong end of a municipal drainpipe.'
>
> Winston Churchill

CHURCHILL'S HOUR COMES

The question was who would take over – Churchill or Lord Halifax, the Foreign Secretary. To the King, the Labour leaders, the Civil Service, in fact to everyone but Churchill and the man himself, Halifax seemed the better choice, but in the event it proved impossible to persuade him. On the evening of 10 May, with Hitler's troops swarming across the Dutch and Belgian borders, Neville Chamberlain tendered his resignation and George VI invited Winston Churchill to become Prime Minister of a truly national government, in which both the Labour and Liberal leaders were prepared to serve. The country had a war-worthy leader at last.

The 'miracle of Dunkirk'

As Churchill busied himself Cabinet-making, the war news quickly went from bad to worse. The German forces were smashing relentlessly through the Low Countries in their *Blitzkrieg*, or lightning war. Early in the morning of 15 May Paul Reynaud, the French premier, telephoned Churchill with the news that his front had broken at Sedan. German panzers were pouring through the gap and on into France. 'We are beaten', Reynaud declared. 'We have lost the battle. The road to Paris is open.' In fact, the German objective at the time was the Channel coast, but it looked certain that the thrust would succeed. On 22 May Lord Gort, commander-in-chief of the British Expeditionary Force (BEF), took the decision to retreat towards Dunkirk. Four days later the order went out to start Operation Dynamo. This was the codename for the evacuation of the BEF from France.

When the evacuation began, no one expected that very much, if anything, could be saved from the wreckage. It came down to how many men could be rescued. All heavy equipment – tanks, artillery, transport – had to be left behind. The call went out for ships and boats to join the Royal Navy's rescue efforts and an armada of small craft, from trawlers and pleasure steamers to cabin cruisers and yachts, began making its way to and fro across the Channel ferrying troops to safety. The first men were lifted off the beaches on 26 May. By the time the evacuation ended ten days later an amazing 338,000 Allied soldiers had been saved, 218,000 of them British. The *Daily Mirror* summed up what people felt with a headline that was short, sweet and to the point: 'Bloody Marvellous!'

Waiting for Hitler

Back in France the onslaught continued, but Churchill resolutely refused French requests to commit more squadrons of RAF fighters to the fray. Sir Hugh Dowding, commander of Fighter Command, had warned that this would leave Britain defenceless. On 11 June, Italy declared war on Britain and France. The

'ALL BEHIND YOU, WINSTON!'
Cartoonist David Low caught the mood of the moment with this image of Winston Churchill – with Labour leader Clement Attlee and the newly appointed Minister of Labour Ernest Bevin alongside him in the front row – leading a new coalition government rolling up their shirtsleeves ready for the task ahead. Neville Chamberlain, pictured behind Churchill, remained prominent in his support for the country's new leader.

CONJURING SUCCESS FROM DEFEAT
Despite the failure to stop the lightning German advance into France in May 1940, Dunkirk has come to represent Britain's wartime spirit of determined resistance and the will to pull through against the odds. The Royal Navy, with the help of hundreds of 'little ships' and vital support from the RAF in combating the Luftwaffe, succeeded in evacuating the BEF together with around 120,000 French troops from the beaches and port of Dunkirk.

SAUCEPANS FOR SPITFIRES

With the war on Britain's doorstep, the nation rallied behind its new leaders. The appeal broadcast on 10 July by Lady Reading, head of the WVS (Women's Voluntary Service), for 'everything made of aluminium' to be turned into aircraft met with an instant, overwhelming response across the country. Salvage drives for all sorts of materials quickly became part of daily life. Parks, gardens, squares, even churchyards lost their ornamental iron gates and railings, while tins, bones, gramophone records, films, rags, jars, bottles and paper were all grist to the recycling mill. Everyone wanted to be seen doing something to aid the war effort.

One of the steps taken to confuse any invading force was the uprooting of all signposts (above). They did not reappear in towns until autumn 1942 and not until summer 1943 in rural areas.

French government fled Paris, leaving the undefended capital to the Germans. Five days later, the exhausted Reynaud resigned, to be replaced by the veteran Marshal Pétain, who promptly sued for an armistice, which was signed on 22 June.

Britain stood alone, braced for invasion. 'In three weeks', prophesied General Weygand, the Allied commander-in-chief, 'England will have its neck rung like a chicken.' Churchill calmly replied: 'What General Weygand called the Battle of France is over. I expect the Battle of Britain is about to begin.' But Hitler seemed in no hurry. It was not until 16 July that he ordered his forces to start preparing for invasion, and not until after August that they moved into top gear.

Britain took full advantage of the respite. Arms factories worked day and night. Large parts of the east and south coasts became Defence Areas, where machine gun nests sprouted from piers, beaches were mined, pillboxes were hastily erected and barbed wire straggled everywhere. All enemy aliens – even victims of Nazi persecution – were interned. Recruits to the Home Guard started pouring into local police stations even before Anthony Eden, the Secretary of State for War, had finished the radio broadcast calling for volunteers. In less than a month, nearly a million-and-a-half men came forward, but with equipment in short supply, they could barely be armed. Even uniforms could not be provided until the autumn, when the first battalions were finally issued with battledress.

ENEMY ALIENS

'COLLAR THE LOT'

Britain started rounding up enemy aliens on 1 September, 1939, and by the end of that year some 73,000 German and Austrian nationals – the majority of them anti-Nazi refugees – had appeared before special tribunals to determine whether or not they were a danger. Most were released under licence, but in 1940, with defeat in France looming, procedures were tightened. On 21 June, the Home Office ordered the immediate arrest and internment of all male enemy aliens, who now also included Italians. Churchill was determined to 'collar the lot'. Those considered high risk were candidates for swift deportation, many being shipped to Canada and Australia. Others were dumped in makeshift camps, such as this one set up in a half-built housing estate at Huyton, near Liverpool (right). On the Isle of Man, 11 such camps were established – six for Germans and Austrians, two for Italians, two for women and one for Britons considered to be a threat to national security. Almost all of the internees were totally innocent and posed no danger whatsoever.

For an invasion of Britain to be launched at all, the Luftwaffe first had to drive the RAF from the skies. On 2 August, the order went out 'to overpower the English air force in the shortest possible time'. The Battle of Britain had begun.

THE BATTLE OF BRITAIN

Over the following weeks, the RAF battled it out against the Luftwaffe in the summer skies over southern England. On paper, German air strength was clearly superior, but in practice this was not necessarily so. The Messerschmitt Me 109, their main fighter plane, was as good as the Spitfire and superior to the Hurricane with which Fighter Command was equipped, but its operational endurance allowed it to spend only minutes in British air space before it had to turn back to refuel. The British also had the priceless asset of radar, which gave them warning of German attacks. There were 21 radar stations arranged in a vast arc stretching from the Isle of Wight to the Shetlands, and these constantly scanned out to sea for the approaching enemy, then fed the information to a highly developed ground control system that directed – or vectored, in the jargon – the RAF fighters onto their targets to make the most of available resources.

The fighting reached a crescendo on 15 August, when the Luftwaffe flew nearly 1,800 sorties against Britain. Despite all its efforts, it failed to make the breakthrough it had expected. The RAF stood defiant and, as rising German air losses indicated, successful. The Luftwaffe's answer was to change tactics. They launched feint raids to confuse the defenders, while targeting their main attack efforts on the air bases themselves. It was effective. For the first time, the RAF seemed in real danger of losing. Its own fighter casualties were mounting, and it was losing pilots at an unsustainable rate. Then, one of the great accidents of history changed the course of the battle.

continued on page 479

SHELTER FROM THE STORM
The Anderson shelter was developed in 1938, before war broke out, and named after Sir John Anderson, who commissioned it after being put in charge of Air Raid Precautions by Neville Chamberlain. It was made from corrugated iron sheets with a steel plate door, but was only suitable for people with gardens as it had to be half buried to a depth of 4ft. The soil unearthed by digging the hole was then used to cover the shelter with a thick protective layer. The first shelters were delivered in February 1939 and before long 2,250,000 had been erected in areas thought likely to be bombed. They were remarkably effective against anything other than a direct hit, but they were also cold and often wet and not very appealing, especially at night. In March 1941 the Morrison shelter was introduced, which could be erected indoors.

THE FIGHT OF THE FEW

DEFENDING THE SKIES

Only the men flying the Spitfires and Hurricanes of RAF Fighter Command could stop the Luftwaffe attaining mastery of the skies that blazing summer of 1940. At the start of what Churchill christened the Battle of Britain, the RAF's notional fighter strength was 768 aircraft, but only 520 were operational. Soon, thanks to Herculean efforts by Lord Beaverbrook at the Ministry of Aircraft Production, an average of 33

Spitfires and 61 Hurricanes were rolling out of the factories each week. By the end of 1940, Britain had built 4283 fighters – over twice as many as Germany. What Fighter Command lacked were adequate reserves of skilled pilots. As the battle intensified, casualties mounted. By the end of August raw replacements were rushed into the air with a bare two weeks of fighter training.

The RAF relied on a sophisticated ground control system to get its fighters up and on course to intercept enemy planes. Coastal radar was supported by 30,000 volunteers in the Observer Corps, who manned 1000 observation posts inland. Their plots were fed through to the operations rooms of Fighter Command HQ at Stanmore, to the four Fighter Command Group HQs around the country and to any sector under specific threat of attack. The Sector Controllers ordered the fighters into the air. Once an order to scramble went out, the pilots lost no time in getting airborne, here (above) in Spitfires. The squadrons were guided to their targets by radio, here over the south coast (right), but pilots had to be alert to spot the enemy. Actual combat was at very close quarters. Here (left), a Spitfire flies beneath the rear gun turret of a Heinkel HE-111 bomber after attacking it.

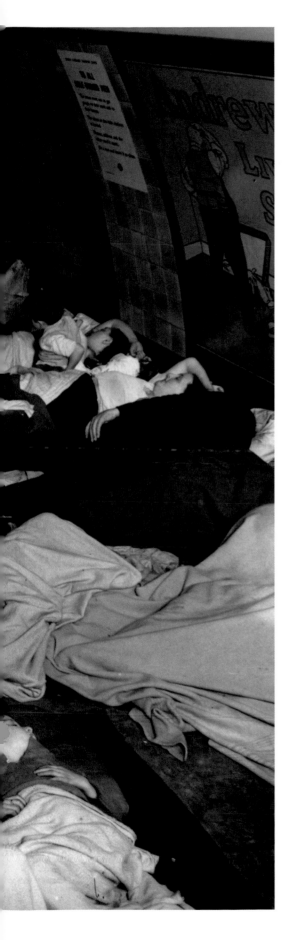

On 24 August, a few German pilots bombed central London by mistake – and against Hitler's express orders. The next night, the RAF hit Berlin in retaliation. Hitler was outraged. Goering, the Luftwaffe's commander, had assured Berliners that it was impossible for enemy aircraft to reach their capital deep in the heartland of Germany. On 7 September, German bombers streamed back towards London. The vital airfields had the reprieve they so desperately needed.

To Goering, it seemed that British resistance was weakening and that one final effort would bring the RAF to its knees. On 15 September – commemorated since as Battle of Britain Day – the Luftwaffe launched what it intended to be its knockout blow. It was a German disaster, even if RAF claims to have downed 185 enemy aircraft that day were later shown to have been exaggerated. The RAF lost only 26 aircraft and 13 pilots, and the tide had definitely turned in its favour. Over the last ten days of the battle – the final major daylight attack took place on 30 September – Fighter Command shot down more than double the number of aircraft it lost. Hitler postponed the invasion indefinitely.

THE BLITZ

Londoners were to remember 7 September, 1940, as 'Black Saturday'. It was the first raid of an all-out bombing blitz that went on for 57 nights without a break. The initial target was the East End – in particular, the docklands area. Arriving at about 5 o'clock that Saturday afternoon, the first bombers set the docks alight

GOING UNDERGROUND
The first mass air raid hit London in September 1940, creating a firestorm that burned for a week. Londoners were swift to take nightly refuge in the Underground.

At the height of the Blitz, 177,000 people were using the Tube for shelter at night. More than 25,000 bombs were dropped on London's docks during the war, making it the most bombed civilian target in Britain.

with incendiaries. Guided by the flames – and the unmistakable U-bend of the River Thames – subsequent waves of bombers poured high explosives onto the fires below. The scale of the inferno was incredible. At the height of the attack, the Fire Officer in charge on the docks sent a terse request to his superiors: 'Send all the bloody pumps you've got. The whole bloody world's on fire!'

That first raid lasted until around 4.30am the next day. Then, night after night, the bombs rained down – and sometimes during the day, too. Londoners took shelter, but there was precious little sleep to be had. As well as the constant explosions, the deafening sound of the anti-aircraft barrage was all pervading, as was the sinister drone of the engines of the attacking bombers high overhead. No one was immune, not even the Royal Family. When a lone German raider struck Buckingham Palace, Queen Elizabeth commented: 'I'm so glad we've been bombed. It means that I can look the East End in the face!'

Other cities around the country became victims of the Blitz in their turn. On 14 November, Coventry was blasted continuously for ten hours. The city centre, including its celebrated cathedral, were razed to the ground. Nearly a third of the city's houses were left uninhabitable. Nazi propagandists coined a new verb,

BEDTIME ROUTINE
A poster issued in 1940 warns civilians of sensible precautions to take before bed. Opening the windows and inner doors reduced the blast damage if a bomb went off nearby, water and sand were in case of fire, and the gas mask, clothes and torch were kept handy in case a trip to the air-raid shelter was necessary.

UNHOLY MESS
Coventry's 600-year-old medieval cathedral lies in ruins after the city became one of Britain's first provincial cities to be thoroughly blitzed. The Luftwaffe launched Operation 'Moonlight Sonata' against the city on the night of 14 November, 1940. The first wave of bombers arrived around 7.20pm, with hundreds more following through the night. By the time the 'all clear' was sounded at 6 o'clock the next morning, the city had been utterly devastated. One Coventry resident wrote that it seemed like 'a city of the dead'.

coventrieren (to coventrate), to define the scale of the destruction they had wrought. Bristol, Birmingham, Southampton and Leicester all suffered, together with places as far removed as Manchester, Sheffield and Portsmouth. Then to end the year, on 29 December, came a devastating raid that sparked the second Great Fire of London. Much of the City of London, including its priceless heritage of Wren churches, was badly damaged or destroyed. The raids continued well into the spring of 1941.

There was some good news to alleviate the gloom. In North Africa, General Wavell was taking the offensive against Mussolini's luckless Italians. The Italian fleet had been hit by Fleet Air Arm torpedo bombers, while the Greeks – Britain's new and only active European ally – were proving more than a match for the invading Italian forces. At home, despite the seemingly never-ending bombing raids, public morale remained for the most part high. 'I think we have won the war', wrote author and politician Harold Nicolson to his wife Vita Sackville West, even as the Blitz raged around him. 'But when I think how on earth we are going to win it, my imagination quails.'

GLASGOW AIR STRIKE
Shipbuilding areas were a major target of the Luftwaffe. A civil defence worker diverts traffic in Glasgow after a night-time bombing raid on Clydeside, in March 1941, caused severe damage to the city.

A NATION IN ARMS

Conscription became part of British life as early as April 1939, when the Military Training Bill made men aged 20 liable to short-term call-up. With the outbreak of war, the National Service (Armed Forces) Act decreed that all fit men between 18 and 41 were liable to military service, and the upper age limit was extended to 51 in December 1941. By 1945, around a quarter of all adult British men under 50 were in the services. Some 5 million Britons were exempted as being in what were termed reserved occupations, such as engineering.

ARMY

BASIC TRAINING
Though conscripts could express a preference for which branch of the services they wished to join, the army took the lion's share of recruits. Whichever service they were drafted into, the first months were spent in learning the basics. This group of raw beginners (left) are being given a foot inspection in the Aldershot Command. As far as the army was concerned, the war-time recruits were treated just like pre-war regulars, such as these men of the King's Own Yorkshire Light Infantry, seen here in hand grenade training in March 1940. The three months of rigorous basic training was, as one wartime Tommy put it, designed to turn 'sloppy civilians into soldiers'.

In September 1939, there were 897,000 troops under arms; this rose to 1,656,000 by June 1940 and 2,221,000 a year later. For most of the war, many remained stationed at home – it was not until after D-Day, in June 1944, that the majority saw overseas action.

AIR FORCE

TALLY HO!

Among the conscripts themselves, the RAF was the most popular choice, followed by the Royal Navy, which was perhaps surprising given the casualty rates in both of those services. At the start of the war, most RAF recruits dreamed of becoming fighter pilots, but many were weeded out during training. By the time the Battle of Britain was approaching its height, the Operational Training Units were turning out 320 pilots a month – which was still not enough to keep pace with Fighter Command's mounting losses. As a short-term measure, pilot training was first cut from six months to four, and then slashed to a totally inadequate two weeks in a desperate attempt to bridge the gap. And practising formation flying on bicycles (above) was no substitute for real air experience.

Training bomber crews (right) took much longer, especially as the aircraft grew in size and complexity. By Spring 1942 there were six jobs for which recruits could be considered: pilot, navigator, engineer, bomb aimer, wireless operator and air gunner.

NAVY

THE SILENT SERVICE

There was no such thing as the 'Phoney War' for the Navy. There were convoys to escort and troops to carry, while contending with U-boats, the Luftwaffe and the German surface fleet. As diarist Constance Miles recorded, 'every day there is some fresh sinking of some vessel … we are losing track of the names'. By May 1940, 268 British ships had been lost, among them the battleship *Royal Oak* with her crew of more than 800 men, torpedoed in Scapa Flow, the Home Fleet's supposedly impregnable base. Training was in deadly earnest from the start. These recruits are learning how to transfer from ship to ship by breeches buoy (right) and to recognise enemy aircraft with the aid of Bakelite models strung on a line (below).

HOME GUARD

DAD'S ARMY

Raised when invasion seemed imminent, the Local Defence Volunteers – or Home Guard as they were later renamed – attracted nearly 1.5 million recruits by the end of June 1940. Anyone between the ages of 17 and 65 was eligible. Initially, half the volunteers – like these recruits practising with Tommy guns – were on the older side and had seen service in the First World War, but by 1943 the average age in the Home Guard was under 30.

It took upwards of a year to equip the volunteers with arms and uniforms; one platoon in the summer of 1940 counted itself lucky to have a rifle, 10 cartridges, a revolver and a shotgun. Many Home Guard groups improvised – pickaxes, crowbars and golf clubs were all pressed into service. In the absence of anti-tank weapons, volunteers were taught to make Molotov cocktails – bottles filled with resin, petrol and tar – and how to fuse and hurl them at an invading enemy.

GETTING READY

The novelist Ernest Raymond recalled how he and his fellow volunteers spent 'the long hot summer evenings of 1940 gambolling about the country in extended order, sometimes throwing ourselves onto our bellies so as to practise firing …'. These volunteers (left) are learning how to tackle a dive-bomber with rifles. Other training taught close combat skills in defence and attack (right). General Sir Edmund 'Tiny' Ironside, commander of the Home Forces, noted: 'We just want the courage of men. No defence is any good if the men behind it run away.'

The first training school especially for the Home Guard was set up in Osterley Park, Middlesex, in December 1940. The idea came from Tom Wintringham, military correspondent of the *Picture Post*, who persuaded Edward Hulton, the magazine's proprietor, and the Earl of Jersey, who owned Osterley Park, to back him. The Earl told him that they could do anything in the grounds, but hoped that they 'wouldn't blow up the house … as it had been in the family for some time'. The government took over the enterprise in 1941.

'The Home Guard must now become capable of taking the burden of home defence onto themselves and thus set free the bulk of the trained troops for the assault on the strongholds of the enemy's power.'

Winston Churchill

1940 TO 1945
STANDING
ALONE

With the start of another year, 1941, a change of mood swept through the nation. Despite all the reverses and hardships of the previous months – perhaps because of them – there was now a steely determination to see things through to a victorious conclusion, no matter what the cost.

BUSINESS AS USUAL A postman on his round in Watling Street, London, in May 1941. St Paul's Cathedral is visible in the background.

DIGGING DEEP FOR VICTORY

By the beginning of 1941, the constraints of the war economy were starting to bite. Every household was forced to recognise that sacrifices must be made, and food shortages were a particular problem. Despite all the efforts of British farmers, the national diet in the early months of 1941 was the poorest of the entire war. Much of the food shortfall was the result of enemy action, as German U-boats embarked on an all-out campaign to sever Britain's trading lifelines. The battle began in earnest in February, when Hitler ordered the intensification of U-boat attacks on ships bound for Britain. Shipping losses rose from 400,000 tons in February, to more than 500,000 tons in March, to a devastating 700,000 tons in April. In May, U-boats sank 142 merchant ships and German air attacks accounted for a further 179.

This was by no means the only potential disaster facing Britain. Gold and dollar reserves were draining away to pay for the stream of armaments being ordered from the USA under the terms of the so-called 'cash and carry' scheme. As national bankruptcy loomed, Churchill appealed to the Americans to 'give us the tools and we will finish the job'. In March, President Roosevelt's Lend-Lease Act passed into law. The vital supplies would keep flowing. In addition to arms, shipments of dried eggs, evaporated milk, bacon, beans, cheese, lard and tinned meat began that summer and were crucial in the battle to keep the nation fed.

Growing our own

One thing that people could do for themselves was to take the advice of the Ministry of Food and dig for victory. Allotments began to sprout in open spaces everywhere, in public parks and private squares, on football pitches and recreation grounds – even in the ruins of bombed-out buildings. By 1942 there were 1,450,000 allotments in England and Wales, up from 815,000 in 1939. And vegetables were not the only foods to come from allotments and gardens. Many people kept hens – by the middle of the war, it was estimated that these were laying a quarter of the nation's fresh egg supply – and rabbits became a backyard favourite. Others tried keeping goats, while some 6900 pig clubs were founded. Every spare bit of land, it seemed, was being used to yield a harvest.

Keeping informed

In homes throughout the land, family life revolved around the wireless, and in particular the BBC's news bulletins, which brought the latest news from the fighting fronts directly into the sitting room. From May 1940, newsreaders began to give their names over the air, and they swiftly became firm family favourites. There was Freddie Grisewood on *The Kitchen Front*, affectionately nicknamed 'Ricepud' by listeners to the popular daily programme, which also made the name of Charles Hill, the avuncular 'Radio Doctor', who went on to become a Cabinet minister and chairman of the BBC.

Then there was John Snagge, who was entrusted with such major announcements as the news of France's surrender, and Bruce Belfridge, who won immediate acclaim for the imperturbable way that he carried on reading the news

VEGETABLES EVERYWHERE
'Let "Dig for Victory" be the motto of everyone with a garden.' This was the message broadcast by Sir Reginald Dorman Smith, Minister for Agriculture, and the nation swiftly responded. Across the land, new allotments sprouted up – by June 1941, Bristol alone had more than 15,000 – and millions of people turned their lawns and flowerbeds over to the raising of vegetables. No patch of land was sacrosanct. In the capital, the wife of the Keeper of Coins and Medals at the British Museum planted rows of beans, peas and onions in the forecourt of the museum, while the moat of the Tower of London became a giant vegetable patch (right).

continued on page 494

THE BATTLE OF THE ATLANTIC

Hitler was swift to realise that Britain's survival depended on its imports. Without them, the country's war industry would grind to a halt and the people would starve. Between the fall of France in June 1940, which gave the German navy an additional 2000 miles of Atlantic coast to operate from, and December 1940, some 3 million tons of British merchant shipping were lost to the combined attacks of German U-boats, surface ships, aircraft and mines. In early 1941, losses reached such a pitch that, in April, Churchill himself ordered that they should no longer be reported in the press.

Nothing could disguise the effect that the loss of food imports was having on individual rations. In February 1941, the weekly meat ration was almost halved, from 2s 2d per person to 1s 2d.

Most of the merchantmen that were sunk were the victims of so-called 'wolf packs' of U-boats operating in the Atlantic. These new aggressive tactics were introduced early in 1941. Rather than attacking individually once a convoy was sighted, as was previously the practice, the U-boat making the sighting tracked the convoy until other submarines had the time to join it. A mass surface

attack was then launched at night. Despite the efforts of the defending escort ships, German successes in the Battle of the Atlantic continued. The U-boat commanders christened this period 'the happy time'.

Then, in May 1941, the British had a stroke of luck. A destroyer in a convoy off Greenland captured a U-boat and discovered a Kriegsmarine Enigma code machine on board, with a full set of code books. The intelligence boffins at Bletchley Park would soon be decoding German navy signals and helping to route convoys around the marauding U-boats.

CONVOYS VERSUS U-BOATS

Britain's ability to continue fighting the war against Germany depended on convoys like this one (above) getting through with vital supplies, in particular with armaments and food from North America. The biggest danger faced by the ships were from 'wolf packs' of U-boats that prowled the waters of the Atlantic – this one (above right) is off the northeast coast of America. The main weapons that ships had against submarines were depth charges. Once the presence of a submerged submarine was suspected, a depth charge of explosives would be launched (right) in the hope of sinking it or forcing it to the surface where it could be finished off by the big guns.

RECYCLING WASTE
Salvage drives featured heavily in wartime daily life. Large bins and boxes labelled 'paper', 'tins' and so on became a fixture along every street and road in the kingdom, with the Ministry of Supply urging householders to fill them to the brim. The women of the WVS – the Women's Volunteer Service – played a major role in the campaign, patriotically collecting old batteries and fishing in ponds for worn-out tyres for scrap rubber. Children, too, were given a job to do. They were enrolled in the so-called Cog Scheme as official salvage collectors. As a correspondent pointed out in *The Times* in 1941, 'there are not many things that small boys can do, but this is one'.

when a bomb fell on Broadcasting House halfway through his bulletin. Later, Wilfred Pickles joined them and his pronounced Yorkshire accent gave his broadcasts an especially individual tone.

BBC war correspondents, such as the young Richard Dimbleby, Frank Gillard and Wynford Vaughan Thomas, became celebrated for their battlefront reports. Eyewitness broadcasts and semi-dramatised documentary features also had huge audiences. One of the most popular was succinctly titled *The Battle of Britain*. Broadcast in May 1941, it had Germanic voices gabbling phrases like 'Achtung Schpitfeur', and RAF ones countering with calls of 'Tally Ho!' and 'Good Show'.

Make them laugh …
News was not the only draw. As the *Radio Times* noted, people were 'looking to the radio for amusement and diversion to refresh them and help them to carry on'. The result was the launch of live shows like *Workers' Playtime*, broadcast from war factories, and popular variety programmes such as *Band Wagon*, starring 'Big Hearted Arthur' Askey and Richard 'Stinker' Murdoch. Then there was *Garrison Theatre* and *Happidrome*, which ran from 1941 into peacetime. The same year saw the BBC's first soap opera, the saga of the Robinsons, a 'front line family', while *Saturday Night Theatre* took to the studio boards for the first time.

Above all, there was *It's That Man Again*, with Tommy Handley and a cast of inspired supporting characters, who had the entire nation in fits. The characters included such immortals as Funf, everyone's favourite German spy, Colonel

Chinstrap, who was swift to respond to any suggestion of a drink with 'I don't mind if I do!', and Mrs Mopp with her catchphrase 'Can I do you now, sir?'.

... and make them think

From modest beginnings in January 1941, *The Brains Trust* garnered a regular audience of between 10 and 12 million people a week – nearly one in three of the adult population. The three resident pundits – Professors Cyril Joad, Julian Huxley and Commander Campbell, a much-travelled retired naval officer – became national celebrities. Even the Ministry of Food jumped on the *Brains Trust* bandwagon with a new dish called 'Joad in the Hole'. Each week the panel answered questions sent in by its listeners, ranging from deep philosophical concerns such as 'Who made God?' to more mundane ones such as 'What is a sneeze?' and 'How does a fly land on a ceiling?' Whatever the topic, millions of loyal listeners accepted what the speakers said more or less as gospel.

Radio apart, most people looked above all to the cinema and dance halls for entertainment, but for the more culturally minded there were concerts, art shows and theatrical performances organised by CEMA – the Council for Education in Music and the Arts. Though Ernest Bevin, the pugnacious Minister of Labour, confided that he found CEMA's efforts 'too 'ighbrow', they were very popular. The BBC Symphony Orchestra broke all records for takings when it played for the troops, even the one set by Gracie Fields. 'Our Gracie' and the young Vera Lynn, 'the Forces' Sweetheart', were the two best-loved popular singers of the day.

PROUD PORKER PARENTS
Private pig-owning became a popular activity as the meat ration dwindled. By the middle of the war, it was officially estimated that there were 6900 pig clubs throughout the country, many of them run by policemen and firemen, like these men from an AFS (Auxiliary Fire Service) station in southwest London. Most pigs were reared on allotments or in back gardens, but some had more unlikely homes, such as the drained swimming pool of a bombed-out London club. The pigs were mainly fed from scraps collected in 'pig bins' in the streets, and were lovingly fattened up before being slaughtered for pork, bacon and ham.
A young woman from Catford later recalled how she and some friends had each taken a 5-shilling stake in a pig being fed at their local Fire Station: 'How we watched those pigs and gladly paid our money when it came round to Christmas and we were given permission to kill them... I don't think pork has tasted the same since.'

THAT'S ENTERTAINMENT

People found all sorts of ways of keeping entertained. At home, there was the wireless: as well as being a vital source of news, the BBC broadcast programmes to suit every taste. Then there was the cinema – between 25 and 30 million seats were being sold every week – and the dance halls, where people were quick to conga, rumba and do the hokey-cokey, as well as take their partners for more traditional ballroom dances.

TAKE YOUR PARTNERS
Dance halls were places where people 'unwound in an atmosphere of gaiety, bright lights, friendliness and humour', as one 17-year-old London girl described it, recalling her almost weekly trips to the Hammersmith Palais. Quicksteps, 'excuse me' dances and noisy novelties, such as the Palais Glide and the Lambeth Walk, were universally popular, but the greatest dance sensation of the war was the arrival of jitterbugging – jiving as it is now better known – which came with the first Americans in 1942. The new dance swept like wildfire across the nation.

DOWN THE PUB
For three-quarters of the nation's men and around half of its women, the pub was home from home – even though beer was in short supply and what was available was watered down and adulterated with oats and potatoes in lieu of barley. From 1941 the doleful notice 'No Beer' was often on display, while many pubs rationed even their regulars to just a pint a head. The cost rocketed as well. Pre-war beer had been 6d a pint, but by 1944 the price had more than doubled. Still, the local was an ideal place to listen in to the radio, especially when someone important like Churchill was broadcasting, as here in August 1941.

A NIGHT AT THE MOVIES
The cinema appealed to everyone. As one observer noted, 'the pictures is the one event of the week which the factory girls really do look forward to and enjoy'. The top film of the war was undoubtedly *Gone With The Wind*, Margaret Mitchell's blockbuster tale of the American South and the Civil War, starring 'King of Hollywood' Clark Gable and British actress Vivien Leigh. It ran to packed houses from early 1940 right up to D-Day. British war movies went down well with audiences, too, the most popular being *In Which We Serve*. Filmed in 1942, it starred Noël Coward as the captain of a ship based on the real-life HMS *Kelly*, which was sunk during the Battle of Crete. The story is told through flashbacks as survivors cling to a life-raft. *Casablanca* was a potent piece of Hollywood anti-Nazi propaganda made during the war. Many of the actors involved were real-life refugees from Europe, which gave the film an added poignancy.

'CAN I DO YOU NOW, SIR?' Dorothy Summers as Mrs Mopp, the Corporation Cleaner, delivering her immortal catchphrase to Tommy Handley, playing the avuncular 'His Wash-out the Mayor' of the resort of Foaming-at-the-Mouth, in a 1942 broadcast of *It's That Man Again*. Known to listeners simply as ITMA, it was the most popular radio comedy series of the war, with more than 16 million devoted fans. Other characters who became household names included Ali Oop the peddler, Cecil and Claude, the two polite brokers' men, the Diver with his 'I'm going down now, sir', and the perpetually bibulous Colonel Chinstrap, always on the look-out for a free drink or two.

LIGHT RELIEF
A queue forms outside the Lyric Theatre for a performance of a hit revue. 'What people need', said *Punch* Magazine, 'is a show which will make them laugh' – and the theatre did its best to give them what they wanted. The two comedy hits of the war were Noël Coward's *Blithe Spirit*, in which a young author and his second wife find themselves facing the inconsiderate return of the ghost of his previous wife from the grave, and Terence Rattigan's *While the Sun Shines*. Set in wartime London in the flat of a millionaire earl serving as an ordinary seaman in the Navy, Rattigan's hit ran to more than 1000 performances. Several Agatha Christie thrillers also enjoyed long runs, as did *Arsenic and Old Lace* after it arrived hotfoot from Broadway in December 1942.

BATTLING ON

Beyond Britain's shores, the war was not going well, to say the least. Victory over the Italians in North Africa turned to defeat and retreat with the arrival of Rommel and his Afrika Korps in the desert in March 1941. The decision to send troops to help the Greeks backfired when the Germans launched armies into the Balkans. Yugoslavia fell to them, too. When the British, having hastily evacuated the Greek mainland, were then driven off the island of Crete in May, the exasperated Henry 'Chips' Channon recorded that many people were now saying that BEF stood not for British Expeditionary Force but for 'Back Every Friday'.

That same month, May 1941, the crack German battleship *Bismarck* sunk the *Hood*, pride of the Royal Navy, in a brief encounter in the Denmark Strait. Only three men survived from the *Hood*'s crew of more than 1400. The *Bismarck* in turn was brought to bay and sunk by the British Home Fleet before it could reach the safety of a French port.

Unexpected relief from Russia

The picture began to improve somewhat for Britain when Hitler turned on Soviet Russia. The German assault on its erstwhile ally was massive, and with most of the Luftwaffe engaged on the new front, the bombing of Britain slowed to a trickle. Experts predicted that Soviet resistance would be crushed in a matter of

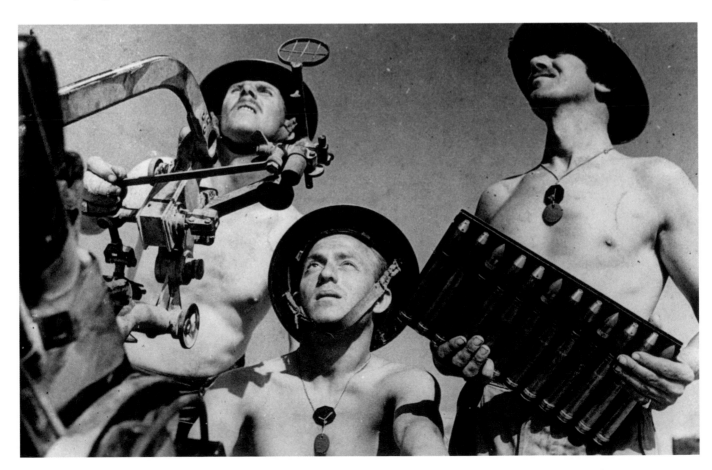

WAR IN THE DESERT

One of the few bright spots of the land war at the start of 1941 was in the North African desert, where, in two months, General Sir Archibald Wavell (far right) drove a larger force of Italians back 500 miles from the Egyptian frontier. The British captured a string of important towns, including Benghazi (below), and took 130,000 Italian prisoners. Success was not to last, as Wavell and General Sir Claude Auchinleck (near right) discovered when Rommel and the Afrika Korps arrived. The battle seesawed across the inhospitable desert. These British Eighth Army soldiers (left) are manning a captured Italian anti-aircraft gun outside Tobruk. The town withstood one German siege, but when it was besieged again in 1942 it swiftly surrendered, to Churchill's consternation. 'Defeat is one thing', he wrote. 'Disgrace is another.'

NEW ALLIES

Churchill and Roosevelt met for the first time on board the battleship *Prince of Wales* at Placentia Bay, off Newfoundland, in August 1941 (left). The two men agreed and signed what became known as the Atlantic Charter, a mutual statement of war aims. Peace, they declared, should bring 'freedom from fear and want' and complete disarmament of the Axis aggressors. Yet despite the practical American support that, thanks to Roosevelt, was pouring into Britain, the USA was still officially neutral. It was not until December, when the Japanese attacked Pearl Harbor, that it joined the war.

By then, back in Europe, Britain had already found a new ally. On 22 June, 1941, Hitler's armies launched a surprise attack on Soviet Russia. Churchill was swift to welcome the Russians as allies. As the Soviet forces fought desperately to resist their attackers, their popularity soared in the UK. When Clementine Churchill launched a personal appeal for Aid to Russia, £8 million was rapidly subscribed to the fund. This lady (right) representing the Red Cross is selling flags on the Strand in London to raise money for the appeal.

weeks, but the Russians hung on grimly, despite horrendous casualties. They were forced back into their heartlands, where winter brought the German onslaught to a halt. The Russians then launched a counter-offensive that drove the Germans back from the gates of Moscow and inflicted on Hitler his first major defeat.

The British public wholeheartedly welcomed their new ally. 'Uncle Joe', as Stalin, the Soviet leader, was affectionately nicknamed, ranked second only to Churchill in popular esteem. Thousands were soon calling for the launch of a Second Front in Europe and prompt despatch of aeroplanes and tanks to re-equip the battered Russian armies. *The Times* declared, 'We cannot afford to neglect anything that may help Russia', while the *Daily Mirror* summed up the popular mood in the bluntest of headlines – 'Russia bleeds while Britain blancoes!'

Across the Atlantic, although the friendship of Churchill and President Roosevelt continued to flourish – in August the two met to sign the Atlantic Charter, a joint declaration of war aims – the USA was still neutral. Yet this, too, changed on 7 December when Japan inflicted a devastating air attack on the US Pacific Fleet anchored in Pearl Harbor in Hawaii. They also struck at British possessions throughout the Far East. Hitler and Mussolini promptly declared war on the USA in support of their faraway ally. From here on, in the long run if not in the short term, the tide of war would turn inexorably and decisively against the Axis powers.

CALLING ALL WOMEN

At home, the British faced a new restriction with their by now customary stoicism. On Whit Sunday, clothes rationing came into effect and Oliver Lyttelton, the President of the Board of Trade, appealed to the nation to accept becoming shabby. From then on, making do and mending were the order of the day.

Make do and mend

The Board of Trade invented Mrs Sew and Sew, a puppet with clothes-peg legs and a cotton-reel body, to explain 'how to patch a shirt' and 'what Mother can do to save buying new'. In response, socks were religiously darned and darned again, and clever improvisation became the order of the day. In Shropshire, one mother kitted out her offspring in cardigans made from dishcloths. A Woking housewife bleached blackout material to make a smart evening top and skirt. The same material was generally recognised to be a godsend when it came to replacing worn-out petticoats and knickers.

Everyone was issued with 66 clothing coupons, which had to last for a year. Each item of clothing was given a points value, fixed according to how much material and how much labour it took to make. After an initial bout of panic buying – people feared, rightly as it turned out, that the number of coupons might be cut later – the system settled down.

The government went on to introduce the Utility Clothing scheme, which provided shoppers with a range of simple, carefully designed clothes of guaranteed quality, available at affordable prices. This went some way to mitigating the effects of the decision by the Board of Trade to do away with turn-ups on men's trousers, which proved to be one of their most unpopular moves of the entire course of the war. Women were far more adaptable to change. Slacks took the place of skirts, hats gave way to headscarves and turbans. A similar utility scheme would be applied to furniture.

Making do seemed to become a national obsession. Smokers turned to all kinds of substitutes as tobacco became harder to obtain. When cosmetics began to run short, women in their thousands resourcefully came up with a host of weird and wonderful improvisations. Glycerine on the lips was said to be a good substitute for lipstick, as was a solution of cooked beetroot, sealed in place with Vaseline. Shoe polish and burned cork were pressed into service to take the place of eyelash mascara, and perhaps most famously silk stockings were replaced by painted legs, with a line drawn up the back to imitate the stocking seam. Scent, though, vanished almost completely, as practically all of it had been imported.

'When you feel tired of your old clothes, remember that by making them do you are contributing some part of an aeroplane, gun or tank to the war effort.'

Oliver Lyttelton, President of the Board of Trade

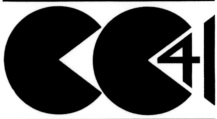

The Board of Trade commissioned leading fashion designers to come up with a range of clothing that would ensure women could buy good quality clothes at affordable prices. Each designer was asked to submit four outfits – coat, suit, afternoon dress and cotton overall dress – and the most suitable were selected for production.

The designs had to conform to strict guidelines and the finished clothes were made from specified fabrics and labelled with the utility mark (above) – two Cs denoting civilian clothing and the number 41 for the year of introduction. There were limits on the number of buttons, pockets, pleats and tucks, the depth of hems and length of skirts – generally short to save material. There were no superfluous trimmings or decoration. These suits (left) saved material by doing away with the collar and cutting away the bottom of the jacket fronts. The original designer suit is on the left, its mass-produced copy on the right. Perhaps surprisingly, women generally loved the clothes, but they disliked the term 'utility'. Ann Seymour, editor of *Women and Beauty*, wrote that 'the word "utility" is awful, but it'll just have to be got over'.

Hats were unofficially frowned upon as an unnecessary luxury, and they were both expensive and hard to find. Many women – unable to afford the natty berets, smart pillboxes and wide shallow cloche hats that became the fashion – struck out and improvised for themselves. A turban provided good protection for the hair at work, while patterned headscarves – some decorated with regimental badges – became widely popular. Begrudgingly, the Board of Trade eventually authorised the production of two utility hats. There were 'one star' and 'two star' versions, which had to cost no more than a guinea and £1.5s respectively. Both were made from wool felt.

Your country needs you

For the vast majority, there was little time to sit back and reflect upon such minor woes. By July 1941, the manpower shortfall was so bad it became clear that drastic steps had to be taken. That December, the call-up for the armed forces was extended downwards to include 18-year-olds and upwards to men aged 51. All people aged between 18 and 60, regardless of sex, were obliged to undertake some form of part-time 'national service'. Most revolutionary of all, women were to be conscripted for the first time in any modern civilised nation.

Things had been heading in this direction for some time. Back in March, Bevin had broadcast an appeal 'for a great response from our women to run the industrial machine'. But despite a promising reaction from some, dubbed 'Bevin Beauties', simply not enough came forward to meet the ever-increasing demands of the armaments machine. Compulsion, it was reluctantly recognised, was the only answer. It was for this reason that conscripted women were encouraged to work in industry, rather than opt for the armed forces. Women soon made their mark in every type of factory. They worked on the buses and on the railways. They took over milk rounds. They tilled the land as part of Britain's great volunteer Land Army, which also included the Timber Corps – Doris Benson, a typical volunteer, thought that 'most of the girls really loved the life'. Local councils recruited women to work as labourers.

All in all, women played an essential part in winning the battle for production. It was total mobilisation on a scale never dreamed of by the Third Reich and it played a vital part in Britain coming through to eventual victory.

WOMEN AT WAR
In December 1941 Britain became the first nation in history to conscript women when it was decreed that unmarried women aged between 20 and 30 were to be called up (above). The age limit was lowered to 19 the following year. Many joined the forces – the women below are observers; thousands more found themselves despatched to work in war industries (right).

1940 TO 1945
THE END
OF THE
BEGINNING

Though Churchill believed that, with the entry of the USA into the war, the tide of battle had turned inevitably against the Axis powers, the dark months that followed the Japanese attack on Pearl Harbor were without question the most dismal of the entire conflict. In the Far East the Japanese seemed unstoppable, as the fall of Hong Kong was followed by the unthinkable – the surrender of Singapore.

OVER HERE A quartet of American GIs enjoy their first taste of English beer outside a country pub in the summer of 1942.

FROM BAD NEWS TO WORSE

Essential supplies of all kinds in Britain were running short once more. As Germany was now officially at war with the USA, its U-boats could take full advantage of American waters, and as a result shipping losses were soon worse than ever. In the Far East, meanwhile, the Japanese were sweeping all before them. In less than two hours on 10 December, 1941, Japanese bombers sank both the *Prince of Wales* and *Repulse*, two of the Royal Navy's biggest and best ships, which had been sent to Singapore in a vain effort to deter Japan from coming into the war. The aircraft carrier that was supposed to afford them air protection never arrived, having been damaged when it ran aground in the West Indies. This left the two ships almost sitting ducks when they were attacked by a large force of Japanese bombers and torpedo planes. The sinkings deepened the shock of Pearl Harbor, blasted in a lightning attack three days earlier.

The shock of surrender

On Christmas Eve, the British garrison at Hong Kong surrendered after a battle that began on 9 December. A far greater bombshell was soon in store from Japanese land forces who were speedily advancing down the long Malay peninsula towards Singapore. Churchill had pledged that this supposedly impregnable fortress island would be defended to the last man, but to the commanders on the ground the situation looked very different. On 15 February, Lieutenant-General Percival surrendered and his 80,000 troops – British, Australian and Indian – went

> 'Our wildest guesses did not take into account the possibility of abandoning the territory to the enemy – we had been told that the island must be held at all costs.'
>
> Len Burgess, Singapore survivor

FAR EASTERN DISASTER
British servicemen are marched from Hong Kong as prisoners of war (above) after the colony's surrender to the Japanese on Christmas Eve 1941. Singapore was soon to follow, despite the efforts of its defenders, like these Indian troops (right) demonstrating prowess with a trench mortar to General Wavell, overall British commander in the region, in January 1942. Many, including Churchill, believed that the island of Singapore was impregnable, but the great guns in its defences all faced out to sea, not towards the hinterland. No one had envisaged the possibility of an invading force fighting its way down the Malayan peninsula to attack the island from the landward side across the Straits of Johor. Above all, no one had imagined the merciless ferocity of a battle-hardened Japanese fighting force.

But in the depths of Britain's woes in the Far East, there was a glimmer of hope because the Japanese had already over-reached themselves. On 7 December, 1941, they attacked the US fleet in its base at Pearl Harbor, Hawaii, triggering the wartime alliance between Britain and the USA.

into Japanese captivity, many of them to slave in brutal conditions on the Burma railway. And the victors marched on: on 8 March they entered Rangoon, the Burmese capital. It looked as through the road to India would soon be open.

Churchill described Singapore's fall as the 'largest capitulation in British history'. It was just one of a litany of disasters. Three days before, the navy and RAF had been humiliated in their own backyard, when the German battlecruisers *Scharnhorst* and *Gneisenau* broke out of the port of Brest together with the heavy cruiser *Prinz Eugen* and steamed up the Channel more or less unmolested. *The Times* magisterially denounced it as 'the most mortifying episode in our naval history since the Dutch got into the Thames in the 17th century'.

In North Africa, British fortunes were also starting to look distinctly bleak. Things had started well enough, when General Sir Claude Auchinleck, who had replaced Wavell the previous November, raised the siege of Tobruk and drove the Afrika Korps and its Italian allies back into Libya. Rommel, though, was swift to counter, forcing the Eighth Army into retreat. On 26 May, the Afrika Korps broke through the British defences. On 16 June, to Churchill's consternation, Tobruk's 33,000-strong garrison surrendered to an attacking force barely half its size.

By July, the seemingly unstoppable 'Desert Fox', as Rommel was now nicknamed on both sides of the lines, was heading for Alexandria, Cairo and the Suez Canal. At home, the more cynical wiseacres were starting to say what the battered British army needed was a new commander – a good German one.

SLIPPED THROUGH THE NET
Another disaster for British arms in February 1942 was the escape of three German cruisers – the *Scharnhorst*, *Gneisenau* and *Prinz Eugen* – from the French port of Brest in Brittany. All three steamed swiftly up the Channel back to Germany. The RAF had made repeated attempts to pummel the ships in harbour, as here (left) in December 1941, but without scoring an effective strike.

DEFEAT UPON DEFEAT
Erwin Rommel, the 'Desert Fox' (above, on left), questions captured British officers after the surrender of Tobruk. Following this defeat in North Africa, Churchill's popularity plummeted to a wartime low, although he still managed to trounce his critics in Parliament when they tabled a motion of censure against his conduct of the war.

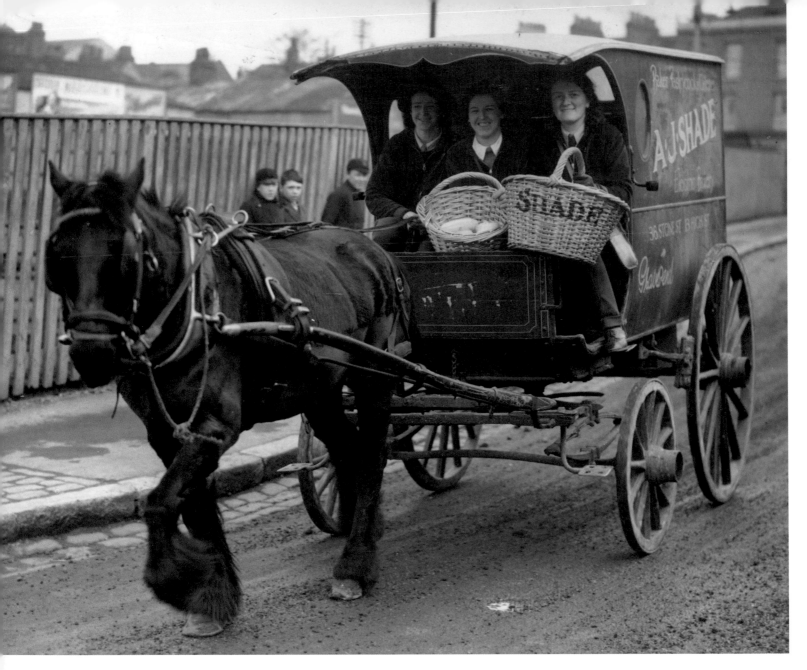

IS YOUR JOURNEY NECESSARY?

Back in Britain, the problems of getting from place to place were on everyone's mind. On 13 March, 1942, it was announced that from July there would be no more petrol at all for private motoring, except in cases of proven necessity. Any driver could be stopped and required to show that his or her journey was essential and that the shortest route possible was being taken. The results were dramatic. In August 1939 there had been 2 million private cars on the roads and even in October 1940 there had been 1.4 million, but from October 1942 no more new cars were produced for civilian use. Their number dwindled until there were only about 700,000 on the roads, all getting shabbier by the mile.

Train travel was a nightmare. The railways struggled to cope with a 70 per cent increase in the number of passengers, plus a 50 per cent rise in goods traffic.

LIFE ON THE HOME FRONT
The mobilisation of the country's womanpower rapidly gained pace as women took over more and more jobs that previously had been a male preserve. Delivering the bread was just one of them. By the end of 1942, 10 million women aged between 19 and 50 were registered for war work. This crew (above) would have been doubly welcome, because they were travelling by horse power. Travel became more and more of a nightmare as the war progressed. At Bank Holidays, notices were posted to discourage the war-weary public from taking even a short break, warning 'you may be stranded if you travel'. The amount of baggage that could be carried was drastically restricted as well – at one stage, even taking a bunch of flowers on board a train was banned.

Locomotive shortages meant that, by the winter of 1942, between 1000 and 1500 trains were being cancelled a week. Those that did run were often hours late. They were all dramatically overcrowded – even more so as there were hundreds fewer passenger carriages available. A woman making the trek from Wales to London recalled how 'each person who was seated in the compartment had someone else seated on their knee', while 'the corridor was a solid mass of people'.

Everyone, it seemed, had a travel saga to relate, with accounts of slow, crowded rail journeys swiftly becoming as common as bomb stories. Long-distance

KEEPING THINGS MOVING
Cutting travel to the minimum became something of a national preoccupation, as this 1943 protest at Paddington station demonstrates (below right). Some people looked for substitutes that would enable them to keep their cars on the road, but this early attempt at fuel improvisation proved short-lived (below left). The huge bags in roofracks on these taxis in Birmingham in 1940 are full of coal gas. The drawback was that the 202 cubic feet of gas that such bags contained was the equivalent of just a single gallon of petrol. On average, this fuelled a distance of just 15 to 20 miles, before it was necessary to fill up again.

'The time has come for every person to search his conscience before making a railway journey. It is more than ever vital to ask yourself: "Is my journey really necessary?"'

Railway poster, 1943

travellers suffered the most, not least because of the decision not to run extra trains at holiday times and to cut back on all other services. Cheap day returns and excursion tickets were withdrawn, while the amount of luggage that could be carried was strictly limited. Comfort was at a premium. Seat reservations were no longer allowed and there were virtually no restaurant cars. On stations, most buffets were crowded out – and, anyway, they often were forced to close early, due to lack of food or crockery. Such was the shortage of cups that, by August 1942, notices were posted urging people to 'Bring your own'.

Every railway station in the land was bedecked with posters, asking sternly 'Is Your Journey Really Necessary?' First coined to deter evacuated civil servants from returning home for Christmas, the message was now universal. Another poster proclaimed, 'Food, Shells and Fuel Must Come First' and asked, rhetorically, 'If Your Train is Late or Crowded – Do You Mind?'

Things were no better on the buses, where shortages of staff, spare parts, rubber and petrol all hit hard. In the autumn of 1942 off-peak services were drastically cut, with a night-time curfew of nine o'clock being imposed across the country – in large cities the last buses ran an hour later. People walked or bicycled, while in the countryside the horse came back into its own. In some rural areas doctors took to making their calls on horseback, medical bag slung from the saddle, just as their predecessors had done a century before. One Cambridgeshire doctor even persuaded the Inland Revenue to concede an income tax allowance of £90 a year to pay for his horse's keep.

PEDAL POWER
Men of the RAF take to the road by bicycle on their way back to their billets, a warrant officer in the lead. Even the forces did their best to economise on the use of petrol where they could. It took 2000 gallons of aviation fuel to get a Lancaster bomber to the Ruhr and back, while a single Spitfire on just a short flight used a civilian motorist's basic petrol ration for a year. Britain's surviving motorists struggled on until July 1942, when even the basic petrol ration was withdrawn. The vast majority of the country's motorists now had no choice but to lay up their beloved cars for the duration. That October, it was announced that no new cars for civilian use would be produced until the war was over.

OVER HERE

Acre by acre, much of Britain was being transformed as army camps, training facilities and air bases sprang up seemingly everywhere. The first US troops started arriving in Britain in January 1942. The majority sailed across the Atlantic on large, purpose-built 'Liberty' ships, or on great British ocean liners, such as the *Queen Mary* and *Queen Elizabeth*.

By the end of 1942 there were almost 250,000 US troops in Britain. By May 1944, as the build-up to the D-Day invasion of occupied France intensified, their number reached 1.5 million.

Both ships had been converted to carry up to 15,000 GIs, as opposed to the 2,000 passengers they carried in peacetime. Then there were the airmen of the 8th Air Force, the majority of whom were stationed on airfields in East Anglia. By the end of 1944, most of the 426,000 US airmen in Britain were squashed into Norfolk and Suffolk, where, on average, there was a new airfield every eight miles.

Nylons, gum – and food

On the whole, the British reacted to this friendliest of invasions well, although some grumbled that the Americans 'seem to treat Britain as an occupied country rather than an ally'. GIs were the highest-paid soldiers in the world and they were lavishly supplied. Their PX (Post Exchange) stores were packed with things that were scarce or rationed in Britain. There were razor blades, Lucky Strike cigarettes at just 3d a packet, soap of pre-war quality, chewing gum and chocolate – Hershey bars were particularly popular – and nylons, an immediate hit in a country where women had not seen silk stockings since their manufacture was banned at the end of 1940. One wartime schoolgirl recalled a glimpse she caught of an American storeroom. 'It was like looking into Aladdin's cave. There were things there that I had forgotten even existed.'

Every GI was reminded that the British were on short rations, but few of them grasped what this really meant. A woman who helped out at an American Red Cross Club was critical of the waste: 'I saw "boys" help themselves to what would have been a week's ration for me, eat a few mouthfuls and then – horror of horrors – stub out a half-smoked cigarette in the middle of the plate.' What defused any potential tension was the Americans' apparently effortless ability to put people at their ease, plus their good nature and lavish open-handedness. Children found out that a quick chorus of 'Any gum, chum' as a troop convoy drove by would trigger a shower of candy, while young women discovered that the GIs were happy to supply them 'with luxuries we hadn't seen for years'.

Making the GIs feel at home

Families were encouraged to invite GIs to their homes, particularly over Christmas. Soldiers who accepted such invitations were issued with special rations for each day's stay – these ranged from fruit or tomato juice, evaporated milk, peas, bacon, sugar and coffee, to lard, butter and rice. Once word got out, over 50 invitations were being received for every soldier available. Americans were also encouraged to take 'hospitality rations' when they went visiting. Supplies bought from the PX or scrounged from the cookhouse frequently augmented these. A GI could arrive laden with cans of ham and peaches, boxes of chocolates, the ever-welcome cigarettes and candy – plus sometimes even cigars and Bourbon whiskey.

SECOND FRONT NOW!

Even before the arrival of the Americans, the British had been getting used to having foreign soldiers in their midst. There were the Free French, Poles, Czechs, Dutch, Belgians, Danish and Norwegians who had fled German occupation, plus substantial contingents from the Dominions – Canada, Australia, New Zealand and South Africa – and from the colonies: after the US and British forces, Indian troops made up the third largest Allied contingent in the Italian campaign.

Russia was the nation's favourite ally. The fact that before Russia was invaded the Kremlin had signed a non-aggression pact with the Nazis was forgotten. Harold Nicolson noted how his references to China and the USA at public meetings won him perfunctory applause, but 'one only has to mention Russia and … one feels upon one's cheek the wind of passion'. One London borough ordered its dustbins repainted red in an orgy of pro-Russian emotion.

Arctic convoys carried arms to ice-free Soviet ports. Despite any misgivings Churchill and his colleagues might privately express, the Bolsheviks were officially 'our valiant allies'. It was the sheer scale of the Russian struggle that gripped the popular imagination. The Russians were fighting flat out, while for the British the chances to get to grips with the enemy seemed few and far between. A clamour for the launch of a Second Front to relieve the pressure on hard-pressed Soviet forces was the result, especially after the Wehrmacht took the offensive again, heading for Stalingrad and the oil-rich Caucasus.

Lord Beaverbrook, maverick Conservative politician and owner of the *Daily Express*, banged the drum. Speaking in New York in April he promised that, provided the Allies took action, 'the war can be won in 1942'. He praised 'Communism under Stalin' for having produced 'the most valiant fighting army in Europe' and 'the best generals in this war'. In May, 50,000 demonstrators packed London's Trafalgar Square to call for an immediate Second Front.

The turning of the tide

Of course, there was no hope of launching a Second Front in Western Europe in 1942. Militarily, it would have been suicide, as the British Chiefs of Staff made clear in July when, despite American pressure, they ruled out any landing in France. Instead, plans were drawn up to land more than 100,000 British and American troops in French North Africa later in the year.

All depended on what was happening in Egypt, where the Eighth Army was grimly hanging on at El Alamein. Stopping Rommel's advance there was the first sign that the tide of battle in the desert was shifting in Britain's favour, but what

UNITED WE STAND
Churchill was constantly reinforcing his message that victory would be achieved. This poster proclaiming confidence in Britain's military prowess – on land, sea and in the air – was released in 1942.

Churchill and General Sir Alan Brooke, now Chief of the Imperial General Staff, wanted was a decisive victory. They descended on Cairo, sacked Auchinleck and replaced him with General Sir Harold Alexander. To command the army in the field, they chose General Bernard Montgomery. 'Alex' and 'Monty', as the two men were soon known, were to prove a winning team, especially as Montgomery insisted on waiting until the Eighth Army outnumbered the enemy by two to one in tanks and had total air supremacy. Despite all Churchill's prodding, this meant that the British did not take the offensive until 23 October. Even then, the first attack went badly, but a second one, which started on 2 November, overwhelmed the exhausted Axis forces. It turned out that Rommel was absent from the battlefield at the time – he had flown back to Germany on sick leave.

News that the battle had been launched reached Churchill as he dined at Buckingham Palace with the King, Queen and Eleanor Roosevelt, wife of the US president. When he returned to the room after taking a telephone call from Downing Street, he was singing a rousing chorus of 'Roll Out the Barrel'. As the BBC prepared to break news of the victory at home, the announcer, his voice literally shaking with excitement, advised listeners not to switch off their sets 'as at midnight we are giving the best news we have heard for years'. Newsreader Bruce Belfridge announced jubilantly that 'the Germans are in full retreat'. It was Britain's first real victory on the battlefield and church bells were rung in celebration. Churchill told a City of London audience that the victory was 'not even the beginning of the end', but it was 'perhaps the end of the beginning'.

DESERT VICTORY
General Bernard Montgomery in typical desert pose, watching the action from the turret of a tank (above). Montgomery and his 'Desert Rats' of the British Eighth Army had one aim – 'to hit Rommel for six'. Below: British Crusader tanks pursue the retreating German forces in the wake of victory at El Alamein.

There was soon more good news. A few days earlier, British and American forces had landed in Morocco and Algeria and were now preparing to take the Axis forces in the rear. The two armies joined up the following May. In July 1943 Allied forces invaded Sicily and two weeks later Mussolini resigned. What Churchill had christened 'the soft underbelly of the Axis' was finally penetrated when the Allies landed on the Italian mainland. At six o'clock on 8 September, Stuart Hibberd announced 'the best news of the war so far' – the unconditional surrender of Italy. The Germans, though, had other ideas and threw reinforcements into the battle. There was to be no swift march on Rome.

On 26 January, 1943, Field Marshal von Paulus and the starving remnants of his army surrendered to the Russians at Stalingrad. That autumn, as the Soviet armies drove the Germans back along the entire Eastern Front, the Sword of Stalingrad, George VI's personal gift to the city's 'steel-hearted people', began a triumphal tour. In London, where it was exhibited in Westminster Abbey, thousands queued for a glimpse of the handcrafted blade.

TARGET FOR TONIGHT

The Battle of the Atlantic now swung decisively in the Allies' favour. In July shipping losses were cut to less than a third of previous levels, while no fewer than 37 U-boats were sunk. Grand Admiral Doenitz was forced to withdraw his remaining submarines. But there was still only one way the British could strike directly at Hitler's Reich. Though the Germans had turned mainland Europe into a fortress, they could not make it safe from the air. As early as September 1940, Churchill had told his colleagues that 'the bombers alone provide the means of victory'. The twin-engine Whitleys and Wellingtons, with which the RAF had begun the war, were followed by four-engine giants – Sterlings, Halifaxes and Lancasters – which could inflict destruction on an unprecedented scale. Night after night, they made the hazardous journey across the North Sea into enemy skies.

BOMBER BOYS
The crew of a Lancaster bomber return from a raid in April 1943 and ground crew move in to check the aeroplane for damage. The Lancaster was a masterpiece of military aviation design, carrying bomb loads of up to 14,000 pounds at a speed of nearly 290mph.

DAMBUSTERS
Wing Commander Guy Gibson (above centre) with members of 617 Squadron, which was formed to carry out *Operation Chastise*, as the Dambusters raid was officially called. Air Vice-Marshal Ralph Cochrane told the squadron: 'You have been selected to give the rapier thrust which will shorten the war if it is successful.' The operation was top secret, so their nickname the 'Dambusters' was bestowed only after their attack on the three great Ruhr dams in May 1943. The 'bouncing bombs' used in the raid were designed specifically for the purpose by Barnes Wallis.

Sir Arthur Harris, chief of Bomber Command from early 1942, was the single-minded apostle of the all-out bombing offensive. Nicknamed 'Bomber' by his men, Harris's aim was the total destruction of Germany's cities. This, he argued, would break civilian morale, so halting war production and bringing the Reich to its knees. In pursuit of this ultimate goal, Bomber Command was to drop more than 850,000 tons of bombs on Germany. It lost 55,000 airmen in the process.

The offensive began in earnest in March 1942 with raids on Lübeck and Rostow. At the end of May came the first 1000-bomber raid on Cologne, which destroyed 12,840 buildings, razing 600 acres to the ground. Similar attacks on Essen and Bremen followed. The next year a ten-day attack on Hamburg, code-named *Operation Gomorrah*, culminated in a firestorm following the night raid of 27 July which killed more than 50,000 civilians and injured 40,000 more. Then came Berlin itself. From November 1942 to March 1944 the city was bombarded continually, but it proved too big to tackle. With the date for the invasion of Europe fast approaching, Harris was ordered to change targets to ones of more immediate military concern.

Looking forward

As the war news improved, people's minds began to turn to what sort of country they wanted to live in when the victory was won. They were determined above all not to see a repeat of the poverty and mass unemployment that afflicted ordinary Britons following the empty promises at the end of the First World War.

FROM CRADLE TO GRAVE

In December 1942, a report laying down guiding principles for the creation of a welfare state was published. It was the work of Sir William Beveridge, a former Director of the London School of Economics, and it was greeted with public acclaim. Within a fortnight, a Gallup poll revealed that 19 out of 20 Britons had heard of the report's proposals and nine out of ten believed that these should be adopted unreservedly.

Beveridge argued that it was the government's duty to guarantee a minimum standard of living, so that people need no longer fear unemployment, illness and old age. He proposed state child benefit, a free national health service and 'full use of the power of the state to maintain employment and reduce unemployment'. In Beveridge's brave new world, the evils of 'want, disease, ignorance, squalor and idleness' were all to be banished as the nation marched along the road towards a 'just society', as Beveridge defined his ultimate goal.

Though the report had been commissioned by the government, its revolutionary content led to immediate dithering. Many Conservatives – and even some Labour dignitaries – believed that it might prove unaffordable. The rank-and-file of the Labour Party, however, were solidly in favour of the plan. When the government proposed to defer any action on it until after the war, Churchill faced his biggest parliamentary rebellion of the entire war. It was not until 1945, though, that the people got their chance to speak.

TOWARDS BETTER HEALTH
Pupils from Slough Girls High School enjoy their milk and buns during the morning break. Britain's children were actually better nourished during the war than before it, largely thanks to the provision of free milk, plus orange juice and cod liver oil under the terms of the Vitamin Welfare Scheme. In England and Wales, the infant mortality rate fell from 51 per thousand in 1939 to 46 per thousand in 1945.

1940 TO 1945
ROAD TO
VICTORY

As winter gave way to the spring of 1944, the whole nation was filled with anticipation. D-Day and the long-awaited Allied invasion of Western Europe was on its way at last. By May 1945 the war in Europe would be over. The Japanese surrender followed in August. Britain could now start to count the cost and begin shaping its future in the post-war world.

V E DAY Jubilant Londoners dance in Piccadilly Circus to celebrate the end of the war in Europe, on 8 May, 1945.

D-DAY ARRIVES

In a broadcast at the end of March 1944, Winston Churchill warned his war-weary fellow countrymen that 'the hour of our greatest effort and action is approaching'. He went on: 'The flashing eyes of all our soldiers, sailors and airmen must be fixed upon the enemy on their front. The only homeward road for all of us lies through the arch of victory.' Everyone was aware that the Second Front was finally coming. From late February onwards, 150,000 US troops a month were arriving to join their comrades. By the end of May, 2,876,600 men were awaiting the order to move. 'England is expectant, almost hushed', wrote the author J L Hodson in his diary. 'Every time we turn on the radio we expect to hear that the great invasion of Europe has begun. Every morning while I am still abed, I am wakened by a dull roaring in the heavens, which tells me that our aircraft are going over – some days seven thousand of them go.'

The launch of this great air offensive – diverted from the usual target of Germany to attack the French railway system and Hitler's much-vaunted Atlantic Wall defences – was not the only sign of the imminent invasion. In April the entire coast from Land's End to the Wash was declared a no-go area for non-residents. Practically the whole of southern England was turned into one huge armed camp, with every port from Falmouth to Tilbury packed to capacity with invasion shipping. In the docks at Southampton ships were berthed up to seven and eight abreast, while not far from the heart of London the southern reaches of the Thames were crowded with tank landing craft. The roads and railways were constantly clogged with convoys of tanks, trucks, jeeps and other military vehicles, all streaming towards their marshalling points.

D-Day dawns

By 4 June, preparations were complete. The US Western Task Force was ready to sail from a coastal strip that stretched from Salcombe in Devon to Poole in Dorset. The British and Canadians of the Eastern Task Force were in position along the Solent and Southampton Water. What they were all waiting for was better weather.

Three days earlier, Group Captain James Stagg, chief meteorologist to the invasion force, had given an ominous weather report to General Dwight D Eisenhower, the Allied commander-in-chief. Fierce storms were predicted in the Channel. In the light of the worsening conditions, Eisenhower ordered that the invasion be postponed. Then Stagg reported the possibility of a 36-hour lull in the storms, during which the weather would clear. Having consulted with General Montgomery, in command of Allied forces on the ground, and his other top commanders, Eisenhower took the gamble with a terse statement: 'OK – we'll go.'

At 12.16am on 6 June, aeroplanes and gliders began to drop paratroops on both flanks of the 50-mile-long invasion front – the US 82nd and 101st Airborne on the west flank and the British 6th Airborne Division on the east. By 3am the invasion fleet was off the coast of France. The Americans began storming ashore on their beaches in the western sector at 6.30am; the British and Canadians had to wait a little longer for the tides before coming ashore in their sector further east. American troops were scheduled to land on two beaches code-named Omaha and

GETTING READY FOR ACTION
US soldiers accept a welcome cup of tea somewhere in southern England. Seemingly endless convoys clogged the roads ferrying troops – mainly British, American and Canadian – towards their embarkation points in the early summer of 1944.

'It was a miracle it all worked as tens of thousands of men and their vehicles slowly funnelled down to the south coast …'

Bob Sheenan, US infantry 1944

ASHORE AT LAST
British troops file ashore on Gold Beach, each carrying a bicycle along with the more usual gear. After securing the beachhead, their objective was to seize Bayeux and the road to Caen, but this was not to be accomplished without heavy fighting – the bicycles were soon abandoned. L G Holden, a wireless operator in the Royal Hampshire Regiment, recalled how he and his comrades 'were in the sea to the tops of our thighs. Floundering ashore, we were in the thick of it … mortar bombs and shells erupting in the sand and the "breep-brup" of Spandau machine guns cutting through the din'. What impressed him was the calm way the troops went about their business. 'There were no shouts, everyone knew his job and was doing it without saying anything. There was only the occasional cry of despair as men were hit and went down'.

Utah; the British target beaches were Gold and Sword; the Canadians landed between the two on Juno Beach. The fighting was fierce – especially on Omaha Beach – but by nightfall 156,000 troops had reached France, the beachheads had been secured and the advance off the beaches was beginning. What Field Marshal Erwin Rommel had predicted would be 'the longest day' was over.

Breaking the news
Back in Britain, the military camps that had sprung up everywhere fell strangely silent. As one observer noted: 'It was so quiet that it was as if the whole country had upped and gone across the Channel to settle with Hitler once and for all.' An exception to this was the airfields, where wave after wave of fighters and bombers were continually landing, refuelling and taking to the skies again to support the troops in France. Officially, news of the invasion had not as yet broken – in fact, it was German radio that broadcast the first report of the Allied landings. Then, at 9.30am, the calm, authoritative voice of the BBC's John Snagge announced 'D-Day has come'. A quarter of an hour later, Eisenhower himself issued the official news to the world.

The word swiftly spread. Esther MacMurray, working her shift in an aircraft factory, recalled how she and her fellow workers heard the news. They were attending a lunchtime concert in their canteen. 'Suddenly the Managing Director came on to the stage and everything stopped. "Ladies and gentlemen", he said quietly, "we have landed in France". There was a stunned silence, then a quavering solitary voice started to sing *Land of Hope and Glory*. In a moment everybody had joined in a great crescendo of sound. Some of the women whose sons and husbands were in the forces were singing with the tears streaming down their faces, while the men were trying to control their emotions. Then we went quietly back to work – for victory.' That victory was still distant. Though the Allied armies were firmly established in Normandy, their progress inland proved to be painfully slow as they confronted determined German resistance.

VENGEANCE WEAPONS

A week after D-Day, the public found themselves once again directly in the line of fire as Hitler turned his V1 flying bomb against Britain. The V1 was the first of Hitler's so-called 'vengeance weapons' – a small, fast, unmanned aeroplane powered by a pulse-jet and armed with a ton of high explosive in its warhead. Its course was preset: when its fuel was exhausted, the engine cut out and the weapon simply dived to the ground, where it exploded.

The first salvo consisted of ten V1s, only one of which reached its intended target – London. Then the pace of attack quickened. Within three days, a heavy, sustained bombardment had begun, with a steady stream of V1s falling on the city throughout the day and into the night. At its height, around 150 flying bombs a day were raining down on London. Experts predicted that, if the attack continued on that scale, it would take only two months to inflict the same amount of destruction as had been suffered during the entire Blitz. And the capital was not the only place to feel the force of vengeance: by mid-September, 2622 flying bombs had fallen on Kent, 886 on Sussex, 512 on Essex, 295 on Surrey.

A dip in morale

Civilian morale slumped under such an impersonal, continuous and, worst of all, unpredictable onslaught. Once the sirens sounded, people could find themselves spending most of the day and night taking shelter. Ears seemed permanently cocked, listening out for the distinctive sound of a V1 approaching – 'a grating, sinister drone' that rapidly inspired the nickname 'doodlebug'. The throbbing of a V1 powering through the sky was enough to daunt the bravest of hearts, as was the agonising silence that fell when the engine cut out and the missile began its final plunge. Many fled London. By September 1944, more than a million in the so-called 'priority classes' – mothers with children under five, schoolchildren, pregnant women, the old, the infirm – had been officially evacuated.

There was not even the comforting sound of anti-aircraft guns to reassure Londoners that at least the V1s were not sailing through unchallenged. One of the frustrations of dealing with the missiles was that, if they were brought down in a

built-up area, they did as much damage as if they had been left to fly on to their intended targets. Accordingly, on 21 June, the decision had been taken to shift all of London's anti-aircraft guns to the North Downs where they had an unrestricted field of fire, while squadrons of the latest and fastest fighters patrolled between coast and capital in what was quickly dubbed 'flying bomb alley', bringing down as many V1s as they could before they reached London. On the southern outskirts of the city, a network of 2000 barrage balloons was massed as a last defence.

The change in tactics was effective. Soon, more than half of the V1s that the Germans launched against Britain were being destroyed before they could reach their targets. Even more decisively, the long-awaited breakthrough in Normandy forced the Germans to abandon their V1 launch sites.

Breaking through in France

On 25 July, the Americans began the breakthrough. Within a week or so, the German front had collapsed and the survivors were in ignominious flight. On 25 August, Paris was liberated. Four days later, Montgomery and his Second Army launched an offensive that in just five days took the British from the River Seine to the outskirts of Antwerp in Belgium, overrunning the remaining V1 launch sites along the way. The news from the east was equally spectacular. The Russians had broken through the German line on a 450-mile front and within a month reached the gates of Warsaw in Poland.

To many, it seemed as if the end of the war must finally be in sight. The V1 menace had been dealt with. On 7 September, Duncan Sandys, the young minister to whom Churchill had delegated the V1 problem, confidently proclaimed that 'the battle for London is over, except possibly for a last few shots'. He was wrong.

The V2 terror

On the evening of 8 September, an ear-shattering 'mystery explosion' echoed through Chiswick in west London. It was swiftly followed by another, equally powerful detonation to the east of London, in Epping Forest. Hitler's second vengeance weapon – the terrifying V2 rocket – had arrived. Carrying about a ton of high explosive in its warhead, it had a range of 225 miles and a supersonic speed of 3600mph. Launched from mobile sites in German-occupied Holland, V2s could easily strike at London or other targets in Britain. There was absolutely no defence against them – it was not even possible to hear a V2 approaching, as it had been with the V1, since it travelled faster than the speed of sound. And as there was no advance warning, people had no chance to seek shelter.

The government did its best to keep the V2 secret. Word was passed down that the explosions were to be attributed to 'air raid incidents', 'plane crashes' or 'gas main explosions'. But such stories were increasingly hard to swallow and Londoners were soon sceptical. Some 36 rockets hit London in September 1944, 131 in October and 284 in November. Neverthless, it was not until 10 November that Churchill finally admitted to Parliament that 'for the last few weeks the

V1 AND V2
Somewhere in the British countryside, an unexploded V1 provides a seat for two Canadian soldiers. This was one of the many German 'vengeance weapons' that failed to reach its target. Nevertheless, within three days of the first V1 attack, 499 people had been killed, 2000 injured and 137,000 buildings damaged. The V2 rocket was an even deadlier weapon.

UNDER ATTACK
Farringdon Street Market in London on
9 March, 1945 (far left). The previous day
a single V2 fell on the market and killed
360 people in an instant. Dazed and injured
survivors (below) are rescued from the
scene. By the time Hitler's rocket offensive
on Britain finally ended, more than 1100 V2s
had been launched against Britain, most of
them aimed at London, killing 2800 people
and seriously injuring 6500.

Civilian morale took a nosedive. Home
Secretary Herbert Morrison warned that this
was not surprising: 'After five years of war,
the civilian population are not as capable of
standing the strains of air attacks as they
were during the winter of 1940–41. I will do
everything to hold up their courage and
spirit – but there is a limit and the limit will
come.' One of the problems with V2
rockets was that there was no advance
warning of an attack. Once launched, a
V2 travelled at supersonic speed to its
unsuspecting target. Many of the capital's
children were evacuated once more to
safer areas in the face of this 'Second
Blitz'. Others stayed to play among the
ruins, however, like these boys having fun
on a decapitated lamppost (left).

enemy has been using his new weapon – the long-range rocket – against us'. The
V2 bombardment continued into 1945. In January there were 223 V2 'incidents',
as these were now officially termed, 233 in February, 228 in March. The final
V2 to be launched successfully against Britain fell on 1 April, 1945. Its blast killed
Ivy Millichamp, a 34-year-old Orpington housewife – she was the last civilian in
Britain to die as a direct result of enemy action.

THE FINAL PUSH

It was not simply the renewed aerial bombardment that lowered people's spirits.
Everyone practically without exception was sick and tired of war, and sick and
tired of waiting. Following the Allied break-out from the Normandy beachhead,
hopes had been high that victory would be won by the autumn, but the advance
in the west had eventually ground to a halt. In September Montgomery launched a
daring but risky airborne assault involving British airborne divisions. The aim was
to capture the bridges over the Rhine at Arnhem, then link up with the British
Second Army to cross the river into the Ruhr, the German industrial heartland.

THE ALLIES LIBERATE EUROPE

THE WAITING IS OVER

The King had put a stop to Churchill's plans to witness the D-Day landings from HMS *Belfast*, a Royal Navy cruiser, but only a few days later Winston crossed the Channel to see how the battle was going. He was greeted with acclaim – here, one happy Frenchman lights his cigar.

German resistance took time to break down, but by late summer the Allies were making good progress. The Americans raced towards Paris, while the British advanced equally speedily across northern France and into Belgium. This British tank below is being greeted with cheers in the Belgian village of Antoing. Similar scenes took place time and again as the Allies drove the Germans back towards their own borders. In Italy, too, Allied troops were on the march north, having captured Rome.

After the rigours of occupation, the French were particularly effusive in their greetings – especially since there were Free French forces among their liberators. However, there was a darker side. They were swift to take revenge on those who had collaborated with the Nazis and Marshal Pétain's puppet Vichy regime. After the war, Pétain was tried and sentenced to life imprisonment. Pierre Laval, his one-time premier, was executed for treason.

Had the venture succeeded it might have considerably shortened the war, but it ended in falure. By the end of the month, the Germans had stabilised all their main battlefronts. It now seemed to many – Montgomery included – that the chance of a decisive Allied breakthrough into the Reich had been missed.

It was small wonder, then, that little signs of life starting to return to normal on the home front had relatively little impact on the public mood. In September, the black-out gave way to what was officially referred to as 'half lighting'. In popular parlance, this was dubbed the dim-out. On 2 December, the Lord Mayor of London held a banquet to mark the standing down of the Home Guard. Just as one of the speakers reached uttered the word 'victory', he was drowned out by the noise of a V2 exploding in the River Thames, just a few yards away.

> ## 'I think that everyone these dark autumn days is truly unhappy. Partly war-weariness, partly sadness at things not going right and partly malnutrition.'
> Harold Nicolson, 1944

The war, it was clear, was not yet over and a fortnight later, the Germans showed that they still had the ability to take the offensive. On 16 December, they struck at weakly held American positions in the Ardennes region of Belgium. This was the start of what became known as the Battle of the Bulge. Taken by surprise, the Americans fell back in disorder; in three days, the Germans advanced 45 miles. This unexpected and unwelcome news took most of the pleasure out of Christmas that year in Britain.

The Allies back on track

The battle now turned decisively against Germany. By risking everything on a last gamble in the west, Hitler had opened the back door to the east. On 12 January, the Russians launched a new offensive; by February, the Soviet army was just 40 miles from Berlin. Meanwhile, the German advance in the west was reversed; by 16 January, the last remnants of the bulge had been pinched out.

In February 1945 the Allied 'big three' – Churchill, Roosevelt, Stalin – met at Yalta on the Black Sea to settle the post-war shape of Europe. Germany would be divided into zones of occupation, but Stalin refused to make any concessions on the future of Poland and other countries in the east. Reluctantly, Britain and the USA agreed to recognise the pro-Communist regime the Russians had installed in Warsaw as the country's legitimate government. Negotiations were not helped by the fact that Roosevelt was clearly ill. In April he died of a stroke.

Unconditional surrender

On the battlefronts, the Allied advance was gathering pace. In early March, the Americans forced their way across the Rhine, to be followed by Montgomery's men further to the north later that same month. On 23 April, American and Russian forces joined hands on the River Elbe, cutting what remained of Hitler's fast crumbling Reich in two. The Führer himself was penned up in a bunker in Berlin – now under constant shellfire from the besieging Russian forces getting ready for their final assault on the Reich's capital. He committed suicide a week later. That night, an unmistakably drunk Lord Haw Haw broadcast to Britain for the last time from a makeshift studio in the ruins of Hamburg. 'You may not hear

from me again for a few months', he announced, concluding portentously: 'Es lebe Deutschland (long live Germany), Heil Hitler and farewell.'

The German collapse rapidly gathered momentum. Even before Hitler's death, his armies in Italy were negotiating surrender. On 4 May, German land forces in northwest Europe threw in the towel. Finally, the German supreme command signed the articles of unconditional surrender at Eisenhower's headquarters in Rheims on 7 May. The war in Europe was over at last.

The news of Germany's capitulation was delayed by a procedural dispute between the Allies – Russia wanted to wait until a formal surrender could be signed in Berlin with all three powers represented – but word seeped out. By the afternoon, flags and bunting were sprouting in the streets, even though there still had not been an official announcement. Eventually, at 7.40pm, the BBC interrupted a piano recital to break the news. The next day was to be celebrated as VE Day. Both it and the day following would be national holidays.

A day to remember

The morning of 8 May was wet and stormy, but by afternoon the sun had broken through to gladden the hearts of the vast crowds that gathered throughout the kingdom to celebrate Hitler's downfall. One of the highlights of the day was Winston Churchill's broadcast, transmitted by the BBC at 3pm from the same room in Downing Street where Chamberlain had announced the outbreak of war. Churchill confirmed that German land, sea and air forces had surrendered unconditionally. 'The evildoers are now prostrate before us', he proclaimed. 'Advance Britannia! Long live the cause of freedom! God save the King!'

Churchill's words echoed across the world. Some of the Eighth Army men listening in to the Prime Minister had crossed into Austria only the day before, following their dogged two-year advance up the spine of Italy. In Singapore, the broadcast was picked up on hidden radios secreted in Changi prison. It gave new hope to the 7000 sick, maltreated prisoners the Japanese held there.

The victorious Prime Minister then drove slowly back to the House of Commons, standing erect in an open-topped car and giving his trademark V sign to the joyful cheering crowds. Later, together with leading members of his Cabinet, he spoke again from the balcony of the Ministry of Health. 'This is your hour. This is your victory', he told his audience before leading them in a rousing chorus of *Land of Hope and Glory*.

In the streets, the partying continued well into the night. Public buildings were floodlit and searchlights played across the skies. All over Britain, there were similar scenes of rejoicing, albeit on a smaller scale. In Oxford, a huge bonfire blazed in St Giles by the Martyr's Memorial, while in Belfast long lines of revellers danced the conga in and out of the immobilised trams. Back in London, the crowds fell silent as midnight drew near, for at 12.01 all fighting officially was to cease. As Big Ben struck the hour, a great cheer went up and people broke into tumultuous applause. It was the end of an unforgettable day, which those taking part would remember for the rest of their lives.

VE DAY

As the great day dawned, people started taking to the streets early. Churchill lunched with the King at Buckingham Palace before departing to broadcast to the nation, then on to the House of Commons. He was 40 minutes late for his appearance on the balcony of the Ministry of Health, but everyone took it in good part. The prevailing cry was simple – 'We want Winnie!'

CELEBRATION!
The Royal Family, joined by Winston Churchill, acknowledge the cheers of the crowds from the balcony of Buckingham Palace. Every time the royal party turned to go in, they were met with roar after roar of 'We want the King! We want George!' It was 11pm when, picked out by spotlights, the King and Queen made their final appearance. The young princesses went out incognito into the crowds.

The West End was bursting at the seams with people partying. They waved flags and streamers, sporting paper hats, ribbons and rosettes. They sang. They danced. In Trafalgar Square 'a very pretty girl about 18 in a red frock with white polka dots' was spotted 'shoeless and stockingless' as she lifted her skirt to paddle in the fountain. Two young officers of the Norfolk Regiment rolled up their trousers to join her and a British Movietone cameramen captured the moment as they climbed to the top of the fountain, carrying the girl, and she kissed them. 'I'll bet she'll catch it when her mother sees the pictures', commented one older woman in the crowd.

UNITED FRONT
An RAF officer, two members of the Women's Royal Air Force and a civilian form a united happy front in normally august Whitehall. Among the millions counting their good fortune that day were more than 13,000 former prisoners of war who arrived back in Britain that morning in time to take part in the festivities, ferried by 200 Lancaster bombers. Among their number was the legendary RAF fighter ace, the legless Douglas Bader, newly released from a POW camp in Germany.

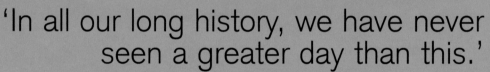

'In all our long history, we have never seen a greater day than this.'

Winston Churchill

WE'VE WON THE WAR!
Police struggle to hold back the crowds in Parliament Square to allow official cars as well as MPs on foot to reach the House of Commons.

There was little drunkenness and almost no rowdyism – for most of the crowds, just joy and perhaps pure relief at having won through and survived. In Piccadilly, Britons of all classes and ages celebrated together, together with their allies. As Churchill inimitably put it in his victory broadcast: 'In all our long history, we have never seen a greater day than this. Everyone, man or woman, has done their best'.

UNFINISHED BUSINESS

On 10 May, it was business as usual. As Churchill had already warned in his VE-Day broadcast, 'Japan, with all her treachery and greed' remained to be subdued. The official estimate was that it would take up to 18 months to bring the Japanese to the point of surrender and that invading their home islands would cost the Allies hundreds of thousands of casualties.

Then there was the future of the great war-winning government to be decided. Churchill had suggested to his Labour partners that they should continue to serve with him until Japan's surrender, and although some of the Labour Party leaders – notably Clement Attlee – were in favour, the party's rank-and-file were not. Accordingly, on 23 May, what Churchill called 'that famous coalition' was dissolved. He formed a Conservative and Liberal caretaker government to hold the fort until a general election could be held. Polling day was set for 5 July, but it was agreed that results would be delayed for a further three weeks to allow the votes cast by forces overseas to be brought back to Britain and counted.

The campaign trail

The approach of the two main parties, Conservative and Labour, to the election campaign could not have been more different. Despite hastily cobbling together a 'Four Year Plan' for Britain in what Churchill somewhat cumbersomely called his 'Declaration of Policy to the Electors', the Conservatives were determined to try to turn the election into a vote of confidence in their leader. After all, he was 'the man who won the war' as their campaign literature proudly proclaimed. On walls and hoardings, the familiar face looked down from posters, captioned

COMING HOME
Demobilisation was already in full swing by the time war came to an end. These wives and relatives were waiting excitedly to welcome their men back home on 21 April, 1945.

'Help him finish the job – Vote National'. Half of their candidates featured the same portrait on their election addresses, this time with the almost Biblical abjuration 'Don't let Him down!'

Labour, by contrast, produced a carefully worked out manifesto, with its policies clearly outlined. Entitled *Let Us Face the Future*, it committed a Labour government to implementing the Beveridge Report in full. It promised an end to unemployment, a massive housing drive, the introduction of family allowances, the setting up of a National Health Service and the nationalisation of coal, gas, electricity, the railways, road haulage and the iron and steel industries. Experts would plan everything in Labour's brave new Britain. 'Labour', the manifesto assured its readers, 'will plan from the ground up.'

From close colleagues to electoral enemies

The battle was hard and, for men who until recently had been close working colleagues, surprisingly bitter. In his first party political radio broadcast, Churchill launched into an astonishing attack on his erstwhile Labour partners in the wartime coalition government. 'I declare to you', he told the listening audience, 'that no socialist system can be established without a political police … they [the Labour leaders] would have to fall back on some type of Gestapo.' Even Margaret Thatcher, then at university in Oxford, recalled thinking that he had gone too far. As the election outcome would show, the British public thought so, too – or simply did not believe him.

Attlee was quite capable of sticking up for himself. The next day he responded with the quietly biting comment that 'the voice we heard last night was that of Mr Churchill, but the mind was that of Lord Beaverbrook'. The right-wing Conservative politician and owner of the *Daily Express* was one of Churchill's closest advisers in the conduct of the Conservative election campaign.

THE 1945 ELECTION BATTLE
The Conservatives campaigned under the label 'National' and relied almost entirely on Churchill's prestige as 'the man who won the war' to sweep them back to power in the 1945 General Election (above left). They were misguided. Labour, with the wartime Deputy Prime Minister Clement Attlee at the helm, won by a landslide. One of the key personalities in Attlee's new government was the bluff, plain-speaking Ernest Bevin, here canvassing a voter of the future. Attlee had intended to make Bevin Chancellor of the Exchequer, but at the King's urgent suggestion switched him round with Hugh Dalton to become Foreign Secretary.

A LANDSLIDE FOR LABOUR

The outcome came as a complete surprise – at least to the Conservatives. In an audience with George VI, Churchill had confidently assured the King that he expected to win with a majority of between 50 and 80 seats. Three days before polling day, the *Daily Express* declared 'Socialists decide they have lost'. Even Attlee did not expect to win a majority – the most he hoped for was a draw. But from the moment that the first results were declared, it was clear that the people had decided who was going to take charge of post-war Britain.

By 10.25am, the first Conservative minister – Harold Macmillan – had lost his seat and another 12 soon followed, including Leo Amery, Brendan Bracken and Duncan Sandys, Churchill's son-in-law. By 10.40 it was clear that Birmingham, a Conservative stronghold since the days of Joseph Chamberlain, was falling to Labour. By noon, the quiet middle-class London suburbs were going the same way. When all the votes were counted Labour had 393 MPs against 213 Conservatives and 12 Liberals, giving them a staggering majority of 146. Even in Churchill's own constituency, where Labour and Liberals did not contest the seat, a local farmer won a quarter of the votes as an Independent.

At 7.00pm Churchill, flourishing the inevitable cigar, drove to Buckingham Palace to tender his government's resignation. Half an hour later, the Attlee family's modest Standard 12, piloted by Mrs Attlee, made its way into Palace Yard. Her husband's opening words to the King were reportedly 'Sir, I've won the election', to which George VI replied, 'I know, I heard it on the six o'clock news'.

In hindsight, the Labour triumph does not seem that surprising. And like all electoral landslides, it was distorted by Britain's first-past-the-post voting system: the Labour Party won 47.8 per cent of the vote, against the Conservatives' 39.8 per cent. Even so, it left no doubt whatever who the British public trusted to tackle the peace. The Conservative Party was hopelessly identified with the dark years of the 1930s – the Britain of dole queues, 3 million unemployed and craven appeasement of dictators. And though Churchill was 'the man who won the war', Attlee was generally thought of as 'the man who ran the country' while he did it – and ran it very well. Labour promised a better future in a better world, reflecting the nation's desire for change, peace and reform.

Japan capitulates

Together with Ernest Bevin, the new Foreign Secretary, Attlee now flew to Berlin for a conference at Potsdam with Stalin and Harry S Truman, who had taken over from Roosevelt as President of the USA. Despite Bevin's confident promise that 'Left understands Left', the outcome, as far as the future of war-torn Europe was concerned, was deadlock in the face of Russian obduracy. Stalin did eventually commit to joining the war against the Japanese, but in the event this came to an end sooner than almost everybody had predicted.

On 2 August, President Truman sanctioned the use of the new atomic bomb against Japan. Four days later the first bomb, nicknamed 'Little Boy', was dropped on Hiroshima, razing the city to the ground. A second bomb, 'Fat Man', destroyed Nagasaki on 9 August. Japan had no choice and surrendered on 15 August (still

VJ DAY

A Chinese waiter joins in the celebrations in London as the news of Japan's surrender breaks. China had been officially at war with Japan since 1937. The Chinese, of course, were not the only people in Britain to be gladdened by the news. In the mining districts of South Wales, the *Merthyr Express* recorded how, though 'the news was almost unbelievable at first, many women were in tears at the thought of again seeing a husband or son soon to be released from prisoner-of-war camps', while 'all our South Wales colliery hooters, train whistles, detonators, fireworks and rattles were used to swell the great chorus of celebration. Many bonfires were lit in the streets and on the mountain-sides, and shone out as symbols of peace and freedom.' Up and down the land, servicemen and their families were relieved not to have to continue to fight.

As on VE Day, the streets of London's West End, such as Piccadilly Circus (below), were packed with revellers. One couple, who had dashed back from holiday in the West Country for the celebrations, recorded that although things started off quieter than they expected, the night-time party more than made up for it: 'So far as revelry by night was concerned, VE Day had nothing on VJ Day. It was London with the lid off.'

14 August in the USA further west). Attlee broadcast the news at midnight. 'The last of our enemies is laid low', he said. 'Here at home you have earned respite from the unceasing exertions which you have all borne for so many dark years.'

Like VE Day, VJ Day was celebrated with a two-day public holiday. In London, the crowds filled the streets – notably Trafalgar Square and Piccadilly Circus, where 100,000 people danced to the music of six barrel organs. At midnight, a vast crowd gathered outside Buckingham Palace. In Liverpool, celebrations went on for a marathon ten days. An Oxfordshire housewife summed up the popular mood when she wrote: 'Today there's just the rejoicing of the whole world – and the glorious knowledge that the killing is over.'

COMING HOME

Home-made signs were already hanging in many streets to greet returning service personnel. For thousands, particularly the released prisoners of war, this would be their first sight of Britain for years. Many wondered how easy the transition from military to civilian life would be, though, in the event, life in the forces and civilian life proved surprisingly similar. The queues were different, but that was about all.

Planning for demobilisation had started as far back as September 1942, the aim of the planners being to avoid the delays and injustices that had created so

THE DEMOB SUIT
A troupe of ENSA entertainers put the new demob suits through their paces in front of an audience of soldiers in Cairo. As well as the suit itself, each demobilised serviceman was issued with a shirt, two collars, two pairs of socks, one pair of shoes, a pair of cufflinks, a hat and a tie.

TOP PRIORITY
Demobilised builders leave Olympia, London, in November 1945 carrying their issue of civilian clothes in cardboard suitcases. Building skills were desperately needed to tackle the housing shortage brought about by enemy bombing, the wartime halting of slum clearance programmes – and years of peacetime neglect. But as Aneurin Bevan, the minister responsible for the housing drive, was to find, shortages of skilled labour, raw materials and funding meant that the targets were unrealistic and unattainable. The housing waiting lists grew and grew.

much bitterness and resentment in the aftermath of the First World War. Its basis was simply length of service, though additional priority was given to people with skills that were needed urgently for post-war reconstruction. Demobilisation began in earnest on 18 June 1945; by Christmas, a third of the 4 million conscripts in the forces or working in war industries had been demobilised relatively smoothly.

The first step back to 'civvy street' was a visit to one of the so-called Dispersal Centres and, for men, the issuing of a 'demob suit' and everything needed to wear with it, from a shirt to socks and shoes. With it came a large, flat cardboard box which folded to make a suitcase to carry the clothes. Next came a trip to the nearest Resettlement Office – there were 400 of these scattered around the country in all – which guided servicemen and women through the

necessary steps for a smooth re-entry to civilian life. As an additional bonus, everyone was granted eight weeks paid Resettlement Leave, with an extra day for every month that had been spent serving overseas.

Evacuees were also coming home. Children had been returning from their safe 'reception areas' across the country since late 1944, though it took until March 1946 to complete the final stages of the process. Coming back to live at home was not without its problems. Some children had been away since September, 1939, when the first great evacuation started, and came back as almost complete strangers to their parents. Quite a few were reluctant to return at all.

'Work or want'

What everyone was hoping for was simple. It was the better tomorrow that they had been promised – but they wanted it today. Few were disposed to pay real heed to Attlee's clipped, precise tones as he warned of the 'difficult years' that lay ahead. Yet almost as soon as Labour had taken office, the terrifying extent of the nation's underlying economic crisis was starkly revealed.

On the very day that President Truman announced the dropping of the first atomic bomb, Lord Keynes, the chief economic adviser to the Treasury, summoned top British and American officials to a crucial meeting. Its purpose was to draft an appeal for peacetime financial assistance from the USA to take the place of Lend-Lease, on which Britain was utterly dependent. Without such aid, Keynes warned, the nation faced 'an economic Dunkirk'. A week later, Truman unilaterally announced the immediate suspension of Lend-Lease. The news fell on Whitehall like a V2 – without warning.

HOME TIME
Two of the hundreds and thousands of children who had been evacuated to safety finally make the return journey (above left). The London Return Plan was put into operation on 2 May, 1945, with the first trainload of children arriving in the capital in early June. Over the next four to five weeks, convoys of trains running seven days a week brought the children and other evacuees back to the city. They carried the old as well as the young. This 80-year-old lady was one of a group of 400 refugees returning from Leicester.

Bankrupt Britain

Britain was staring bankruptcy in the face. By the time Lend-Lease terminated on 21 August, 1945, the country had received upwards of £5 billion dollars worth of goods from the USA and spent another £1.2 billion on what were termed 'Reverse Lend-Lease' transactions. Its exports had collapsed, its gold and foreign currency reserves were virtually wiped out and it owed other vast sums around the world. Victory had cost Britain everything it had – and more.

Lord Keynes had faith that the country could recover. If exports increased in volume by at least 50 per cent over their pre-war level and government expenditure – particularly overseas – was ruthlessly cut, he believed that the enormous deficit could be eliminated by 1949. What it all depended on, though, was the immediate negotiation of a loan from the USA – Keynes thought $5 billion would do it – to buy time for economic recovery to get under way.

Keynes flew to the USA to start negotiations. He came back with a loan of $3.75 billion, which was expected to last until 1950. Britain was to pay interest on its borrowings at a rate of 2 per cent a year and repay the loan in 50 annual instalments, starting on 31 December 1951. But there was a sting in the tail. The Americans insisted that holders of sterling, the sale of which had been tightly controlled during the war, must be free to convert it into dollars a year after Congress approved the loan. As subsequent events would demonstrate, this was a ticking time bomb, just waiting to explode. Some MPs from both parties

BACK TO BLIGHTY
Newly liberated prisoners of war arrive back in Britain by air, and are welcomed by volunteers from the Women's Royal Air Force. Life for returning POWs and servicemen alike was not always easy, particularly when it came to re-establishing relationships with their families. The divorce rate soared and children often found the presence of a stranger in the home hard to handle. 'I did not like this tall, weird old man', one little girl later recorded when she reached adulthood. Another described her newly returned father as 'moody and very demanding'.

opposed the terms of the loan – the Conservative Robert Boothby exclaimed 'we have sold the Empire for a packet of cigarettes!' But in truth there was little alternative. The money had been found. The big questions now were how would it be spent and would it be enough?

Tough choices

Hugh Dalton, the Chancellor of the Exchequer, argued that Britain's vast overseas commitments were something that 'we cannot possibly afford'. Financial pressure rapidly led to the fusion of the UK and US zones in Germany and Britain withdrew its support elsewhere. Within two years, it would be gone from India. But it was hard to give up the belief that Britain was still a world power, which perhaps explains why, in the depths of such a financial crisis, the government decided to build Britain's own atomic bomb. And what of the housing, health and welfare policies that had been so boldly promised? The government was determined to stick to its cherished programme of domestic reform. The British people had voted for implementation of the Beveridge report – and Labour would deliver. One of the prices would be austerity and rationing into the next decade.

WAVING GOODBYE
GI brides on board the *Queen Mary* in Southampton leaving behind their old lives in Britain for a new life in America. Such marriages were frowned on by both the British and US authorities – and by many parents into the bargain. Some fathers refused to sign the necessary papers, while others did so only extremely reluctantly. Others gave their daughters wholehearted support. 'They felt', said one, 'that I would have a much better life in the States.'

INDEX

Page numbers in *italic* refer
to the captions and/or
illustrations.

PICTURE CREDITS

All images in this book are courtesy of Getty Images, including the following which have additional attributions:
Abbreviations: t = top; m = middle; b = bottom; r = right; c = centre; l = left

1900s
George Eastman House: 96bl
Popperfoto: 13, 26t, 27, 32, 38, 39, 65, 70, 72, 75b, 92t, 106, 112, 114, 115, 119b, 121
Sean Sexton: 28, 57, 61
Time & Life Pictures: 22, 35b, 58

1910s
George Eastman House: 209

Popperfoto: 124, 127, 130r, 134b, 148, 163, 166tl, 166bl, 168, 198, 200, 203, 204-205, 220b, 225, 226-227, 229
Roger Viollet: 167b, 220t
Time & Life Pictures: 159, 173, 190, 206, 210

1920s
John Kobal Foundation: 320-321, 323b
Popperfoto: 265t, 269t, 304t, 307b, 331b

Redferns: 323m
Sean Sexton: 259, 287

1930s
Imagno: 358, 361
Popperfoto: 350, 354-355, 360l, 394, 406, 407r, 414t, 415, 416, 425b, 433tl, 439, 442, 451, 452-453
Lytton Strachey: 404t
Time & Life Pictures: 447, 455

1940-45
AFP: 528, 534t
Time & Life Pictures: 498l, 501, 512, 519t, 539, 543l, 549l
Warner Bros: 498r
With thanks to David Low/Solo Syndication for their kind assistance in supplying the cartoon on page 470

Popperfoto: 7 (Foreword)

PICTURES WITHOUT CAPTIONS

FRONT COVER: George VI and Princess Elizabeth photographed in his study at Windsor Castle as the King goes through the Royal boxes on 11 April, 1942.
BACK COVER: A Bat bi-plane with a Mr Mines at the controls during Doncaster Flying Week, October 1909.
PAGE 2: Two young women enjoying themselves on a ride at Southend Fair. The photograph, by Kurt Hutton, was originally published in the Picture Post in 1938.
PAGE 7: A British soldier on a Rudge Multi motorcycle, with two of his colleagues behind, shortly before going out to France in 1914.
PAGE 8-9: A picnic party in the picturesque setting of ruined Netley Abbey in Hampshire, c1900.
PAGE 122-3: A machine gun regiment of the Royal Northumberland Fusiliers, also known as 'The Fighting Fifth', in April 1916 after the Battle of St Eloi, south of Ypres. They are equipped with the Lewis Gun, a US-invented light machine gun powered by gas.
PAGE 240-1: Construction workers take their lunchbreak perched high up a half-finished building in London in April 1929.
PAGE 346-7: A parade of bathing beauties at the open air swimming pool in Blackpool in August 1936.
PAGE 458-9: A soldier home on leave from the BEF kisses his young son, who is about to be evacuated from London in June 1940.

PORTRAIT OF AN ERA
An Illustrated History of Britain 1900 to 1945
Published in 2011 in the United Kingdom by
Vivat Direct Limited (t/a Reader's Digest) in association
with Getty Images and Endeavour London Limited

Vivat Direct Limited
(t/a Reader's Digest)
157 Edgware Road
London W2 2HR

Original colour origination by Chroma Graphics,
    Singapore
Printed and bound in China

**Portrait of an Era: An Illustrated History of Britain
1900 to 1945** is based on material taken from five
volumes of **Looking Back at Britain**, an illustrated
series of books produced in association with Endeavour
London Limited and published by Reader's Digest
Association Limited between 2007 and 2010.

We are committed both to the quality of our products and
the service we provide to our customers.
We value your comments, so please do contact us on
08705 113366 or via our website at
www.readersdigest.co.uk

If you have any comments or suggestions about
the content of our books, email us at
gbeditorial@readersdigest.co.uk

CONTRIBUTORS

Written by:
Foreword: Juliet Gardiner
1900s: Tony Allan
1910s: Jeremy Harwood
1920s: Jonathan Bastable
1930s: Brian Moynahan
1940-45: Jeremy Harwood

Project editor: Christine Noble
Art editors: Conorde Clarke, Tea Aganovic
Original picture research: Jennifer Jeffrey,
    Franziska Payer Crockett
Indexer: Marie Lorimer
Proofreader: Ron Pankhurst

For Vivat Direct
Editorial director: Julian Browne
Art director: Anne-Marie Bulat
Managing editor: Nina Hathway
Picture resource manager: Sarah Stewart-Richardson
Technical account manager: Dean Russell
Product production manager: Claudette Bramble
Production controller: Jan Bucil

BOOK CODE: 400-527 UP0000-1
ISBN: 978-1-78020-011-8